T0047355

HUDSON VALLEY & THE CATSKILLS

NIKKI GOTH ITOI

Contents

DISCOVER

Hudson Valley
& the Catskills

A bundant natural beauty and diverse communities across the Hudson River Valley have inspired quiet contemplation for centuries. What better place than a secluded riverbank or mountaintop vista to ask big questions—and hopefully find some answers? It is here that John Burroughs penned his most thoughtful nature essays and Thomas Cole created landscape paintings that marked the dawn of the Romantic era.

At the center of our modern-day environmental and food movements, the valley today is shaping what it means to be sustainable, connected, and authentic. People increasingly care about not only what they eat but also how it's made. Industrial is out; artisan and heritage are in. Clean water and fresh air matter to us, more than ever before. From Beacon to Bovina Center, entire Hudson Valley towns have embraced this ethos, and a younger generation is coming back to work the land.

Measured by numbers, the Hudson River itself is unexceptional—only 315 miles long, 3.5 miles across at its widest point, and 216 feet at its deepest. Carved by a glacier 75 million years ago, the river originates from Lake Tear of the Clouds in the rugged Adirondack Mountains and becomes navigable at Troy, north of

Clockwise from top left: making maple syrup in the northern Catskills; the Vanderbilt Estate in Hyde Park; fall colors on a Catskill High Peaks trail; basil for sale at a farmers market; hiking in Delaware County; enjoying the Hudson River in Tarrytown.

BASIL
$1.00/Bunch

Albany. From the Federal Dam at Troy all the way to New York Harbor, the Hudson is a 150-mile-long estuary that ebbs and floods with ocean tides, mixing saltwater with fresh as far up as Kingston in Ulster County. The Algonquin people called it "Muhheakantuck," meaning "the river that flows both ways," or, "great waters constantly in motion."

The constant mixing supports the largest single wildlife resource in New York State. Deciduous trees, rocky bluffs, and gentle foothills line both shores. Mallard ducks paddle across narrow inlets, while fishing boats troll for striped bass. Beyond the river's edge, narrow country lanes lead to historic parks, working fruit and dairy farms, and mountains that stretch 4,000 feet into the sky. From distilleries to farm stays, the valley has a way of adapting to the changing interests of its people.

At its heart, the Hudson River Valley is a place of contrasts—where dairy farmers mingle with concrete factory workers, where hunters share the forest with conservationists, and where the cosmopolitan meets small-town America. Wherever you choose to go, a trip through the region today promises a chance to discover and reflect. To taste and breathe. And to meet the entrepreneurs and innovators who are—quite literally—betting the farm on a vision for the future.

Clockwise from top left: start of the Escarpment Trail, near Windham; Shunpike Dairy in Millbrook; gazebo overlooking the Hudson Valley; Kaaterskill Falls.

9 TOP EXPERIENCES

1 **See the fall colors:** New York's deciduous forests put on quite a show for a few weeks between late September and mid-October. Grab your camera and head out for a walk in the woods, or a scenic backroads drive (page 27).

2 **Go for a bike ride:** Pedal along endless miles of country roads through rolling hills and farmland, or along any of the paved rail trails. Or take it off-road for some technical loops in one of the valley's new single-track trail networks (pages 21 and 22).

3 **Taste the valley's bounty:** From peaches and apples to wine and whiskey, it's all grown and made among the farms of the Hudson Valley. Each day, graduates of the Culinary Institute turn the local harvest into the most memorable of meals (page 25).

>>>

4 **Experience a working farm at Stone Barns:** At this four-season farm and educational center, you can tour vegetable gardens, collect eggs, and even help farmers shear sheep in spring (page 42).

<<<

5 **Ski the Catskill Mountains:** Plan a winter retreat to the slopes of the Catskills. Rent the gear, take a lesson, and enjoy the lively après-ski scene (page 22).

 >>>

6 **Explore military history at West Point:** History and tradition come alive on a tour of the 200-year-old United States Military Academy campus (page 81).

<<<

7 **Tour the grand estates:** Experience several centuries of architectural trends by touring majestic residences that are now museums (page 20), such as the Rockefeller Estate at Kykuit (pictured).

8 **Relive Woodstock at Bethel Woods:** Learn about the music of the 1960s and catch the latest bands on tour at this museum and performing arts center (page 193).

9 **Hit the hiking trail:** Numerous state parks and rail trails have gentle terrain to explore, while the ridges and peaks of the Catskill Mountains and Shawangunk Range will challenge the most experienced backpackers (page 28).

Planning Your Trip

Where to Go

Lower Hudson Valley

The Hudson River Valley stretches north from New York City and the New Jersey border, leading to many densely populated bedroom communities of **Westchester and Rockland Counties.** The area is not a destination in itself, but several attractive **mansions** and **gardens** are worth a stop. The best of the bunch is **Kykuit,** the former Rockefeller family residence near **Tarrytown.** The food and entertainment are on par with what you'll find in Manhattan.

The Hudson Highlands

The Hudson Highlands encompass **Orange and Putnam Counties** along the most dramatic-looking stretch of the river. A solid granite mountain range called the **Appalachian Plateau** crosses the Hudson here, and the river has carved a narrow and deep path through the range. A dreamy mist often clings to the peaks of **Storm King Mountain** and **Breakneck Ridge** on opposite shores. It's an easy daytrip from New York City to browse the antiques shops along Main Street in **Cold Spring,** or visit the **West Point** campus for a military history refresher.

Mid-Hudson Valley and the Southern Catskills

Part commuter district, part bucolic getaway, the middle section of the valley starts to resemble a traveler's destination. The **Shawangunk Mountains** of **Ulster County** and the riverside mansions of **Dutchess County** define the landscape. Rolling hills and farm fields intersperse with lakes, streams, and forests. The towns of **New Paltz, Saugerties,** and **Woodstock** make a convenient base for exploration. **Dia:Beacon** exhibits artwork from the 1960s to the present, and the **Culinary Institute of America** trains first-rate chefs.

Western Catskills to the Delaware River

Wellness resorts and farm stays have replaced yesterday's summer boarding houses in the Western Catskills region. Many visitors head here to try an **off-the-grid** existence. Small communities include young farmers, artists, and second-home owners. Historic **covered bridges** span the Willowemoc Creek and Beaver Kill, while hundreds of lakes and streams create a playground for anglers and bird-watchers. Spend an hour inside the **Catskill Fly Fishing Center and Museum,** even if you're not the fishing type.

Upper Hudson Valley and the Northern Catskills

The **Catskill and Berkshire Mountains** frame the upper section of the Hudson River Valley in **Greene and Columbia Counties.** Adventure-seekers come here to mountain bike, hike, and ski; but there are pockets of culture too, especially in the towns of Hudson and Catskill. **Leaf peeping** is arguably the best in this forested region. The topography of the Catskills inspired the first generation of the Hudson River School of painters. The Livingston family home at **Clermont** and the Persian-style **Olana,** which belonged to painter Frederic Church, are well worth a visit. Farm-to-table experiences are everywhere, and mountain biking is on the rise.

The Capital-Saratoga Region

The Capital-Saratoga region marks the end of the navigable Hudson River and the gateway to the rugged **Adirondack wilderness.** Business travel brings most people to **Albany,** while

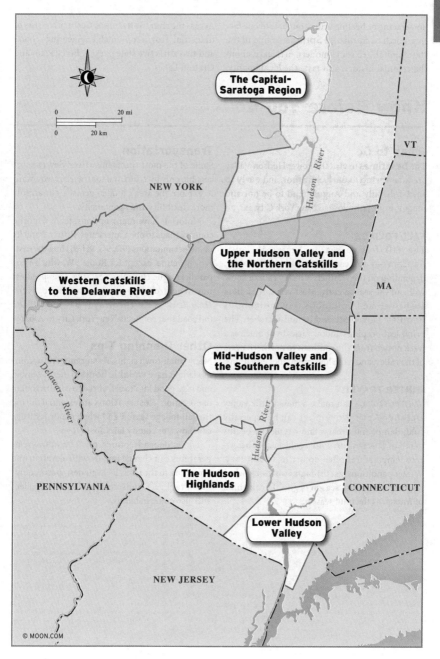

The Capital-
Saratoga Region

VT

NEW YORK

Hudson River

Upper Hudson Valley and
the Northern Catskills

MA

Western Catskills
to the Delaware River

Delaware River

Mid-Hudson Valley and
the Southern Catskills

Hudson River

PENNSYLVANIA

The Hudson
Highlands

CONNECTICUT

Lower Hudson
Valley

NEW JERSEY

0   20 mi
0   20 km

© MOON.COM

horseracing or healing waters might lead one farther north to **Saratoga Springs.** While in the state capital, see some modern art, learn about the colonial history, and taste the local bounty.

Across the river, **Rensselaer County** consists of industrial Troy, a top-notch engineering school, and two attractive state parks, Cherry Plain and Grafton Lakes.

Know Before You Go

When to Go

The **best times** to visit the Lower Hudson Valley are **late spring** to **early summer,** and **early to mid-fall.** July and August tend to be hot and muggy, especially close to New York City.

FALL FOLIAGE

The fall foliage season begins in **mid-September** and can last until **late October,** depending on the weather. A heavy rain or snow will end the season early. Most years, the colors are best around **Columbus Day/Indigenous Peoples' Day weekend** in mid-October. The prime leaf-peeping window varies by as much as a week or two from the southern to northern parts of the valley, and from lower to higher elevations.

WINTER TRAVEL

Winter storms can make a mess of the valley **October-April. November** can be especially cold, damp, and dreary. Snow typically begins to fall in **December,** with a cold snap of below-zero temperatures often occurring in **January.** Winter conditions last through **February,** when the maple-sugaring season begins. Locals think of **March** as the mud season.

Transportation

Some of the most spectacular river views are accessible only by **train,** but for travelers who want to explore the area's hidden gems, a **car** affords more flexibility and spontaneity.

Motorists have many options, from winding country roads to open interstates. **Route 9** and its many permutations (9D, 9G, 9H, 9J) hug the eastern shoreline, except for Route 9W, which runs parallel on the Hudson's west side. The speediest way to get from the wilderness to the sea is the **New York State Thruway (I-87),** a multilane toll road that connects New York City to Albany.

Other Planning Tips

Many small-town sights, restaurants, and accommodations have **variable hours** in the off-season, and it's a good idea to call ahead to confirm hours of operation. **Reservations** are essential during the fall foliage season and when major festivals, car shows, or county fairs are in town.

For outdoor adventures, **pack layers,** as temperatures can change rapidly with elevation and proximity to the river. Field guides, sports equipment, rain gear, sunscreen, and insect repellent will also come in handy.

Day Trips from New York City

Tarrytown and the Rockefeller Estate

Plan ahead for this trip by prebooking your preferred Kykuit tour online. Start your day at Grand Central Station and catch an early morning train on the Hudson Line north to **Tarrytown.**

Walk up **Main Street** and grab a cup of coffee at Coffee Labs. Take a cab or shuttle to the Kykuit Visitor Center in neighboring **Sleepy Hollow.** Check in for your tour of the **Rockefeller Estate** at Pocantico Hills.

After the tour, head to **Stone Barns Center for Food and Agriculture** to see a working sustainable farm in action. The next stop is **Sunnyside,** Washington Irving's romantic-era estate on the border between Tarrytown and Irvington. After the house tour, browse the museum shop and pick up one of Irving's books for the train ride home.

Boscobel and Cold Spring Village

If you want to browse antiques shops, tour a neoclassical mansion, or paddle around the river, stay on the train until it arrives at Cold Spring Station in **Putnam County.** Exit the station and stop at the visitors booth on Main Street to pick up a map and inquire about the shuttle to Boscobel House and Gardens, the site of the annual Hudson Valley Shakespeare Festival.

Grab picnic supplies at **Hudson Hil's Café & Market,** then walk down to the riverside gazebo to take in the view of **West Point** and the surrounding cliffs across the river.

Hop on the shuttle to **Boscobel House and Gardens** and admire the apple trees, river views, and collections of silver, china, and glassware inside. Later, if the tides are right, rent a kayak in town and head down to the boat launch

a spooky scarecrow on display in Sleepy Hollow

Grand Estates

Home of Franklin D. Roosevelt National Historic Site in Hyde Park

A handful of majestic estates line the Hudson River, representing several centuries of architectural and cultural trends, including American Renaissance, Georgian, Federal, Romantic, Greek Revival, and Gothic Revival. Many have been turned into interpretive museums that are open to the public. Here are some of the most popular mansions to visit:

- **Kykuit (The Rockefeller Estate):** The sprawling hilltop estate of the Rockefeller family is a must-see in the Lower Hudson River Valley. The three-hour Grand Tour is well worth the time investment.

- **Union Church of Pocantico Hills:** After a Kykuit tour, stop here to admire stained glass windows designed by Henri Matisse and Marc Chagall for the Rockefeller family.

- **Sunnyside:** The Romantic-style home of Washington Irving, America's first man of letters, is a whimsical place right on the river's edge just south of Tarrytown in Westchester County.

- **Lyndhurst Mansion:** Financier Jay Gould's former residence, also near Tarrytown, is considered the finest example of Gothic Revival style in the United States.

- **Boscobel House and Gardens:** This restored neoclassical mansion near Cold Spring is the home of the Hudson Valley Shakespeare Festival.

- **Home of Franklin D. Roosevelt National Historic Site:** FDR's presidential library and museum are just up the road from the Culinary Institute of America in Hyde Park.

- **Vanderbilt Estate:** Fifty rooms range from Renaissance to rococo, and the lawn is a great place for a summer picnic in the Mid-Hudson River Valley.

- **Montgomery Place:** Built in the Federal style, this riverside estate, now part of Bard College, presents scenic views of the Catskill Mountains.

- **Clermont State Historic Site:** The Georgian-style estate of Robert Livingston Jr. reflects the influence of seven generations of the prominent Livingston family.

- **Olana State Historic Site:** Romantic landscape painter Frederic Church designed his Persian-style home after a trip to the Middle East.

at **Foundry Dock Park** to paddle around Constitution Marsh.

Return to **Cold Spring Village** to browse the antiques shops along Main Street. Stay for dinner at **Brasserie Le Bouchon,** or make a reservation at **Valley Restaurant at The Garrison.** When the sun has set, it's time to catch the return train south to Grand Central.

Dia:Beacon

River views and the innovative restoration of an old factory make for an enjoyable day of modern art at this **Dutchess County** museum. (An added plus is the location within walking distance of the Beacon Metro-North train station.) Catch an early morning train from Grand Central to **Beacon** and allow a few hours to explore the galleries. Plan ahead to time your visit with a museum event, such as a gallery talk or film screening. A café on-site serves light breakfast and lunch fare, or you can call a ride share to **Main Street** to eat at Beacon Pantry or the Beacon Falls Café. Spend the afternoon browsing galleries and boutiques, or tackle the short hike to the casino ruins of Mount Beacon.

Cycling the Hudson River Valley

TOP EXPERIENCE

In a six-day tour, riding 35-45 miles per day, you can cover the length of the Hudson River Valley, hitting key sights, vistas, and attractions on both sides of the river. Total distance is approximately 200 miles. This suggested itinerary starts in the town of Hudson, in the Upper Hudson River Valley. Use your arrival day to get oriented, stock up on supplies, and check out your gear. Steiner's Sports on Warren Street can see to all your last-minute needs. If you have extra time, take a warm-up ride over to Olana (12 miles) to tour Frederic Church's historic estate. Book accommodations in or near the towns of Hudson, Kingston, Hyde Park, Garrison, and Nyack.

Day 1: Hudson to Kingston

Get an early start for the first ride of the week, which starts in Hudson (Columbia County) and finishes in Kingston (Ulster County). Along the way, stop to visit **Montgomery Place** and refuel in Rhinebeck. Cross the river at the Kingston-Rhinecliff Bridge. When you reach downtown Kingston, walk through the **Stockade District,** check in to your hotel, and then look to the **Rondout Creek** area for dinner.

Day 2: Kingston to Hyde Park

Ride along part of the **Wallkill Valley Rail Trail** and through the college town of **New Paltz.** Be sure to see the historical homes along **Huguenot Street** and stop at a **winery** or two. End the day by crossing the river on the **Walkway Over the Hudson** and looping back north to Hyde Park.

Day 3: Hyde Park Rest Day

Take a day off to visit **FDR's home and library,** the **Vanderbilt Estate,** and the **Culinary Institute of America.** Or add an optional loop through the countryside and wineries of **eastern Dutchess County** instead.

Day 4: Hyde Park to Garrison

Fuel up for an action-packed ride through **Poughkeepsie, Beacon,** and **Cold Spring.** Optional side trips include the **Dia:Beacon modern art museum** and a **paddle on the river** from a launch near Cold Spring. Finish the day in **Garrison** (Putnam County).

Day 5: Garrison to Nyack

Ride across the **Bear Mountain Bridge** and head south over **Storm King Mountain** to **West Point.** Take a tour of the **military academy,** and

Outdoor Adventures

Fresh air and challenging terrain for a wide range of sports are two primary factors that draw visitors to the more remote parts of the Hudson River Valley. Whether you choose to hike, bike, or ski, you'll have plenty of choices for a memorable outdoor adventure.

CYCLING AND MOUNTAIN BIKING

Piermont and New Paltz are popular cycling hubs, and many local clubs plan group rides on summer weekends. You might tour one county at a time, or attempt the 180-mile multiday ride from New York City to Albany. Include as many bridge crossings as possible, and allow time to take in some of the sights along the way. Several companies offer guided bike tours of the area; an amateur bike race is another way to discover many of the back roads.

Several counties have converted long stretches of abandoned train tracks into paths for walking, jogging, or biking. (Hybrids or gravel bikes are best for these trails.) The Wallkill Valley Rail Trail in Ulster County is a flat, easy ride ideal that begins at the popular Rail Trail Café in Rosendale and includes views from the Rosendale Trestle Bridge. For longer excursions, you can go as far as Kingston to the north and past Gardiner to the south, for a total of 22 miles (one-way).

Networks of mountain biking trails also are popping up across the region, from Peekskill to Windham Mountain. Singletrack trails feature tough climbs, flowy berms, and plenty of rock gardens. Elm Ridge Wild Forest in Greene County is a well-maintained trail system outside of Windham has several loops of singletrack for beginner and intermediate riders. Along Route 23, parts of The Escarpment Trail in Catskill Park offer a technically challenging ride for more experienced bikers.

SWIMMING AND BOATING

The Hudson and its tributaries lure water-sports enthusiasts for fishing, sailing, tubing, kayaking, and more. Tubing on the Esopus in Ulster County is especially popular in summer. Sailing school is an option out of Kingston. Greenwood Lake in Orange County, Lake Taghkanic in Columbia County, and several lakes near Saratoga Springs have beaches for swimming and facilities for boats.

mountain biking in Catskill Park

In Dutchess County, kayakers can paddle The Great Swamp, plus many lakes, ponds, creeks, and the Hudson River. Several shops in the region rent gear and offer guided trips.

SKIING

Falling temperatures mean one thing to winter sports enthusiasts: the possibility of powder. Ski resorts in the Catskills and Adirondacks start making snow as soon as it will freeze, and then hope for a little help from Mother Nature as the season progresses. Whether you prefer the thrill of downhill or the serenity of the open trail, the greater Hudson River Valley has much to offer December-March.

Downhill thrills can be found in the Catskills at Belleayre Mountain Ski Center, great for beginner and intermediate skiers, and Windham Mountain Resort, with more terrain for experienced skiers. Hunter Mountain Ski Bowl and Plattekill Mountain, also in the Catskills, and Catamount Ski & Snowboarding Area, in the Berkshires, are also fun options.

For more solitude on Nordic trails, choose the Capital-Saratoga region: John Boyd Thacher State Park near Albany and Lapland Lake near Saratoga Springs are good bets.

have lunch at the **Thayer Hotel.** For more mileage, add an optional route through **Bear Mountain State Park.** Or get off the bike for a few hours to hike along a section of the **Appalachian Trail.** Overnight in Nyack or Piermont.

Day 6: Nyack to New York City

Finish the ride along the Hudson with a ride under the **cliffs of the Palisades** and end at the **George Washington Bridge.** Alternatively, cross the river at Nyack to explore **Tarrytown** and the **Rockefeller Estate.** From Tarrytown, you can catch Amtrak back to Hudson, or plot a new cycling route for the return trip, with stops in Peekskill, Red Hook, and Catskill, for example.

Revolutionary War Route

The outcome of the nine-year struggle for independence from the British hinged largely on who controlled the Hudson River. From the boycott of British tea to the turning point at Saratoga, many of the war's pivotal events took place in the surrounding valley. Today, a number of interpretive museums and historic sites preserve and commemorate various events and decisions that took place in those long years between 1774 and 1783.

The following itinerary identifies major Revolutionary War sights along the river, from south to north. Other options are to follow the Henry Knox Cannon Trail through Saratoga Springs, Albany, and Columbia County; or to trace the Washington-Rochambeau Revolutionary Route, through the Lower Hudson Valley.

Day 1

This tour begins at the former home of loyalist Frederick Philipse III, who was arrested by General George Washington in 1776, after signing the Declaration of Independence. Both the family residences, **Philipse Manor Hall** in **Yonkers**

Van Cortlandt Manor

and the **Philipsburg Manor** in **Sleepy Hollow,** were confiscated by the state and later preserved as museums. Situated in the neutral zone, **Van Cortlandt Manor** hosted loyalists and patriots alike during the war.

An American victory at **Stony Point Battlefield** in 1779 boosted morale and severely damaged British forces. To reach this state historic site, cross the Hudson at the Bear Mountain Bridge and head south into Rockland County.

Retrace your steps north to the **United States Military Academy** at **West Point,** a training ground for army officers since 1802. The academy sits on the bluffs overlooking the narrow stretch of the river that was chained to keep the British out. You can begin your tour with a walk through the museum (outside the gate), which includes Washington's pistols among its exhibits. Next, book a bus or river tour at the visitors center and have lunch at the stately Thayer Hotel just inside the campus gate. Add half a day for a visit to **Constitution Island.**

Day 2

The first Purple Heart was issued at the Hasbrouck family farmhouse, where George Washington stayed for 16 months at the end of the war. **Washington's Headquarters** in **Newburgh** became the first national historic site in the United States. His army camped at New Windsor Cantonment in Vails Gate, now also the site of the **National Purple Heart Hall of Honor.**

In the afternoon, visit the **Mount Gulian Historic Site** outside Beacon, an 18th-century Dutch stone barn that once belonged to the Verplanck family and served as headquarters for Revolutionary War General Friedrich Wilhelm Augustus von Steuben.

In keeping with the historic theme, join the likes of George Washington, Philip Schuyler, Benedict Arnold, and Alexander Hamilton in spending the night at the 1766 **Beekman Arms** in Rhinebeck, where local townspeople gathered inside for safety while the British burned Kingston to the ground across the Hudson.

Day 3

Today begins with a drive across the river to visit **Kingston,** a colonial city that the British burned to the ground. They landed at Rondout Landing, where periodic reenacts now take place. In Kingston's Stockade District, the **Senate House** hosted the first Senate of New York State in 1777.

Cross the river on the Kingston-Rhinecliff Bridge and make your way north to **Clermont,** colonial estate of the Livingston family. The British torched it in 1777, but the family promptly rebuilt the home during the war.

Day 4

Start the day with a drive across the **Rip Van Winkle Bridge** and continue north along Route 9W to the **Bronck Museum,** where New Yorkers signed the Coxsackie Declaration of Independence in 1775. From there, it's about 25 miles north to **Albany** and the **Schuyler Mansion,** home of Major General Philip Schuyler and the place where British General Burgoyne was imprisoned after his defeat at Saratoga.

Complete the trip at the **Saratoga National Historical Park,** which commemorates the Battle of Saratoga. Here, you can follow a 10-stop auto tour that interprets the battle.

Many Hudson Valley chefs were among the pioneers of the locavore trend. A love of fresh food prepared with a creative flair is a prerequisite for enjoying all that the Hudson Valley has to offer.

FARM STAYS

Learn how sustainably produced pasture-raised food gets from farm to table by helping with the everyday chores. At a place like **Stone & Thistle Farm,** you might collect eggs from the chickens, bottle feed the goats, or move the sheep to fresh pasture.

HEIRLOOM FRUITS AND VEGGIES

Every county in the region has its share of apple orchards, berry patches, organic farms, and cornfields. Flavors differ from one hillside to the next, in what farmers call microterroirs. **Farmers markets** and **farm stands** bring the local harvest to a central location each week, building a sense of community in the process.

In early spring, fernlike fiddleheads appear on many menus. Spring rains bring wild mushrooms. In summer, the local garlic harvest begins in Saugerties, and farm stands overflow with corn, tomatoes, eggplant, and other vegetables. Strawberries and cherries ripen through June and July, and blueberries last July-September. You can pick apples July-November, and pumpkin patches do a steady business in September and October.

DESTINATION RESTAURANTS

You'll find mind-blowing cuisine all across the Hudson Valley. The towns of **Hudson, Rhinebeck, Albany,** and **Saratoga Springs** are places you might travel just to eat. Plan well ahead to dine at the best of the best: **Blue Hill at Stone Barns** in Westchester, **American Bounty** on the CIA campus, **Valley Restaurant at The Garrison,** and **The DeBruce** are travel destinations on their own, and advance reservations are a must.

WINERIES AND DISTILLERIES

Hudson Valley grape growers introduced French-American hybrid grapes in the 1970s to please an increasingly sophisticated consumer base. The switch put the region on the New York State wine map, producing award-winning Italian-style whites, as well as pinot noirs and cabernet francs.

summer harvest of beefsteak tomatoes

The **Dutchess Wine Trail** includes **Clinton Vineyards** and **Millbrook Vineyards & Winery** and covers miles of pretty countryside. Meanwhile, the wineries themselves produce some of the highest-quality labels in New York State.

On the other side of the Hudson, the **Shawangunk Wine Trail** runs along back roads between the New York State Thruway, I-84, and Route 17 between New Paltz in Ulster County and Warwick in Orange County. Some of the most popular stops include **Applewood Winery** and the **Warwick Valley Winery & Distillery.**

Passage of the New York State Farm Distillery bill in 2008 opened the door to a wave of **microdistilleries** across the valley, with new tasting rooms in Albany, Gardiner, Roxbury, Ancram, and Warwick. Local grains and fruits are used to make high-end whiskey and bourbon as well as creative spirits such as apple brandy and other fruit liquors.

COOKING CLASSES

The main campus of the nation's premier culinary college sits on 80 acres overlooking the river at Hyde Park. The **Culinary Institute of America** runs five restaurants, a bookstore, and courses for cooking professionals and enthusiasts. For serious training, enthusiasts can enroll in one of the CIA's Boot Camp programs.

Contemporary Art, Indoors and Out

The arts scene is alive and well in the Hudson River Valley. Artists-in-residence can arrange long-term retreats, while the public gets to experience the results of their creativity. Several premier museums, galleries, and outdoor sculpture parks can anchor a multiday tour of the region. This tour starts in the Capital District and makes its way to the Lower Hudson Valley.

Day 1

Start this itinerary in Albany and head north to the college town of **Saratoga Springs,** where the **Tang Teaching Museum and Art Gallery** serves as an integral part of the curriculum for Skidmore College students. Rotating multimedia exhibits combine objects like Hudson River School landscapes or Shaker furniture with new works of international contemporary art. Spend the rest of the day enjoying a leisurely lunch on Broadway, or get outside to tour Saratoga Spa State Park. Spend the night at the **Saratoga Arms,** or head back to accommodations in Albany.

Day 2

Walk the Empire State Plaza in downtown **Albany** to see the **New York State Art Collection.** A legacy of former Governor Nelson A. Rockefeller, the sculptures are considered one of the most important collections of modern art found anywhere in the United States. Stay at **Morgan State House** or the **State Street Mansion Bed & Breakfast** for the evening.

Head to **Angelo's 677 Prime** for a steak dinner or catch a show in the theater district.

Day 3

In the morning, pack the car and head east to the town of **Ghent** and the 120-acre **Art Omi Sculpture & Architecture Park,** which currently features works by Alicja Kwade and Jean Shin, among more than 60 other contemporary artists from all over the world. Have lunch at the museum café, then continue the journey south to the river town of **Hudson,** a revived artist's mecca. Walk the length of Warren Street, noting the mix of old and new. Stay over at **The Hudson Whaler Hotel** and plan dinner at **Wm Farmer & Sons,** or catch a show at **Club Helsinki** dinner theater.

Day 4

Start the day with a hot cup of tea at **Verdigris Tea & Chocolate Bar,** and point the GPS to the south. Your destination is **Dia:Beacon** to view the light installations by Mary Corse and other modern works in a converted factory along the river. Head to Main Street, Beacon, after the museum tour for lunch at **Beacon Pantry.** Alternatively, skip Dia:Beacon and walk the grounds of the **Storm King Art Center,** an outdoor sculpture garden on the other side of the river. For dinner, try **MacArthur's Riverview Restaurant** at West Point or **Valley Restaurant at The Garrison.**

Fall Foliage Tours

If you time your visit to the changing of the seasons, you can catch one of the most spectacular displays of color anywhere on the planet. The leaves begin to turn in mid-September and peak around Columbus Day in October. The clear, crisp days of autumn offer prime conditions for hiking.

On Foot

The hardwood forests of the **Catskill** and **Shawangunk** ranges explode in shades of red, orange, and yellow each autumn.

CATSKILLS HIKE

One of the most difficult but rewarding fall hikes is a triple-summit over the Catskill High Peaks of **Thomas Cole, Black Dome,** and **Blackhead peaks.** Windham and Hunter make equidistant launching points for the day. You'll need two vehicles to complete this one-way hike. Park the pickup vehicle at the eastern end of Big Hollow Road, off Maplecrest Road (County Rd. 40) in the town of **Jewett.** Then drive to the eastern end of Barnum Road, also off Maplecrest Road (County Rd. 40), to begin the hike (6.1 miles one-way) on an old logging road. A mixed hardwood forest of oak, maple, and beech trees puts on the initial display.

SHAWANGUNKS HIKE

Fall colors are all the more striking against a pair of sparkling lakes in the **Minnewaska State Park Preserve.** For an easy day hike on a network of carriage trails, park at the upper Gertrude's Nose lot off Route 44 and follow the Minnewaska Lake Loop (2 miles) around **Lake Minnewaska.** To extend the hike, add a loop up the Beacon Carriage Road (0.7 mile) and down the Beacon Hill Trail (0.9 mile). After the hike, drive to **High Falls** for a casual dinner at **The Egg's Nest Saloon.**

Minnewaska State Park Preserve

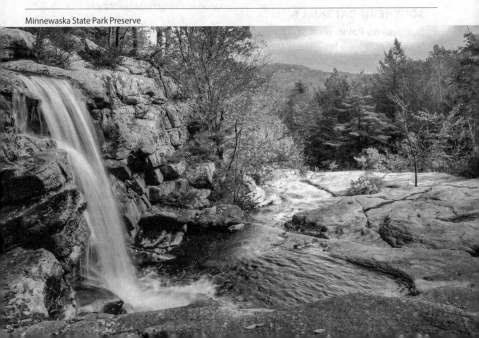

Best Hikes

The most difficult part of planning a Hudson Valley hike is choosing where to go. Should you head to the Catskills or Hudson Highlands, Shawangunks or Taconic Range? Happily, interesting bits of history, wildlife sightings, and panoramic views await on almost every route. Watch the weather, pack some layers, and get out into the woods.

HUDSON HIGHLANDS

Mount Beacon, Beacon

When you want to combine nature and exercise with art and good eats, try this strenuous hike (4.4 miles round-trip) up to the ruins of an old casino, then head to Main Street in Beacon to refuel.

THE SHAWANGUNKS

The Labyrinth and Lemon Squeeze, Mohonk Mountain House

Scrambling is a technical term in the Gunks. You'll do a good bit of it on this challenging hike (5.6 miles round-trip). Keep an eye out for native dwarf pines along the trail and peregrine falcons soaring overhead, when you're not climbing ladders and squeezing yourself through narrow cracks in the ledges.

a rocky scramble in the Shawangunks

SOUTHERN CATSKILLS

Huckleberry Point, West Saugerties

Moderately strenuous by Catskills standards, this out-and-back route (4.5 miles round-trip) begins with a drive up to Platte Clove. After a stream crossing and some elevation gain, the trail rewards hikers with river and valley views from the edge of a cliff. Afterward, allow time for a mug of hot cocoa at the Circle W in nearby Palenville.

NORTHERN CATSKILLS

Escarpment Trail, Catskill Park

Plan an overnight adventure or hike a short section out-and-back along a challenging 24-mile route through the High Peaks area. You can start at the Elm Ridge parking area near Windham or at North Lake in Hainsville.

TACONIC RANGE

Bash Bish Falls, Taconic State Park

At the New York-Massachusetts state line, near the town of Copake Falls, a fairly flat trail (1.5 miles round-trip) leaves a parking lot on the New York side and meanders beside a creek to the 80-foot waterfall and great photo ops.

THE CAPITAL-SARATOGA REGION

Five Mile Trail, Saratoga Spa State Park

Ideal for a morning run before the races, this loop connects several nature trails within the park. Sample the mineral water at each station along the way and see if you can taste the differences.

By Car

TACONIC STATE PARKWAY

This tree-lined road offers changing scenery around every bend, with occasional vistas across the surrounding valley. The stretch from Route 55 north to Chatham is beautiful in the fall and takes about an hour to drive. Along the way, **Clinton Vineyards** and **Millbrook Vineyards & Winery** make easy side trips.

ROUTE 9W

Hugging the river's western shoreline, Route 9W passes through long stretches of hardwood forest between Newburgh and Coxsackie. Begin the day's drive at the **Bear Mountain Bridge** and make your way north, stopping for lunch and antiques shopping in **Saugerties.** Allow about three hours of driving time to reach downtown **Albany.**

ROUTE 23/23A

This is a good route for an early-season tour, as the elevation means color will peak a bit sooner than lower in the valley. Begin the drive in the village of **Catskill,** after grabbing a cup of coffee at HiLo Catskill on Main Street. Follow Route 9W south to pick up Route 23A west. At **Palenville,** you'll begin to climb. Look for a trailhead on the right for **Kaaterskill Falls** if you want to hike; otherwise, continue the winding road uphill to **Hainsville,** where you can tour the **Mountain Top Arboretum** and walk along the **Kaaterskill Rail Trail.** Grab lunch at Hunter Village or wait until Windham; then complete the loop by following Route 23 down the mountain and back to the village of Catskill. Total distance is about 80 miles.

ROUTE 44

Pick up Route 44 from the Taconic State Parkway heading east and follow it through **Millbrook,** taking the **Millbrook Vineyards & Winery** detour if time permits. Browse the boutiques in Millbrook, or continue east through Amenia to Millerton. In **Millerton,** park near the Harney & Sons tea company and walk part of the **Harlem Valley Rail Trail.** Afterward, warm up with a cup of tea at the **Harney & Sons Tea Shop &**

bridge along Route 9W near Fort Montgomery, with a footbridge below

Hawk's Nest

Tasting Room. Total driving time will be about an hour from the Taconic State Parkway to the state line. Retrace your steps at day's end to have dinner at Millbrook's **Café Les Baux.**

HAWK'S NEST

This drive begins in western Orange County, near the **Delaware River.** Exit I-84 at Port Jervis and pick up **Route 97 north.** It's about a two-hour scenic drive along the Delaware, past Minisink Battleground and Narrowsburg to Hancock, where you'll pick up Route 17 heading back east and south. Stop for lunch in **Narrowsburg** at **The Heron** overlooking the river. When you reach Roscoe and Livingston Manor on Route 17, consider a visit to the **Catskill Fly Fishing Center and Museum** on your way through Livingston Manor, then finish the day with dinner at **The DeBruce** (or the inn's more casual Club Room) along the **Willowemoc Creek.**

Lower Hudson Valley

The Hudson River Valley's most populous coun-
ties border New York City, with a complex maze of highways, bridges,
trains, and buses to shuttle residents in and out of the five boroughs
every day. Although no longer the rural destination it once was, the
Lower Hudson Valley is packed with historic mansions and restored
gardens at every bend in the road. John Jay, Frederick Philipse, the
Vanderbilts, and the Harrimans all left their mark, but the grandest estate of all was Kykuit, the sprawling Rockefeller residence at Pocantico
Hills near Tarrytown. As a legacy of these large estates, Westchester
and Rockland Counties were able to preserve wilderness areas that rival
many upstate parks and preserves, even as they struggled to cope with
rapid industrial and housing development. More than a dozen gardens

Highlights

Look for ★ to find recommended sights, activities, dining, and lodging.

© MOON.COM

★ **Lyndhurst Mansion:** Part castle and part church, this stunning Gothic Revival estate once housed the family of railroad baron Jay Gould (page 39).

★ **Kykuit (The Rockefeller Estate):** John D. Rockefeller built this six-story, 40-room mansion with breathtaking views of the Hudson River and the Palisades (page 41).

★ **Stone Barns Center for Food and Agriculture:** Tour a working farm, shop the farmers market, or make reservations for an unforgettable meal at Blue Hill, the center's Michelin-star restaurant (page 42).

★ **Katonah Museum Mile:** Katonah is home to three first-rate museums, all located within a mile of each other: the Caramoor Center for Music and the Arts, the Katonah Museum of Art, and the John Jay Homestead (page 46).

★ **Piermont Village:** Three miles south of the Tappan Zee Bridge, on a steep hillside between Route 9W and the riverbank, this upscale community is a haven for cyclists, foodies, and creative types (page 61).

★ **Harriman State Park:** The first section of the Appalachian Trail was cleared here in 1923; today, hikers can access several lakes, plus 200 miles of trails, inside the park (page 64).

★ **Hook Mountain-Nyack Beach Bikeway:** This five-mile trail connects three state parks, Hook Mountain, Rockland Lake, and Nyack Beach (page 68).

Lower Hudson Valley

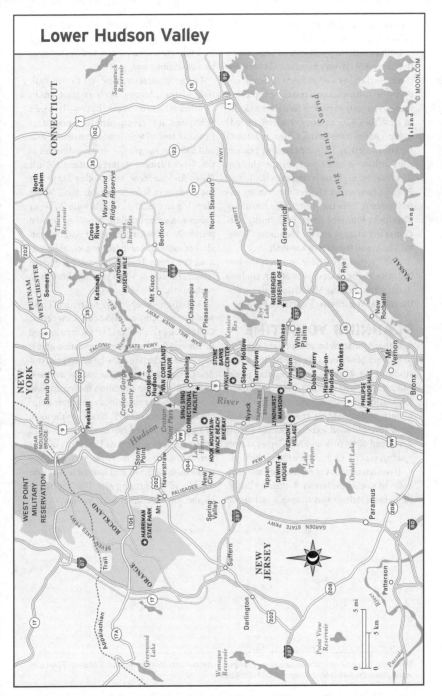

© MOON.COM

are open to the public and easily accessible in a day trip from New York City.

Both counties support diverse populations that represent the very highest and lowest income brackets, as well as many different nations and cultures. Local restaurants prepare menus you only expect to find domestically in New York City or San Francisco, including specialties from Brazil, China, India, and Japan, as well as Italy, Spain, and France. And unlike in other parts of the Hudson River Valley, night owls who visit the Lower Hudson have many choices for evening entertainment, from the Westchester Broadway Theatre in Elmsford to the Performing Arts Center in Purchase and the Caramoor Center for Music and the Arts in Katonah.

The Tappan Zee Bridge connects the two counties at the widest part of the Hudson River, while the Bear Mountain Bridge spans the river at Westchester's northern border.

PLANNING YOUR TIME

Whether you want to add an easy day trip to a longer New York City stay or find a new stopover on your way to a regular weekend getaway farther north, Westchester and Rockland Counties offer many choices for historic tours, outdoor entertainment, and farm-to-table food experiences. The well-developed New York and New Jersey transit systems make it easy to leave the car behind.

If you have one day to explore the area, book a tour of Kykuit, the former Rockefeller Estate, in Sleepy Hollow, and choose a restaurant for dinner in Tarrytown. Alternatively, in Rockland County, head to Piermont Village for a bike ride, hike, or river paddle, followed by a satisfying meal.

Longer itineraries allow you to visit multiple historic homes, such as Jay Gould's Lyndhurst and Washington Irving's Sunnyside, or to contemplate the works of art in one of several well-funded museums. Add half a day to sample the wild mushrooms at the Nyack Farmers Market or attend a White Plains Antique Show. Add another day to tour the gardens in Somers and Purchase. When planning an overnight visit, beware that your choices in accommodations will be limited primarily to business hotels or Airbnb rentals. For more choice in lodging, consider visiting the Lower Hudson on a day trip from New York City or when passing through to parts north.

A Hudson Valley college tour might bring you to the campus of **Sarah Lawrence College,** a private liberal arts school located in Yonkers, with a student population of just over 1600, including a few hundred grad students. Founded in 1926, the college was early to the progressive education movement and has expanded its curriculum over time to include the sciences as well. Nearby in the town of Purchase, **SUNY Purchase** is one of 13 public colleges in the State University of New York higher education system, with a student enrollment of 3,500 and a notable focus on visual and performing arts. Don't miss the Neuberger Museum of Art if you go.

Three Days in Westchester County

With Tarrytown as a base, this plan offers a good mix of art, history, gardens, and good eats.

DAY 1

Fly into Westchester County Airport or any New York City airport and transfer to the Tarrytown area via rental car, Uber, or the Metro-North Hudson Line. Book a hotel room at the Marriott or DoubleTree, or reserve a guest suite, cottage, or house through Airbnb. Browse the shops along Main Street and grab a casual farm-to-table dinner at Sweet Grass Grill. Check the performance schedule at the Tarrytown Music Hall.

Book a tour of Kykuit, the Rockefeller Estate, for your first morning; then head to the Bridge View Tavern in Sleepy Hollow for lunch. In the afternoon, walk the grounds of Lyndhurst, Jay Gould's former estate. A guided tour of the Gothic Revival mansion takes about an hour. Enjoy an evening of fine dining and entertainment at the Westchester Broadway Theatre in Elmsford.

DAY 2

Head east to see the Caramoor Center for Music and the Arts, then shop your way through downtown Katonah. Later, drive through the PepsiCo Sculpture Garden or visit the Neuberger Museum of Art in Purchase. Reserve a table months in advance for dinner at Blue Hill at Stone Barns. Be sure to arrive early enough to tour the working farm to see where your food is grown.

DAY 3

Tour Washington Irving's Romantic estate, Sunnyside, then grab lunch on the waterfront in Irvington and wrap up your trip with a walk along the Old Croton Aqueduct.

Westchester County

Bordering the Bronx, the southern edge of Westchester County is just 15 minutes from Manhattan by train. The county boasts the largest population and the highest population density in the Hudson River Valley—and a surprising blend of wealthy suburbs, ample green space, and historic sites. Yonkers, Mount Vernon, New Rochelle, Rye, and White Plains are the largest cities, and White Plains is the county seat.

Westchester County became a commuter base as early as the 19th century, when rail travel made it possible to reach New York City in just a few hours. As transportation evolved from steamboat to rail to car, Westchester grew at a frenzied pace. Its river towns began to produce medicines, cars, beer, sugar, and elevators, among other goods. Expansion of the New York City watershed created more jobs and further accelerated growth. While many business travelers find themselves in the area for meetings, the main draw for visitors is Tarrytown, with its grand estates, farm-fresh food, live music, and boutique shopping.

ALONG THE RIVER: ROUTE 9
Yonkers

Start a tour of Westchester's river towns from the West Side Highway in Manhattan and follow Route 9A north to Yonkers. This diverse city of approximately 200,000 people is a major transportation hub and is the fourth-largest city in New York State. Its name derives from *jonkheer*, the Dutch word for "young nobleman," in reference to Dutchman Adriaen van der Donck, who built a sawmill where the tiny Nepperhan River (later renamed the Saw Mill River) empties into the Hudson. Four miles of frontage on the eastern bank of the

Hudson offer beautiful views of the Palisades in New Jersey and Rockland County.

Two notable museums are within walking distance of the train station. Two blocks east on Warburton Avenue is **Philipse Manor Hall State Historic Site** (29 Warburton Ave., at Dock St., 914/965-4027, http://parks.ny.gov, noon-5pm Tues.-Sat. Apr.-Oct., noon-4pm Tues.-Sat. Nov.-Mar., adults $5, seniors and students $3, under age 12 free, on-site parking free). This Georgian mansion housed three generations of the Philipse family until loyalist Frederick Philipse III was arrested in 1776 and forced to flee to England. The building dates to 1682, and the exhibits inside trace the history of Yonkers.

Also on Warburton Avenue, the **Hudson River Museum** (511 Warburton Ave., 914/963-4550, www.hrm.org, noon-5pm Thurs.-Sun., adults $8, youths $4, seniors and students with ID $5, members free) was founded in 1919 with a focus on Hudson River art, history, and science. Recent exhibitions focus on environmental conservation and the role of the river in shaping local communities. The permanent collection includes landscape paintings from the Hudson River School of painters, historic photographs, sculpture, and prints. A summer amphitheater hosts a variety of performances from Shakespeare to modern dance to international musicians.

Inside the Glenview Mansion, which is also part of the museum, six rooms are furnished in turn-of-the-20th-century style. The sitting room holds one of the highlights of a house tour: a delicately carved and inlaid sunflower pattern in the woodwork, representative of the rare American Eastlake interior style. In addition to these varied exhibits, the museum hosts an annual jazz series each summer.

Three River Towns: Hastings-on-Hudson, Dobbs Ferry, and Irvington

If you have only one day to spend on the **Old Croton Aqueduct** (Park Office, 15 Walnut St., Dobbs Ferry, 914/693-5259, http://parks. ny.gov), choose the section that connects the three river towns above Yonkers: Hastings-on-Hudson, Dobbs Ferry, and Irvington. Artists and commuters have made these towns their home, and the route leads from historical homes and shady lanes to local parks and river views, with the Palisades always looming in the distance. Farmers markets, bookstores, antiques stores, and other shops provide good diversions from the trail. The Ossining aqueduct tunnel is open June-October by reservation only; the rest of the park is open sunrise-sunset year-round.

The most famous resident of Hastings-on-Hudson began his career as an architect and later became a painter associated with the first generation of the Hudson River School. Like his fellow Romantic artists, Jasper Francis Cropsey (1823-1900) depicted the Hudson River, Catskill Mountain House, and Lake George, as well as other natural wonders in the northeast, in a series of colorful and fantastical landscapes. The **Newington Cropsey Gallery** (25 Cropsey Lane, Hastings-on-Hudson, 914/478-7990, www. newingtoncropsey.com, permanent collection and gallery tours by appointment Tues.-Thurs. Feb.-July and Sept.-Nov., call for admission), located near the train station, contains an exhaustive collection of Cropsey's works, including oil paintings, watercolors, drawings, and architectural renderings. A guided tour of the gallery takes about 45 minutes. Also in town, the yellow 1835 **Cropsey Homestead** (49 Washington Ave., Hastings-on-Hudson, 914/478-7990, www.newingtoncropsey.com, tours available by appointment 10am-1pm Mon.-Fri. Feb.-July and Sept.-Nov., call for admission), called Ever Rest, has been furnished and decorated to reflect 19th-century sensibility. The separate art studio dates to 1885, and many of Cropsey's sketches and studies are on display inside the home and studio.

During the same period, a 19th-century photographer and astronomer named John William Draper (1811-1882), who took some of the earliest pictures of the moon, built a federal-style farmhouse on 20 acres in Hastings. His two sons later built a famous

Old Croton Aqueduct State Historic Park

Yonkers is the southern terminus for the most unique outdoor space in all of Westchester County: the Old Croton Aqueduct State Historic Park. In the early 19th century, a thirsty New York City, plagued by fire and illness, turned to abundant upstate resources for a clean and ready supply of water. The Croton River delivered, and the city has feuded with rural upstate towns over rights to water ever since.

Engineers diverted the river through a 26.2-mile aqueduct to the Bronx. They built a stone tunnel 8.5 feet tall by 7.5 feet wide that sloped just enough to use the force of gravity. They then laid the length of it with brick, adding a stone shaft at every mile for ventilation. Completed in 1842 at a cost of $12 million, the Old Croton Aqueduct served the growing city well until the turn of the next century. When New York needed more, a replacement in 1905 tripled its capacity.

The oldest aqueduct in the New York City watershed is now a national historic landmark and a long corridor of a state park. It's also just the perfect length, surface, and terrain to prepare for a marathon. In fact, joggers hit the trail at dawn most days of the year. Historic mansions, riverside villages, and Hudson River views distract them from the work at hand, while the stone markers at every mile ensure they stay on pace.

You don't have to be an endurance athlete to appreciate the trail: Cyclists, walkers, cross-country skiers, and horseback riders of all levels enjoy the path and its ever-changing scenery. Access is convenient to most of the train stations along the Metro-North Hudson Line, including Hastings-on-Hudson, Dobbs Ferry, Irvington, and Greystone in Yonkers. Parking is available at the train stations and also at the Ossining Heritage Area Visitor Center. The community organization **Friends of the Old Croton Aqueduct** (www.aqueduct.org) publishes two detailed color maps of the trail for $5 each. New signs posted in 2018 clarify some of the trail section connections.

observatory that hosted the likes of Thomas Edison and Samuel Morse. Today, the **Draper Observatory Cottage** (41 Washington Ave., Hastings-on-Hudson, 914/478-2249, www.hastingshistorical.org, 11am-2pm Mon. and Thurs., 2pm-4pm 1st Sat. of the month Sept.-June, call for admission) holds the Hastings-on-Hudson Historical Society, with an archive of books, maps, paintings, and other town memorabilia. After browsing the museums, enjoy a picnic and the riverside views at MacEachron Waterfront Park, next to the train station.

Much of the 2002 movie *Unfaithful*, starring Diane Lane and Richard Gere, was filmed in neighboring Dobbs Ferry, a town that locals affectionately call the Sausalito of the east, referring to its setting on a hillside overlooking the Hudson River. Settled by Irish, Italian, and other European immigrants during the Industrial Revolution, this town of 11,000 residents was named for a ferry service that operated in the 1700s. Journalist and railroad

financier Henry Villard (1835-1900) joined the well-to-do here in 1879. Many of the original homes feature long-lasting Vermont slate roofs. A handful of art galleries are located along Main Street and Broadway.

Irvington takes its name from Washington Irving, but the town is better known as the home of the first African American millionaire and philanthropist, Madam C. J. Walker (1867-1919), who made her fortune selling hair and beauty products. Walker commissioned Vertner Woodson Tandy, considered the first licensed black architect in New York State, to build her dream home on Broadway in 1917. The resulting Italianate structure, called Villa Lewaro, featured river views from the dining room and hosted many black leaders of the time, from Langston Hughes to W. E. B. Du Bois. Villa Lewaro is privately owned today by Helena and Harold Doley.

Tarrytown and Sleepy Hollow

Soon after he moved to the neighboring

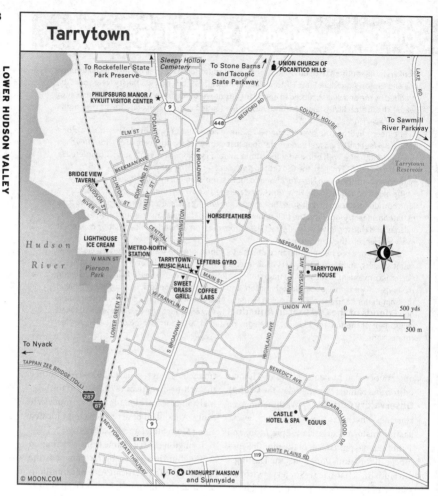

Tarrytown

hamlet of Sleepy Hollow, John D. Rockefeller reportedly tried to purchase and shut down Tarrytown's only tavern. It was a rare instance in which the Puritan business mogul was unable to impose his will on those around him, and Tarrytown remained a lively center for commerce and the arts.

Today, a stroll along Main Street, with its coffeehouses and antiques shops, is the perfect interlude between tours of the surrounding homes and gardens, and it is a convenient stop for nourishment while exploring the Old Croton Aqueduct. At the river's edge, **Pierson** **Park** (238 W. Main St., Tarrytown) has picnic tables, tennis courts, and a play structure for kids. This is a good place to park and pick up the mile-long Tarrytown-Sleepy Hollow section of the **Westchester RiverWalk.** For motorists, Route 9 turns into Broadway as you approach the center of town. Follow Main Street toward the river to find a public parking lot.

Sunnyside

A few miles south, **Sunnyside** (W. Sunnyside Lane, Tarrytown, 914/631-8200, www.

hudsonvalley.org, admission by timed tours only 10am-5pm Wed.-Fri. and 9:30am-5pm Sat.-Sun. early May-Sept., adults $10, seniors $8, children $8, under age 3 free), the Romantic-era home of celebrated author Washington Irving, known as America's first man of letters, comes right out of the pages of a children's storybook. Set among rolling hills, a babbling brook, and the purple and white flowers of wisteria that climb all the way up to the gabled roof, Sunnyside captures the imagination in much the same way that Irving's tales "Rip Van Winkle" and "The Legend of Sleepy Hollow" did.

After a life of international travel and diplomacy, Irving found this peaceful retreat near Tarrytown, a place he remembered well from his childhood. Irving purchased the future site of Sunnyside in 1835 and settled here a year later. After a brief stint as minister to Spain, he returned to Sunnyside to live until his death in 1859. John D. Rockefeller acquired the property in 1945 and opened it to the public two years later.

In Sunnyside, Irving happily mixed and matched architectural styles according to the Romantic philosophy: Stepped gables and weathervanes reflect the writer's Dutch heritage, while steeply pitched rooflines, irregular window sizes, and a facade of cut stone were borrowed from the Scottish home of Sir Walter Scott, a contemporary of Irving's. Later, Irving added a Spanish-style tower to remind him of the time he had spent living in Spain. The surrounding gardens and grounds were as important to the writer as the design of his home.

Today, guides in Victorian-era costumes welcome visitors into the enchanted home to experience a day in the life of the writer. A pair of Gothic Revival-style benches line the entrance to the home. Among the furnishings on display are Irving's desk and many of his books. In the kitchen, visitors can admire the cast-iron wood-burning stove and cast-iron pedestal sink, which featured both hot and cold running water, modern conveniences during Irving's time.

Nationally known and loved in his own lifetime, Irving wrote far more than the stories we remember today: Among his last works was an exhaustive biography of his namesake, George Washington. Visitors can tour the inside, walk the grounds, and picnic under the trees. Tours begin with a short film, and visitor services include a café and museum shop stocked with books by and about Irving as well as some of his contemporaries.

★ Lyndhurst Mansion

The Old Croton Aqueduct trail connects Sunnyside to the adjacent **Lyndhurst** estate (635 S. Broadway, Tarrytown, 914/631-4481, www.lyndhurst.org, grounds 9:30am-4:30pm daily Apr.-Dec., mansion tours 9:30am-4:30pm Fri.-Sun. and holidays May-Nov., grounds pass $10, tours adults $20, seniors $18, ages 6-16 $15, under age 6 free). When former New York City mayor William Paulding was ready to retire in 1838, he commissioned architect Alexander Jackson Davis to design a modest 7,000-square-foot country villa in the Gothic Revival style. Twenty-five years later, Davis was brought back to the estate to double the size of the mansion when businessman George Merritt bought it from the Paulding family. Then, in 1880, railroad baron Jay Gould purchased the estate as a summer home and left it to his eldest daughter, Helen, who added a bowling alley and recreation center and a circular rose garden that still blooms today. Helen's younger sister Anna was the last member of the family to oversee the estate, and she left it to the National Trust for Historic Preservation when she died in 1961.

Today, the landscape remains much as it was planned in the 19th century, including groves of linden trees and river views from several different angles. Inside, all the art, books, and furnishings are original to the estate, many of them designed by the architect himself, and the collection reflects the aesthetic of each of the three families who lived at Lyndhurst.

You can stroll the grounds with a pass purchased in advance for $10. The classic

mansion tour takes about an hour. Backstairs Tours show the butler's pantry, servants' quarters, and other behind-the-scenes areas. Sunday jazz concerts on the lawn provide entertainment during the summer months.

Philipsburg Manor

A tour of the white three-story **Philipsburg Manor** (381 N. Broadway/Rte. 9, Sleepy Hollow, 914/631-8200, www.hudsonvalley. org, admission by timed tours only 10am-3pm Wed.-Sun. May-Nov., adults $12, seniors $10, ages 3-17 $6, under age 3 free), at Upper Mills, is an interactive production, with theatrical guides dressed in colonial garb. It is also a sobering experience, designed to give visitors an appreciation for the manual labor required to run an international trading company in the 19th century. The Philipse family was one of the earliest and largest slaveholders in the northeast, and today's museum exhibits address the African American experience on the farm. The tour begins in the basement kitchen and former slave quarters, and then progresses through the house with a narrative that brings the enslaved perspective to life.

Philipsburg Manor is also the departure point for all tours to Kykuit, the Rockefeller Estate. A small café sells basic breakfast fare, snacks, and paninis; the adjoining gift shop stocks a variety of relevant books and souvenirs. Across Route 9 from Philipsburg Manor is the **Sleepy Hollow Cemetery,** with the gravesites of Washington Irving, William Cullen Bryant, Andrew Carnegie, Walter Chrysler, William Rockefeller, and others. The property runs for several miles along Route 9, surrounding the **Old Dutch Church** and its historic burial ground.

★ Kykuit (The Rockefeller Estate)

Land prices were at a historic low in 1893 when John D. Rockefeller bought his first 400 acres in the **Pocantico Hills** (po-CAN-tee-co,

1: guided tour of Lyndhurst Mansion 2: Philipsburg Manor

meaning "water rushing over rocks") north of Tarrytown. Stunning views of the Hudson River and surrounding hills and mountains drew the oil magnate to an area he described as "a place where fine views invest the soul and where we can live simply and quietly." The family's country estate expanded to 1,600 acres by the turn of the 20th century and 3,000 at its peak. Today, it remains an extraordinary place where visitors can absorb some history, admire a modern art collection, learn about local flora, and reflect on a bygone era.

Rockefeller built 75 homes and 70 miles of roads, all strategically placed to show off the surrounding views. He designed much of the landscape himself, and except for a central private area, he insisted that the grounds be kept open to the public, as long as visitors abided by his rules: no cars, no drinking, and no smoking. As the estate grew, Rockefeller paid handsomely to relocate a small college, a neighborhood of homes, and even a stretch of the New York Central Railroad to the outskirts of his property. A small farm supplied food for the family, and golf became Rockefeller's preferred pastime at Pocantico. He designed a 12-hole course and played year-round, rain or shine.

For the first decade, Rockefeller lived in and remodeled the modest home that had come with the property. When that residence burned down in 1902, the family built a hilltop mansion two miles from the Hudson called Kykuit (pronounced KYE-cut), which means "lookout." It was designed to maximize sunlight in winter. Conceived as an English country house, the structure evolved into a six-story, 40-room ordeal in the American Renaissance style. It was completed in 1913.

Rockefeller's son, Junior, commissioned the estate's garden design to architect William Welles Bosworth, who crafted one of the finest surviving examples of beaux arts gardens found anywhere in the United States. Among the unusual flora are a split-leaf maple and weeping cherry trees. Wisteria blooms in May. A hedge is trimmed to mirror the profile of Hook Mountain in the distance. A table and stools in the form of mushrooms are set back in an overhang. Made of rough-cut stone, the Grotto features a Guastavino tile ceiling and Moravian tile floor. In a characteristic installation, Junior's son, Nelson Rockefeller, added the yellow and green *Futuristic Flowers* by Italian artist Giacomo Balla.

In fact, it was Nelson Rockefeller who first added a sense of fun to the estate, introducing modern art, a card table, and a bowling alley. His collection of modern art is a highlight of any Kykuit tour. A dozen tapestries by Pablo Picasso are hung in lower-level galleries, and sculpture works by Alexander Calder and other 20th-century artists complement the formal Italian-inspired gardens and challenge golfers on the putting green. *The Bathers*, a series of six figures Picasso originally made of driftwood, were cast into bronze and set against a background of white pine near the brook garden and adjacent to the former tennis court. Having a bit of fun with the placement of the installation, Nelson Rockefeller decided to elevate the diver onto a platform.

Five different walking tours—led by knowledgeable guides who cover art, plants, and architecture as well as the family history—allow visitors to tailor their experience to the areas of the estate that interest them most. The two-hour **house and inner gardens tour** (914/631-8200, www.hudsonvalley.org, 9am-5:15pm Thurs.-Fri., 9am-6pm Sat.-Sun. May-Nov., adults $25-40) is oriented toward first-timers. A three-hour **Grand Tour** ($45) includes more of the sculpture and gardens, as well as a tour of the second floor of the home. The first group of the day gets the best view of the river from inside the house; later in the day, other groups a few minutes ahead tend to block the views. Book tours on the website.

The only access to **Kykuit** (200 Lake Rd./Rte. 448, Pocantico Hills, Tarrytown, www.hudsonvalley.org) is via shuttle bus from the visitors center at Philipsburg Manor. The adjoining **Rockefeller State Park Preserve** (Rte. 117, 1 mile east of Rte. 9, Tarrytown, 914/631-1470, http://parks.ny.gov, 7am-sunset daily, parking $6) is open year-round for hiking, fishing, horseback riding, and cross-country skiing.

Route 442 out of Sleepy Hollow leads to Bedford and the **Union Church of Pocantico Hills** (Rte. 448/Bedford Rd., Sleepy Hollow, 914/631-2069, www.hudsonvalley.org, 10am-4:30pm Fri.-Sat., noon-4pm Sun. Aug.-Nov., $9). Take the Eastview exit from the Saw Mill River Parkway. This church features stained glass windows designed by Henri Matisse and Marc Chagall to serve as Rockefeller family memorials. Just days before Matisse died, he completed the design for a rose window honoring Abby Aldrich Rockefeller, the founder of the Museum of Modern Art in New York City. The series of one large and eight small windows, completed in 1965, are the only church windows Chagall ever created.

TOP EXPERIENCE

★ Stone Barns Center for Food and Agriculture

Just up the road from the Union Church, families, foodies, and backyard gardeners flock to Stone Barns, a nonprofit four-season farm and educational center that is committed to changing the future of our food system. Set on 80 acres of rolling hills adjoining the Rockefeller State Park Preserve, the center trains young farmers to grow produce and livestock sustainably, while also educating the community about what it takes to build an ecological food culture. A longstanding partnership with the on-site restaurant **Blue Hill** at Stone Barns is part of what makes this center unique among agricultural programs.

Visitors to **Stone Barns** (630 Bedford Hills Rd., Pocantico Hills, 914/366-6200, www.stonebarnscenter.org) can tour the vegetable gardens, collect eggs, observe the beehives, participate in scavenger hunts, visit the livestock, watch chickens take a dust bath, and help farmers shear sheep in spring. There are classes in beekeeping, soil fertility, farm-to-table cooking, and more. Guest speakers have included authors Michael Pollan and Bill McKibben, and Amanda Hesser of the *New*

York Times. The summer farm camp program is popular for kids. In 2020, Stone Barns introduced a Chef in Residence program to deepen its exploration into the intersection of cooking and farming—along with connections to culture, identity, community, and health.

Reservations are required for all activities, and the tickets do tend to sell out most weekends. Once you've selected a day online, you can add on specific programs. For example, a 90-minute session in the Innovation Lab ($75) focuses on the link between healthy soil and nutritious food. Or a 60-minute guided farm tour costs $25. Alternatively, you can just pay $25 for a parking pass and explore the grounds on your own. Food options include a pre-fixed lunch tray ($35) or afternoon snacks ($40) prepared by **Blue Hill Café & Grain Bar** (914/366-9600, 10am-4:30pm Wed.-Sun.). A gift shop on the premises sells farm-themed goodies such as beeswax candles, gardening gifts, and books about growing green.

Ossining and Croton-on-Hudson

Continuing north along Route 9, Ossining is best known as the location of **Sing Sing Correctional Facility,** which you can see from a small riverfront park near the train station. Ossining's Main Street is busy and attractive in a no-nonsense sort of way, although a Bikram yoga studio suggests the town may be shedding its working-class image. The Old Croton Aqueduct runs straight through the middle of town. And just beyond, **Teatown Lake Reservation** (1600 Spring Valley Rd., Ossining, 914/762-2912, www.teatown.org, trails open dawn-dusk year-round, admission and parking free) is a nature preserve with 14 miles of secluded trails and environmental exhibits. The nature center is open 9am-5pm daily.

The next river town, Croton-on-Hudson, is a major point of transfer for rail commuters coming to and from the northern counties. Croton also boasts the third-largest reservoir in the New York City Watershed. By the turn

of the 20th century, New York City needed more water than the original aqueduct could provide, and work began anew. Irish, German, and Italian immigrants labored hard to build the dam that created the **New Croton Reservoir.** It measures nine miles long—touching the towns of Cortlandt, Yorktown, Somers, Bedford, and New Castle—and holds 19 billion gallons at full capacity. The dam is located on Route 19, off Route 9A north of the village of Croton.

At the junction of the Croton and Hudson Rivers and within walking distance of the Croton-on-Hudson train station, the fieldstone **Van Cortlandt Manor** (S. Riverside Ave., Croton-on-Hudson, 914/631-8200, www. hudsonvalley.org, admission by timed tours only 10am-4:30pm Fri.-Sun. July-Aug., adults $12, seniors $10, children $6, under age 3 free) hides behind a row of hardwood trees. As the Dutch-style home of a prominent colonial family, the museum contains many original Georgian and Federal period furnishings. On the grounds outside, caretakers plant seasonal heirloom vegetable and herb gardens.

Croton Point Park (Croton Point Ave., Croton-on-Hudson, 8am-dusk daily) occupies a 508-acre peninsula on the Hudson River just outside of town and hosts Clearwater's Great Hudson River Revival festival each June. Camping, hiking, swimming, and sunbathing are all possible here, and there is a small nature center at the top of the hill.

Follow Grand Street (Rural Rte. 129) east out of town for a couple of miles to get to **Croton Gorge County Park** (Rural Rte. 129, Cortlandt Manor, 914/827-9568) at the base of the New Croton Dam. This 97-acre park has a long grassy lawn, picnic tables, restrooms, and views of the falls. Fishing and cross-country skiing also are permitted. Follow a dirt road by foot or bike to reach the road at the top of the dam. From there, you can follow the Old Croton Aqueduct trail through the woods. The trail has several road crossings between Croton-on-Hudson and Ossining, so watch for traffic.

Peekskill

At the northern edge of Westchester County and just below the Hudson Highlands lies the city of Peekskill, yet another strategic location during the American Revolution. It later became a large manufacturing center and busy river port. After some tough years of decline, Peekskill is attracting artists and small businesses again. The **Peekskill Coffee House** (101 S. Division St., 914/739-1287, http://peekskillcoffee.com, 7am-7pm daily) is a great place to soak up the local vibe.

On the same block, **Flat Iron Gallery** (105 S. Division St., 914/734-1894, 3pm-6pm Fri., noon-6pm Sat., appointment only Sun.) specializes in contemporary fine art and handcrafted jewelry. This is a good place to look for Hudson River landscapes. In June, you can tour local artist studios in the downtown area. Guided and self-guided tours are available. Contact the **Peekskill Arts Alliance** (914/737-1646, www.peekskillartsalliance. org) for info. If you're in search of books about the history and outdoors of the Hudson Valley, pop into **Bruised Apple Books** (923 Central Ave., 914/734-7000, www.bruisedapplenooks. com). Call ahead, as business hours vary.

Peekskill's **Riverfront Green** is a suitable place to launch a kayak for a paddle around Peekskill Bay. The 1,600-acre **Blue Mountain Reservation** (Welcher Ave., Peekskill, 914/862-5275, http://parks. westchestergov.com, 8am-dusk daily year-round, parking $10) has 20 miles of bike trails signed for beginner, intermediate, and advanced riders, as well as hiking and picnic grounds. Exit Route 9 at Welcher Avenue and head east to the park entrance.

CENTRAL WESTCHESTER COUNTY

Several old highways traverse the length of central Westchester County, following smaller rivers that empty into the Hudson: The Saw Mill River Parkway connects Manhattan's Upper West Side to the Taconic State Parkway in Mount Pleasant; the Bronx River Parkway connects Mount Vernon to the Taconic at I-287; and the Hutchinson River Parkway runs from Pelham Manor to I-684. In the center of all the traffic is White Plains, a land of corporate headquarters, chain hotels, shopping galleries, and business conference centers.

Named for the fog that hung over its wetlands when the first settlers arrived, White Plains has secured its place in history: It was the site of a major Revolutionary War battle, and George Washington set up a command from the 1720 **Jacob Purdy House** (60 Park Ave., White Plains, 914/328-1776, www. westchestertourism.com, by appointment only). Unless you seek upscale stores outside of New York City, however, you'll find few sights that require a special trip.

Purchase

East of White Plains, near the Westchester County Airport, is an outstanding modern art museum, the **Neuberger Museum of Art** (735 Anderson Hill Rd., Purchase, 914/251-6100, www.neuberger.org, noon-5pm Wed.-Sun., adults $5, seniors and students $3, under age 12 free, free 1st Sat. of the month). In 1969, Purchase College, part of the State University of New York, received a generous donation of 20th-century American art. Roy R. Neuberger enabled the college to begin a collection that now features contemporary and African art, as well as its initial base of modern masterpieces. The permanent collection at the Neuberger Museum of Art includes works by Edward Hopper, Georgia O'Keeffe, Jackson Pollock, and Mark Rothko. Occasional solo exhibitions feature artists who have had a significant impact on the contemporary art world but have not yet been recognized for their contributions. Take exit 28 from the Hutchinson River Parkway.

While you're in the area, don't miss the chance to tour the **Donald M. Kendall Sculpture Gardens at PepsiCo Headquarters** (700 Anderson Hill Rd.,

---

1: sunflowers in Stone Barns' garden
2: flour for sale at Stone Barns' café 3: Stone Barns Center entrance

Purchase, 914/253-3150, 10am-4pm Sat.-Sun. Mar.-Oct.). The company has placed 45 sculptures by 20th-century artists, including Auguste Rodin, on 168 landscaped acres. You can walk or drive the grounds free of charge. Allow about 90 minutes for a complete tour.

Katonah

New York City's need for water left an indelible mark on the hamlet of Katonah. When city officials flooded the Cross River in the 1890s to add new capacity to the Croton Watershed System, they threatened to swallow the homes that had stood on its bank since the first Europeans arrived. A group of resolute townspeople pooled their resources and moved dozens of buildings to the opposite shore. They planned a simple grid, and the new town thrived as a place of commerce and leisure. As a result, present-day Katonah blends a Victorian look and feel with a modern sensibility. More than 30 Victorian-era buildings make up the Katonah Historic District on Bedford Road, between Edgemont Road and the Terrace. Near the Bedford Village Green at the junction of Routes 22 and 172 are the 1878 courthouse, schoolhouse, general store, post office, and old burying ground.

On Route 35, **Lasdon Park and Arboretum** (914/864-7268, www.lasdonpark. org, park hours 8am-4pm daily, conservatory hours 10am-3pm Wed.-Sun.) is the largest publicly owned arboretum in the county, with 234 acres of woods, meadows, and gardens originally designed as a country estate for philanthropist William Lasdon. It has been owned by Westchester County since 1986 and boasts one of the largest collections of lilac trees in the region, with more than 90 different species that bloom in purples, whites, and pinks each May. Three acres of rare American chestnut trees and a historic tree walk bring researchers and amateur botanists alike. The park hosts a summer concert series, annual plant sale, and twice-yearly antiques shows.

★ Katonah Museum Mile

This community of 3,000 people supports a remarkable group of cultural institutions, three of which make up the town's Museum Mile, along Route 22. The **Caramoor Center for Music and the Arts** (149 Girdle Ridge Rd., Katonah, 914/232-1232, www.caramoor. org, 10am-4pm daily summer, 10am-4pm Fri.-Sun. fall-spring) began as the summer home of Walter and Lucie Rosen, both passionate musicians and patrons of the arts. The Rosens purchased the estate in 1928, and they had exquisite taste in furniture, tapestries, china, and jewels—many of which are on display in the many rooms that are used for public concerts and lectures today. They invited musicians to perform in the old-world setting of a Spanish courtyard, and over the years, their private concerts evolved into an annual summer festival. It's free to tour the grounds during the concert season. In the off-season, you can tour the Rosen House (Fri.-Sun., $15 pp), enjoy afternoon tea, and stroll the formal gardens. The Sense Circle is an especially peaceful place to collect your thoughts. But to really experience the place, you must attend a performance. Recent concerts have focused on flamenco, jazz, string quartets, and "rising stars."

North of Caramoor on Route 22, the **Katonah Museum of Art** (Rte. 22 and Jay St., Katonah, 914/232-9555, www. katonahmuseum.org, 10am-5pm Tues.-Sat., noon-5pm Sun., adults $10, seniors and students $5, under age 12 free) hosts three major exhibits per year, plus a series of smaller shows and outdoor concerts. In this way, the museum draws a large following while giving exposure to newer works. Don't overlook the sculpture garden outside.

Katonah's third museum is a good place to dive into the early history of the nascent U.S. government. At the conclusion of a distinguished career, diplomat and negotiator John Jay retired to his family's farm in Katonah. A descendant of the Van Cortlandt family, Jay had worked with the Founding

1: Chinese Friendship Pavilion and Culture Garden at Lasdon Park and Arboretum **2:** the New Croton Dam in Croton Gorge County Park

Fathers to ensure the future of the new republic. After Jay held a succession of international posts, George Washington appointed him first chief justice of the U.S. Supreme Court. His former residence is now the **John Jay Homestead State Historic Site** (400 Jay St./Rte. 22, Katonah, 914/232-5651, www. johnjayhomestead.org, visitor center 10am-4pm daily, grounds sunrise-sunset daily, free), located on Route 22 between Katonah and Bedford Village. Shaded by three linden trees, the main home remains much as it was in Jay's time. Outside, you can view the formal gardens and walk the steep Beech Allee to imagine how it felt to arrive at the estate by carriage. Local farmers bring their harvest to the homestead for a farmers market (10am-2pm Sat. June-Oct.).

The site is arranged into six **discovery centers** (free), each in its own historic building with interactive exhibits. The Carriage Barn serves as the main visitor center, while the Red Barn (9am-4pm Sat. May-Oct., other days by reservation) focuses on the agricultural history of the estate.

Cross River

Westchester County's largest park has been a wildlife sanctuary since 1924. Located east of Katonah at the junction of Routes 35 and 121, **Ward Pound Ridge Reservation** (Rte. 35 and Rte. 121, Cross River, 914/864-7317, http://parks.westchestergov.com, 8am-dusk daily, parking $10) encompasses 4,315 acres of wildflowers, hiking trails, campsites, and picnic grounds, plus an interpretive **Trailside Nature Museum** (9am-4pm Tues.-Sat., closed some Fri.) with Native American exhibits that are a popular destination for school field trips.

Somers

IBM and PepsiCo draw business travelers to the suburban town of Somers, but at least one unusual sight is worth a peek if you happen to pass through. Apply the concept of heirloom vegetables to fauna, and you've got **Muscoot Farm** (51 Rte. 100, 914/864-7282, www.

muscootfarm.org, 10am-4pm daily, fees vary). Its rare farm-animal breeds and vintage-equipment exhibits on 777 acres portray the life of the American farmer in the early 20th century. In something of a cross between a petting zoo and a museum, the farm raises pigs, horses, sheep, and ducks. It is also a good place to look for wild butterflies. Self-guided Farmyard Visit tours are offered by appointment only Monday-Tuesday. From exit 6 on I-684, follow Route 35 west to Route 100. The entrance is a mile down the road, on the right.

North Salem

The **Hammond Museum and Japanese Stroll Garden** (28 Deveau Rd., 914/669-5033, www.hammondmuseum.org, noon-4pm Wed.-Sat May-Nov., adults $8, seniors and students $6, under 12 free) blends Eastern and Western aesthetics to create an enchanting outdoor experience. Workshops introduce visitors to the Japanese tea ceremony, how to make sushi, and origami for children. Water lilies, a reflecting pool, and the red maple terrace take visitors back to sixth-century Japan. And a delightful combination of rock, sand, waterfalls, and evergreens stimulates the senses. Inside the Hammond Museum is a collection of Mandarin fans, as well as several hundred portraits taken by music and theater critic Carl Van Vechten. Occasional twilight hours events (4pm-7pm, adults $15, seniors and students $12, under age 12 free) give visitors a chance to experience the gardens under stars. Croton Falls is the nearest Metro-North station for those arriving by train.

RECREATION
Winter Sports

Despite its population density, Westchester maintains 17,000 acres of public parks for recreation throughout the year. Many of them are ideal for cross-country skiing after heavy winter storms. Take a loop around the lake on three miles of trails at **Cranberry Lake Preserve** (Old Orchard St., White Plains, 914/428-1005, http://parks.westchestergov. com, dawn-dusk daily). Some sections of the

Gardens of Westchester County

Westchester County boasts some of the largest and most elaborate outdoor gardens in the Hudson River Valley. Here is a sampling of the very best:

- **Caramoor Center for Music and the Arts, Katonah:** Stroll through the Sunken Garden, Butterfly Garden, Iris & Peony Garden, Sense Circle, and Tapestry Hedge on this 90-acre property dedicated to the arts.

- **Donald M. Kendall Sculpture Gardens at PepsiCo Headquarters, Purchase:** Drive or walk the grounds to see 45 sculptures on 168 acres.

- **Hammond Museum and Japanese Stroll Garden, North Salem:** Think of Japan as you walk among water lilies, a reflecting pool, and the red maple terrace.

- **John Jay Homestead State Historic Site, Katonah:** Formal gardens designed in the 19th century are set around a sundial and fountain. Several more flower gardens surround the historic home.

- **Kykuit, The Rockefeller Estate, Sleepy Hollow:** With so many formal and historic gardens, there is a tour dedicated to plants and sculpture. Learn about classic garden design while viewing contemporary sculptures in a stunning hilltop setting.

- **Luquer-Marble Memorial Wildflower Garden, Ward Pound Ridge Reservation, Cross River:** Behind the Trailside Nature Museum in Westchester's largest park, a small wildflower garden honors two conservationists who were instrumental in securing funding for the museum. Best visited in April and May when spring flowers bloom.

- **Lyndhurst Rose Garden and Fern Garden, Tarrytown:** View 500 roses on a historic 19th-century estate.

- **Van Cortlandt Manor, Croton-on-Hudson:** Heirloom veggies and herbs grow outside one of the Hudson River Valley's preserved river mansions.

- **Lasdon Park and Arboretum:** Head here in May to see an incredible display of lilacs blooming, or anytime to take the Historic Tree Walk. The Chinese Friendship Pavilion and Cultural Garden was gifted by the city of Jingzhou.

gently graded **Old Croton Aqueduct** are also skiable. Try Croton Dam Plaza in Croton or North Tarrytown, near Rockefeller State Park Preserve.

Hiking

Westchester wilderness lends itself more to a walk in the woods than a backcountry experience. But several large green spaces make it possible to get well away from the bustle of everyday suburban life. Many of Westchester's parks are open to residents only and require the purchase of a county park pass (http:// parks.westchestergov.com, $75 per year). The **Westchester Trails Association** (www. westhike.org) organizes weekend day hikes year-round. Here is a sampling of the top 100 routes:

Cranberry Lake Preserve (Old Orchard St., White Plains, 914/428-1005, parks.westchestergov.com, dawn-dusk daily) has an easy three-mile trail through an old quarry. Allow a couple of hours to complete the loop.

For a moderate all-day hike, head to **Ward Pound Ridge Reservation** (Rte. 35 and Rte. 121, Cross River, 914/864-7317, http://parks.westchestergov.com, 8am-dusk daily, $10) and follow the **Rocks Trail** (7-mile loop). Alternatively, the **Star Loop** (5 miles) is an easier route.

You can take in both peaks of **Blue Mountain Reservation,** Blue and

Spitzenberg Mountains, on a moderate hike (7 miles round-trip) from Depew Park in Peekskill.

Cycling and Mountain Biking

Westchester County maintains a network of trailways for cyclists—paths that are mostly paved and closed to motorists. The **South County Trailway** is a 14.1-mile path that runs north to south in the southern part of the county. Pick up the northern end by the Eastview park-and-ride at Route 100C. The **North County Trailway** starts at the same park-and-ride and runs north for 22 miles, connecting to the Putnam Trailway. There is a relatively steep climb up from the Croton Reservoir. The **Bronx River Parkway** also closes to traffic for free Bicycle Sundays (10am-2pm Sun. May-June and Sept.), from exit 22 at the Westchester County Center (parking $7) to exit 4 at Scarsdale Road in Yonkers. The distance is 13 miles round-trip.

The **Westchester Cycle Club** (www. westchestercycleclub.org) hosts the annual Golden Apple Tour in September. Routes from 25 to 60 miles traverse the countryside in Westchester and Putnam Counties.

Mountain biking is on the rise across the Hudson Valley, and each region has a club that is actively working with the state's Department of Environmental Conservation (DEC) to build and maintain trails. The Trailforks app is the best way to find established trails and routes. The **Westchester Mountain Biking Association** (www. wmba.org) posts trail reports, group rides, and upcoming events in the Lower Hudson Valley. It also hosts the Fat Tire Festival in June.

Peekskill has a gem of a park for mountain biking enthusiasts: **Blue Mountain Reservation** (Welcher Ave., Peekskill, 914/862-5275, 8am-dusk daily year-round, parking $10) has 20 miles of trails designated for beginner, intermediate, and advanced riders. Local NICA high school teams practice here. Note that Blue Mountain Peak (680 feet) is accessible only on foot.

Run by a pro-level mountain biker, **Trail Masters Touring** (914/325-5916, www. trailmasterstouring.com) offers tours and clinics for riders of all levels. Owner and instructor Tom Oakes offers bike rentals as well as guided tours. He is a Certified Mountain Bike Instructor who is active in local trail building and maintenance, and offers frequent free skills clinics. One of the most popular and scenic rides for visitors begins in Croton Gorge Park and follows the Old Croton Aqueduct through the towns of Croton-on-Hudson and Ossining. Tom also can meet guests at the train station with bikes. **Endless Trail Bikeworx** (56 Main St., Dobbs Ferry, 914/674-8567, www.endlesstrailbw. com, 11am-5pm Tues.-Fri., 10am-5pm Sat., noon-5pm Sun.) is a short walk from the Dobbs Ferry Metro-North train station and rents bikes by the day. Ticket-and-rental packages are available through the **Metro-North Getaways Program** (http://web.mta.info).

Golf

New York City executives support some 50 public and private golf courses across the county. **Hudson Hills Golf Course** (400 Croton Dam Rd., Ossining, 914/864-3000, www.hudsonhillsgolf.com, Sat.-Sun. $115, Mon.-Fri. $85, reduced rates with county park pass) is one of six public courses run by Westchester County. Architect Mark Mungeam, who led the overhaul of Chicago's Olympia Fields Country Club for the 2003 U.S. Open, designed the 7,000-yard par 71 championship course in 2004. You'll have to fight the city crowd for tee times.

Dunwoodie Golf Course (Wasylenko Lane, Yonkers, 914/231-3490, http://golf. westchestergov.com, Sat.-Sun. $48, Mon.-Fri. $43, not including cart, reduced rates with county park pass) is county-owned, and some patrons say it shows in the greens. The short 5,778-yard par-70 course offers plenty

1: historic Old Croton Aqueduct **2:** Ward Pound Ridge Reservation

of challenges, with elevation changes and a deep rough.

Designed by Tom Winton, **Maple Moor Golf Course** (1128 North St., White Plains, 914/995-9200, http://golf.westchestergov.com, Sat.-Sun. $48, Mon.-Fri. $43, not including cart, reduced rates with county park pass) has been in operation since 1927. Some greens are slow on this 6,374-yard par-71 course, but there's enough action to keep it interesting. Don't let the highway noise on the front nine distract you.

Boating

Hudson River Recreation (299 Palmer Ave., Sleepy Hollow, 914/682-5135, www.kayakhudson.com) takes paddlers on guided trips departing from Croton River, Croton Point Park, and Tarrytown Lakes. You can book a kayak or SUP lesson or simply rent the gear for your own adventure. This outfitter does not maintain a public storefront. All activities are booked online, and clients meet at one of the three launch points. Croton Point Park in Croton-on-Hudson has a boat launch for larger watercraft.

Fishing

Freshwater fishing in Westchester revolves around the reservoir system. With a New York Watershed permit, you can catch large bass and the occasional trout. Rent a canoe to open up the possibilities. **Mohansic Lake** (201 Hawley Rd., North Salem, 914/864-7310) is a zoo on summer weekends, but it is known to have aggressive bass, smallmouth, and black crappie. **Crom Pond**, next to Mohansic, has a good top-water bite for largemouth bass. The **Kensico Reservoir,** three miles north of White Plains, has rainbow, brown, and lake trout up to 15-20 pounds. **Cross River Reservoir** reportedly has good-size brown trout, largemouth bass, and smallmouth bass. If you're in southern Westchester County, try **Tibbet's Brook Park** for largemouth bass.

Yoga and Spas

After a day of touring historic estates, unwind with a fast flow or restorative session at **YogaWorks Westchester** (50 S. Buckhout St., Irvington, 914/591-9642, www.yogaworks.com, drop-in $28). The studio is walking distance from the train station. You can sweat it out or try Candlelight Yin at **Riverstone Yoga** (2 Hudson View Way, Tarrytown, 914/332-9642, www.riverstoneyoga.com, drop-in $25, new students 2 weeks unlimited $49), noted a favorite studio among locals. **Day Spa Westchester** (50 Hamilton St./25 Stanley Ave., Dobbs Ferry, 914/409-1900, www.oasisdayspanyc.com, 9am-7pm Sun.-Mon., 9am-8pm Tues.-Sat.) is the place to pamper yourself with an organic seaweed facial. Deep-tissue massage is the signature treatment at **Sankara Spa** (400 Benedict Ave., Tarrytown, 914/524-6392, www.castlehotelandspa.com, from $145 for 60 minutes) at the Castle Hotel. Facials and body scrubs use Naturopathica products. Enjoy the steam room and whirlpool before or after your treatment. Head to the top of Fort Hill in Peekskill for a treatment at **The Abbey Inn Spa** (900 Fort Hill Rd., Peekskill, 914/736-3261, www.theabbeyinn.com), where massages start at $160 per hour and facials at $180.

ENTERTAINMENT AND EVENTS
Performing Arts

Built by music lovers for music lovers, the **Caramoor Center for Music and the Arts** (149 Girdle Ridge Rd., Katonah, 914/232-1252, www.caramoor.org) features classical and jazz performances in two theaters. The **Performing Arts Center** at SUNY Purchase College (735 Anderson Hill Rd., Purchase, 914/251-6200, www.artscenter.org, noon-6pm Tues.-Fri.) holds hundreds of chamber orchestra, string quartet, comedy, dance, and jazz events annually.

Another popular evening venue is Elmsford's **Westchester Broadway Theatre** (1 Broadway Plaza, Elmsford, 914/592-2222, www.broadwaytheatre.com, $59-89), a dinner theater that produces musicals, comedy, and children's shows. Choose from matinee or evening performances. The standard dinner menu includes chicken marsala, fillet of sole, prime rib, or roast pork loin.

Musicians from Dave Brubeck to Bruce Springsteen have performed on the stage of the 1885 **Tarrytown Music Hall** (13 Main St., Tarrytown, box office 877/840-0457, www.tarrytownmusichall.org, 11am-6pm Mon.-Thurs., 11am-4pm Fri.). A local nonprofit rescued the theater from near demolition in the 1970s, and although the building is showing its age outside, it continues to host concerts, plays, musicals, operas, dance performances, and recordings inside. In 2004, the theater began showing movies again after a 27-year hiatus. For tickets, call ahead or visit the box office up to two hours before a show.

Jazz Forum Club (1 Dixon Lane, Tarrytown, 914/631-1000, www.jazzforumarts. org, 6pm-midnight Fri.-Sat., 3pm-11pm Sun., tickets $15-25) is the county's only jazz club, hosting concerts in a 2,000-square-foot space that opened in 2017. Recent performers have included Denise Reis, Barry Harris, and Bill O'Connell. If you show up hungry, order cured meats, cheeses, olives, and breads from the Italian-themed menu. The bar serves Italian wines, beer, and cocktails.

Bars and Nightlife

Tarrytown has some good options for music and drinks. Choose from more than 100 types of domestic and imported beer at **Horsefeathers** (94 N. Broadway, Tarrytown, 914/631-6606, www.horsefeathersny.com, 3pm-8:30pm Tues., noon-8:30pm Wed.-Thurs., noon-9pm Fri.-Sat., noon-8pm Sun.), including the local Saranac Pale Ale. The beautiful bar at **Sweet Grass Grill** (24 Main St., Tarrytown, 914/631-0000, www. sweetgrassgrill.com) was carved from an oak tree that was felled in the Rockefeller State Park Preserve. Enjoy a cocktail or microbrew before your meal. **The Tapp** (17 N. Broadway, Tarrytown, 914/418-5454, www.theetappny. com, noon-midnight Mon.-Thurs., noon-1am Fri.-Sat.) is a local's place with a basic bar-food menu and Tuesday Night Trivia.

In Katonah, the bar at **The Whitlock** (17 Katonah Ave., Katonah, 914/232-8030, www. thewhitlockny.com, 11:30am-9pm Tues.-Sat., 11:30am-8pm Sun., kitchen closes daily 3pm-5pm) stays open all day. Try a pint of the Peekskill Brewery Eastern Standard draft or a bottle of Vienna Lager from the Yonkers Brewing Co. Quality wines by the glass and some creative cocktails complete the lineup.

For a family-friendly night out, **Grand Prix New York** (333 N. Bedford Rd., Mount Kisco, 914/241-3131, www.gpny.com, 3pm-9pm Wed.-Thurs., noon-10pm Sat., noon-6pm Sun.) is an indoor go-kart racing track and bowling alley. Racers have a choice of multiple tracks, including a kids' track, and prices are $8-35 depending on the track and if you come during the track's peak hours (Fri. evening-Sun.). The bowling alley offers regular bowling along with leagues and private lessons, and there is a restaurant and full bar on-site. Other activities for kids include an arcade, art studio, and bounce house.

Festivals

Caramoor International Summer Music Festival (149 Girdle Ridge Rd., Katonah, 914/232-1252, www.caramoor.org, 10am-4pm daily summer, 10am-4pm Mon.-Fri. fall-spring) is a summer concert series with a wide range of productions, from classical music to Latin jazz fusion. Many shows sell out, so check the website early for tickets. Arrive early to enjoy a stroll through the gardens before your performance begins.

Yonkers Hudson Riverfest (Yonkers Waterfront, Yonkers, 914/969-6660, www. yonkersriverfest.com) is a daylong environmental and multicultural festival held every September. Tens of thousands of visitors come each year for a free day of music, fireworks, and arts and crafts. Also on the river, **Clearwater's Great Hudson River Revival** (www.clearwater.org) takes place at Croton Point Park each June.

Once a year, Historic Hudson Valley invites artists of all ages and abilities to work on the grounds of Sunnyside, Washington Irving's estate during **Artists on the Hudson** (914/631-8200, ext. 618, www.hudsonvalley. org, free), which takes place in May. In April, the **Annual RiverArts Studio Tour** covers about 50 studios in Ardsley, Irvington, Hastings-on-Hudson, and Dobbs Ferry (914/412-5120, www.riverarts.org, free).

The area's biggest Halloween celebration takes place at Van Cortlandt Manor from late September to late November. **The Great Jack O'Lantern Blaze** (adults $22-27, children $16-20) features thousands of pumpkins carved, lighted, and arranged into sculptures that are set about the estate grounds. Tickets go on sale in early September and sell out fast. Contact **Historic Hudson Valley** (914/631-8200, www.hudsonvalley.org) for information and tickets for both events.

SHOPPING

Westchester and shopping go all the way back to the Great Depression, when the first department store opened in White Plains. Today you can find it all, from antiques and flea markets to Neiman Marcus. If you're on a quest for unusual antiques, head to Bedford Hills, Cross River, Tarrytown, or Larchmont.

With more than 100 stores, the **Cross County Shopping Center** (8000 Mall Walk, 914/968-9570, www.crosscountycenter.com, 10am-9:30pm Mon.-Sat., 11am-7pm Sun.), in Yonkers, is one of the oldest and largest malls in the county, while **The Westchester** (125 Westchester Ave., 914/421-1333, www.simon. com, 10am-9pm Fri.-Sat., 11am-6pm Sun.), in White Plains, and **Vernon Hills Shopping Center** (700 White Plains Post Rd., 914/472-2000), in Eastchester, are among the most upscale.

In Katonah, the **Charles Department Store** (113 Katonah Ave., 914/232-5200, www. charlesdeptstore.com, 10am-5pm daily) is a throwback to the era of the family-owned department store. The store is managed by the grandsons of the founder and sells everything from shoes to coffeepots.

Antiques and Galleries

Post Road Gallery (2128 Boston Post Rd., Larchmont, 914/834-7568, www. postroadgallery.com, 10:30am-5pm Mon.-Fri. summer, call for hours fall-spring) specializes in fine art, including Hudson River School works, and English antiques, especially clocks.

More than a dozen antiques shows take place year-round in Westchester County. Check www.westchestertourism.com for dates and locations. Each Sunday, hundreds of vendors set up outdoor booths at the **Yonkers Raceway Market** (914/963-3898, 9am-4pm Sun. Mar.-Dec.). Goods for sale include new merchandise as well as antiques and collectibles. From the New York State Thruway, take exit 2 northbound or exit 4 southbound.

Riverrun Books & Manuscripts (12 Washington Ave., Hastings-on-Hudson, 914/478-1339, www.riverrunbookshop.com, by appointment) is a haven for bibliophiles, with 200,000 titles in two stores and two warehouses. The collection includes signed books, vintage paperbacks, and modern first editions.

Peekskill's **Flat Iron Gallery** (105 S. Division St., 2nd Fl., Peekskill, 914/734-1894, www.flatirongallerypeekskill.com, 3pm-6pm Fri., noon-6pm Sat.-Sun.) specializes in contemporary fine art and handcrafted jewelry. This is a good place to look for Hudson River landscapes.

Farm Stands

The largest event of its kind in Westchester, the **Pleasantville Farmers Market** (www. pleasantvillefarmersmarket.org) takes place at Memorial Plaza next to the Metro-North station Saturday mornings April-November. An indoor market runs December-March at the Pleasantville Middle School (40 Romer Ave.). More than 50 vendors set up each week, with music, crafts, fresh produce, and good eats. Elsewhere in the county, the **Irvington Farmers Market** runs on Sunday mornings in the parking lot of the Main Street School (101 Main St., Irvington, www.irvmkt.org).

A group of 13 farms and orchards make up the official Westchester Farm Trail—most of them family-run, and some hundreds of years in the making. Depending on the time of year, you might be able to help with the animals, make maple syrup, pick your own apples, or do real farm chores. At the north end of the trail, **Harvest Moon Farm and Orchard** (130 Hardscrabble Rd., North Salem, 914/485-1210, http://harvestmoonfarmandorchard.com, Sept.-Oct.) offers U-pick apples, as well as its own blueberries, pastured chicken, and quail eggs for sale. At **Fable** (1311 Kitchawan Rd., Ossining, 914/862-0205, http://fablefoods.com, 11am-3pm Fri.-Sun. year-round), you can browse the day's vegetable harvest and pick up eggs and honey. For a complete **trail map** visit www.visitwestchesterny.com.

Vendors sell artisanal cheese, bread, tomatoes, ice cream, barbecue, and kimchi. Some 30 vendors of the **Tarrytown and Sleepy Hollow Farmers Market** (914/923-4837, http://tashfarmersmarket.org, 8:30am-1:30pm Sat. June-mid-Nov.) take over the lawn at Patriot's Park off Route 9 on Saturday Memorial Day to Thanksgiving. Special events include cooking classes, arts and crafts, and the usual assortment of locally grown foods.

If you can't make it to market day in Tarrytown, family-owned **Mint Premium Foods** (18 Main St., Tarrytown, 914/703-6511, noon-7pm Thurs.-Sun.) carries gourmet cheeses, olive oils, and meats, as well as organic teas and honey. **Rochambeau Farm** (214 W. Patent Rd., Bedford, 914/241-8090, www.rochambeaufarmny.com, 9am-4pm Wed.-Fri., 10am-4pm Sat.-Sun.) is not certified organic, but grows its produce sustainably and without the use of pesticides. Stop by for fresh vegetables and specialty crackers, granola bread, popcorn, and the like.

FOOD

Restaurants are plentiful and diverse in Westchester, serving cuisines from Indian to Southwestern. French and Italian themes are most common, and the county offers a number of casual cafés and local farm stands. That said, there are a lot of expense-account traps to avoid—unless, of course, you're on an expense account.

Along the River: Route 9

Bread and Brine (19 Main St., Hastings-on-Hudson, 914/479-5243, www.breadandbrinehoh.com, noon-8:30pm Mon., Wed., Thurs., and Sun., noon-9pm Fri.-Sat., $14-29) is the place for a seafood fix. Choose from the raw bar menu, market fish, or other Maine-inspired delights.

Tarrytown's Main Street has a full menu of choices for casual and fine dining. The "Labs" in ★ **Coffee Labs** (7 Main St., Tarrytown, 914/332-1479, www.coffeelabs.com, 6:45am-5pm Mon.-Fri., 6:45am-6:30pm Sat.-Sun., drinks $2-5) refer to Labrador retrievers, which the owners evidently adore. With a 15-year track record, this roaster and café is serious about sustainability. Among a long list of green decisions, the company sends all of its coffee grounds to the Stone Barns compost program. Stop in for a cup of fair-trade brew or choose from a great selection of loose-leaf teas.

Lefteris Gyro (1 N. Broadway, Tarrytown, 914/524-9687, www.lefterisgyro.com, 11am-10pm daily, $5-16) packs in the crowds at the corner of Main and Broadway. Neighboring shop owners use this busy Greek restaurant as a barometer for the business level on any given day. Sit outside and enjoy platters of Greek specialties—souvlaki, gyros, or salads—served with warm pita bread. Service is quick and the food is reliably good.

Locavores head to ★ **Sweet Grass Grill** (24 Main St., Tarrytown, 914/631-0000, www.

Calling All Food Changemakers

Many of the Hudson River Valley's small farms are playing a vital role in changing the way we think about what we eat. At the **Stone Barns Center for Food and Agriculture** (630 Bedford Hills Rd., Pocantico Hills, 914/366-6200, www.stonebarnscenter.org, 10am-5pm Wed.-Sun.), young farmers are learning the value of resilient, restorative farming techniques, and children are forming vital connections to the sources of their food. Combine a historic setting near Kykuit (the Rockefeller Estate) with cutting-edge research and you get 200 varieties of fruits and vegetables on 6.5 acres of cultivated fields. There are no pesticides, herbicides, or chemical additives here. Composting is a full-time job for the center's soil nutrient manager. From heirloom beans to heritage turkeys and Berkshire pigs, the center is helping to make the farm-to-table mantra a way of life for everyone.

sweetgrassgrill.com, dinner 4pm-8:30pm Tues.-Sun., lunch noon-3pm Tues.-Fri., brunch 11am-3pm Sat.-Sun., $14-24) for seasonal soups, salads, and entrées. In summer, you might start with a chilled golden beet soup and move on to the littleneck clams or grilled arctic char. In winter, go for the roast chicken. Small plates and sides include spinach risotto, couscous quinoa salad, and sweet potato fries. Browse the farm board for specials. This restaurant sources its food from the nearby Stone Barns Center as well as other local farms. The menu changes frequently. For the same high-quality food in a more casual setting, check out its sister restaurant down the hill, **Grass Roots Kitchen** (124 Wildey St., Tarrytown, 914/909-5588, https://grassroots.kitchen, 9am-8pm daily, $8-17).

Also centrally located, **Horsefeathers** (94 N. Broadway, Tarrytown, 914/631-6606, www.horsefeathersny.com, 3pm-8:30pm Tues., noon-8:30pm Wed.-Thurs., noon-9pm Fri.-Sat., noon-8pm Sun., $10-30) is known for its literary decor and a tome of a menu, which is arranged by chapters and includes 100 types of beer. Burgers and pub fare prevail.

Blue Hill at Stone Barns (630 Bedford Rd., Pocantico Hills, 914/366-9600, www.bluehillfarm.com, 5:30pm-10pm Wed.-Sun., $378-428 pp) is a once-in-a-lifetime kind of place that takes the concept of farm-to-table to new heights, night after night. It is here that founding chef Dan Barber, author of *The Third Plate*, reinvented what it means to eat local and seasonal. There are no menus, as the available harvest changes daily. In a nine-course tasting menu during the summer, you might try a "tortilla" made of kohlrabi, a single perfect cherry tomato, quail eggs served over house-made tagliatelle, and a single lamb chop. Each course can be paired with a glass of wine or a nonalcoholic infusion—and the latter are actually more memorable. The presentation is exquisite, start to finish. This dining experience takes a minimum of three hours, not counting the insider tour beforehand. Prepare to be amazed.

In Peekskill, start your day at the ★ **Peekskill Coffee House** (101 S. Division St., 914/739-1287, http://peekskillcoffee.com, 7am-7pm daily, mains $5-10), a gathering place for local artists and the community at-large. Order a sweet or savory crepe (including gluten-free) to accompany your fresh-roasted brew. Grab a sign from the counter if you're willing to share your table during busy times. Another Peekskill find for local food and craft beer is **Birdsall House** (970 Main St., Peekskill, 914/930-1880, www.birdsallhouse.net, noon-10pm daily, $15-25). All of the pork, beef, chicken, rabbit, and duck that appear on the menu come from nearby Hemlock Hill Farm in Cortlandt Manor, and many of the beers on the restaurant's drink menu are from

1: works of pumpkin art at the Great Jack O'Lantern Blaze 2: the Katonah Village Library 3: shops along Katonah Avenue 4: a colorful farm-fresh salad at Sweet Grass Grill

New York breweries. Munch on Cajun-spiced popcorn or smoky almonds while you down a drink or two. Then sample the house-made charcuterie, or go all out for the buttermilk fried chicken and biscuits. Brunch is offered on Sundays (noon-3pm).

Located on the Riverfront, **Peekskill Brewery** (47-53 S. Water St., Peekskill, 914/734-2337, www.peekskillbrewery.com, noon-8pm Mon.-Thurs., noon-9pm Fri.-Sat., 11am-8pm Sun., $13-20) operates a taproom on its first floor that stays open late and features a number of house beers. The second floor is home to a pub that is open for lunch and dinner daily as well as a Sunday brunch featuring oysters, poutine, and pierogi. Gluten-free and vegetarian options are labeled on the menu. Reservations are recommended for pub dining.

In Sleepy Hollow, **Bridge View Tavern** (226 Beekman Ave., Sleepy Hollow, 914/332-0078, www.bridgeviewtavern.com, noon-8pm Tues.-Sun., 3pm-9pm Mon., $15-26) serves a long list of burgers with just about every topping imaginable. Pulled pork empanadas are a tasty way to begin the meal. The BVT Beer Garden serves a rotating selection of craft beers and several house-made sangrias.

Sushi Mike's (146 Main St., Dobbs Ferry, 914/591-0054, www.sushimikes.com, 3pm-9pm Tues.-Thurs. and Sun., 3pm-9:30pm Fri.-Sat., $15-29) is a small Japanese restaurant on the corner of Main and Cedar in Dobbs Ferry. It's usually packed with locals. Order from a menu of creative rolls, or go for one of the hot dishes, such as *gyoza*, teriyaki, or a soba noodle stir-fry. Order online for faster takeout.

Croton-on-Hudson has several unique dining experiences. **Mex-to-go** (345 S. Riverside Ave., Croton-on-Hudson, 914/271-8646, www.mextogo-croton.com, 11am-10pm daily, mains $7-13) makes tortas, burritos, tacos, and other Mexican staples, with reasonably priced lunch specials. For ice cream, head to the **Blue Pig** (121 Maple St., Croton-on-Hudson, 914/271-3850, www.thebluepigicecream.com, 1pm-8pm Tues.-Thurs. and Sun., 1pm-9pm Fri.-Sat.). Its homemade, locally sourced

flavors and soft-serve sorbet are still the talk of the town.

On the pier in Yonkers, **X2O Xaviars on the Hudson** (71 Water Grant St., Yonkers, 914/965-1111, www.xaviars.com, noon-2pm and 5:30pm-10pm Wed.-Fri., 5pm-10pm Sat., noon-2pm and 5pm-9pm Sun., $32-40) brings local ingredients to the plate in the form of a chilled gazpacho, roasted beets and burrata, locally raised quail, Hudson Valley pasture-raised pork chops, and house-made spaetzle. You can top it off with a slice of the carrot layer cake.

Central Westchester County

Coromandel (30 Division St., New Rochelle, 914/235-8390, www.coromandelcuisine.com, lunch noon-2:30pm Mon.-Fri., noon-3pm Sat.-Sun., dinner 5pm-10pm Sun.-Thurs., 5pm-10:30pm Fri.-Sat., $16-25) is part of a chain of six restaurants that ranks among Westchester's best for Indian-inspired fare.

A stroll along Katonah's main thoroughfare reveals another handful of tempting places to grab a bite. **Blue Dolphin Ristorante** (175 Katonah Ave., Katonah, 914/232-4791, www.thebluedolphinny.com, lunch 11am-3pm Mon.-Fri., 11:30am-3:30pm Sat., dinner 5pm-9:30pm Mon.-Thurs., 5pm-10pm Fri.-Sat., $17-24) prepares fresh daily seafood specials, raviolis, and other Italian specialties. Expect to wait for a table on weekends.

Around the corner from Little Joe's Books and co-owned by the same couple, the inviting ★ **Katonah Reading Room** (19 Edgemont Rd., Katonah, 914/232-1010, www.katonahreadingroom.com, 6:30am-6pm Mon.-Fri., 8am-5pm Sat., 9am-4pm Sun., $5-13) makes egg sandwiches, avocado toast, salads, and a gluten-free crustless quiche of the day. Ingredients come from a long list of local farms, and many of the products are for sale in the adjoining market. Stop in to pick up a cold brew, *kombucha*, grass-fed yogurt, gluten-free crackers, and other picnic supplies.

An early adopter in the farm-to-table movement, ★ **Crabtree's Kittle House** (11 Kittle Rd., Chappaqua, 914/666-8044, www.crabtreeskittlehouse.com, 12:30pm-9pm Tues.-Thurs., 12:30pm-10pm Fri.-Sat., 11:30am-2:30pm and 3pm-8pm Sun., $21-36) has a 30-year track record of serving classic American cuisine. A new Clean Eating menu highlights the simplest dishes made only from whole foods. Vegetarians and gluten-free eaters will find plenty of choices here. The restaurant is known for an unparalleled selection of wines, with nearly 60,000 bottles in the cellar. Order a special bottle in advance to have it brought up to temperature or let sediment settle out. For a special occasion, reserve a chef's tasting in the Wine Tasting Room.

Fresh fish and reasonable prices bring in the crowds at **Eastchester Fish Gourmet** (837 White Plains Rd., Scarsdale, 914/725-3450, www.eastchesterfish.com, lunch 11:30am-2:30pm Thurs.-Fri., dinner from 5pm daily, $15-21). It's both a restaurant and market, in business since 1981. Expect a wait unless you show up early.

★ **Purdy's Farmer & The Fish** (100 Titicus Rd., North Salem, 914/617-8380, noon-9pm Sun.-Thurs, noon-10pm Fri.-Sat.) is the happy result of a fishmonger partnering with a chef who studied agriculture. The majority of produce needed for its menu comes from the restaurant's own four-acre farm right next door. Growing practices are modern and sustainable, from start to finish. You can start with Maine mussels or try the duck fat fried potatoes, and then move onto the cedar planked Scottish salmon. The atmosphere is casual and porch-side seating is a popular request in warmer months. And if you don't have time for a meal, at least pop into the **Farm Shop** (noon-7pm Mon.-Sat., 11:30am-7pm Sun.) and grab some ingredients or prepared foods to go. The owners also have a second restaurant called **Hudson Farmer & The Fish** (11 River St., Sleepy Hollow, 914/631-8380, http://farmerandthefish.com, noon-9pm Mon., Wed., and Thurs., noon-10pm Fri.-Sat., noon-8pm Sun.). It's located along the Westchester RiverWalk in Sleepy Hollow, and the menu features a raw bar, pizza, and seafood classics.

ACCOMMODATIONS

Westchester has mastered the science of the business-conference hotel. There are a few exceptions, and more short-term rentals popping up all the time, but for more choice and charm in accommodations, you're better off heading north to Putnam County or into New York City.

Under $150

Inn on the Hudson (634 Main St., Peekskill, 914/739-1500, www.innonthehudson.com, from $75) is an upgraded motor lodge with river views, a swimming pool, and 53 basic rooms that make for a good value.

$150-200

Crabtree's Kittle House (11 Kittle Rd., Chappaqua, 914/666-8044, www.crabtreeskittlehouse.com, from $175) is first and foremost an outstanding restaurant, but its 12 moderately priced rooms are an added convenience if you plan to sample more than a taste from its enormous wine cellar. Rooms are decorated simply in pastels and floral linens, and with white trim and dark wood furniture.

Tarrytown House (49 E. Sunnyside Lane, Tarrytown, 914/591-8200, www.tarrytownhouseestate.com, $90-200) is a full-service conference center set on 26 acres in two 19th-century mansions. More than 200 rooms and suites are designed to accommodate business travelers but also make for a pleasant weekend getaway. The 10 Georgian-era rooms in the King Mansion have the most character. Inquire about the Pooch Package if you're bringing a dog along.

Over $200

Built by the son of a Civil War general on a hilltop outside of Tarrytown, the **Castle Hotel & Spa** (400 Benedict Ave., Tarrytown, 914/631-1980, www.castlehotelandspa.com, from $350) features a 75-foot tower that is the highest point in Westchester County. Its rooms have high ceilings and plenty of natural light. Elegant drapery and furnishings create a decidedly old-world atmosphere. Dinner at its Equus restaurant will be an experience to remember, if only for the views and the bill. **The Abbey Inn & Spa** (900 Fort Hill Rd., Peekskill, 914/736-1200, www.theabbeyinn. com, from $349) sits on a hilltop overlooking Peekskill and the Hudson Highlands area. Formerly a convent and chapel, this historic property has been restored and transformed into a boutique hotel with its own spa and a restaurant called **Apropos** (914/739-3546, http://aproposrestaurant.com, 5pm-8pm Tues.-Thurs., 5pm-8:30pm Fri.-Sat., 9am-2pm Sun., $21-56) that serves its own rendition of Hudson Valley-Mediterranean cuisine. Enjoy starters like sliced porchetta and bone marrow, and entrées like branzino and rack of lamb.

For unlimited budgets, the **Bedford Post Inn** (954 Old Post Rd., Bedford, 914/234-7800, www.bedfordpostinn.com, from $675) is a Relais & Chateaux property with eight luxury rooms, a yoga studio, and two farm-to-table restaurants. Most rooms have working fireplaces, and some feature terraces with forest views.

INFORMATION AND SERVICES

The **Westchester County Office of Tourism** (222 Mamaroneck Ave., White Plains, 800/833-9282, www. westchestertourism.com) also runs a seasonal tourism information center in July-August at exit 9 off the Bronx River Parkway, near Leewood Drive. The **Katonah Village Library** (26 Bedford Rd., Katonah, 914/232-3508, www.katonahlibrary.org, 10am-5pm Mon.-Tues. and Thurs.-Fri., 10am-7pm Wed., closed Sat.-Sun.) has free Wi-Fi, visitor information, restrooms, and comfortable tables in a 1930 building that also houses the Katonah Historical Museum.

GETTING THERE AND AROUND
Bus
The **Bee-Line System** (http://transportation. westchestergov.com) is a countywide bus service with more than 55 different routes and express service. Routes serve many of the county's recreational facilities and also provide connection to trains. The fare is $2.75 (seniors $1.35) in coins, exact change required, on most routes. The Westchester-Manhattan express costs $7.50 (seniors $3.75 off-peak).

Train
It's hard to avoid the **Metro-North** (www. mta.info) commuter line in Westchester. It was practically built to serve this county's suburbs, and today, there are 43 station stops on three lines providing continual service to Manhattan's Grand Central Station and points within the county. Tarrytown, Croton-on-Hudson, and all of Westchester's riverside towns are easily accessible via the Hudson Line.

Car
You can rent a car at the **Westchester County Airport** (240 Airport Rd., Suite 202, White Plains, http://airport.westchestergov. com). But be forewarned: Traffic is bad and getting worse in Westchester—both from visitors' cars and those of local residents. The Tappan Zee Bridge regularly backs up during the rush hour commute. Drive off-peak whenever possible, and allow extra time to reach your destination at any time of day.

Rockland County

With the Hudson River, New Jersey, and Orange County as its borders, Rockland County is the smallest county in the state outside the five boroughs of New York City. Located just 16 miles from New York City, Rockland has protected almost one-third of its 176 square miles from development, thanks in part to generous donations from the wealthy families who built the first mansions along its riverbank. The terrain encompasses approximately 30 miles of Hudson River frontage, plus Bear Mountain and Harriman State Parks, which contain most of the Ramapo Mountain Range.

Although city dwellers think of Rockland as a place you pass through on the way to mountains and open space, its state parks and historic sites may be worth a stop for some. Also, numerous immigrant communities have helped create a vibrant scene for restaurants, performing arts, and museums, especially around Clarkstown, Haverstraw, Ramapo, and Stony Point.

ALONG THE RIVER: ROUTE 9W

Rockland County begins about 10 miles north of the George Washington Bridge (I-95), a main artery out of New York City. From the bridge, the Palisades Interstate Parkway cuts diagonally across the county, and Route 9W hugs the riverbank. Near the New Jersey state line, the dramatic Palisades cliffs plunge into the river, creating a playground for geologists and rock climbers alike.

Rockland's major river crossing, the Tappan Zee Bridge (I-287), is the longest span across the Hudson, connecting Rockland residents to Westchester County and points east. With more than 140,000 cars a day passing through, the bridge is the busiest crossing in the region. A reconstruction is in progress; roadway finishing work is ongoing, with frequent lane closures.

★ Piermont Village

Three miles south of the Tappan Zee Bridge, on a steep hillside between Route 9W and the riverbank, is the village of Piermont, population 2,500, where you can savor contemporary farm-to-table cuisine, paddle a canoe through 1,000 acres of salt-water marsh, and then return to town for an evening of live music. Piermont has long been a haven for creative types. These days, many residents commute daily into Manhattan and ride their Italian-made bicycles on the weekends. A row of lively bistros and boutiques takes up most of Piermont Avenue in the village center, where a mile-long pier juts out over the marsh and into the Hudson. The **Piermont Pier** is a public park that attracts anglers, walkers, and anyone in search of a cool breeze. Just south of the pier is **Tallman Mountain State Park** (Rte. 9W, Bear Mountain, 845/359-0544, www.parks.ny.gov, vehicles $6), a favorite spot for viewing birds and wildflowers on land that once belonged to John D. Rockefeller's Standard Oil Company. Additional facilities include a recently renovated public pool (day pass $10) and tennis courts. Take exit 4 from the Palisades Interstate Parkway to reach the Piermont area.

Piermont Marsh (www.dec.ny.gov) is a two-mile stretch of protected shoreline and tidal flats best reached by canoe or kayak or viewed from Tallman Mountain State Park. A unique ecosystem in the region, the marsh is managed by the Hudson River National Estuarine Research Reserve. The New York Department of Environmental Conversation has approved an "environmental remediation" plan to get rid of invasive plants and restore native species to the area. Residents are concerned about the use of herbicides in the plan.

Tappan

Students of the Revolutionary War must pay a visit to several sites in the village of

Nyack

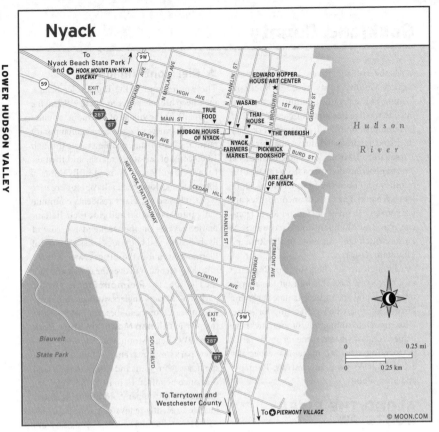

Tappan, a few miles southwest from Piermont. George Washington turned the Dutch colonial **DeWint House** (20 Livingston Ave., 845/359-1359, www.dewinthouse.com, 10am-4pm Tues.-Sun., free)—now a national historic landmark and the oldest building in Rockland County—into temporary headquarters during the trial of Major John André, the British spy who was accused of conspiring with Benedict Arnold. The trial took place at the county courthouse, which stood on the Village Church Green, next door to the 1835 **Reformed Church of Tappan** that stands today.

Near a stoplight at the center of town is **The '76 House** (110 Main St., Tappan, 845/359-5476, www.76house.com), built in 1755. André

was held captive here until his execution. The building is now a restaurant and tavern.

Nyack

On the other side of the Tappan Zee Bridge lies the busier commercial center of Nyack (meaning Point of Land), part of the Clarkstown township. Home to a vibrant mix of artists, immigrants, and commuters (many of whom know each other by name), Nyack draws day-trippers out of the city with the **Edward Hopper House Art Center** (82 N. Broadway, Nyack, 845/358-0774, www. edwardhopperhouse.org, noon-5pm Sat.-Sun., adults $8, seniors $6, students $3, under age 16 free), as well as dozens of galleries, shops, and restaurants. Most of the businesses are gathered around the intersection of Main Street (which slopes downhill toward the river), and Broadway, which runs parallel to it. Look for a visitor information booth near the Clock Tower, where Main Street crosses Cedar Street.

Realist painter Edward Hopper spent his childhood in a modest clapboard house on Broadway, a few blocks north of the main retail strip. After attending high school in Nyack, he moved to New York City but returned home frequently throughout his career. A small museum in the family home, now a restored New York state historic site, documents Hopper's life and displays works by local artists. In summer, jazz concerts are often held in the garden.

A short drive beyond the Edward Hopper House leads to a row of riverside mansions—many of them owned by celebrities—protected by imposing brick and stone fences. At the end of this exclusive neighborhood is **Nyack Beach State Park** (Broadway, 845/358-1316, www.parks.ny.gov, year-round, vehicles $6), where local residents come to walk, relax, and fish. A two-mile trail for jogging and biking follows the river north to Hook Mountain. Trains rumble in the distance, and to the south, you can see the Tappan Zee Bridge.

The **Historical Society of the Nyacks** offers guided walking tours (845/418-4430, nyackhistory.org, 2pm select Sun., $5) on a handful of Sundays April-October. The meeting place depends on the theme of the tour. **Hopper's Nyack** is a popular tour, as it brings the city to life through the artist's eyes.

Haverstraw Bay

Natural resources and innovation in the process of brickmaking positioned Haverstraw at the forefront of the construction industry through most of the 19th century. In 1771, clay was discovered in the Hudson offshore from Haverstraw, and the ability to mold bricks into a standard size allowed Rockland County to play a pivotal role in the building of New York City. At its peak before the advent of steel and the Great Depression, the local industry supported 42 independent brickyards. The **Haverstraw Brick Museum** (12 Main St., Haverstraw, 845/947-3505, www. haverstrawbrickmuseum.org, 1pm-4pm Sat.-Sun. or by appointment, $2) documents the history of the industry. The museum was closed for renovations in 2018 but continues to host occasional events and programs. A ferry to the Ossining Metro-North station departs from Short Clove Road.

River access is possible at three small parks: **Bowline Point Park** (1 Bowline Plant Rd., Haverstraw, 845/429-4099) at the mouth of Haverstraw Bay; **Emeline Park** (1st St., Haverstraw, www.scenichudson.org); and **Haverstraw Beach State Park** (200 Riverside Ave., Haverstraw, 845/568-3020, www.palisadesparks.org).

New City

Between Rockland Lake State Park and Haverstraw, Route 304 West leads to New City, where the **Historical Society of Rockland County** produces historical exhibits inside the **Jacob Blauvelt House** (20 Zukor Rd., New City, 845/634-9629, www. rocklandhistory.org, noon-4pm Wed.-Fri. and Sun. during museum gallery exhibitions, admission varies). This two-story brick farmhouse was built in 1832 in the Dutch style with six rooms and an 1865 carriage house, which you can view on a guided walking tour of the property. Exhibits cover a broad span of time and address a range of topics relevant to the local experience. Native American culture, Dutch bibles, Civil War diaries, 19th-century furnishings, the agrarian lifestyle, and former industries (such as brickmaking, harvesting ice, mining, and quarrying) are all represented. To get here, take exit 10 from the Palisades Interstate Parkway.

The **Rockland Farm Alliance** (www. rocklandfarm.org) saved a historic farm and turned it into an organic grower of produce and a leader in the move to sustainable agriculture. **Cropsey Community Farm** (220 S. Little Tor Rd., New City, 845/634-3167) has a state-of-the-art geothermal climate battery greenhouse. There are several ways to experience the farm: Sign up for a workshop and learn to make lip balm, infused oils, or healing salves from herbs. Join the CSA and buy a share of the harvest. Shop the Nyack Farmers Market on Thursday or the Cropsey Farm Stand on Saturday. Or get tickets to the Annual Twilight Dinner, held each September.

Also at Cropsey Farms, **Rockland Bee Tours** (220 S. Little Tor Rd., New City, 845/202-2575. www.rocklandbeetours.com, $15) leads informative and up-close tours of hives on the farm. If you're brave enough, you can put on a bee suit and see what it's like to be a beekeeper. Tours last about an hour. Reservations are required.

Between the Hudson River and New City, a three-mile-long waterway, **Lake DeForest Reservoir** (845/620-3328, www. suezwatershed.com) is part of the local watershed. Permits are available for recreational activities April-November with seasonal membership for customers of the Suez water company ($40 adults, $100 family) and non-customers ($50).

Stony Point Battlefield State Historical Site

Located on Haverstraw Bay is an all-important Revolutionary War site: The **Stony Point Battlefield State Historical Site** (44 Battlefield Rd., Stony Point, 845/786-2521, https://parks.ny.gov, 10am-4:30pm Wed.-Sat., noon-4pm Sun. mid-Apr.-Oct., free) is a riverside park and museum that includes the oldest lighthouse on the Hudson (1826). On the night of July 15, 1779, Brigadier General Anthony Wayne led a small group of colonial soldiers in a midnight assault on the British troops who had taken control of the point. In a textbook operation, Wayne's men waded silently through marsh and mud to catch the British by surprise. A small but important win, the victory restored morale among American troops.

It takes about 10 minutes to walk from the parking lot to the lighthouse, where you'll be rewarded with a view of Haverstraw Bay.

Interpretive signs inside the park document the battle, and staff members occasionally dress up in colonial costumes to set the mood. There are two entrances to the park from Route 9W: A historic marker indicates the southern turnoff, while the northern one is more difficult to spot.

THE RAMAPO MOUNTAINS

Rockland's greatest outdoor treasure is an enormous green space that straddles the border with Orange County, running southwest from the Bear Mountain Bridge almost to the New Jersey state line. Thanks in part to families that include the Rockefellers, Vanderbilts, and Harrimans, more than 50,000 rugged acres are divided into two adjoining state parks: Harriman (46,000 acres) and Bear Mountain (5,000 acres).

★ Harriman State Park

The first section of the Appalachian Trail was cleared here in 1923, and today, hikers can access 200 miles of trails and more than 30 lakes and reservoirs inside the second-largest park in the New York state system. **Seven Lakes Drive** runs the length of **Harriman State Park** (Rte. 9W, Bear Mountain, 845/786-2701, www.parks.ny.gov) and provides access to the main recreation areas, including Lake Sebago, Lake Welch, Lake Tiorati, and the Anthony Wayne Recreation Area. There is no gate or fee to enter the park, but parking costs $10 to access the beaches at Lake Welch or Lake Tiorati. A once-popular beach on Lake Sebago has closed indefinitely since Hurricane Irene blew through the area in 2011. The boat launch remains open. Find a free PDF trail map at www.myharriman.com.

Wilderness accommodations include shelters, cabins, and campsites. There are two entrances to the park: from Route 17 in Sloatsburg or from the Palisades Interstate Parkway near West Haverstraw. Park only in designated areas, or take the Tuxedo-Harriman shuttle bus from the train station to a trailhead or other destination in the park.

Harriman often fills to capacity on busy holiday weekends; a midweek visit affords more tranquility, but if you do arrive with the masses, you can quickly escape by heading into the backcountry.

Bear Mountain State Park

Formed in 1910 as a reaction against the proposed relocation of Sing Sing prison from Ossining, the smaller but well-developed Bear Mountain (Rte. 9W, Bear Mountain, 845/786-2701, www.parks.ny.gov, dawn-dusk daily, parking $10) sees as many visitors per year as the most popular national parks. The sprawling parking lot gives an indication of how crowded the park can get on hot summer weekends.

Near the entrance, a stone lodge overlooking Hessian Lake houses the Bear Mountain Inn (3020 Seven Lakes Dr., 845/786-2731, www.visitbearmountain.com, $150-230)—which was *the* place to stay in 1920s New York. Prospective guests had to complete an application and provide a personal recommendation for the privilege of spending the night. The price of $3.50 a day bought a room with all meals. The lodge reopened in 2012 after a six-year closure for extensive renovations totaling $12 million. The renovations added 15 guest rooms and suites, a restaurant, a spa, a 20,000-square-foot event space, and a souvenir shop.

Behind the inn, Perkins Memorial Drive winds its way to the top of Bear Mountain and a commanding view of the highlands from Perkins Memorial Tower. Hikers can reach the summit in about three hours, starting at Hessian Lake. The Bear Mountain Trailside Museums and Zoo (845/786-2701, www.trailsidezoo.org, 10:30am-4:30pm daily, $1 pp, parking $10) entertains kids with exhibits on black bears, beavers, coyotes, and other animals. The Merry-Go-Round Pavilion (845/786-2731, 11am-5pm Wed.-Sun. mid-June-Labor Day, 11am-5pm Sat.-Sun. and holidays Sept.-mid-June, $1 pp per ride) is decorated with hand-painted scenes of the park and has 42 seats, each hand-carved in

the shape of a native animal. Additional activities include swimming, paddleboats, ice-skating, and numerous seasonal festivals. Look for the entrance to Bear Mountain State Park on Route 9W, about 0.5 miles from the traffic circle at the Bear Mountain Bridge.

Inside the state parks, Iona Island National Estuary (access from Palisades Pkwy. or Rte. 9 north, 845/786-2701, http://parks.ny.gov) is a protected tidal wetland where narrow-leaved cattails provide habitat for a variety of shorebirds, fish, and bald eagles.

Common wisdom said it would take the Bear Mountain Hudson River Bridge Company 30 years to build a span across the narrowest part of the Hudson—it was expected to be the longest suspension bridge in its day. Engineers finished in 20 months, and the first crossing over the river opened to traffic in 1924. The Appalachian Trail crosses the river at this point, and many hikers stop to admire the views of the highlands from the span.

ROUTE 59 CORRIDOR

The old Nyack Turnpike, built to transport manufactured goods from the Ramapo Mountains to the Hudson River, is now a busy thoroughfare that connects the towns of Suffern, Spring Valley, and Nanuet to Nyack. Along Route 59 are several suburban communities with sprawling shopping centers.

Historic Suffern has a handful of shops and restaurants, as well as Rockland County's largest movie complex, the 1924 Lafayette Theatre (97 Lafayette Ave., Suffern, 845/547-2121, www.lafayettetheatersuffern.com, adults $10, under age 12 and seniors $8). To the northeast in Montebello, Rockland County maintains Kakiat Park (584 Haverstraw Rd., Montebello), where you can hike the Kakiat Trail, which leads across the Mahwah River and into Harriman State Park.

At the southern edge of Harriman State Park, near Ramapo, Torne Valley Vineyards (Torne Valley Rd., Hillburn, 845/712-5505, www.tornevalleyvineyards.com, 11am-5:30pm Sat.-Sun.) sits between the Ramapo

River and Torne Brook. Weekend tastings include eight wines ($8). The owners purchased an 1875 Victorian Gothic mansion that had fallen into disrepair and planted their first vines in the early 2000s. The varietals range from a sweet dessert wine to a couple of drier reds.

Nestled in the Ramapo Highlands, **Sloatsburg Village** retains a country feel in close proximity to a busy commercial corridor. The Jacob Sloat House, or **Harmony Hall** (15 Liberty Rock Rd., Sloatsburg, 845/712-5220, http://friendsofharmonyhall.org) is an 1846 Greek Revival structure that hosts occasional special events, such as the **Annual Bluegrass Music & Craft Festival** in September.

RECREATION

With two large state parks and numerous smaller green spaces, Rockland offers a surprising variety of possibilities for outdoor entertainment. You can do just about everything in Bear Mountain and Harriman State Parks: hike, bike, boat, camp, picnic, swim, fish, skate, ski, and play.

Winter Sports

When the Hudson ices over and snow blankets the highlands, cross-country skiers head to the two-mile trail at **Nyack Beach State Park** for a morning of exercise. **Bear Mountain State Park** has an ice rink and hosts public skating hours ($5 entrance, rentals $4).

Hiking

Harriman State Park is a great place to hike in mid- to late fall, since no hunting is allowed within its boundaries. But there are a great many trails in the park and it's surprisingly easy to get turned around. Visit http://nynjtc.org to order a printed trail map. The **Almost Perpendicular, Claudius Smith's**

1: Bear Mountain Inn 2: signs at Bear Mountain State Park 3: hiking in Harriman State Park 4: lighthouse at the Stony Point Battlefield State Historical Site

Den, and Dutch Doctor Shelter Loop (5.2 miles, 800 feet elevation gain) begins in Sloatsburg and leads to panoramic views of the Ramapo Mountains. From the parking area on Johnsontown Rd., follow the Blue Disc Trail. The "den" is actually a cave that served as the hideout of a Revolutionary War-era outlaw. There is some scrambling along the way, and the hike will be moderately challenging for most leisure hikers.

For a navigation challenge, hike the moderately challenging **Lemon Squeezer to Lichen Trail Loop** (7.4 miles, trail map strongly recommended) for some cool rock formations, open meadows, ponds, wildlife, and a day-long adventure. Allow 4-5 hours to complete this route. You will gain 1,800 feet of elevation throughout the day. The trail begins in the Elk Pen parking lot at the intersection of Route 17 and Arden Valley Road in Tuxedo (Orange County). Visit http://hikethehudsonvalley.com for step-by-step directions.

For an easy hour-long hike in Bear Mountain State Park, head to **Iona Island** (2.5 miles round-trip), off Route 9W. The easternmost part of the island is a protected research reserve that's closed to the public, but you can walk through marshy meadows in search of bird sightings and enjoy views of the river, Bear Mountain Bridge, and Anthony's Nose on the opposite shore. Visit http://dec.ny.gov for a map of the reserve.

Hook Mountain State Park (Rte. 9W, Nyack, 845/268-3020, www.nynjtc.org, dawn-dusk daily, fees vary by season) is well known as a place to watch hawks soar above the treetops. Enter through Rockland Lake State Park and follow signs to the Landing Road parking area. From there, proceed to a barricade where the Long Path (aqua blazes) crosses the road. Follow the trail about a mile north to the summit of Hook Mountain (730 ft.). You can make this hike a six-mile loop by connecting to the white-blazed Upper Nyack Trail, which leads down to the river and into Nyack Beach State Park.

Just north of Tallman Mountain State

The Long Path

A project of the **New York-New Jersey Trail Conference** (http://nynjtc.org) hiking club, the **Long Path** traverses some 350 miles of New Jersey and the Hudson Valley, beginning at the George Washington Bridge and hugging the western bank of the Hudson River through Rockland County. There are about 60 miles of road-walking needed to connect various sections of the trail, but through-hikers will experience numerous state and county parks as well as many scenic vistas before ending in John Boyd Thatcher State Park outside Albany. Future plans call for extension of the trail through the Adirondacks to connect with the Northville-Lake Placid Trail.

In Harriman State Park, the Long Path crosses the Appalachian Trail. Then it travels to the Shawangunks in Ulster County and continues north through the Catskill Forest Preserve, where the route becomes more rugged and rises to bag a few 3,000-foot peaks, then ultimately crosses the Schoharie Valley. Volunteers maintain an online trail guide (http://nynjtc.org), which includes up-to-date information for backpacking and camping. Look for turquoise-colored blazes marking the trail.

Park and bordered by several county parks, **Blauvelt State Park** (Rte. 303 north to East Greenbush Rd., Blauvelt, 845/359-0544, http://parks.ny.gov) is an undeveloped expanse that once served as a rifle range for the National Guard. It has a few miles of hiking trails, including a 2.5-mile section of the **Long Path** (350 miles), which connects to sections in Tallman Mountain State Park to the south and Hook Mountain State Park to the north. This part of the Long Path is mostly forested and easy to navigate.

Order trail maps from the **New York-New Jersey Trail Conference** (201/512-9348, www.nynjtc.org). In any of these areas, park only in designated areas for hikers and camp only in public camping areas.

★ Cycling and Mountain Biking

Piermont's scenic roads are popular with cyclists, but beware of the steep fine for riding double file. Stop in to chat with the knowledgeable crew at **Piermont Bicycle Connection** (215 Ash St., Piermont, 845/365-0900, www.piermontbike.com, 9am-6pm Tues.-Sun. summer, 11am-6pm Thurs.-Tues. winter) and pick up maps and supplies before you ride. None of the shops in the area rent road bikes. The **Rockland Bicycling Club** hosts the Rockland Century in September

(www.rocklandbike.org). The club also posts other routes and cue sheets for local and visiting cyclists.

The **Hook Mountain-Nyack Beach Bikeway** runs five miles through three state parks with surfaces that vary from pavement to crushed stone to dirt and rock. The southern part is a flat stretch that goes along the river, but the northern section gets steep and bumpy. You'll want fat tires with some traction for this route, and road bikes are not advised. Parking is easiest at Nyack Beach State Park.

For a 10-mile (round-trip) scenic bike ride with options for food and history along the way, check out the **Esposito Trail** that runs between Nyack and Piermont and connects to the **Old Erie Path** and the **Joseph B. Clark Rail Trail**, as well as the new bike path over the Tappan Zee Bridge. This route is best for hybrid or mountain bikes. It begins at the intersection of South Franklin and Clinton Avenue. in Nyack, taking in river views, the restored Piermont Train Station, and the DeWint House in Tappan. See the Rockland Bicycling Club newsletter (www.rocklandbicyclingclub.org) for route details.

Golf

Rockland County has more than a dozen golf courses to test your skills. **Spook Rock Golf**

Course (233 Spook Rock Rd., Montebello, 845/357-6466, www.spookrockgolfcourse. com, $35-59) has large, fast greens with tight fairways. The course consistently ranks in the top public courses in the state. **Rockland Lake State Park Golf Course** (Rte. 9W and Lake Rd., Congers, 845/268-7275, https:// rocklandlakestategolf.com, Sat.-Sun. $31- 36, Mon.-Fri. $25-30) is a 6,864-yard par-72 course with 18 holes. A second nine-hole executive course has plenty of bunkers to keep golfers on their toes.

Swimming and Boating

Piermont Marsh is a unique aquatic habitat within walking distance of Piermont's shops and restaurants. The best way to explore it is by canoe or kayak, which you can rent from Captain Bill at **Paradise Boats** (15 Paradise Ave., Piermont, 845/359-0073, www. paradisecanoeandkayak.com, 9am-5pm Sat.- Sun. and holidays May-June and Sept.-Oct., 8am-5pm Wed.-Sun. July-Aug., $50 for two hours, $12 each additional hour). Make an appointment before you go and look for a sign at the corner of Piermont and Paradise. September and October are the best months to go for a paddle.

Nyack Boat Charter (11 Burd St., Nyack, 845/535-1675, www.nyackboatcharter.com) runs speedboat and sailboat trips on the Hudson for two hours, half a day, all day, or overnight.

You can rent paddle and row boats by the hour on **Hessian Lake** in Bear Mountain State Park (11am-5pm Mon.-Fri., 11am-6pm Sat.-Sun.). A permit is required to put any type of boat in the water here. **Lake Sebago** in Harriman State Park also has a boat launch.

The large outdoor swimming pool in Bear Mountain Park (10am-5:30pm daily from mid-June, parking $10) gets insanely crowded on summer weekends, but kids may enjoy a dip. **High Tor State Park** (415 S. Mountain Rd., New City, 845/634-8074, www.parks. ny.gov, 10am-5:30pm Wed.-Sun., $6 per vehicle, $5 pool wristband) has an inviting swimming pool that's open to the public mid-June through mid-August. On the Hudson River behind the power plant, **Bowline Point Park** (Samsondale Ave., Haverstraw, 845/429-4099, www.townofhaverstraw.org, noon-7pm Mon.- Fri., 11am-7pm Sat.-Sun., nonresidents $11 Mon.-Fri., $15 Sat.-Sun.) has an Olympic-size pool, a diving pool, and water slides as well as tennis courts and a fishing pier.

Hessian Lake in Bear Mountain State Park

Fishing

The best spots to cast a line in Rockland County include the Mahwah River, which is stocked with trout; Bowline Point Park for river access; and Lake DeForest Reservoir for largemouth, smallmouth, carp, yellow perch, white perch, sunfish, and catfish.

Yoga and Spas

The Spa at Bear Mountain (3020 Seven Lakes Dr., Bear Mountain, 845/233-2152, http://bearmountainspa.com) came with the extensive hotel renovations of 2013. Choose from Swedish, deep tissue, or a custom massage for runners, cyclists, and hikers, or go for the organic facial. The spa will reimburse 50 percent of the parking fee if required.

Wholeness Center (7 New Lake Rd., Valley Cottage, 845/268-7532, www.wholenesscenter.com, 10am-5pm Mon.-Tues. and Fri.-Sat., 10am-8pm Wed.-Thurs.) has an infrared sauna, steam room, and crystal salt meditation room that clients can book along with any massage or facial. Hot stone, shiatsu, deep tissue, and other styles of massage are provided, along with a number of advanced skincare treatments.

ENTERTAINMENT AND EVENTS
Performing Arts

Rhino Comedy (96 Lafayette Ave., Suffern, www.rhinoimprov.com, 7pm-9pm Wed.-Fri., 7pm-11pm Sat., noon-6pm Sun., $10-20) has opened in a historic Suffern playhouse with weekly shows, improv classes, comedy writing workshops, and open mike nights. **Children's Shakespeare Theater** (Palisades, 845/262-0278, www.childrensshakespeare.org) is an organization of children and teens (ages 8-18) who produce and present a number of Shakespeare plays each season, all with the intention of fostering an interest in the dramatic arts from a young age.

Bars and Nightlife

The Turning Point (468 Piermont Ave., Piermont, 845/359-1089, http://piermont.

club) lures acclaimed jazz performers to a cozy space in Piermont Village. You can have dinner on the porch before the show. The **Pier 701 Tiki Bar** (701 Piermont Ave., Piermont, 845/848-2550, www.pier701ny.com, noon-10pm Mon.-Thurs., noon-11pm Fri.-Sat., 11:30am-3pm Sun.) has a waterfront "beach" area and tables that are literally at the river's edge. It hosts Rockland County Live Music on Friday and Saturday nights, and the adjoining restaurant serves dependable Mediterranean fare (small plates $10-21, large plates $29-37). Daily drink specials include mojitos on Mondays, tequila on Tuesdays, and wine on Wednesdays.

Most evenings, Nyack has something going on for every kind of night owl. **The Hudson House of Nyack** (134 Main St., 845/353-1355, www.hudsonhousenyack.com, 5pm-10pm Wed.-Thurs, 5pm-11pm Fri.-Sat., 5pm-9:30pm Sun.) occupies the former village jailhouse, and two cells now hold the restaurant's wine cellar. Creative cocktails showcase local spirits like Warwick cider and Beacon whiskey, while the wine list includes a good mix of European and California whites and reds. Dinner ($28-43) and bar snacks are available.

Local artists and musicians frequent **Casa del Sol** (104 Main St., Nyack, 845/353-9846, www.casaofnyack.com, noon-9pm Tues.-Sun., mains $15-21). The bar shakes up a good many margaritas, mojitos, and mules on weekend nights. Order the Mexican Lollipops (chorizo meatballs), table-side guacamole, or brisket burrito to accompany your cocktail. Taco Tuesdays feature $3 Coronas and $3 tacos. Thursdays are for live music Casa Jams, and bands play on Friday and Saturday nights.

On Friday and Saturday nights, **Art Café** (65 S. Broadway, Nyack, 845/353-4230, http://artcafenyack.com, 9am-9pm Mon.-Thurs., 8am-9pm Fri.-Sat., $10-15) transforms itself from a coffee shop to a speakeasy, with impromptu performances, late night espresso, and beer, wine, and prosecco cocktails. Israeli-style dishes such as grain bowls and *malawach* are made from organic ingredients with some gluten-free options.

For live jazz in a small venue, check out **Maureen's Jazz Cellar** (2 N. Broadway, Nyack, 845/535-3143, http://maureens jazzcellar.com, Tues.-Sun., tickets $10-25). Shows typically begin at 6pm or 8pm. **Seven Lakes Station** (80 Orange Turnpike, Sloatsburg, 845/712-5586, www. sevenlakesstation.com, noon-10pm Tues.-Thurs. and Sun., noon-midnight Fri.-Sat.) pours craft beers from across New York State and elsewhere. Try the flight of seven local selections for $20. The kitchen ($14-22) serves up panini sandwiches, house-made chili, and a few lighter snacks. Live music often plays on Saturday.

Festivals

The **Highlands Bluegrass Festival** has become a September tradition in Sloatsburg, hosted at Harmony Hall, the Jacob Sloat House (15 Liberty Rock Rd., 845/712-5220, http://friendsofharmonyhall.org, free).

Hosted by the Redhawk Native American Arts Council, the **Annual Bear Mountain Powwow** ($12) takes place at the Anthony Wayne Recreation Area in Harriman State Park each August. More than 1,000 artists, performers, and educators participate. The event culminates in a dance competition that draws competitors from across North and South America. The **New York Triathlon Club** (Apr.-Oct., www.nytri.org) runs a triathlon at Lake Welch in Harriman State Park.

Bear Mountain State Park puts on a lively **Octoberfest** (845/786-2701, noon-6pm Sat.-Sun. Sept.-Oct.) at the Anthony Wayne Recreation Area, with traditional music and polka dancing in the crisp fall air. The **Rockland Audubon Society** (www. rocklandaudubon.org) runs field trips to Doodletown on Iona Island, Tallman State Park, and other open spaces for wildlife observation.

SHOPPING
Farm Stands

Don't miss the Thursday **Nyack Farmers Market** (845/353-2221, www.nyackchamber.

org, 8am-2pm Thurs. Apr.-Nov.), in the municipal parking lot at the corner of Main and Cedar Streets. You can buy 20 different types of mushrooms from a single grower, plus the usual assortment of locally grown fruits and vegetables. In winter, the market moves indoors to the Nyack Center (55 Depew Ave., 8am-2pm Thurs. Dec.-May). The **Cropsey Farm Stand** (220 S. Little Tor Rd., New City, 845/634-3167) is open on Saturday with the fresh-picked harvest of the week.

Additional Rockland County farmers markets include:

- Wednesday in Spring Valley (8:30am-3pm Wed. mid-July to mid-Nov.)

- Saturday at Stony Point (9am-2pm Sat. early July to late Oct.) and Suffern (8:30am-1pm Sat. mid-May to late Oct.)

- Sunday in the Village of Haverstraw (9am-1pm Sun. early July to late Oct.)

Check http://rocklandgov.com for current farmers market schedules, as hours and locations tend to change with every season.

For a traditional apple-picking experience, try **Dr. Davies Farm** (306 Rte. 304, Congers, 845/268-7020, www.drdaviesfarm.com, 9am-4pm daily Sept.-Nov.). Grab a half-bushel (25 pounds) bag or a half-peck (7 pounds) bag and a picking pole to reach fruit at the top of the trees. The farm grows 15 different varieties, including some for eating and others ideal for baking.

Hungry Hollow Co-op (841 Chestnut Ridge Rd., Chestnut Ridge, 845/356-3319, http://hungryhollow.coop, 8am-6:30pm Mon.-Fri., 10am-6pm Sat., 10am-4pm Sun.) stocks fresh produce from local organic farms, milk and yogurt from Duryea Farm, and Hudson Valley cheeses.

Antiques and Galleries

Art galleries and antiques shops abound in Nyack and Piermont. Book lovers will find contemporary and classic titles piled floor-to-ceiling at **Pickwick Bookshop** (8 S. Broadway, Nyack, 845/358-9126, http://pickwickbookshop.wordpress.com,

Antiques Advice

Collectors, casual shoppers, and bargain hunters all can find interesting shopping throughout the Hudson River Valley. The list includes vintage clothing, jewelry, furniture, artwork, glassware, home decorations, and more.

Some stores are set up as beautiful galleries, while others are run as auctions or sprawling multiple-dealer affairs with a maze of different rooms to explore. A few even have cafés on-site.

Cold Spring, Hudson, and Millerton have a high concentration of upscale shops; the dealers in Tannersville, Warwick, and Saugerties meet a wider range of price points. Most businesses are open during standard retail hours, but some are by appointment only. If you're looking for something specific, call ahead.

9:30am-7pm Mon.-Fri., 9:30am-8pm Sat., 11am-6pm Sun.). **Sillage of Piermont** (510 Piermont Ave., Piermont, 814/523-7097) allows you to blend a unique personal fragrance from 30 different perfumes. To look for hidden treasure, browse the goods inside the **Tappan Zee Thrift Shop** (454 Piermont Ave., 845/359-5753, 10am-4pm Thurs.-Sat., 1pm-5pm Sun.).

On the Route 59 corridor, the **Palisades Center** (1000 Palisade Center Dr., West Nyack, 845/348-1000, www.palisadescenter. com, 10am-9:30pm Mon.-Sat., 11am-7pm Sun.) is a four-level destination shopping center with 200 stores, anchored by Lord & Taylor, Macy's, Target, and H&M.

FOOD

Along the River: Route 9W

The food scene in Nyack evolves each year, with some bold new concepts and a handful of evergreen standouts. **The Hudson House of Nyack** (134 Main St., Nyack, 845/353-1355, www.hudsonhousenyack.com, 4:30pm-10pm Wed.-Sun., $28-43) prepares an outstanding pan-roasted Hudson Valley duck breast. The restaurant occupies the former village hall and jailhouse. You might start with the white peach and cucumber salad or the spice poached beet salad, then try the shrimp and grits or the Hudson House steak au poivre with a side of *shishito* peppers or crabmeat tater tots.

A harrowing refugee experience from Vietnam to Thailand landed chef Doug Chi

Nguyen in Rockland County and shaped the creative force that became **Wasabi** (110 Main St., Nyack, 845/358-7977, www.wasabichi. com, lunch noon-2:30pm Mon.-Fri., dinner 5pm-10pm Mon.-Thurs., 5pm-11pm Fri.-Sat., 4pm-9:30pm Sun., $27-35). This is an excellent longstanding sushi restaurant that blends a bit of other cuisines too. Skip to the Omakase Creations if you're feeling adventurous and inclined to trust your meal to the chef.

Though small and dark on the outside, **Thai House** (12 Park St., Nyack, 845/358-9100, www.thaihousenyack.xyz, 4:30pm-9:30pm Mon.-Thurs., 3pm-9:30pm Fri.-Sun., $16-23) is a nicely appointed restaurant serving a full Thai menu. The *massaman* and *panang* curries come highly recommended. The kitchen does not use MSG.

If you're passing through Nyack, centrally located ★ **Art Café of Nyack** (65 S. Broadway, Nyack, 845/353-4230, www. artcafenyack.com, 9am-9pm Mon.-Thurs., 8am-9pm Fri.-Sun., $10-15) serves Counter Culture brand coffee, which you can get as pour-over, French press, or Turkish style. The food is organic, with Middle Eastern specialties like *shakshooka* (baked eggs), plus grain bowls and very filling salads. Gluten-free substitutions are available. At **Prohibition River** (82 Main St., Nyack, 845/727-7900, http:// prohibitionriver.com, 4pm-9pm Mon.-Wed., 4pm-10pm Thurs., 4pm-11pm Fri., noon-11pm Sat., noon-9pm Sun., $18-34) you can order small plates (empanadas, cauliflower bites, wings), burgers with hand-cut fries, and steak frites or bangers and mash for bigger appetites.

Part restaurant, part gourmet market, ★ **True Food** (166 Main St., Nyack, 845/480-5710, www.truefoodofnyack.com, 9am-8pm daily, $6-14) is the place for people who care deeply about the quality of food they eat. The owner has local, sustainable, and organic choices for just about every way of eating—carnivore, gluten-free, vegetarian, and more. When dining here, your cheeseburger will be grass-fed and the salmon burger wild-caught. You can order a Rainbow Bowl, Bullet Coffee, or Turmeric Tea. Bone broth is available warm or cold, by the mason jar, or by the pint.

Grab a stool at the curvy Copper Bar and sip a glass of wine or seasonal cocktail with Chef Constantine at **The Greekish** (8 N. Broadway, Nyack, 845/353-1200, http://thegreekish.com, noon-10pm daily, $11-30), where Greek-style meze (small plates) are the way to go. Try Hudson Valley smoked salmon or Montauk lobster toast for something different, or stick to the classics of spinach pie, Greek meatballs, and feta croquettes. Watch the events calendar for an occasional three-course prix-fixe special that's served early (2-4pm) for $46. Happy hour (2-3:30pm daily) features two-for-one cocktails and $1 oysters.

The '76 House (110 Main St., Tappan, 845/359-5476, www.76house.com, lunch noon-3pm Mon.-Sat., dinner 5pm-9pm Mon.-Thurs., 5pm-10pm Fri- Sat., noon-8pm Sun., $20-44) is the oldest tavern in New York State. Highlights on the menu include venison medallions, Amish chicken, and Yankee pot roast. Listen to live music most nights of the summer and fall, or try the popular Sunday brunch (11am-3pm).

Freelance Café and Wine Bar (506 Piermont Ave., Piermont, 845/365-3250, www.freelancecafe-piermont.com, noon-3pm and 5pm-10pm Tues.-Sun., small plates $9-19, large plates $26-36) remains a reliable place to meet a friend for lunch or drinks. Order small plates like Asian barbecue lettuce wraps or octopus orzo salad. Notable large plates include steak frites, calf's liver, and brook trout.

Acclaimed chef Peter X. Kelly now runs two restaurants in the Lower Hudson Valley: X2O is on the pier on Yonkers in Westchester County, and out in the country, **Restaurant X** (117 N. Rte. 303, Congers, 845/268-6555, www.xaviars.com, noon-2:30pm and 5:30pm-9pm Wed.-Fri., 5pm-9pm

The '76 House

Sat.-Sun., brunch noon-2pm Fri. and Sun., $32-40) offers an ahi tuna ceviche or chicken liver mousseline to start, and cod with brown butter spinach or classic beef Wellington as entrées.

A Culinary Institute grad, Eric Woods is the owner of ★ **14 & Hudson Kitchen and Bar** (457 Piermont Ave., Piermont, 845/680-0014, http://14andhudson.com, 3pm-8pm Wed.-Thurs., 3pm-9pm Fri, noon-3:30pm and 4pm-9pm Sat., noon-3:30pm and 4pm-8pm Sun., $20-38), an inviting bistro-style restaurant serving modern comfort food like mini meatballs, Baja fish tacos, and a variety of burgers with truffle fries.

Sidewalk Bistro (482 Piermont Ave., Piermont, 845/680-6460, www.sidewalkbistro.com, noon-10pm Wed.-Thurs., noon-11pm Fri.-Sat., noon-9pm Sun., $17-42) is a French-inspired concept, complete with sidewalk seating and a backyard garden. Try the *moules poullette*, Niçoise salad, pizzettes, or Kobe bistro burger.

Popular with the pre-theater dinner crowd, **La Fontana** (95 S. Broadway, Nyack, 845/358-3770, www.lafontanaofnyack.com, $21-45) has an inviting terrace and river views from the dining room upstairs. A simple menu focuses on classic Italian dishes: gnocchi Bolognese, linguini in white whole clam sauce, chicken parmigiana, veal saltimbocca, and shrimp scampi, to name just a few.

Cornetta's Restaurant and Marina (641 Piermont Ave., Piermont, 845/359-9852, www.cornettas.com, noon-9pm Sun., noon-9:30pm Mon., Wed., and Thurs., noon-10pm Fri.-Sat., $21-39) has indoor seating year-round and a waterfront pavilion that's open only in the warmer months. Italian-style seafood, pasta, and meat dishes are the specialty of the house. Gluten-free pasta is an option.

The Hudson Water Club (606 Beach Rd., West Haverstraw, 845/271-4046, www.hudsonwaterclub.com, $16-43) is a seasonal restaurant on the waterfront that's open for lunch and dinner in summer. Created by a CIA grad, the dinner menu features littleneck clams, oysters, and mussels prepared three ways. Small plates include chicken wings and an antipasti platter. For a main course, you can order red or white pizzas, pork chop scarpiello, pan-seared Maine scallops, and the like. Several gluten-free dishes are provided. Also at the river's edge, just south of Emeline Park, **Don Coqui** (16 Front St., Haverstraw, 845/942-1616, www.doncoqui.com, open daily in summer, $15-35) specializes in Puerto Rican and Caribbean-themed cuisine such as coconut shrimp, pan-fried Cajun red snapper, and seafood paella.

The Ramapo Mountains

Characters (formerly The Glenwood, 94 Orange Turnpike, Sloatsburg, 845/753-5200, www.charactersresturant.com, 11:30am-10pm Sun.-Thurs., 11:30am-11pm Fri.-Sat., $16-27) has a down-home feel, with Irish specialties such as chicken pot pie, fish-and-chips, and shepherd's pie.

★ **Valley Rock Cantina** (17 Mill St., Sloatsburg, 845/618-9112, http://valleyrockinn.com, 5pm-11pm Thurs.-Fri., noon-11pm Sat., 11am-5pm Sun., $15-26), part of the Valley Rock Inn, serves up mojo pork tacos, cold soba noodles, hearty chicken soup, and a gourmet grilled cheese. On Sundays, the brunch menu adds French toast, breakfast burritos, and a short rib hash to the entrée options. On the drink menu, you'll find a great selection of fun cocktails and some interesting wines by the glass from around the world.

Just shy of the New Jersey state line, **Mount Fuji Steakhouse** (296 Rte. 17, Hillburn, 845/357-4270, www.mtfujirestaurants.com, lunch noon-2:30pm Mon.-Fri., dinner 5pm-10pm Mon.-Thurs., 5pm-11pm Fri., 3pm-11pm Sat., 3pm-10pm Sun., $25-48) is perched on a hilltop above Route 17. Seating around a private hibachi station and servers tossing cleavers in the air make it the perfect venue to celebrate a birthday or a family reunion. You'll likely wait for a table, even with a reservation. Arrive in daylight to catch the mountain views.

Route 59 Corridor

Sakana Japanese Fusion (25 Rockland Plaza, Nanuet, 845/623-2882, www.sakanafusion.com, noon-3pm and 4:30pm-9pm Mon.-Thurs., noon-3pm and 4:30pm-10pm Fri., 1pm-10pm Sat., 1pm-9pm Sun., $15-27) offers a large and detailed menu of classic sushi dishes as well as unique creations like the angel roll—shrimp tempura topped with spicy tuna, tempura flakes, and black caviar. A number of cooked rolls, teriyaki dishes, and curries are also available.

Marcello's Ristorante of Suffern (21 Lafayette Ave., Suffern, 845/357-9108, www.marcellosgroup.com, 5pm-9pm Mon.-Wed., noon-9pm Thurs., noon-9:30pm Fri., 5pm-9:30pm Sat., 4:30pm-8:30pm Sun., $20-33) is a white-linen affair with a menu of true Italian specialties. Look for the burgundy awning. Happy hour (2:30pm-5pm Thurs.-Fri.) is available.

The Sanchez family brings the flavors of Guadalajara to Suffern at ★ **Hacienda de Don Manuel** (72 Lafayette Ave., Suffern, 845/369-1633, http://haciendadm.com, 11am-10pm daily, $14-24). Beautiful hand-painted murals decorate the walls inside. Chilaquiles would be a great choice for breakfast, fish tacos for lunch, and any of the mole dishes for dinner. The restaurant hosts an especially festive Cinco de Mayo celebration in May.

Enjoy the all-you-can-eat buffet at ★ **Fink's BBQ and Cheesesteak Roadhouse** (32 Orange Ave., Suffern, 845/533-4033, www.finksbbqroadhouse.com, 11am-10pm Sun.-Thurs., 11am-11pm Fri.-Sat., $13-28). Munch on some pork cracklings or fresh-cooked potato chips, then move on to one of the famed cheesesteak sandwiches. The Classic comes with pit-roasted sirloin thinly sliced with a choice of cheese. Crispy pork belly makes for an especially filling meal.

ACCOMMODATIONS

Accommodations with personality are surprisingly hard to come by in Rockland County. Notable mentions in the chain hotel category include a Marriott Residence Inn in Orangeburg, Hilton Pearl River, and the DoubleTree in Nanuet. Travelers who seek a more unique lodging experience may prefer to continue on to Orange County or cross the river to Putnam.

$150-200

Next to Hessian Lake in Bear Mountain State Park, the **Bear Mountain Inn** (Bear Mountain, 845/786-2731, www.visitbearmountain.com, from $169) has updated kings, queens, and suites in a historic building that was renovated top to bottom in 2013. In a separate building on the property, **Overlook Lodge** (from $169) has basic but comfortable motel-style rooms that are simply furnished with two double beds and private baths. The location and views are the most appealing quality of this property; however, be prepared for a noisy environment on weekends in the high season. Rates include continental breakfast.

Now a Hyatt property, **Hotel Nyack** (400 High Ave., Nyack, 845/675-8700, http://hyatt.com, from $360) manages to create an artist's loft vibe in a restored factory building. Some rooms have river views, and the fitness room stays open late. Enjoy the heated outdoor pool and bar during the summer months. The hotel is pet-friendly, and you can dine at the on-site restaurant, **The Grille at Nyack** (noon-10pm Mon.-Fri., 9am-10pm Sat.-Sun., $22-50).

Over $200

In the Ramapo Mountains, ★ **Valley Rock Inn & Mountain Club** (17 Mill St., Sloatsburg, 845/618-9112, http://valleyrockinn.com, $795 per night for two people) has 17 guest rooms spread across four historic buildings. This thoughtfully designed property specializes in fitness retreats with a lap pool and state-of-the-art gym, as well as organized hiking, biking, and kayaking programs. The organic market and antiques store (10am-6pm Mon.-Tues., 10am-7pm Wed.-Fri.,

8am-7pm Sat., 8am-6pm Sun.) sells fresh produce and special vintage finds. Also on the premises, **66Orange Art Gallery** showcases the works of local artists. The **Valley Rock Cantina** (5pm-11pm Thurs.-Fri., noon-11pm Sat., 11am-5pm Sun., $15-26) is an excellent new option for outdoor dining, drinks, or Sunday brunch.

For a contemporary B&B experience, book one of the three guest rooms in a restored 1850s villa, now known as ★ **Casa Hudson Penzione** (34 First St., Haverstraw, 845/219-1698, www.casahudsonny.com, $300). You can walk to village restaurants, or simply enjoy the beautifully designed space inside and take in views from a chair on the porch.

INFORMATION AND SERVICES

The **Rockland County Office of Tourism** (18 New Hempstead Rd., New City, 845/708-7300 or 800/295-5723, https://explorerocklandny.com) is headquartered in New City. In Nyack, look for a visitors information booth by the Clock Tower at Main and Cedar Streets.

GETTING THERE AND AROUND

Bus
Several companies run buses in Rockland County: **Transit of Rockland** (845/364-3333, http://rocklandgov.com) and the **Spring Valley Jitney** (845/352-1100, http://rocklandgov.com) provide local service, while ShortLine Bus and Adirondack Trailways connect to parts north.

Train
The **Metro-North** (800/638-7646) Spring Valley and Port Jervis lines run through Rockland County. A ferry connects Haverstraw (30-34 Dr. Girling Dr.) with the **Hudson Line train station** (800/533-3779, www.nywaterway.com) in Ossining. Ride-share services operate in all the major towns, including Nyack. Stewart Airport is the best place to rent a car.

Car
The Palisades Interstate Parkway (exits 4-15) connects Rockland County to the George Washington Bridge, and the Garden State Parkway heads to New Jersey. I-287 crosses the Tappan Zee Bridge to Westchester County.

The Hudson Highlands

Between the towns of Peekskill in Westchester

County and Beacon in Dutchess County—a 15-mile stretch—a solid granite mountain range called the Appalachian Plateau crosses the Hudson. Here, the river has carved a narrow and deep path through the range to form the Hudson Highlands, a fairytale landscape that recalls the signature banks of the Rhine. Storm King Mountain on the west and Breakneck Ridge on the east rise up on opposite shores near Cold Spring and West Point, giving Orange and Putnam Counties some of the most beautiful vistas—and colorful history—of any county in the region.

During the Revolutionary War, it was here, in the narrowest part of the river, that American troops stretched an iron chain—each link

Highlights

Look for ★ to find recommended sights, activities, dining, and lodging.

★ **West Point:** A gold mine of American military history sits in one of the most beautiful spots along the Hudson (page 81).

★ **Storm King Art Center:** This outdoor sculpture museum features works from well-known American and British artists (page 83).

★ **Sugar Loaf:** One of the region's most unusual attractions is this small village of artisans who craft handmade ceramics, soaps, and other goods (page 91).

★ **Boscobel House and Gardens:** The home of the annual Hudson Valley Shakespeare Festival is a restored neoclassical mansion called Boscobel (page 105).

★ **Cold Spring Village:** Visit antiques shops and gourmet restaurants just steps from the Metro-North commuter line (page 106).

★ **The Great Swamp:** Paddle this expansive watershed area covering Dutchess and Putnam Counties to see abundant wildlife surviving in a fragile ecosystem (page 111).

measuring two feet long and weighing more than 140 pounds—across the entire width of the river. The goal was to prevent British ships from sailing north up the Hudson. Though it may well have been an effective deterrent, the chain was never tested because none of the British ships managed to advance as far as West Point after the chain was set.

A few miles north, where the river widens to form Newburgh Bay, tiny Pollepel Island has an abandoned Scottish-style castle and what remains of the former Bannerman Island Arsenal, an unusual family business that dealt in military supplies. You can see what remains of the fortress by taking a river cruise or kayak tour.

Today, the Hudson Highlands area boasts four state parks, a section of the Appalachian Trail, the Black Dirt onion-growing region, and a lively summer scene around Greenwood Lake.

PLANNING YOUR TIME

Few travelers attempt to see all of the Hudson Highlands in one trip. Weekend itineraries are best limited to one museum, park, or village. You might target several sights along the river, or plan to visit one of the expansive state parks. West Point, the Storm King Art Center, and Cold Spring Village can take from a few hours to a full day to explore. In summer, a day at Greenwood Lake followed by an evening of shopping and fine dining in Warwick make

a good combination. Route 17 through western Orange County is a major access route to Sullivan County and the Catskill region.

Putnam County measures less than 20 miles north to south and is well worth a full day's visit. Cold Spring is the county's most popular destination, and a day passes quickly in and around the riverside town. With an early start at the Bear Mountain Bridge, you'll have time for brief stops at Manitoga, Boscobel Restoration, and Constitution Marsh Center & Sanctuary, followed by a walk and a memorable meal along Cold Spring's Main Street. Serious antiques shoppers will need more time, as will anyone who plans to hike the Hudson Highlands or paddle the river.

To add Clarence Fahnestock Memorial State Park and eastern Putnam County to the itinerary, follow Route 301 west out of Cold Spring through the towns of Kent, Carmel, and Brewster.

Scenic Drives
Route 9D in Putnam County, from Beacon to the Bear Mountain Bridge, winds its way through the Hudson Highlands. On the other side of the Hudson, Route 218 leads over Storm King Mountain, with spectacular views of West Point and the Bear Mountain Bridge. This crossing is weather-dependent and often closes after storms when debris collects in the road. Be prepared to turn around and take Route 9W instead.

Previous: grounds of the Boscobel House and Gardens; a summer eve at Greenwood Lake; Breakneck Ridge Trail.

The Hudson Highlands

© MOON.COM

Orange County

The only county in the Hudson River Valley with frontage on both the Hudson and Delaware Rivers begins 50 miles north and across the river from New York City, encompassing 816 square miles of fertile fields, rolling hills, and quiet suburban communities. Orange County's largest commercial centers are Newburgh, Middletown, and Port Jervis. Goshen is the county seat.

History is one of the primary reasons travelers visit Orange County. It is home of the prestigious U.S. Military Academy at West Point and several related sights that draw some three million visitors a year.

ALONG THE RIVER: ROUTE 9W

Orange and Rockland Counties share a border at the Bear Mountain Bridge on the west side of the Hudson River. Several thoroughfares meet here in a traffic circle at the approach to the bridge: Route 9W runs along the riverbank, the Palisades Interstate Parkway heads south toward New Jersey, and Route 6 runs west to join Route 17 (the Quickway). Appalachian Trail hikers also pass through on their way to or from Harriman State Park. (The AT crosses the Hudson at the Bear Mountain Bridge.)

Fort Montgomery State Historic Site

A few miles south of West Point, you can view the remains of an old fort, from which American soldiers sought—unsuccessfully—to prevent the British from advancing up the Hudson during the Revolutionary War. A visitors center contains artifacts found in the area of the fort, including shoe buckles, cuff links, glasses, and flatware. Visits to **Fort Montgomery** (690 Route 9W, 845/446-2134, http://parks.ny.gov, grounds 8am-sunset daily, visitors center 9am-5pm Wed.-Sun. mid-Apr.-Oct., group tours $5) begin with a

short film about the site and its role in early American history. Thematic tours and events focus on Native American archeology as well as reenactments and demonstrations of historical events.

TOP EXPERIENCE

★ West Point

A few miles north of the Bear Mountain Bridge, the Hudson flows through its narrowest and deepest stretch (more than 200 feet), creating the strategic military position of West Point. In revolutionary times, American forces strung a 40-ton chain 500 yards across the river to keep the British at bay. After the colonial victory, President Thomas Jefferson believed the young nation needed to build its own military capability and wean itself from dependence on foreign expertise. He signed the United States Military Academy into law in 1802.

The academy's first curriculum produced civil engineers, who went on to build much of the nation's transportation infrastructure. West Point established its reputation for military excellence during the Civil War, when graduates, including Robert E. Lee and Ulysses S. Grant, fought against each other during almost every battle. Superintendents during the 20th century broadened the program to include academic, physical, and military education, and the first woman graduated from the academy in 1980.

Today, the **United States Military Academy at West Point** (www.usma.edu) develops cadets in academics, athletics, and military training in preparation for serving their country as officers. For visitors, **West Point Tours** (Highland Falls, 845/446-4724, www.westpointtours.com) runs guided bus tours daily, except on football Saturdays, holidays, and during graduation week. The 75-minute tour ($16) begins at the visitors center, off the West Point Highway, where you can view a model cadet barracks room and gather information about the academy. Note that tour requests must be made online at least 7 days before your visit, and there are no rest stops during the drive around campus.

Extended two-hour tours, offered twice daily June-October, add stops at the Old Cadet Chapel (8:15am-4:15pm daily) and West Point Cemetery. Built in 1836, the chapel is one of the oldest buildings still used on campus. The cemetery holds graves that date back to 1782 and represent casualties of almost every war the academy's graduates have fought. Inquire about combination bus and river tours. The West Point Band plays on Sunday evenings in an outdoor amphitheater near the North Dock in West Point.

Behind the visitors center stands the West Point Museum (845/938-3590, www.usma. edu/museum, 10:30am-4:15pm daily, free), which houses four floors of warfare exhibits covering 135 U.S. military conflicts. A large weapons display in the basement has a World War I tank, while the small weapons include axes, clubs, and swords that date all the way back to the Stone Age. Tours often stop at Fort Putnam, a key position in defending the fortress, with panoramic views of the river and campus. Trophy Point offers a postcard-perfect view of the Hudson Highlands.

Familiar names grace the monuments across the central part of the campus: Patton, Marshall, MacArthur, Eisenhower, Schwarzkopf. More than 2,000 names are inscribed on the massive granite shaft of the striking Battle Monument (1897), designed by Sanford White, who also built and furnished the opulent Vanderbilt Estate in Hyde Park.

The Gothic Thayer Hotel (674 Thayer Rd., West Point, 845/446-4731, www. thethayerhotel.com, from $175), built in 1926, overlooks the Hudson at the south entrance to West Point. It was named for Colonel Sylvanus Thayer, superintendent of West Point from 1817 to 1833. A $26 million face-lift in 1996 restored the hotel to its former glory. Portraits of military leaders decorate the walls in the formal dining room, which is popular for holiday gatherings.

From the back lawn of the hotel, you can see Constitution Island, the first place George Washington chose to fortify at West Point. Unfortunately, the British had the same idea and established a stronghold in 1777; the Americans won it back a year later. By the 1830s, the island fell into private hands. Henry Warner and his two daughters built a family estate, and for years the daughters invited cadets to the island to study the Bible. The Warners donated their house and gardens to the academy in 1908. Today's cadets complete many of their training exercises here.

The nonprofit Constitution Island Association (845/265-2501, www. constitutionisland.org) organizes tours (10am Wed., 9am Sat. late June-Sept., $15). Each tour takes about two hours, and reservations are required. Boats depart from the South Dock inside West Point, past the Thayer Hotel. For special events, the association runs a shuttle bus from the Cold Spring Metro-North train station.

Call before you head to West Point for any of these activities because the visitors center may cancel tours at any time. Photo identification is required for entry, and your vehicle will also be searched. Allow extra time if you are taking a cruise or attending an event. To get here, exit the New York State Thruway at exit 16.

Cornwall and Cornwall-on-Hudson

After West Point, Route 9W winds its way north to the base of Storm King Mountain and the quiet hamlet of Cornwall-on-Hudson. Alternatively, follow Route 218 north for a white-knuckle drive over Storm King Mountain, with gorgeous views of the fjord-like highlands. The Hudson Highlands Nature Museum has two locations about 1.5 miles apart. The Outdoor Discovery Center (120 Muser Dr., Cornwall, 845/534-5506, www.hhnm.org,

Tips for Exploring the Hudson Valley

Proximity to a major metropolitan area brings large crowds to the best places in the region. Here are some tips to avoid the masses:

- **Get off the thruway:** I-87 is straight with many lanes, and usually the fastest route through the valley, but older parkways and highways often make for a more pleasant drive.

- **Get out of the car:** Go ahead and stop at scenic overlooks and roadside stands. Follow handmade signs. They often lead to cool places.

- **Eat something fresh off the farm:** Try an heirloom tomato, fresh-picked strawberries, or an antique apple. You will taste the difference.

- **Talk to the innkeeper:** Bed-and-breakfast hosts in the country know a lot about the area—who's harvesting what that week, which businesses have opened and closed, and which have changed hands.

- **Get dirty:** Roll up your sleeves and feel the dirt. Volunteer on a farm, camp in the woods, or pick your own fruit.

- **Take to the river:** The land looks different when you're cruising on a small ship. Travel by boat to see fall colors, historic mansions, and birds of the Hudson.

10am-4pm Sat.-Sun. mid-Apr.-mid-Nov.) maintains hiking trails and a visitors center with a variety of nature programs throughout the year. For example, you might learn about the soil under your feet, the habitat of wild turkeys, the world of mushrooms, or predator behavior. Its **Grasshopper Grove** ($5) is a nature play area designed for younger children. The museum entrance is on Angola Road; there is no access from Route 9W. A separate **Wildlife Education Center** (25 Boulevard, Cornwall-on-Hudson, 845/534-7781, www.hhnm.org, noon-4pm Sat.-Sun., $5) has rabbits, turtles, owls, and other wild critters and offers occasional "Meet the Animals" sessions. The Ogden Gallery features local artists and interactive exhibits that focus on the natural world. This location also has a gift shop.

★ Storm King Art Center

The Quaker Avenue exit off Route 9W leads to the expansive sculpture gardens of the **Storm King Art Center** (1 Museum Rd., New Windsor, 845/534-3115, www.stormking.org, 10am-6pm Wed.-Mon., adults $20, under age 5 free). The museum stays open until 8pm

on summer Fridays and Saturdays. This is the perfect site for a summer picnic, but you'll have to leave your barbecue, balls, Frisbees, pets, and radios at home. In this outdoor museum, you can walk along tree-lined paths and view larger-than-life sculptures against the dramatic landscape and ever-changing light of the Hudson Highlands. The collection represents British and American artists, both postwar and contemporary. Some of the sculptures were designed expressly for their sites in the 500-acre park. *The Arch,* one of Alexander Calder's "stabiles," measures 56 feet high. The *Joy of Life,* a monumental piece by Mark di Suvero, weighs 20 tons and stands 70 feet tall.

Lately, exhibits have focused on the theme of climate change. Storm King is a popular place for organized singles' outings from New York City. The center offers guided, self-guided, and audio tours. Wear good walking shoes and dress for the weather. The museum café serves light lunch fare, including Applegate hot dogs, chicken kebabs, a hummus sandwich, and vegetarian soup. If leaving the city by train, you can take a shuttle from the Beacon Metro-North station.

Newburgh

Farther up the river at the intersection of Route 9W and I-84 lies Newburgh, a city that has struggled with its legacy as a manufacturing center. Many of the old buildings look sadly neglected, but the city retains a deep sense of history, and a few of its blocks are coming back to life as centers for food and the arts.

George Washington established his Revolutionary War headquarters in the home of Jonathan Hasbrouck, a fieldstone fortress on a hill overlooking the river. **Washington's Headquarters** (84 Liberty St., Newburgh, 845/562-1195, www.parks.ny.gov, 11am-4pm Wed.-Sat., 1pm-4pm Sun. mid-Apr.-Oct., 11am-3pm Fri.-Sat. Nov.-Apr., adults $7, seniors and students $5, under age 12 free) has been a national historic site since 1850. Guides in period dress lead groups through a half-hour tour of Hasbrouck House, which has been restored to reflect its setup as military headquarters. Before or after a tour, you can walk through a separate interpretive exhibit to learn more about the Revolutionary War. Across the lawn and overlooking the river is a monument built in the 1880s to honor the peace treaty that ended the Civil War.

The parking lot is somewhat tricky to find. If you're coming from I-84, follow Route 9W/32 south until Broadway. Turn left on Broadway and go about 10 blocks. Turn right on Liberty Street, and after a block, look for the fenced lawn on the left and an alleyway just before Washington Street that leads to a parking lot.

The 1839 **Crawford House** (189 Montgomery St., Newburgh, 845/561-2585, www.newburghhistoricalsociety.com, 1pm-4pm Sun. Apr.-Oct., $5), once the residence of a shipping merchant, houses the **Historical Society of Newburgh Bay & The Highlands.** On display inside the classic revival building are 19th-century antiques and Hudson River School paintings. Views of

Newburgh Bay are as memorable as the collection inside.

In addition to many private restorations under way, Newburgh has revived a section of its waterfront by turning several abandoned factories into an attractive boardwalk with a handful of upscale restaurants and shops. People now arrive at **Newburgh Landing** (Front St., Newburgh, 845/565-3297) by the boatful on summer weekends, where a variety of cuisines and trendy bars are just steps away from a slip in the marina. Fake palm trees—and some real ones too—are all part of the experience. Serious partiers often sleep on their boats after a night of revelry at one of the nearby clubs.

From the water's edge, you can see the beginning of the narrow Hudson Highlands to the south. Several river cruises, including **River Rose Cruises** (845/562-1067, http://riverrosecruises.com), depart from the landing. To find Newburgh Landing, exit I-84 at Route 9W and turn left at the second light onto North Plank Road. Go 1.25 miles and make a left onto 2nd Street to go under the train trestle.

If you continue on Route 9W instead of heading to the landing, you'll soon reach the intersection of South Street and the edge of Newburgh's landmark green space: 35-acre **Downing Park** (Rte. 9W and 3rd St., Newburgh, 845/565-5559, www.downingparknewburgh.org, visitors center open year-round, 11am-5pm Wed.-Sun. summer). It was named for architect Andrew Jackson Downing and designed by Frederick Law Olmsted and Calvert Vaux, the creators of Central Park in New York City. The restored Downing Park Shelter House serves as the city's visitors center, and the Newburgh Symphony Orchestra plays here in summer; local yoga instructors sometimes offer free classes in the amphitheater.

Hundreds of bikes have been carefully restored by a father-son duo for display in an old lumber warehouse at **Motorcyclepedia** (250 Lake St., Newburgh, 845/569-9065, www.motorcyclepediamuseum.org,

---

1: West Point Museum **2:** Downing Park Shelter House

Newburgh

© MOON.COM

5pm-8pm Thurs., 10am-5pm Fri.-Sun., $15)—a two-story museum dedicated to two-wheeled transportation from 1897 to the present. There are choppers, vintage models, and military and police motorcycles. Nearby, **The Velocipede** (109 Liberty St., 10am-4pm Sat.) carries on the theme with antique bicycles and tricycles dating all the way back to 1820.

This same block of Liberty Street, just steps from Washington's Headquarters, is seeing development in other ways too. A few boutique shops are mixed in with eateries like **Liberty Street Bistro** (97 Liberty St., Newburgh, 845/562-3900, libertystreetbistro.com, noon-9pm Wed.-Thurs., noon-10pm Fri.-Sat., noon-8pm Sun.), started by a

graduate of the Culinary Institute of America in nearby Hyde Park.

New Windsor Cantonment and the National Purple Heart Hall of Honor

The history lesson continues a short drive from Newburgh, at the **New Windsor Cantonment** (374 Temple Hill Rd./Rte. 300, Vails Gate, 845/561-1765, www.nysparks.com, 10am-5pm Wed.-Sat., 1pm-5pm Sun. Apr.-Oct.), where George Washington's army stayed. You can view a replica of the Temple of Virtue, where Washington delivered one of his most moving speeches to troops who were losing faith in the war. The purposes of slanted bed frames, the use of charcoal for toothpaste, and the wonders of hard bread are just some of the trivia you'll pick up on a walk through the grounds and museum.

With the addition of the **National Purple Heart Hall of Honor** (374 Temple Hill Rd./ Rte. 300, Vails Gate, 845/561-1765, www. thepurpleheart.com, 10am-5pm Tues.-Sat., 1pm-5pm Sun. Apr.-Oct.), the Cantonment offers an appealing blend of old and new. A visit here is an interactive experience that makes full use of the latest audiovisual technology. There are high-definition films to watch and computer stations set up for visitors to find or add their loved ones. Although the hall is designed to honor all 1.7 million recipients collectively, museum staff bring individual stories to life through a series of Roll of Honor interviews recorded in an on-site video studio. An outdoor courtyard is set aside as ceremonial grounds for quiet reflection. The gift shop sells Hall of Honor souvenirs plus colonial-themed toys and games for children.

CENTRAL ORANGE COUNTY: ALONG ROUTE 17

Greenwood Lake

The Appalachian Trail enters New York State from New Jersey at Greenwood Lake, a long, narrow body of water that joins the two states. Surrounded by dense forest and mountains, the natural lake is shallow with a maximum depth of 57 feet and wetlands at each end. Visibility is generally good, except after heavy storms. A narrow local road hugs the eastern shore of the lake, and busy Route 210 heads into New Jersey on the western side.

The Erie Railroad brought the first wave of visitors to the lake in the 1870s, and Babe Ruth was a frequent vacationer. A number of year-round residences and second homes of city-dwellers crowd the shoreline today, but several access areas are open to the public for swimming and boating.

From Greenwood Lake, Route 17A climbs over Sterling Mountain to the east, winding through a 19,000-acre state park that is the site of a small ski resort and the **New York**

Renaissance Faire (845/351-5171, https:// renfair.com/ny, 10am-7pm Sat.-Sun. Aug.- Sept., adults $30, children $13) before meeting up with Route 17 and the New York State Thruway at the town of Tuxedo.

Fifties-era billboards and now-closed diners like the battered Red Apple Rest line this stretch of Route 17. During the peak of the Catskill summer resorts in the 1960s, traffic leaving New York City poured through en route to cooler air in the mountains. Two developments could bring renewed interest to the area: The **Resort World Catskills Casino & Hotel** opened in 2018 in Monticello, 50 miles to the north. And the new **Legoland New York Resort** (6 N. Church St., Goshen, legoland.com) opened in summer 2021.

Legoland New York Resort

Legoland (1 Legoland Way, Goshen, 845/410-0290, www.legoland.com/new-york, 10am-6pm daily, closed in winter, from $68) opened the first major theme park in the northeastern United States in more than 40 years. Youngsters ages 2-12 will have a blast exploring all seven themed worlds, named for the various Lego product lines: Brick Street, Bricktopia, Ninjago, Castle, City, Pirates, and Miniland for the littlest guests. Between the rides, shows, and in-park dining, families can easily spend a couple of days here. For a complete experience, grab a room at the resort hotel and take advantage of vacation packages that include admission. Note: Most of the park is closed in the winter months, but the hotel stays open.

Harriman State Park

Established in 1910 through a land grant from the Harriman family, Harriman State Park is the second largest park in the state of New York, with dozens of lakes, reservoirs, ponds, and 200 miles of trails. Look for the entrance to **Harriman State Park** (Rte. 9W, Bear Mountain, 845/786-2701, www. nysparks.com, parking $6-10) on the east side of Route 17A. A much larger neighbor to Bear Mountain State Park at the Rockland County line, Harriman boasts the oldest stretch of the Appalachian Trail, which was cleared in 1923. The Reeves Meadow Visitor Center (Seven Lakes Dr., 845/753-5122, weekends and holidays 8am-5pm) near Sloatsburg on the west side of the park has maps, books, toys, and hiking essentials.

Because of its proximity to New York City, the park attracts considerable crowds on summer weekends. Most people head for the areas around Lake Welch, Bear Mountain, and Hessian Lake, and the network of trails that depart from Reeves Meadow. Avoid these areas and you can find solitude in the woods. Dogs are allowed inside the park on leash.

The facilities at Lake Sebago have been closed since 2011 following damage from Hurricane Irene. Lake Welch has a popular swimming beach and cabins for camping. Lean-to shelters on a dozen of the trails are available on a first-come, first-served basis, free of charge.

You can get to the park by train from Harriman station, Tuxedo station, Manitou station (limited service), or Peekskill station and call a ride-share service or cab to cross the river. There is no entry fee to the park; however, parking in one of the larger lots costs $6-10 per day, depending on the lot and the time of year.

Warwick

In the opposite direction from Sterling Mountain on 17A—just minutes from the New Jersey state line—lies Warwick, a Victorian village with art galleries, antiques shops, and gourmet restaurants along its Main Street. The effect is a little bit like New York City's SoHo district, on a smaller scale.

From May through December, the surrounding farmland produces a constantly changing harvest: vegetables and berries in summer; pears, apples, and pumpkins in fall; evergreen Christmas trees in winter. The annual Warwick Applefest (www. warwickapplefest.com) in early October is not to be missed; however, you should be prepared to battle the crowds. The Warwick

Valley Farmers' Market (South St. at the railroad tracks, 845/988-7912, https://www. warwickvalleyfarmersmarket.org, 9am-2pm Sun. May-Nov.) has been going for decades and represents dozens of nearby farms. Local residents come by to pick up pastured eggs, fresh milk, microgreens and other organic veggies, and cold-pressed oils. Most of the vendors come every Sunday.

Nightlife is lively, especially in summer, when several local cafés and galleries offer live music. Parking will challenge even the most seasoned urbanites on weekends.

Black Dirt Region

The township of Warwick encompasses much of the 14,000-acre Black Dirt Region, an agricultural anomaly formed by glacial activity some 12,000 years ago. Polish and German immigrants cleared fields in present-day Pine Island and Florida by hand in the 1880s and discovered that the soil was well suited to growing onions. The region still produces about a quarter of all the onions consumed in the United States. During the August harvest season, the sweet aroma seeps into the car the moment you cross into the area. You can sample the local harvest at the Pine Island Black Dirt Farmers Market (Kay Rd. and Treasure Lane, 10am-2pm Sat. June-Oct.), which takes place in Pine Island Town Park.

Rogowski Farm (327-329 Glenwood Rd., Pine Island, 845/258-4574, www. rogowskifarm.com) offers classes in healthy eating. Learn about dealing with food sensitivities and improving your lifestyle through food, or take a private cooking class. Occasionally, the farm opens the doors to its greenhouse, farm kitchen, and fields to show the public how real crops and animals grow without the use of harmful chemicals.

Rise & Root Farm (Chester, no tel., www. riseandroot.com) is owned by four women who describe themselves as Black and white, queer and straight, working together to

1: River Rose Cruises at Newburgh Landing 2: the New York Renaissance Faire 3: Greenwood Lake

Warwick

INN AT STONY CREEK · 41

SPANKTOWN RD

UNION CORNERS RD

JESSUP RD

MEADOW LARK FARM BED AND BREAKFAST

Warwick Town Park

DISTILLERY RD

94

17A

E RIDGE RD

OLD RIDGE RD

W RIDGE RD

BELCHER RD

APPLEWOOD WINERY

4 CORNERS RD

DEMAREST RD

Durland

13

WARWICK MUNICIPAL AIRPORT

Warwick Lake

THE LANDMARK INN

WARWICK VALLEY WINERY & DISTILLERY

ACKERMAN RD

13

To Pine Island and the Black Dirt Region

PINE ISLAND

TURNPIKE

94

17A

KINGS HWY

LOWER WISNER RD

DETAIL (inset):
WELLING PL
MAIN ST
MCEWEN ST
NEWHARDS
WEST ST
FRAZZLEBERRIES
GRAPPA RISTORANTE
RAILROAD AVE
1ST ST
SOUTH ST

WARWICK VALLEY BED AND BREAKFAST

Warwick

SEE DETAIL

SANFORDVILLE RD

WEST ST

FORRESTER AVE

Bellvale

BELLVALE LAKES RD

KAIN RD

Warwick Valley Country Club

GALLOWAY RD

BRADY RD

BALL RD

Warwick Park

BELLVALE FARMS CREAMERY

17A

To Greenwood Lake

94

CHATEAU HATHORN

New Milford

WARWICK DRIVE-IN

21

0   1 mi

0   1 km

© MOON.COM

---

create a more just and sustainable food system. You can get involved by volunteering for a community farm work day or donating to help the team rebuild after Hurricane Ida. The farm's address is given out to people once they sign up to volunteer. Look for this farm's vegetables, flowers, herbs, and seedlings at the **Chester Ag Center Farm Store** (8 Greycourt Ave, Chester, 845/445-7393, https://www.chesteragcenterfarmstore.com, noon-6pm Fri., 10am-2pm Sat.) and at the **Kingston Farmers Market** (285 Wall St, Kingston, https://kingstonfarmersmarket.org). Order by Wednesday night to pick up on Saturday.

To reach the Black Dirt Region from Warwick, follow the Pine Island Turnpike (Rte. 1B) west to Pine Island, or Route 17A north to Florida.

Monroe

Back on Route 17, schoolchildren have been visiting the historic **Museum Village at Old Smith's Clove** (1010 Rte. 17M, 845/782-8248, www.museumvillage.org, 11am-4pm Thurs.-Sun. Apr.-Nov., closed Memorial Day weekend, July 4, and Aug. 31, adults $15, children $10) in Monroe since the 1940s to learn about the wonders of colonial life, such as making wagons and candles. Walk from the red barn to the firehouse, weaver, and blacksmith in the shade of stately sugar maples. The museum is located behind a park-and-ride lot off exit 129. Turns are well marked from the exit ramp.

★ **Sugar Loaf**

Farther west, off Route 17M, is the village of **Sugar Loaf** (Kings Hwy., Sugar Loaf, 845/469-9181, www.sugarloafnewyork.com, hours vary by shop Wed.-Sun.), a collection of boutique shops selling handmade goods that include ceramics, clothes, and soaps. Pick up orange and eucalyptus loofah soaps at **Rosner Soap** (1373 Kings Hwy., 845/469-5931, www.rosnersoap.com, 11am-5pm Thurs.-Sun.). Find creative ways to use herbs at **Sugar Loaf Mountain Herbs** (1361 Kings Hwy., Sugar Loaf, www.sugarloafherbs.com, 11am-5:30pm Thurs.-Sat.). Stores keep slightly different hours, but if you arrive between 11am and 5pm, you should be able to visit most of them. You can grab a bite to eat at **Anne Marie's Country Deli** (1398 Kings Hwy., Sugar Loaf, 845/610-5044, www.annemariescountrydeli.com, 6am-3pm daily). Most shops close Monday-Tuesday. Sugar Loaf hosts a fall festival on Columbus Day weekend in October with crafts, food, music, and more.

Shawangunk Wine Trail

A 13-winery route through Orange and Ulster Counties meanders along country roads with stops in Warwick, Pine Island, Washingtonville, and Pine Bush. Tastings include barrel-fermented chardonnay, sweet ice wines, sparkling hard ciders, and locally distilled spirits paired with whatever is in season on nearby farms. Visit www.shawangunkwinetrail.com for information about live music and other events. **The Little Wine Bus** (917/414-7947, www.thelittlewinebus.com, $150 pp) shuttles tasters

from one winery to the next, so you can leave your own car behind. Tours include stops at three wineries, with 5-6 tastings at each place.

WESTERN ORANGE COUNTY: I-84 TO THE DELAWARE RIVER

From the Route 17 intersection, I-84 heads southwest toward Middletown and Port Jervis at the southern end of the Shawangunk Mountains. The Neversink and Delaware Rivers meet here, a stone's throw from both New Jersey and Pennsylvania.

A onetime hub for road, rail, and canal transportation, Port Jervis was named for John Bloomfield Jervis, an engineer who built the D&H Canal and Croton Aqueduct. Although the name suggests a major shipping port, the river is better suited to canoes than freighters. Today, a population of 10,000 supports several small- to midsize industrial businesses, and Port Jervis serves as a gateway to the Upper Delaware River in Sullivan and Delaware Counties. Beginning in the town of Sparrowbush, about five miles outside Port Jervis, Route 97 twists and turns and climbs over the **Hawk's Nest** to present breathtaking views of New York, Pennsylvania, and the Delaware River. At a height of 150 feet above the river, the road has several lookouts, called bay windows, that were built into the original design. Car companies like to film commercials along this stretch of winding road.

RECREATION

Although more developed than the Upper Hudson Valley, Orange County has preserved a number of open spaces that are ideal for a variety of mountain and aquatic adventures.

Winter Sports

Orange County enjoys a mild climate compared to other parts of the Hudson River Valley, receiving only a foot of snow on average each winter. But the Hudson Highlands and Ramapo Mountains create ideal terrain for beginner skiers, and a couple of local ski areas offer weekend and evening entertainment for families. For example, to the west of Greenwood Lake, on Route 17A, is the **Mount Peter Ski Area** (Rte. 17A, Warwick, 845/986-4940, www.mtpeter.com, adults $35-67, juniors $35-63).

Hiking

Backpackers can follow the **Appalachian Trail** (AT) from the New Jersey state line at Greenwood Lake (Orange County) through the Bear Mountain Wildlife Center to the Bear Mountain Bridge, a distance of 35 miles. Along the way is the oldest section of the AT, completed in 1923 in Harriman State Park. Moderate elevation changes provide valley and lake views.

For a day-hike along the AT, try the 7.6-mile section that begins at the Elk Pen parking area off Arden Valley Road and follow the white blazes into Harriman State Park to the end point of Seven Lakes Drive. Highlights include the Lemon Squeezer rock formation and the peak of Surebridge Mountain. This route will be moderately strenuous for most recreational hikers. The **Appalachian Trail Guide to New York-New Jersey** is a good printed reference for this section of the AT, and trail maps are available from the **New York-New Jersey Trail Conference** (www.nynjtc.org).

Schunnemunk State Park (845/351-5907, http://parks.ny.gov) has more than 3,000 acres of lush meadows and the tallest peak in Orange County, Schunnemunk Mountain (1,600 feet). The Long Path passes through, and there are half a dozen additional marked trails totaling 20 miles. The best access points within the park are at the Otterkill Road Trail Head and the Sweet Clover Trail Head. To summit **Schunnemunk Mountain** (http://hikethehudsonvalley.com, 6.4 miles round-trip, 1,723-foot elevation gain) in a strenuous day-hike, park at Taylor Road and head up the Jessup Trail to the Sweet Clover Trail.

In the western part of Sterling Forest above Greenwood Lake, the **Sterling Ridge Trail** (5.3 miles round-trip) leads to views of Sterling Lake and the Sterling Fire Tower,

while the **Indian Loop Trail** (4 miles), an offshoot of the AT, climbs to views of Route 17 and the surrounding valley. Both of these routes are moderately challenging for recreational hikers.

Near Cornwall, the **Stowell Loop Trail** (1 mile) is an easy walk through the Hudson Highlands Nature Museum's Outdoor Discovery Center. For a longer hike, this trail connects to the **Highlands Trail** (1.8 miles round-trip) and **McKeon Loop Trail** (2.2 miles), which crosses into **Black Rock Forest,** a wilderness research area managed by the Black Rock Forest Consortium (www.blackrockforest.org).

The **Delaware River Heritage Trail** (6-mile loop) is an interpretive walking tour through the city of Port Jervis, set up by the Minisink Valley Historical Society. It begins and ends at Fort Decker and takes in river views, historic stops, and local parks along the way. A printed guide is available from the society for $7 (http://minisink.org/trail.html).

Some parks are closed to hikers during hunting season in November-December. Contact the **Department of Conservation** (845/256-3000) for details.

Cycling and Mountain Biking

On the access road to Museum Village is a treasure of a bikeway, the 15-mile **Heritage Trail,** which follows the bed of the old Erie Railroad, connecting Monroe to Goshen. You can rent electric mountain bikes ($100 per day) at **Bryan's Bikes** (240 Main St., Cornwall, 845/534-5230, www.bryansbikes. com, 11am-5pm Tues.-Fri., 10am-4pm Sat.). The **Orange County Bicycle Club** (www.ocbicycleclub.org) coordinates several group rides each week, starting from Harriman Park in Sloatsburg, Pine Island, Florida, Goshen, and Chester. The club also puts on the Country Roads Tour in September each year.

Mountain bike riders can access several great trail systems in Orange County: **Camp Orange** in Middletown has around 20 miles of trails on a mix of single track and double track. There are some technical sections with

Appalachian Trail

steep climbs and rock gardens to navigate, and the downhills are flowy and fun. **Goose Pond** in Monroe has another 20 miles of intermediate trails. **Stewart State Forest** (55 miles, intermediate) in Newburgh has 55 miles of rolling trails with loops as long as 20 miles. **The Red Trail** (7 miles) in Tuxedo climbs 900 feet along a well-marked out-and-back forest trail.

Golf

A round of golf at the **Mansion Ridge Golf Club** (1292 Orange Turnpike, Monroe, 845/782-7888, www.mansionridgegc.com) begins in the stone barn clubhouse and meanders through forest and across hills, with incredible views of the countryside. The championship course is the only Jack Nicklaus Signature Design course in New York State that's open to the public. Fees have changed to a dynamic pricing system, so the rates change daily according to demand. Another good option is the **Falkirk Estate & Country Club** (206 Smith Clove Rd., Central Valley, 845/928-8060, www.falkirkestate.com, $35-63), where golfers play with the Ramapo Mountains as a scenic backdrop.

Outside Middletown in the western part of the county, **Green Ridge Golf Club** (204 Gregory Rd., Johnson, 845/355-1317, http://greenridgegolfclub.com, dawn-dusk daily, weather permitting, $25-70) is an 18-hole par-71 public course with plenty of hills, woods, and water—plus a historic clubhouse with vintage golf gear on display.

Swimming and Boating

Orange County offers easy access to a bunch of aquatic activities. **Silver Canoe & Whitewater Rafting** (37 S. Maple Ave., Port Jervis, 800/724-8342, www.silvercanoe.com, 8am-7pm daily Apr.-Sept., $37-50) leads trips down the Delaware River and has canoes and kayaks for rent ($50 pp per day). Rates include transport and pickup.

Sailing and waterskiing are summer pastimes on Greenwood Lake. There are four marinas on the lake, and a public beach on

Windermere Avenue on the east shore. At Willow Point Marina, **Jersey Paddleboards** (622 Jersey Ave., Greenwood Lake, 845/554-0787, jerseypaddleboards.com, 10am-6pm daily) rents stand-up paddleboard (SUP) equipment and kayaks. Try the SUP Yoga Lessons for something different. The **Paddlepoloozza** is a September tradition, with courses from 1 mile for beginners up to 12 miles for pros.

Lake Welch in Harriman State Park is a popular destination for a summer swim or boating excursion. Several other lakes in the park offer swimming, but not beaches or boating.

Several marinas along the Hudson River have boat ramps and services: **Highland Falls RV Park & Marina** (72 Station Hill Rd., Highland Falls, 845/839-0361, www.highlandfallsrvpark.com, 9am-9pm daily May-Oct.), within walking distance to West Point, has 44 slips and five moorings. In Newburgh, **Front Street Marina** (40 Front St., Newburgh, 845/661-4914, www.riverfrontmarinanewburgh.com, mid-Apr.-mid-Oct.) puts you at the doorsteps of all the new restaurants and shops on the Newburgh waterfront. This is a state-of-the-art marina with every amenity, including an ATM, but no fuel (bulk diesel is available dockside).

Storm King Adventure Tours (187 Hudson St., Cornwall-on-Hudson, 845/534-7800, www.stormkingadventuretours.com) will lead small groups on a guided paddle around Bannerman Castle, Storm King Mountain, Moodna Marsh, Plum Point, and hidden coves along the river's edge. Tours range $60-120 for three- to four-hour paddles.

River Cruises

Hudson River Adventures offers sightseeing cruises aboard the *Pride of the Hudson* (26 Front St., Newburgh, 845/220-2120, www.prideofthehudson.com). Tours depart from Newburgh Landing and the sights include Mt. Beacon, Bannerman's Castle, Breakneck Mountain, Cold Spring Village, Constitution Island, and West Point. Boats depart on

Wednesday-Saturday afternoons and Sunday afternoons and evenings (adults $26, seniors $24, ages 4-11 $18, under age 4 free). **River Rose Cruises** (70 Front St., Newburgh, 845/562-1067, www. riverrosecruises.com) runs tours on the *River Rose*, an authentic stern-driven Mississippi paddle wheeler. The two-hour sightseeing trip ($22 adults, $16 children) includes a full bar and heads south from Newburgh to view Bannerman Island, the Catskill Aqueduct, the village of Cold Spring, and West Point. Enjoy a special two-hour buffet brunch cruise on Sunday ($42 adults, $26 children). Nightly dinner cruises are another option ($48 adults, $26 children), as well as special dance party cruises ($25). Its sister ship, the *Rip Van Winkle II*, sails from Kingston.

Another way to experience Bannerman Castle is a walking tour via boat service from Beacon (11am and 12:30pm Sat. May-Oct., adults $40, children $35), or Newburgh (11am and 12:30pm Sun. May-Oct.) organized by the **Bannerman Castle Trust** (855/256-4007, www.bannermancastle.org). A two-hour trip includes close-up views of the abandoned Scottish-style castle and surrounding gardens. Bring shoes with good tread, as the terrain is rough in spots.

Fishing

Largemouth bass, chain pickerel, and pan-fish are the most popular catches in Orange County's lakes and ponds. **Ceely's Bait Bucket** (436 Shore Rd., New Windsor, 845/534-3495, 6am-6pm daily) sells bait, equipment, and licenses. Stop in for the latest report and advice on the best river access points. You can fish for smallmouth, stripers, and catfish from shore.

Four miles east of Newburgh, **Washington Lake** (207 New Britain Rd., Newburgh, 845/562-5830) is a reservoir with largemouth bass, crappie, and pump-kinseeds. The deepest part is 40 feet, with the steepest drop from shore on the southwest corner of the lake. Practice catch-and-release, since the water has a history of

contamination. Northwest of the intersection of Routes 32 and 300, **Chadwick Lake** (1702 Rte. 300, Newburgh, 845/564-0608, resident vehicle fee $10, non-resident $20) is a clean 207-acre lake that supports largemouth, bluegill, and crappie. You can fish from shore or rent a nonmotorized boat, and there is a small park at the south end of the lake.

O&H Bait Shop (209 Meadow Ave., Chester, 845/469-2566, 6am-6pm daily) is another option for fishing supplies. The business is family owned and operates out of the owner's garage.

Aviation

For a morning adventure, take a champagne hot air balloon flight with **Above the Clouds** (Middletown, 845/692-2556, www.abovethecloudsinc.com, May-Oct., $375, reservations required) and draft over the Lower Hudson Valley. Flights with **Fantasy Balloon Flights** (Middletown, 845/856-7103, www.fantasyfliers.com, $329) depart from Randall Airport and follow pretty much the same format.

Horseback Riding

Several parks in Orange County offer the use of bridle paths by permit. Goosepond Mountain State Park in Chester and Highland Lakes State Park in Middletown both have extensive acreage of undeveloped woods to explore by horseback. **Juckas Stables** (Rte. 302 and Rte. 17, Bullville, 845/361-1429, www.juckasstables.com) has 117 acres of trails and English and Western riding lessons on beautiful horses. Camping is available.

Yoga and Spas

The Spa at Glenmere Mansion (624 Pine Hill Rd., Chester, 845/469-1939, www.glenmeremansion.com, 10am-7pm Wed.-Sat., 10am-5pm Sun.) offers an exhaustive menu of treatments from standard to traditional Turkish hammam experiences. The luxury comes with a hefty price tag; most

60-minute services run $175. If money is no object, make a weekend of it and stay in one of the inn's 18 guest rooms. Reservations are required. **The Spa at Wellness Springs** (489 Rte. 32, Highland Mills, 845/928-2898, www. wellness-springs.com) offers more affordable spa treatments, yoga classes, acupuncture, and other wellness programs to local residents as well as visitors.

On summer weekends, local yoga instructors in Newburgh offer free classes in the amphitheater of Downing Park. Check www. cityofnewburgh-ny.gov for an updated schedule. **Warwick Yoga Center** (54 Main St., Warwick, 845/987-2076, http://warwickyoga. com, drop-in $18) offers several Iyengar classes daily, as well as wellness workshops and retreats.

ENTERTAINMENT AND EVENTS
Performing Arts

West Point's **Eisenhower Hall Theatre** (Eisenhower Hall Theatre Box Office, Bldg. 655, West Point, 845/938-4159, www.ikehall. com) is a top-notch venue for a range of performances, from the musical *Chicago* to the Moscow Ballet. The West Point Band (845/938-2617, www.westpointband.com) plays a free summer concert series at the Trophy Point Amphitheatre. Bring a picnic and enjoy the views.

Wallkill River School of Art (232 Ward St., Montgomery, 845/457-2787, www. wallkillriverschool.com, noon-5pm Fri.-Sun.) is a nonprofit artists' cooperative that runs an art school and fine art gallery as well as a plein air (painting outdoors) art workshop series on local farms and open spaces. The gallery represents about 40 local Orange County-based artists. Adults can sign up for classes in acrylics and portraits or Paint & Sip parties. Children and teens can learn pastels, still life drawing, and advanced cartooning. The school's **Farm Art Trail Geo Tour** matches 15 artists with 15 farm sites to create a geocache challenge for all ages.

Bars and Nightlife

Orange County Distillery at Brown Barn Farms (286 Maple Ave., New Hampton, 845/374-2011, www.orangecountydistillery. com) mixes farm-fresh cocktails in a hundred-year-old barn. Order pulled pork, burgers, fish tacos, and the like from **The Bus** food truck ($10-12) Thursday-Sunday. Live music often plays 6pm-9pm Friday-Saturday. Sugar-beet vodka, wheat vodka, corn whiskey, and maple flavored whiskey are among the house-made labels. Aside from its own spirits, the beer and wine lists are entirely from New York State.

Zulu Time Rooftop Bar and Lounge at the Thayer Hotel (674 Thayer Rd., West Point, 845/446-4731, www.thethayerhotel. com, 4pm-11pm Thurs.-Sat.) overlooks the Hudson River. The signature drink is The Double Tap, a 16-ounce beer with a shot of tequila, a souvenir cup, and a T-shirt. Drinks and some apps are half price 4pm-6pm Thursday and Friday. DJs play 7pm-11pm Friday evenings.

Newburgh Landing puts on a lively—and sometimes downright rowdy—nightlife. **Blue Pointe** (120 Front St., Newburgh, 845/568-0100, www.blu-pointe.com, noon-9pm Mon.-Sat., 11am-2pm and 3pm-8pm Sundays., $18-38) mixes creative cocktails at an outdoor bar on the patio overlooking the river. **River Grill** (40 Front St., Newburgh, 845/561-9444, www.therivergrill.net, lunch 11:30am-3:30pm daily, dinner 5pm-9pm Sun.-Thurs., 5pm-10pm Fri.-Sat., $16-32) serves bottomless mimosas for Sunday brunch. **Golden Rail Ale House** (29 Old N. Plank Rd., Newburgh, 845/565-2337, http://thegoldenrail.com, 3pm-2am Mon.-Thurs., noon-2am Fri.-Sun.) is a sports bar that serves craft beers and stays open until the wee hours. Happy hour runs 3pm-7pm on weekdays.

For a quieter scene, check out **Liberty Street Bistro** (97 Liberty St., Newburgh, 845/562-3900, libertystreetbistro.com). They expanded in 2019, adding a cozy bar and lounge that serves fun cocktails, beer and wine by the bottle, and "elevated" bar fare from the adjoining restaurant kitchen. Creative drinks include That Slaps!—which brings together the flavors of bourbon, rye, maple, and black walnut—and Here Today, Cardamaro, made of cardamaro liquor mixed with sweet vermouth, lemon, and a seasonal jam. Pop in for happy hour 3pm-7pm Wednesday-Sunday.

Warwick locals gather at the bar inside **The Landmark Inn** (Rte. 94, North Warwick, 845/986-5444, www.landmarkinnwarwick.com, 5pm-9:30pm Tues.-Thurs., 5pm-10pm Fri.-Sat., 3:30pm-8pm Sun.). Keep an eye out for live music performances at Warwick's wineries and cafés. The family-owned 1950s-era **Warwick Drive-In Theater** (5 Warwick Turnpike/Rte. 21, 845/986-4440, www.warwickdrivein.com, 7pm-10:30pm daily, adults $12, seniors and ages 4-11 $8, under age 4 free) also is packed on summer nights.

Applewood Winery (82 Four Corners Rd., Warwick, 845/988-9292, www.applewoodwinery.com, 11am-5:30pm Wed.-Sun., weekends only Jan.-Feb.) produces chardonnay, cabernet franc, and a hard cider called Naked Flock. The winery closes January-February. Check the events calendar for events such as wine and chocolate pairings and live music. And **Warwick Valley Winery & Distillery** (114 Little York Rd., Warwick, 845/258-4858, www.wvwinery.com, 11am-6pm daily) makes riesling, chardonnay, pinot gris, cabernet franc, and pinot noir wines, as well as apple and pear ciders under the label Doc's Draft Cider. Pick up a bottle of the award-winning Black Dirt Bourbon if you go. Live music plays most Saturdays and Sundays 2pm-5pm. Located at the winery, **Pane Bakery Café** (11am-4pm Wed., 11am-5pm Thurs.-Sun.) prepares fresh-baked treats from locally sourced ingredients.

Brotherhood Winery (100 Brotherhood Plaza Dr., Washingtonville, 845/496-3661, www.brotherhood-winery.com, 11am-5pm Sun.-Fri., 11am-7pm Sat.) was established in 1839—hence the self-appointed designation, "America's Oldest Winery." Its underground cellars hold more than 200 oak barrels. If you're new to wine trail travel, take the guided tour to learn how the different labels are made. Then head upstairs and put your newly acquired knowledge to the test in the tasting room. Take the tour with a tasting flight ($25), or enjoy a tasting without a tour ($15 per flight). A large reception hall is available for weddings, and there is also a restaurant and small café on-site. This place is very popular with the tour buses.

Festivals and Events

Nothing quite tops the spirited rivalry of an Army versus Navy football game at West Point. West Point Football Saturdays take place at Michie Stadium, with a parade, a cannon salute, and a cadet review to kick off the event. Ferry service is available from Tarrytown.

Cars line the sides of Route 17A over Sterling Mountain during the popular **New York Renaissance Faire** (Sterling Forest, Tuxedo, 845/351-5171, www.renfair.com, 10am-7pm Sat.-Sun. Aug.-Oct., adults $30, children $13). The **Orange County Fair** (100 Carpenter Ave., Middletown, 845/343-4826, www.orangecountyfair.com) takes place in Middletown each July.

Warwick draws 30,000 apple-lovers to the ever-popular (and insanely crowded) **October Applefest** (845/987-2731, www.warwickapplefest.com). The apple pie baking contest is an annual tradition. Nearby Sugar Loaf puts on a **Fall Festival** (845/469-9181, www.sugarloafnewyork.com) to celebrate local artists with food and music. The Hudson Valley Jazz Festival is a weeklong event with shows at multiple venues, including the Warwick Village Green, Glenmere Brewery, and the Warwick Center for Performing Arts.

The **Bear Mountain Native American Festival** (Anthony Wayne Recreation Area, Harriman State Park, www.redhawkcouncil.org) takes place in Harriman State Park in August with singing, dancing, food, crafts, and educational programs.

If you have a bike and like to eat, the Hudson Valley **Farm to Fork Fondo** (www.

Family Fun

Young children and teenage travelers will find many opportunities for entertainment and recreation in the Hudson River Valley, from hiking and swimming to apple and berry picking to educational tours of historic homes and museums. Here are a few family-friendly destinations:

- **Children's Museum of Science and Technology** (250 Jordan Rd., Troy, 518/235-2120, www.cmost.org, 9am-4pm Mon.-Sat. July-Aug., 9am-4pm Tues.-Sun. Sept.-June, $8): In Rensselaer County, view the 75-foot-long Living Indoor Hudson River exhibit, which models the river from the Adirondacks to the Atlantic. Experiences are designed for ages 18 months through the tween years.

- **Museum Village at Old Smith's Clove** (1010 Rte. 17M, Monroe, 845/782-8248, www.museumvillage.org, 11am-4pm Thurs.-Sun., adults $15, seniors $13, ages 4-12 $10, under age 4 free): In Orange County, you can experience life in the 19th century; learn to make a candle, and tour the blacksmith, printing, and pottery shops.

- **New Windsor Cantonment State Historic Site** (374 Temple Hill Rd., New Windsor, 845/561-1765, www.nysparks.com, 10am-5pm Tues.-Sat., 1pm-5pm Sun.): Orange County offers the opportunity to imagine what it was like to be a soldier in the Revolutionary War as you walk the grounds where George Washington's troops spent their final winter and spring. It's best for ages five and up.

- **Zoom Flume** (20 Shady Glen Rd., off Rte. 145, East Durham, 518/239-6271, www.zoomflume.com, 10am-6pm daily June-Sept., some weekends until 7pm, adults $36, ages 3-8 $29, under age 3 free): Older kids will have a blast cooling off in the pools and slides of the area's biggest water park.

- **Stone Barns Center for Food and Agriculture** (630 Bedford Rd., Pocantico Hills, 914/366-9600, www.stonebarnscenter.org, 11am-5pm Thurs.-Sun.): All ages can help gather eggs, walk the trails, and explore this farm in Westchester County.

- **Taconic Outdoor Education Center** (75 Mountain Laurel Lane, Cold Spring, 845/265-3773, www.nysparks.com): Located inside Clarence Fahnestock Memorial State Park in Putnam County, the center offers a variety of summer and winter programs for kids as well as adults.

- **Mid-Hudson Children's Museum** (75 N. Water St., Poughkeepsie, 845/471-0589, www.mhcm.org, 9:30am-5pm Mon.-Sat., 11am-5pm Sun., $9): Set on the banks of the Hudson in downtown Poughkeepsie in Dutchess County, this museum for younger children has a mastodon skeleton, solar and wind energy exhibits, and a horizontal rock-climbing wall.

farmtoforkfitness.com/fondos, adults $50-150, depending on ride length) is a must. Ride from farm to farm, sampling small bites along the way.

SHOPPING

Orange County has everything a shopper could desire, from mega-chains and discount outlets to one-of-a-kind boutiques. One of the county's most unusual attractions is **Sugar Loaf,** a small village of artisans who craft handmade ceramics, soaps, and other goods.

Woodbury Common Premium Outlets

Bargain hunters flock to the **Woodbury Common Premium Outlets** (498 Red Apple Court, Rte. 32, Central Valley, 845/928-4000, www.premiumoutlets.com, 11am-8pm Mon.-Thurs., 10am-9pm Fri.-Sun.), at the edge of Harriman State Park (I-87 exit 16). Dozens of stores are arranged in a campus-like setting, making it less than ideal for rainy-day retail therapy. Look for significant discounts on name brands from Arc'teryx and Armani Exchange to BCBG and Tahari. The long list of stores and often-deep discounts draw crowds on holiday weekends. **Shortline Bus** (201/529-3666, www.coachusa.com) offers weekday service to the outlets (adults $42, children $21), as well as daily "shop and stay" packages that include accommodations at one of several local hotels ($140 pp d).

Farm Stands

Orange County made national TV in 2004 when the Food Network produced a Hudson Valley episode of *FoodNation with Bobby Flay,* featuring several local eateries. Among them was the **Quaker Creek Store** (757 Pulaski Hwy., Goshen, 845/258-4570, www. quakercreekstore.com, 7am-5pm Mon.-Fri., 7am-4pm Sat.) in Pine Island, a must-try for homemade sausages and smoked meats made by a third-generation owner and Culinary Institute graduate. The family-run business has evolved from a 1940s sandwich shop to a gourmet treasure. Onion rings are made from the bounty that makes the region famous.

Chances are you'll have to wait for a parking space at the **Warwick Valley Farmers Market** (South St. parking lot, off Main St., Warwick, www.warwickvalleyfarmersmarket. org, 9am-2pm Sun. mid-May-mid-Nov.). Thirty-something local farms, artists, and other businesses sell homemade pies and candies as well as fresh-picked produce. You can stock up on ingredients for the week or simply taste your way through the market.

Common Ground Farm holds the **Newburgh Farmers' Market** (http:// newburghfarmersmarket.org, 9am-2pm Sat. June-Nov.) at Safe Harbors Green. Elsewhere around the county, at least a dozen other municipal farmers markets take place each week in Cornwall, Monroe, Pine Bush, and other towns. Locations and hours vary with each growing season. Visit www.orangetourism. org for the latest details.

Family-run **Overlook Farm Market and Country Store** (5417 Rte. 9W, Newburgh, 845/562-5780, 8am-6pm Wed.-Mon.) sells a variety of fresh produce, eggs, dairy, honey, syrup, and jams that are ideal for a picnic lunch.

Orchard Hill Cider Mill (29 Soons Circle, New Hampton, 845/374-2468, www. orchardhillcidermill.com) is a farm winery that makes hard cider from the Soons Orchard apple harvest. Located next to the market at Soons, the cidery makes a convenient all-in-one farm stand experience. **Jones Farm** (190 Angola Rd., Cornwall, 845/534-4445, www. jonesfarminc.com, 8am-5pm Wed.-Sun. has several shops in one spot on a family farm near West Point. Pick up homegrown produce and other goodies in the Country Store, order freshly baked goods from Grandma Phoebe's Kitchen, and find decorative gifts for yourself or someone else in the old dairy barn.

Several you-pick farms open during the fall apple- and pumpkin-picking seasons. **Apple Dave's Orchards** (formerly Applewood Orchards, 82 Four Corners Rd., Warwick, 845/986-1684, www.applewoodorchards. com, 9am-5pm daily Sept.-Oct., admission, parking, and entertainment free) and **Apple Ridge Orchards** (101 Jessup Rd., Warwick, 845/987-7717, www.appleridgeorchards.com, 9am-6pm Thurs.-Sun. Sept.-Oct.) are both great places to take the kids for a farm-to-food experience.

Antiques, Galleries, and Boutiques

Warwick is a boutique shopper's delight, with unique places to find apparel, books, gifts, and food. **The Bungalow** (46 Main St., Warwick, 845/987-9885, www.thebungalowny.com, 10am-6pm Mon.-Sat., 10am-5pm Sun., closed Mon. Jan.-Feb.) carries gifts for the home, often made by local artisans. Look for drinkware, serving platters, tea pots, cheeseboards, and more. It's also a fun place to shop for funky handbags, scarves, and socks printed with slogans like "All You Need Is Love and Dog." Pick up a special bottle of EVOO from Italy or Peru and pair it with a traditional balsamic vinegar at **Warwick Valley Olive Oil Co.** (20 Railroad Ave., Warwick, 845/544-7245, www.warwickvalleyoliveoil.com,

11am-6pm Mon.-Sat., 10am-6pm Sun.). If you need a sweet treat, **Fizzy Lifting Soda Pop Candy Shop** (17 Main St., Warwick, 845/544-7400, http://fizzyliftingsodapopcandyshop.com, 11am-6pm Sun.-Thurs., 11am-7pm Fri.-Sat.) has lots of colorful retro candies and sodas on display.

Frazzleberries Country Store (24 Main St., Warwick, 845/988-5080, www.frazzleberries.com, 10am-6pm Mon.-Sat., 10am-5pm Sun.) is loved for its cute country furnishings and festive seasonal displays. The store is stocked with quilted bags and smells like apples. **Newhard's** (39 Main St., Warwick, 845/986-4544, www.newhards.com, 10am-6pm Sat.-Thurs., 10am-8pm Fri.) has been in business for over 30 years and continues to carry a variety of kitchen gadgets and cooking supplies, including pottery and cookbooks, plus a unique selection of toys and games.

FOOD
Along the River: Route 9W
Centrally located near West Point, Storm King, and the Brotherhood Winery, **Painter's** (266 Hudson St., Cornwall-on-Hudson, 845/534-2109, www.painterstavern.com, 4pm-8pm Thurs., 2pm-9pm Fri., noon-9pm Sat., 11am-4pm Sun., $17-27) is a favorite for summer dining with everything from burritos to pad thai. The theme seems to be eating around the world: a little American, a little Mexican, mixed with some Japanese and Italian food. There are plenty of vegetarian and gluten-free options, and kids may order from an extensive children's menu. Do save room for dessert.

Inside the Thayer Hotel at West Point, ★ **MacArthur's Riverview Restaurant** (674 Thayer Rd., West Point, 845/446-4731, www.thethayerhotel.com, 5:30pm-10pm Thurs.-Sun., $25-50) is an old-world dining experience—perfect for celebrating a special occasion. A capable team of CIA graduates serves American-style dishes from field, farm, and sea. The hand-cut tomahawk rib eye for two is worth the wait.

Near West Point and Storm King Arts Center, **Twins Eating House** (30 Quaker Ave., Cornwall, 845/237-7220, https://twinseatinghouse.com, 8am-3pm Sun. and Tues.-Wed., 8am-8pm Thurs.-Sat., $9-17) replaced the former Woody's Farm to Table in Cornwall. At this veteran-owned establishment, named for the proprietor's twin children, you can order breakfast, soups, sandwiches, burgers, and more, any time the kitchen is open. Set inside a cozy house, the restaurant's vibe is casual and family-friendly

In Newburgh, you'll rub elbows with the locals over the famous hot dogs slathered in house-made "Texas Sauce" at **Tony's Newburgh Lunch** (348 Broadway, Newburgh, 845/562-9660, www.tonysnewburghlunch.com, 6:30am-4pm Mon.-Wed., 6:30am-5pm Thurs.-Sat., $5-10), which has been open continuously since 1969. Tony's family will turn you down if you dare ask for the sauce recipe, but if you must bring it home, you can order some online. Besides the signature hot dogs, the kitchen makes a satisfying chicken bacon ranch and patty melt sandwich.

Passengers disembarking from river cruises at Newburgh Landing often head straight to the inviting patio at **Blu Pointe** (120 Front St., Newburgh, 845/568-0100, www.blu-pointe.com, noon-9pm Mon.-Sat., 11am-8pm Sun., $28-55) for lunch, dinner, or just a glass of wine. Dinner highlights include a raw bar with various shellfish platters, whole Maine lobsters, four different cuts of beef steaks, and a charcoal-grilled whole branzino.

For traditional Tuscan fare, try **Il Cenácolo** (228 S. Plank Rd., Newburgh, 845/564-4494, www.ilcenacolorestaurant.com, noon-2:30pm and 5pm-9pm Mon. and Wed.-Thurs., noon-2:30pm and 5:30pm-11pm Fri., 4pm-11pm Sun., $29-35). The menu here is a carnivore's delight, featuring large tube pasta with Bolognese sauce, grilled rack of lamb, Italian pot roast, stewed rabbit, and veal medallions. Under the same ownership, and also on the waterfront, **Café Pitti** (40 Front St., Newburgh, 845/565-1444, www.cafepitti.net, noon-10pm Tues.-Sat., noon-8pm Sun., mains $15-35) serves antipasti, paninis, and pizzettes under a bright yellow awning.

★ **Newburgh Brewing Taproom** (88 South Colden St., Newburgh, 845/569-2337, www.newburghbrewing.com, kitchen 4pm-10pm Thurs.-Fri., noon-10pm Sat., noon-6pm Sun., $10-15) makes craft beers from locally sourced hops in a converted 1850s-era box factory. You'll find more than a dozen beers on tap most nights. Start with the classic Billy's Waterfront Wit and you can always get more adventurous from there. Besides the brews, you can take the edge off by ordering small plates made from locally sourced ingredients. Rosemary and garlic fries with housemade mayo are a must.

River Grill (40 Front St., Newburgh, 845/561-9444, www.therivergrill.net, lunch noon-3:30pm Mon. and Fri.-Sun., dinner 5pm-9pm Sun.-Mon., 5pm-10pm Fri.-Sat., $10-33) does surf and turf with a Latin twist. Try the littleneck clams to start and the seafood paella for an entrée while you take in the river views.

Hidden up the hill from the waterfront, near Washington's Headquarters, the star of the dining scene in Newburgh of late is ★ **Liberty Street Bistro** (97 Liberty St., Newburgh, 845/562-3900, http://libertystreetbistro.com, noon-9pm Wed-Thurs., noon-10pm Fri.-Sat., noon-8pm Sun., $17-35). Founded by a Culinary Institute graduate, the restaurant creates seasonal dishes using local ingredients; the setting is contemporary but understated. The chicken liver mousse comes with locally baked sourdough and house berry jam, while the seared monkfish appears on a bed of celeriac puree with collard greens and bacon for a southern twist.

Hudson Street Café (190 S. Plank Rd., Newburgh, 845/784-4191, 8am-3pm Mon., Thurs., and Sun., 7am-3pm Fri.-Sat., $10-15) is a casual place for breakfast and brunch dishes inspired by the seasonal harvest. On any given day, you might discover avocado toast, the Piggy Hash, a chicken BLT, or Lumberjack Special among the options.

Central Orange County: Along Route 17

New restaurants come and go quickly in the Warwick area, but the ★ **Landmark Inn** (Rte. 94, North Warwick, 845/986-5444, www.landmarkinnwarwick.com, 5pm-9:30pm Tues.-Thurs., 5pm-10pm Fri.-Sat., 3:30pm-8pm Sun., $15-35) remains a local favorite for casual American cuisine and evening cocktails. Sit in the main dining room or the cozier pub. Daily specials put the local harvest in the spotlight. The Maryland crab cakes usually are a hit.

Out-of-towners head to the fancier **Chateau Hathorn** (33 Hathorn Rd., Warwick, 845/986-6099, www.chateauhathorn.com, 5pm-9pm Wed.-Sat., 4pm-8pm Sun., $25-38) for Swiss and French cuisine in a storybook mansion from the 18th century. Start with frog legs à la provençal or escargot, and then move on to the rack of lamb or wiener schnitzel.

Eddie's Roadhouse (18 Main St., Warwick, 845/986-7623, www.eddiesroadhouse.com, noon-10pm Thurs.-Sat., $15-29) pairs craft beer with craft food for the win. Order crispy calamari tacos and steak frites for the table, then a salad of locally picked greens.

Grappa Ristorante (22B Railroad Ave., Warwick, 845/987-7373, www.grapparistorante.com, noon-9:30pm Tues.-Thurs., noon-10pm Fri.-Sat., noon-8:30pm Sun., $24-40) brings northern Italian fare prepared by a graduate of the Culinary Institute to hungry restaurant-goers in Warwick. Dip warm bread in olive oil to start, then move on to cold or hot antipasti such as truffle burrata mozzarella or eggplant rollatini. Mains include a variety of chicken cutlets, veal, and fresh fish. Gluten-free pasta is available, and the chef can sometimes modify other dishes to meet dietary needs. **Opa Greek Grill** (10 Oakland Ave., Warwick, 845/986-8808, www.opagreekgrillwarwick.com, 11am-9pm Sun.-Thurs., 11am-10pm Fri.-Sat., $8-25) makes homemade Greek fries, traditional Greek dips, and super filling platters.

If you like a menu that includes the local farm in its entrée names, ★ **The Grange Restaurant and Local Market** (1 Ryerson Rd., Warwick, 845/986-1170, http://thegrangewarwick.com, 4pm-8pm Mon. and Fri.-Sat., noon-4pm Sun., $25-36) is your place. The owners are a husband-and-wife team; she grows certified organic vegetables and her husband is the chef. This menu changes frequently. On any given night, you might find among the options a La Belle Farm duck breast, HVCC pasture-raised beef burger, or wild-caught mahi-mahi. The market side has Pine Island honey, locally baked goods, and organic coffee for sale.

During the fall harvest, apple pickers enjoy coffee and a cider donut or heartier lunch and dinner fare at **Harvest Grill** (161 State Route 94 South, Warwick, 845/986-1059, www.penningsfarmmarket.com, 11am-8pm Wed.-Mon., $10-15) at Pennings Farm Market. On Tuesdays, the grill is closed, but the farm operates a food truck from noon until 6pm. The adjoining farm market is open daily 10am-7pm.

At Greenwood Lake, the most popular choice for lakeside dining is **Emerald Point** (40 Sterling Rd., Greenwood Lake, 845/477-2275, www.emeraldpnt.com, noon-9pm Mon.-Fri., noon-midnight Sat.-Sun., $8-21)—which serves littleneck clams, wood-fired pizzas, meat lasagna, and fish-and-chips.

On the drive between Warwick and Greenwood Lake, don't miss the homemade ice cream, fresh-baked waffle cones, and valley views at the hilltop ★ **Bellvale Farms Creamery** (1390 Rte. 17A, Warwick, 845/988-1818, www.bellvalefarms.com, noon-9pm daily Apr.-Oct., reduced hours early and late in the season). Choose from 50 flavors, including maple cinnamon and the Black Dirt Blast, a chocolate lover's delight. Locals stockpile the cookies and cream by the quart in their freezers. The creamery also has a pumpkin patch (11am-dusk Sat.-Sun. Oct.).

Glenmere Mansion (634 Pine Hill Rd., Chester, 845/469-1900 or 866/772-2982, www.glenmeremansion.com) has several dining options served by one central kitchen. Frogs End Tavern is a casual option open 11am-3pm and 5pm-9pm daily for soups, salads, and flatbread pizzas ($10-30) and light entrées like sandwiches, pasta dishes, and fish or beef specials ($20-45). The formal Supper Room (5pm-9pm daily, $32-52) serves elegant fare like pan-seared Hudson Valley foie gras, local steelhead trout, and Hudson Valley duck. Several gluten-free and vegetarian dishes are available on this menu, and the kitchen will try to accommodate food allergies if you let them know in advance. Definitely don't miss out on Daryen Cimaglia's sea-salt cured meats.

Saffron Fine Indian Cuisine (130 Dolson Ave., Middletown, 845/344-0005, www.saffronmiddletown.com, noon-10pm daily, $13-22) prepares dishes inspired by the traditional cuisine of both the southern and northern regions of India, "from the Himalayas to the Indian Ocean and the Arabian Sea to the Bay of Bengal," in the restaurant's own words. Tandoori specials are a highlight and the daily lunch buffet is a popular event. Also in Middletown, **El Azteca** (122 North St., Middletown, 845/342-3448, www.elaztecamexicanrestaurants.com, 10am-9pm Sun.-Thurs., 10am-9:30pm Fri.-Sat., $8-18) cooks a complete lineup of traditional Mexican specialties such as chilaquiles, shrimp ceviche, cactus salad, pozole, enchiladas, and just about every kind of tacos you can imagine. The owners, Bernardino and Erica, have a second location in the nearby town of Florida.

Ward's Bridge Inn (135 Ward St., Montgomery, 845/457-1300, www.wardsbridgeinn.com, 4pm-9pm Tues.-Sun., $20-42) is a restored country inn that caters to both visitors and locals with a menu of grilled steaks, rich pasta dishes, filling salads, and more.

ACCOMMODATIONS

The best places to stay in Orange County are clustered near Greenwood Lake and Warwick, and along the river between West Point and Cornwall. Small bed-and-breakfast inns, along with Airbnb-style rentals, are the most common type of lodging, with an assortment of chain hotels located along I-84.

$100-150

Run by the Stoeberl family, **The New Continental Hotel & Restaurant** (15 Leo Court, Greenwood Lake, 845/477-2456, www. thenewcontinentalhotel.com, $100-175) is a comfortable and affordable lakeside option in the tradition of a country inn. Its 15 eclectic rooms have tiled private baths and lake views. Twin and double beds are available. There is a two-night minimum stay July-August. Summer cottages also are available on a weekly or seasonal basis for $550-650 per week.

Meadow Lark Farm Bed & Breakfast (180 Union Corners Rd., Warwick, 845/651-4286, http://meadowlarkfarm.com, $95-120) is an 1800s English farmhouse and a dog-friendly B&B (with prior approval). There are three suites: King, Queen, or Princess. Savor the country breakfast with veggies fresh-picked from the garden.

Tranquility is the theme at ★ **Cider Mill Inn** (207 Glenwood Rd., Pine Island, 845/258-3044, www.cidermillinn.com, $145-175), a bed-and-breakfast housed in an 1865 Victorian farmhouse on land that once served as a dairy farm and apple orchard. Choose from two rooms and one suite—each with its own antiques and floral linens.

$150-200

Close to West Point, **The Dominion House** (50 Old Dominion Rd., Blooming Grove, 845/496-1826, thedominionhouse.com, $175) has three suites. Hospitality is top-notch, and the morning pastries are a special treat.

Less than a mile from the Storm King Art Center, **Storm King Lodge** (100 Pleasant Hill Rd., Mountainville, 845/534-9421, www. stormkinglodge.com, $160-190) is a beautiful and quiet place for a weekend getaway. The innkeepers offer four cozy rooms in a 19th-century lodge near Storm King Mountain. The Lavender and Pine rooms have fireplaces. The two-bedroom cottage goes for $500.

West Point's **Thayer Hotel** (674 Thayer Rd., West Point, 845/446-4731, www. thethayerhotel.com, from $159) has 151 modern but cozy rooms decorated in 19th-century Americana style. Guest rooms and suites inside the imposing granite building offer campus, river, or mountain views. Amenities include flatscreen TVs with DirecTV, high-speed internet access, and a renovated fitness center.

A stay at the **Cromwell Manor Historic Inn** (174 Angola Rd., Cornwall, 845/534-7136, www.cromwellmanorinn.com, $190-380), five miles from West Point, includes a hot breakfast and help-yourself-anytime coffee, tea, and snacks in the guest kitchen. Choose one of nine guest rooms in the main house, an 1820 brick manor, or one of four rooms in the 1764 Chimneys Cottage. Service here is friendly as ever; rooms upstairs in the main house are quite small and showing signs of wear-and-tear.

The colonial ★ **Inn at Stony Creek** (34 Spanktown Rd., Warwick, 845/986-3660, www.innstonycreek.com, $180-199) has seven guest rooms, each with a queen bed, a private bath, and its own special decorative touch, usually involving antiques and lace or floral fabrics. Choose among the brass, wrought iron, four-poster, and canopy beds. Enjoy fresh flowers and robes for your stay. The multicourse breakfast may include fresh fruit smoothies, yogurt with granola, French toast with real maple syrup, or an omelet. Like many historic properties in the Hudson River Valley, this one attracts wedding parties during the summer months.

You can walk to dinner and shopping from the seven-room **Warwick Valley Bed and Breakfast** (24 Maple Ave., Warwick, 845/987-7255, http://wvbedandbreakfast.com, from $144). Dietary preferences can be accommodated with advance notice. Guests can choose to be social—or not—during the farm-to-table breakfast.

The lakefront **Waterstone Inn** (62 Sterling Rd., Greenwood Lake, 845/477-3535, http://waterstoneinn.com, from $170) has five guest rooms with private baths. The main-floor suite, dining room, and deck are accessible to wheelchairs. The owners serve bread, fruit, and a hot breakfast entrée each morning. There is a two-night minimum for summer and fall weekends. A separate two-bedroom cottage and new one-bedroom efficiency with a full kitchen also are available for extended stays.

Over $200

Owners John and Dena serve up a legendary multicourse breakfast at 9am every morning at the ★ Caldwell House Bed & Breakfast (25 Orrs Mills Rd., Salisbury Mills, 845/496-2954, www.caldwellhouse.com, $195-315). All 14 rooms are private and comfortably appointed with antique furniture and modern amenities. Some have fireplaces too. Hot drinks, goodies, and a roaring fire are available all day in the parlor, and the common rooms are stocked with books and games for guest entertainment.

Eighteen guest rooms, including five premium suites, make up the accommodations at Glenmere Mansion (634 Pine Hill Rd., Chester, 845/469-1900, www.glenmeremansion.com, from $675). This boutique Relais & Chateaux resort opened in 2010. Originally built in 1911 as the country retreat of industrialist Robert Goelet, the property now serves as a luxurious hideaway, complete with a full-service spa, two restaurants, and 150 acres of gardens and grounds. Guests often arrive via helicopter, landing on the front lawn. Reservations are required for any activity here; accommodations are limited to guests who are age 18 or older.

Legoland New York Resort Hotel (1 Legoland Way, Goshen, 845/410-0290, www.legoland.com/new-york, from $109 pp) has 250 themed rooms and suites that will appeal to families with young children. Included with the rate are a breakfast buffet, special evening events for kids, character meet-and-greets, and in-room treasure hunts. Check the website for vacation packages that include admission to the theme park. The rides close for a few months in the winter, but the hotel stays open year-round.

Campgrounds

Oakland Valley Campground (399 Oakland Valley Rd., Cuddebackville, 845/754-8732, www.oaklandvalleycampground.com, May-Oct., $40-55) has large, wooded sites for tents, trailers, and motor homes. Amenities include water and electric hookups, flush toilets, firewood, cable TV, a swimming pool, and free hot showers. Or try the full-service glamping option ($60-70), where the campground sets up a three-room tent with air mattresses, water, and electric. Black Bear Campground (197 Wheeler Rd., Florida, NY 845/651-7717, http://blackbearcampground.com, $80-100) has back-in and pull-through sites for even the largest of rigs. The amenities here include a heated outdoor swimming pool, Wi-Fi, cable, barbecue pits, fire rings, and picnic tables.

INFORMATION AND SERVICES

A network of 10 tourist information centers serves Orange County visitors; several of them are open seasonally. The Orange County Tourism (124 Main St., Goshen, 845/615-3860, www.orangetourism.org, 8am-5pm Mon.-Fri.) office can provide a wealth of information before or during a visit. The Palisades Parkway Tourist Information Center (between exits 16 and 17, Palisades Interstate Parkway, 845/786-5003, 8am-6pm daily Apr.-Oct., 8am-5pm daily Nov.-Mar.) stocks a variety of trail guides, local interest books, road maps, and all things Hudson River Valley. This is also the place to pick up your New York State fishing license.

GETTING THERE AND AROUND
Bus

Adirondack Trailways (800/776-7548, www.trailwaysny.com) stops in Newburgh, while Shortline Bus (201/529-3666, www.coachusa.com) stops include Monroe, Middletown, Newburgh, Goshen, Chester, and Central Valley. Main Line Trolley Bus (800/631-8405) offers local service to Chester,

Goshen, Harriman, Middletown, Monroe, and Woodbury Common. **New Jersey Transit** (973/275-5555, www.njtransit.com) also runs bus service to Greenwood Lake and Warwick.

Train

The Metro-North Port Jervis Line stops in western Orange County between Port Jervis and Suffern, with connecting service to Newark Liberty International Airport in New Jersey and Penn Station in New York City. Alternatively, Beacon station along the Hudson Line is a short cab or shuttle ride across the river from Newburgh. The Newburgh Beacon Shuttle bus connects the Beacon station, downtown Newburgh, and Stewart International Airport.

Car

In the eastern part of Orange County, Route 17, I-87, and I-84 form a triangle that encloses many of the most popular attractions in the area. Uber, Lyft, and several taxi services cover Orange County, including West Point, Monroe, Warwick, and Greenwood Lake. Car rentals are available at Stewart International Airport (www.panynj.gov), including Avis, Budget, Enterprise, and Hertz.

Boat

The **Newburgh-Beacon Ferry** (212/532-4900, www.nywaterway.com, adults $1.75, seniors and children $1) connects the cities of Newburgh and Beacon on opposite sides of the Hudson River and provides convenient access to the Metro-North train station in Beacon. Although it's primarily run for commuters, travelers who want to experience both the **Dia:Beacon** museum (3 Beekman St., Beacon, 845/440-0100, www.diaart.org) and Newburgh Landing may find the ferry service to be a good way to avoid driving.

Putnam County

Squeezed between the large and densely populated counties of Westchester to the south and Dutchess to the north are 231 square miles of the most dramatic landscape along the Hudson. On overcast days, a dreamy mist clings to the jagged ridgeline of the Hudson Highlands, creating a landscape reminiscent of a tale from the Brothers Grimm. Just 50 miles from Manhattan and easily accessible by rail, romantic Putnam County features two Victorian-era towns along the river, two large state parks, and hundreds of miles of wilderness trails. The county's many lakes and streams provide a vital source of freshwater for the New York City reservoir system.

Putnam does not have a Hudson River crossing of its own—its borders extend from just above the Bear Mountain Bridge to a point south of the Newburgh-Beacon Bridge—however, two Metro-North rail lines make this area an easy day trip from New York City. The Hudson Line stops in Garrison and Cold Spring along the river, while the Harlem Line stops in Brewster. From Brewster, it's about a 90-minute ride to Grand Central.

In addition to the train tracks, a 20-mile stretch of the Appalachian Trail crosses diagonally through Putnam County, from the Bear Mountain Bridge and Hudson Highlands State Park in the southwest to Clarence Fahnestock Memorial State Park and the Dutchess County line in the northeast.

ALONG THE RIVER: ROUTE 9D
★ Boscobel House and Gardens

Two rows of apple trees frame the view of the Hudson from the entrance to Boscobel (Beautiful Wood), a restored neoclassical mansion dating to the 19th century. Named after an English manor, the home belonged to colonial loyalist States Morris Dyckman, a contemporary of Chancellor Robert Livingston.

The building originally sat on a 250-acre farm in Montrose, about 15 miles south of its present-day location. It was nearly lost to history when the federal government sold it to a demolition contractor in the 1950s for $35. Fortunately, a group of private citizens came to the rescue and moved the building, piece by piece, to a scenic bluff in Garrison.

The structure and details of the home create a light and airy feel that is unique among the Hudson River Valley's riverside mansions. On the outside, wood-carved drapery, complete with bow ties and tassels, decorates the space between columns on the second-floor balcony. Inside, Dyckman furnished Boscobel with exquisite silver, china, and glassware that he purchased in London in the late 18th century.

Home to a number of cultural events throughout the year, **Boscobel House and Gardens** (Rte. 9D, Garrison, 845/265-3638, www.boscobel.org, 9am-7pm Fri.-Mon., adults $17, seniors $14, ages 6-18 $8, under age 6 free, grounds only adults $12, seniors $10, ages 6-18 $6, under age 6 free) hosts the annual Hudson Valley Shakespeare Festival. The museum runs a free shuttle from the Cold Spring Metro-North station on designated weekends. Visitors must pay an entrance fee to wander the formal gardens and the mile-long Woodland Trail, but the variety of roses (more than 150 types) and the views of West Point across the river are well worth the donation.

Directly below Boscobel, the National Audubon Society operates the **Constitution Marsh Audubon Center & Sanctuary** (127 Warren Landing Rd., Garrison, 845/265-2601, constitution.audubon.org). A short but steep and rocky path leads from the small parking lot to a nature center and boardwalk that spans a large section of tidal marsh—an ideal setting for bird-watchers. You can paddle to the marsh from Foundry Dock Park in Cold Spring. The parking lot off Route 9D can accommodate only eight cars at a time, so call ahead or be prepared to change plans if the sign says "Full." Street parking is prohibited along Indian Brook Road.

To the east of Route 9D in Garrison, **Manitoga** (Place of the Great Spirit of Algonquin) and the **Russel Wright Design Center** (Rte. 9D, Garrison, 845/424-3812, www.visitmanitoga.org, tours at 11am and 1:30pm Fri.-Mon., 3pm select Sat. May-Nov.) are a one-of-a-kind nature retreat and residence created by nationally acclaimed designer Russel Wright. With his unique and practical designs for the home, Wright championed easier living and pioneered lifestyle marketing. Beginning in 1942, he transformed an abandoned quarry and lumberyard in Garrison into a 75-acre masterpiece of ecological design, featuring native plants, stones, and streams. Dragon Rock, his experimental home, sits on a rock ledge surrounded by four miles of trails that connect to the Appalachian Trail. Tours start at $30 for general admission. A Collectors Tour is $50 pp and the Sunset Tour costs $100.

★ Cold Spring Village

The timeless village of Cold Spring lies in the shadow of Storm King Mountain, which rises 1,000 feet across the Hudson at the narrowest and deepest stretch of the river. A haven for antiques-lovers, Cold Spring's Main Street is divided into upper and lower sections that slope downhill toward an inviting gazebo at the river's edge—the site of many a marriage proposal. Adjoining it is the **Foundry Dock Park,** with access to the river. Pedestrians can cross the tracks via an underpass, but drivers must take a detour to the south to reach lower Main Street and the riverfront. An easy day trip for city dwellers, Cold Spring lures hikers, shoppers, and diners by the trainful. Treasures from vintage toys to designer jewelry await within walking distance of the station. There is a visitors center booth located directly above the station, next to the Cold Spring Depot.

Nearby, the **Putnam History Museum**

1: Constitution Marsh Audubon Center & Sanctuary **2:** the Boscobel House and Gardens **3:** Bannerman Castle

Cold Spring Village

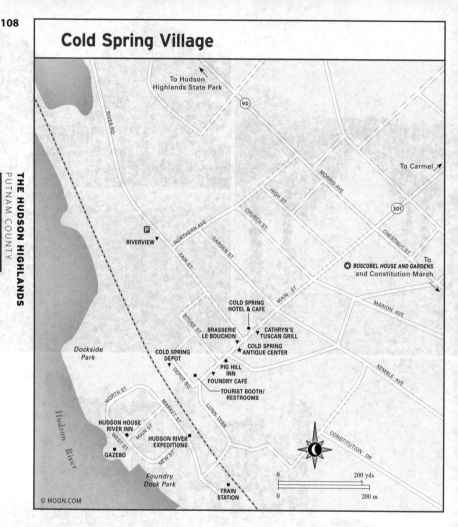

(63 Chestnut St., Cold Spring, 845/265-4010, www.putnamhistorymuseum.org, noon-4pm Wed.-Sun., admission free, $5 suggested donation) is a popular field trip for area schoolchildren. The building was constructed in 1817, when America was reeling from the War of 1812 and the realization that it needed a domestic source of iron to defend its borders, and now contains a collection of tools, letters, blueprints, and decorative ironworks, such as the ornate Washington Irving bench. Outside, you can stroll the grounds of the West Point Foundry Preserve (dawn-dusk daily). A half-mile accessible trail leads from the Cold Spring Metro-North Station to the foundry ruins.

Magazzino Italian Art (2700 Rte. 9, Cold Spring, 845/666-7202, www.magazzino.art, 11am-5pm Wed.-Mon., free) is a relatively new museum and research center that focuses on postwar and contemporary Italian art in the United States.

Outdoor activities are readily accessible from Cold Spring: The most popular pastimes include paddling the river and the Constitution Marsh and hiking trails in the 4,200-acre Hudson Highlands State Park.

Hudson Highlands State Park Preserve

Extending the length of Putnam County, from Westchester to Dutchess, **Hudson Highlands State Park Preserve** (Rte. 9D, Beacon, 845/225-7207, www.nysparks.com, sunrise-sunset daily) encompasses 25 miles of hiking trails that meander along the ridgeline of the Hudson Highland range. Views of the river here are among the best anywhere in the region. Camping, campfires, bikes, and motorized vehicles are not permitted within the park, but you can fish and boat along the shoreline.

Bannerman Castle

As the river widens to form Newburgh Bay, a small island appears just north of Storm King Mountain and about four miles north of West Point. At less than seven acres, the island is made mostly of rock and sits about 1,000 feet from the river's eastern shore. (Though Bannerman Island lies technically within Dutchess County, it is most often viewed from Hudson Highlands itineraries.) It played a role in colonial history, first as part of a plan to stop the British from advancing north along the Hudson, and later as a designated military prison that was built but never used.

The island's most interesting story, however, is connected with a Scottish American entrepreneur named Frank (Francis) Bannerman VI, who collected and sold military goods acquired at government auctions. When he needed a place to store ammunition from the Spanish American War, Bannerman Island Arsenal came to be.

Bannerman acquired the island formerly known as Pollepel from the state of New York in 1900 and built a Scottish-style castle, complete with crenellated towers and turrets. The fortress housed the family business until 1967, when the Bannermans sold the island back to New York State. State officials had planned to open the island to visitors, but a fire in 1969 severely damaged many of the buildings, and the island remained off-limits for four decades, making it the subject of much speculation and mystery.

Today, what remains of the castle is managed by the **Bannerman Castle Trust** (www.bannermancastle.org), which offers guided walking tours (from Beacon 11am and 12:30pm Sat. and 12:30pm Sun., from Newburgh 11am Sun. May-Oct.) by boat or kayak. You can get a glimpse of the island and its abandoned castle from a river cruise or kayak tour—but paddlers, beware of strong currents around the island. Contact **Hudson River Adventures** (Newburgh or Beacon, 845/220-2120, www.prideofthehudson.com, $18-28) for sightseeing cruises, or **Hudson River Expeditions** (Cold Spring, 845/809-5935, www.hudsonriverexpeditions.com, $90 for 3 hours) and **Storm King Adventure Tours** (Cornwall, 845/534-7800, www.stormkingadventuretours.com, $70 adults, $55 child paddle only, $100 paddling and walking tour) for guided paddling trips.

CENTRAL PUTNAM COUNTY: ALONG THE TACONIC STATE PARKWAY

Clarence Fahnestock Memorial State Park

The white sand beach at Canopus Lake in central Putnam County arrived by truck from Long Island in the late 1970s. Today, the completed waterfront complex has everything beachgoers need, save the salty air. A concession stand sells burgers and hot dogs, and there are showers, picnic tables, a boat launch, and campsites.

The beach sits within Putnam County's second state park, **Clarence Fahnestock Memorial State Park** (1498 Rte. 301, Carmel, 845/225-7207, www.nysparks.com, beach 9am-7pm daily, $9 per vehicle), which covers 10,000 acres extending from a few miles east of Cold Spring to beyond the Taconic State Parkway. Swimming is no

For Amateur Geologists

It's hard to imagine that a good part of the Hudson River Valley was once a tropical sea. Over the course of hundreds of millions of years, a continual process of uplift and erosion—and four different ice ages—shaped the mountains and rivers we know today. As a result, geological sites abound along highways, in state parks, and on mountaintops across the region, offering insight for both professional and amateur scientists into the natural forces that have defined the topography over time.

WHERE TO GO

Hudson Highlands
Head first to Harriman State Park in search of rocky exposures along trails in the western part of the park. You can reach the trails directly from the Metro-North station in Tuxedo. Plan for several hours of hiking to reach the best views and geological sites. Nearby, swing through Bear Mountain State Park to view examples of resilient Storm King granite. Then cross the Bear Mountain Bridge to view the road cuts along Route 9D near Anthony's Nose.

Upper Hudson
Start with the road cuts along Route 23 between the towns of Leeds and Cairo in Greene County (New York State Thruway exit 21), a popular destination for college field trips. Continue northwest to Kaaterskill Falls on Route 23A to get an idea of the power of water erosion. In the Albany area, the "Indian Ladder" is a striking 80-foot-high limestone cliff inside John Boyd Thacher State Park.

WHAT TO LOOK FOR

In the Hudson Highlands, you'll encounter glacier-scoured exposures of bedrock, granite gneiss (combinations of sandstone and shale) cut by small veins of quartz, and abandoned iron mines. In the Catskills, look for fossils of ferns, root systems, and marinelife, as well as ripple marks in shale layers.

WHERE TO LEARN MORE

The U.S. Geological Survey (USGS) has published a thorough guide to New York geological sites online, as well as an overview of geological fundamentals at http://3dparks.wr.usgs.gov. In addition, see local geologist Robert Titus's *The Catskills: A Geological Guide, Expanded Edition* (Fleischmann's, NY: Purple Mountain Press, 2016) and *Geology of the Hudson Valley: A Billion Years of History*, by Steven Schimmrich (independently published, 2020).

longer permitted at Canopus Lake, but you can still enjoy a picnic on the beach. Several lakes and ponds present good opportunities for boating and fishing.

Hikes on 42 miles of wooded trails range from easy to moderately strenuous. Mountain bikers and horseback riders have access to additional trails and bridle paths. Access the park from Route 301, which connects Route 9 along the Hudson River to the Taconic State Parkway.

Also inside the park, **Taconic Outdoor Education Center** (75 Mountain Laurel Rd., Cold Spring, 845/265-3773, www.nysparks. com, year-round for group use by reservation) has wildlife exhibits and runs geology, aquatic ecology, astronomy, and outdoor skills programs for groups only. Guests stay in nine heated log cabins. In winter, the center has more than nine miles of groomed cross-country ski trails, along with equipment rentals and lessons. A little farther east on Route 301, **Canopus Lake** has more trails for cross-country skiing. It's about a two-mile drive to the center from Route 301, and the turnoff is well marked.

EASTERN PUTNAM COUNTY: ALONG I-84

Brewster

Named for a local contractor, Walter Brewster, who built a station for the Harlem Line Railroad in the 1850s, this village thrived as an early thoroughfare between New York City and Danbury, Connecticut. Today, however, the town is a mixed bag of 19th-century homes and run-down storefronts.

Unique among regional museums, Brewster's **Southeast Museum** (67 Main St., 845/279-7500, www.southeastmuseum. org, 10am-3pm Tues.-Thurs. and Sat. Apr.-Dec., free) documents a number of seemingly unrelated developments—from the arrival of the early American circus and the Borden Condensed Milk factory to the engineering of the Harlem Line Railroad and the Croton Reservoir—that took place in and around the town of Southeast. Located in a historic building in downtown Brewster, the museum also displays a collection of antique farm equipment, quilts, and other Americana in rotating exhibits throughout the year.

Carmel and Mahopac

On the shores of a small lake at the intersection of Route 6 and Route 301 lies **Carmel** (CAR-mel), the Putnam County seat since 1812. It is home to the second-oldest courthouse in New York State, a Greek Revival structure built in 1814.

Suburban **Mahopac** sits on the shores of Lake Mahopac, once a large resort community. Today, local residents water-ski, sail, and fish the lake during summer months. The town has two marinas for launching and servicing powerboats.

Nearby in Kent is the peaceful **Chuang Yen Monastery** (2020 Rte. 301, Kent, 845/225-1819, www.baus.org, 10am-noon or 1pm-3pm daily Apr.-Dec., reservations required), a Dharma education center featuring the largest Buddha statue in the western hemisphere. The 37-foot Buddha Vairocana towers over thousands of smaller statues inside the Great Buddha Hall, a pagoda-like structure

that was built around the giant statue in the style of the Tang dynasty era (AD 618-917). The Woo Ju Memorial Library on the premises contains 70,000 Buddhist reference texts in many different languages. A pleasant reading room faces Seven Jewels Lake and is open to the public.

★ The Great Swamp

The Great Swamp is a remarkable watershed area spanning more than 19 miles and 6,000 acres of wetlands in Dutchess and Putnam Counties. There are nearly 200 species of birds, 64 species of butterflies and moths, 37 types of fish, and at least 34 kinds of bees and wasps. And that's just the beginning of the ecosystem. Beaver, otter, mink, coyote, bear, and bobcat inhabit the woods, while wood ducks, black ducks, and mallards use it as a migratory flyway. Much of the wildlife in this area is rare, threatened, or endangered in New York State, and the water itself feeds directly into the Croton Reservoir, so a number of local and national environmental organizations have been sounding the alarms about this fragile environment. Salted roads, leaching septic and sewage systems, and chemical run-off coming from commercial parking lots, golf courses, and industrial agriculture operations all pose threats to the delicate balance that sustains wildlife in this special place.

The Appalachian Trail traverses the swamp in Dutchess County near Pawling, but the best way to explore the swamp is by kayak in spring or early summer, when the water level is high. Paddlers can launch from **Patterson Environmental Park** (South St., off Route 311, Patterson, 845/878-6500). Use caution when crossing the train tracks, and note you will start the paddle heading downstream, so allow time for the more difficult upstream paddle on the way back. When school is not in session, you can launch from **Green Chimneys School** (400 Doansburg Rd., Brewster, 845/279-2995, only after 5pm Mon.-Fri.).

Headquartered in Pawling, **Friends of**

The **Great Swamp** (845/350-2669, www. frogs-ny.org) is a local nonprofit organization dedicated to preserving this fragile ecosystem. With a grant from Patagonia, FrOGS produced a beautiful eight-minute video (youtu.be/owcd6C3bBLo) narrated by James Earl Jones to capture the beauty and importance of this unique wetland environment. Check its website for current maps, events, and launch sites.

RECREATION

Putnam County offers a remarkable variety of outdoor activities, given its proximity to the urban sprawl of New York City. Much of the county's land and water is protected from development by the state park system. Trails are well maintained, and rental gear and professional instruction are readily available for a range of sports, including hiking, skiing, paddling, and horseback riding.

Winter Sports

During winter, Clarence Fahnestock Memorial State Park becomes a playground for Nordic skiing, snowshoeing, ice-skating, ice fishing, and snowmobiling.

Family-run **Thunder Ridge Ski Area** (Rte. 22, Patterson, 845/878-4100, www. thunderridgeski.com, 10am-9pm Mon.-Fri., 9am-9pm Sat., 9am-5pm Sun., adults $35-65, under age 12 $35-49) has night skiing and easy slopes that are ideal for beginners. The mountain runs a free shuttle from the Patterson train station during the peak season. They also offer babysitting services for a reasonable price.

The **Brewster Ice Arena** (63 Fields Lane, Brewster, 845/279-2229, www. brewstericearena.com) hosts public skate sessions (adults $8.75) and rentals ($3.75). Open hockey sessions are $15. Hours change by the season.

Hiking

Both **Hudson Highlands** and **Clarence Fahnestock State Parks** maintain extensive trail systems for hikers, including well-traveled stretches of the Appalachian Trail. Water found on the trails within these parks is not safe to drink. Bring your own. Except for the designated camping area at Canopus Lake, camping and campfires are not permitted within the parks.

Bird-watchers frequent 900-foot-high **Anthony's Nose** at the Westchester County line to watch hawks, eagles, and vultures hover over the Bear Mountain Bridge. Park

The Great Swamp

Community Science Volunteer Opportunities

Community participants play an essential role in helping biologists monitor wildlife populations in the Hudson River, its tributaries, and unique environments like The Great Swamp. With the advent of digital technology, people can get involved in many ways—for example, by logging their fishing catch, volunteering to monitor juvenile glass eels, helping with amphibian road crossings in spring, and planting native species to facilitate stream restoration. Search for Community Science Volunteer Opportunities at www.dec.ny.gov to find current programs and special events that may be happening during your visit.

APPS FOR NATURALISTS

The popular iNaturalist and Seek by iNaturalist mobile apps (inaturalist.org) provide a fun way for aspiring naturalists, young and old, to record personal wildlife observations and have them validated by a global virtual community. Watch for occasional nature challenges in this region and see how many of the thousands of plant and animal species on the New York checklist you can find!

along the pullout of Route 9D a short distance north of the bridge. The trail (2.6 miles round-trip, http://hikethehudsonvalley.com) begins on the opposite side of the road from the river and is part of the AT (white blazes). The first half-mile is steep as it climbs a rocky staircase before leveling out along the ridge.

For one of the steepest and most strenuous hikes in the region, try the **Breakneck Ridge Trail** (3.7 miles round-trip, http://hikethehudsonvalley.com), which begins north of the tunnel on Route 9D, two miles north of Cold Spring. This trail leads to the most expansive and memorable views in the park; however, it can be dangerous during inclement weather. Choose a different route in wet or windy conditions. Not advised for children or dogs.

In Clarence Fahnestock State Park, the **Three Lakes Loop** (5.9 miles, 3.2 miles with shortcuts) is a popular easy route that follows the bed of an old railroad line and meets up with the Appalachian Trail at the end. Along the way, hikers meander through forest, wetlands, and dense patches of mountain laurel.

Ninham Mountain State Forest (also spelled Nimham in some places, Gypsy Trail Rd., Kent) has a fire tower that's very easy to reach via a gravel road from the parking area (1.5 miles round-trip). Enjoy views of the Catskills from the top.

You could easily spend a couple of hours exploring the 163-acre **Fred Dill Wildlife Sanctuary** (62 Fair St, Carmel Hamlet, no pets), near Carmel High School. It has several easy, well-marked trails with interpretive stations and a picnic pavilion. The lesser-known 600-acre **Michael Ciaiola Conservation Area** (478-480 Haviland Hollow Rd, Patterson) has several looping trails that lead to a waterfall with a shallow pool for swimming.

Cycling and Mountain Biking

The **Putnam County Trailway** (12 miles, http://putnamcountyny.com) follows the route of the old New York Central Railroad, connecting Brewster to Mahopac (9.7 miles), Somers/Baldwin Place (12 miles), and the North County Trailway in Westchester County (34 miles). From 1881 until 1958, the "Old Put" ushered passengers between the Bronx and Brewster. Today, the tracks are a paved bike- and footpath. Many sections are still under construction.

The annual **Pedal Putnam** (https://goputnam.com, $25-60) cycling event takes place in July. The races (12 miles, 40 miles, or

62 miles) start and finish in Kent, covering many miles of Putnam's prettiest countryside.

The **Michael Ciaiola Conservation Area** (478-480 Haviland Hollow Rd., Patterson) allows mountain bikes on 11 miles of its forested trails, a rare find in this part of the Hudson Valley. **Ninham Mountain State Forest** has another 10 miles of mostly intermediate level trails, plus a few black diamonds for the pros.

Cold Spring Bike Rental & Tours (347-638-7707, www.coldspringbikerentaltours.com, 9am-7pm daily) operates out of Long Dock Park in Beacon and runs guided trail rides on hybrid bikes through the Hudson Highlands, as well as sites in and around Beacon (Dutchess County). Rates for bikes only are $15 for one hour up to $50 for a full day. Guided tours are $35 per person.

Golf

Golfers can choose from four public golf courses in Garrison, Mahopac, and Carmel. The **Highlands Golf Club** (955 Rte. 9D, Garrison, 845/424-3727, highlandscountryclub.net, $22-40) has nine holes and river views. It's open to the public daily in spring and fall. Summer public hours start at 8am Monday-Friday, 7:30am Saturday-Sunday. Its sister property, **The Garrison** (2015 Rte. 9, Garrison, 845/424-4747, www.thegarrison.com, $45-95) is open to the public daily April-November. The **Putnam County Golf Course** (187 Hill St., Mahopac, 845/408-1880, www.putnamcountygolfcourse.com, $20-72) is a 6,800-yard par-71 course that's open to the public daily. **The Centennial Golf Club** (185 John Simpson Rd., Carmel, 845/225-5700, www.centennialgolf.com) has five lakes on the course and is open daily April-November. Dynamic pricing ranges $29-139, depending on the day and the time you book.

Swimming and Boating

Putnam County offers aquatic activities on the Hudson and in several natural lakes located in its two state parks. For a sandy beach, head to **Canopus Lake** in Clarence Fahnestock Memorial State Park. You can launch your own kayaks from **Foundry Dock Park** in Cold Spring, but be sure to check the river tide tables before pushing off.

Hudson River Expeditions (14 Market St., Cold Spring, 845/809-5935, www.hudsonriverexpeditions.com, noon-6pm Mon. and Thurs., 9am-6pm Fri.-Sun. July-Sept.) runs beginner to advanced-level kayak trips on the Hudson to Constitution Marsh, Bannerman Castle, and overnight destinations, as well as guided hikes through the Hudson Highlands. You also can rent kayaks, but contact the shop at least a day in advance to find out about the tides for the hours when you want to paddle. You can enter the marsh only during low tide due to a railroad bridge that you need to paddle under. The shop is a block from the Cold Spring train station. This outfitter has additional locations at Long Dock Beacon (Mid-Hudson region) and Peekskill (July-Aug. only).

Mahopac Marine (897 S. Lake Blvd., Mahopac, 845/628-6550, www.mahopacmarine.com, 10am-5pm Tues.-Sun.) is a full-service boatyard that provides boat slips, fuel, and a marine supply shop on the shores of Lake Mahopac.

Fishing and Hunting

Anglers head to the lakes to catch bass, perch, pickerel, and trout. The DEC stocks **Stillwater Lake** in Clarence Fahnestock Memorial State Park with rainbow and brook trout each spring. Brown trout are common in the streams that feed the New York City Watershed. Thirteen miles of water are open to the public, and the season typically runs April-September. Regulations vary by location and are more protective in Putnam County than elsewhere in New York State. In designated areas, size limits may be higher, daily limits may be lower, and artificial lures may be required. Bow hunting for deer and wild

1: Chuang Yen Monastery **2:** charming storefronts in Cold Spring Village **3:** boat launch at Canopus Lake **4:** hikers ascending Breakneck Ridge Trail

turkey hunting are permitted during limited seasons.

Cranberry Mountain Wildlife Management Area (Stage Coach Rd., Patterson, www.dec.ny.gov) has a network of trails on old wood roads that traverse a hardwood forest of oak and maple trees. Six ponds within the park support healthy populations of largemouth bass, sunfish, bullheads, and chain pickerel.

Horseback Riding
There are bridle paths in Clarence Fahnestock Memorial State Park, and **Hollow Brook Riding Academy** (890 Peekskill Hollow Rd., Putnam Valley, 845/526-8357, www.hollowbrookriding.com) offers lessons to new and experienced riders.

Yoga and Spas
Putnam Yoga (30 Tomahawk St., Baldwin Place, 845/494-8118, www.putnamyoga.com) holds classes in gentle and restorative yoga styles as well as fitness classes for cardio and strength conditioning. Visitors can drop in for $20 or purchase a multiple-class card.

Putnam County still doesn't have any destination spas, but you can make an appointment at **Pure Radiance Day Spa** (854 Rte. 6, Mahopac, 845/803-8129, www.pureradiancedayspa.net, 10am-6pm Mon.-Fri., 10am-4pm Sat.) for a facial or massage with optional hand and foot scrubs.

ENTERTAINMENT AND EVENTS
Performing Arts
The theater event of the summer in Putnam County is the **Hudson Valley Shakespeare Festival** (845/265-9575, www.hvshakespeare. org, $10-94), which started in 1987 and has staged *Richard II* and *The Taming of the Shrew* in recent seasons. This is a world-renowned festival that attracts more than 250,000 people each year. Performances (7:30pm Wed.-Mon. mid-June-early Sept.) take place under a tent at Boscobel House and Gardens. Special offerings include a beer garden, lawn parties,

wine and cheese tastings, and family nights. Children must be age five or older to attend, and no pets are allowed. Locals also adore the **Philipstown Depot Theatre** (10 Garrison's Landing, Garrison, 845/424-3900, www.philipstowndepottheatre.org) at Garrison Landing, a historic venue that dates to 1892. The theater produces plays, children's programs, poetry readings, chamber music, cabaret, film, and other community programs.

Festivals and Events
Winterfest (845/265-3773, www.nysparks.com) takes place at the Taconic Outdoor Education Center on National Winter Trails Days in January, with snowshoeing, nature walks, and crafts. In March, the center celebrates the maple sugaring season with a Maple Sunday Pancake Breakfast and hands-on demonstration of tapping trees and boiling sap into syrup. Brewster and Mahopac hold **street fairs** in October. Boscobel holds **candlelight tours** in December.

The German American Social Club of Peekskill puts on a September **Oktoberfest** (11 Kramers Rd., Putnam Valley, 845/528-5800, www.gac1936.com), complete with polka dancing and a beer stein-holding contest. The annual **Pedal Putnam** (https://goputnam.com, $25-60) cycling event takes place in July. All three courses (12 miles, 40 miles, or 62 miles) start and finish in Kent, covering many miles of Putnam's prettiest countryside.

Bars
The U-shaped bar at the **Cold Spring Depot** (1 Main St., Depot Square, Cold Spring, 845/265-5000, www.coldspringdepot.com, noon-8pm daily) makes for a popular watering hole, with its TV screens and rotating selection of local beers. More craft beers from Chatham, Catskill, Saratoga, and elsewhere around the state can be found at **Doug's Pretty Good Pub** (54 Main St., Cold Spring, 845/265-9500, www.dougsprettygoodpub.com, 4:30pm-9:30pm Wed.-Fri., noon-9:30pm Sat., noon-7pm Sun.). You can order burgers

or "not burgers" ($10-15) to go with your spirits. The kitchen closes at 9pm most nights.

SHOPPING
Farm Stands
The Hudson River Valley's iconic farms and orchards aren't far away from Putnam County. The **Brewster Farmers Market** (15 Mt. Ebo Rd., South Brewster, 10am-2pm Sun. mid-June-late Nov.) and **Cold Spring Farmers Market** (Boscobel House and Gardens, 1601 NY-9D, Garrison, 845/265-3611, www.csfarmmarket.org, 10am-1pm Sat. May-Oct.) are among the most popular foodie events around.

Tilly Foster Farm (Rte. 312, Brewster, www.putnamtillyfoster.com) is a restored farm and education center with an organic garden, nature trail (1 mile, easy), and several breeds of chickens, pigs, and alpacas. Take a self-guided tour (10am-4pm daily). **Tilly's Table** (100 Rte. 312, Brewster, 845/808-1840, www.tillystablerestaurant.com, 5pm-10pm Wed.-Sat., 11am-2:30pm and 5pm-9pm Sun., $17-44) serves farm-to-table food like pork belly, burrata *caprese* with heirloom tomatoes, prosciutto-stuffed Berkshire pork chops, rosemary roasted chicken, and New York strip steak.

Antiques and Galleries
Casual and serious antiques collectors flock to Cold Spring for a day of retail adventure. Dozens of shops line Main Street, inviting shoppers with window displays of vintage toys, coins, jewelry, and home furnishings. Most stores close by 6pm, with some open later on weekend evenings. Many also are closed on Tuesday.

The **Cold Spring Antique Center** (77 Main St., Cold Spring, 845/265-5050, noon-5pm Mon.-Thurs., 11am-6pm Fri.-Sun.) is located just a few doors up from the Pig Hill Inn in a 19th-century bank building. Here you'll find furniture, records, dolls, toys, silver, jewelry, art glass, and other vintage items from multiple dealers. Milk crates, taxidermy, and vinyl are among the latest acquisitions.

Bijou Galleries (50 Main St., Cold Spring, 845/265-4337, www.bijougalleries.com, 10am-4pm Fri., 10am-5pm Sat.-Sun., appointment only Mon.-Thurs.) represents 30 dealers of antiques, collectibles, and art. **Art & Antiques** (40 Main St., Cold Spring, 845/265-4866, www.artantiquegallery.com, 11am-5pm Thurs.-Mon.), another multiple-dealer shop, specializes in vintage clothing, books, magazines, comic books, records, lighting, prints, and costume jewelry. You can easily spend a few hours here reminiscing about the past.

For contemporary gifts for children or the home, visit the **Country Goose** (115 Main St., Cold Spring, 845/265-2122, www.highlandbaskets.com, 11am-6pm daily). You'll find everything from retro calendar towels and candles to games, coffee, and other knickknacks. The owner also prepares beautiful country gift baskets for a loyal clientele of local businesses.

Poor George (64 Main St., Old Spring, 845/666-7451, www.shoppoorgeorge.com, 11am-5pm Mon.-Fri. and Sun., 10am-6pm Sat.) started as an Etsy shop online before opening its brick-and-mortar store in Cold Spring. This lifestyle boutique is all about supporting women-led brands with a focus on sustainability and fair trade. You'll find small batch apparel like cute PJ sets, stylish hoodies, plaid cardigans, lounge dresses, and the like. Mixed in with these great finds are some vintage discoveries, housewares, and jewelry.

FOOD
Putnam County restaurants excel at blending farm-fresh ingredients with international cuisine to please the cosmopolitan palate.

Along the River: Route 9D
Kick off a day of antiquing with a fresh-baked scone at the **Foundry Café** (55 Main St., Cold Spring, 845/265-4504, 6am-3pm Mon.-Tues. and Thurs.-Fri., 8am-5pm Sat.-Sun., $4-15), a popular gathering place for local residents on weekday mornings, except for Wednesday, when the café is closed. **Cold Spring Coffeehouse** (92 Main St., Cold Spring,

845/533-3353, https://coldspringcoffeehouse. square.site, 8am-5pm Mon.-Thurs., 8am-6pm Fri., 8am-7pm Sat.-Sun.) serves locally roasted organic and fair-trade coffee and espresso drinks. Croissants, danishes, and the gluten-free biscuit will be hard to resist.

A little farther up Main Street, **Cathryn's Tuscan Grill** (91 Main St., Cold Spring, 845/265-5582, www.tuscangrill.com, 4:30pm-9:30pm Mon. and Thurs.-Fri., noon-9:30pm Sat.-Sun., $15-35) is a Cold Spring mainstay, serving spinach ravioli, linguini with clams, sautéed calamari, and other Italian dishes. Vegetarians will find plenty of options on the wide-ranging menu. On a warm day, ask for a table in the courtyard. Across the street from the Pig Hill Inn, **Brasserie Le Bouchon** (76 Main St., Cold Spring, 845/265-7676, noon-8pm Mon.-Sat., noon-7pm Sun., $15-25) has garden seating in warm weather and a few tables on the porch, from where you can watch the action on Main Street. On the bistro menu are pâté, terrines, three different preparations of mussels, escargot, steak frites, rack of lamb, cassoulet, and bouillabaisse. Be prepared for cozy seating indoors, as the dining room is very small.

With nine guest rooms on its upper floors, the **Cold Spring Hotel Café** (124 Main St., Cold Spring, 845/264-0824, www. coldspringhotelny.com, 10am-6pm daily, $6-14) serves up a basic menu of fresh salads, pressed sandwiches, and homemade soups.

At the foot of Main Street, the ★ **Cold Spring Depot** (1 Main St., Depot Square, Cold Spring, 845/265-5000, www. coldspringdepot.com, noon-8pm daily, $16-30) actually was a train depot from 1893 until 1954. Today, the restaurant is a first-come, first-served kind of place with an inviting patio that's pet-friendly, and a separate clam bar, plus two fireplaces for winter vibes. Try the beef and pork belly burger, pickled beet salad, or pan-seared salmon. And definitely save room for the Nutella-stuffed brown butter skillet cookie.

Round Up Texas BBQ (2741 Route 9, Cold Spring, 845/809-5557, 11:30am-7:30pm Tues.-Sun., $7-15) cooks up legit brisket, rubs, barbecued chicken, sausage, and catfish for a diehard clientele. Try the two-meat combo with fried okra on the side. After that, head over to **Moo Moo's Creamery** (32 West St., Cold Spring, 845/554-3666, www. moomooscreamery.com, noon-8:30pm Sun.-Thurs., noon-9pm Fri.-Sun.) for ice cream made fresh daily on-site. Flavors change daily and usually aim to surprise the palate. Get the Cake Batter, WalNutella, or Mexican Chocolate if you happen to spy them on the menu that day.

★ **Hudson Hil's Café & Market** (129-131 Main St., Cold Spring, 845/265-9471, www. hudsonhils.com, 9am-3pm Wed.-Fri., 9am-4pm Sat.-Sun., $14-19) serves all-day breakfast and a delightful lunch menu, with everything made from scratch and mostly from local ingredients sourced from Hudson River Valley farms. Eggs come from nearby Feather Ridge Farm, and there are several gluten-free options on the menu. A large porch offers good people-watching when the weather cooperates. This is a great place to fill your picnic basket with treats from the bakery and small market stocked with organic and gourmet foods, including syrups, raw natural honey, premade salads, and teas. Another option: Choose from a menu of prepared meals at Boscobel House and Gardens, which partners with Hudson Hil's, and enjoy the riverside scenery.

A short walk from Main Street, **Riverview** (45 Fair St., Cold Spring, 845/265-4778, www. riverdining.com, 5:30pm-9pm Wed.-Fri., noon-10pm Sat., noon-9pm Sun., $18-30, cash only) occupies an unassuming building with an enclosed terrace. Fresh fish, scallops, and oysters top the list of seafood specials. Starters include a baby arugula, endive, and beet salad. Main courses include steamed littleneck clams and mussels, black seabass, and boneless short ribs. In business since 1941, the restaurant is located next to a large municipal lot for easy parking.

Hudson House River Inn (2 Main St., Cold Spring, 845/265-9355, www.

hudsonhouseinn.com, lunch 11:30am-3:30pm daily, dinner 4pm-9pm Mon.-Thurs., 4pm-10pm Fri.-Sat., 4pm-8pm Sun., $21-42, prix fixe $39 pp) is the place for an old-world dining experience. Black Angus aged western steaks are the main attraction here, and the kitchen will broil them exactly to your liking—just be sure to consult the menu's cheat sheet on levels of doneness before you order. Highlights from the seafood section include Faroe Island salmon and jumbo diver sea scallops. The prix fixe Sunday brunch ($28 pp) begins with your choice of an appetizer followed by an entrée; add a house-made bellini or bloody Mary for $9.50.

Another Culinary Institute of America-trained chef, Vinny Mocarski, runs the kitchen at **Valley Restaurant at The Garrison** (2015 Rte. 9, at Snake Hill Rd., Garrison, 845/424-3604, www.thegarrison.com, 5pm-8pm Thurs., 5pm-9pm Fri., noon-3pm and 5pm-9pm Sat., noon-3pm and 4:30pm-7:30pm Sun., $30-69), a golf resort nestled among rolling hills of the Hudson Highlands. Start with the yellowfin tuna sashimi or East Coast oysters and move on to the ploughman's board of New York cheeses and pâtés. Medium and larger plates include a Wagyu beef burger and Long Island duck breast.

For bistro-inspired fare that follows the seasons, head down to ★ **Dolly's** (7 Garrison's Landing, Garrison, 845/424-6511, www.dollysrestaurant.com, 4pm-9pm Wed.-Thurs. and Sun., 4pm-9:30pm Fri.-Sat., $20-38). Experienced caterers Shelley and Kimball first opened the riverside eatery in 2018. Today, the menu features pork and chive dumplings, clam toast, and cauliflower nuggets to start. Larger plates include spice-roasted lamb shoulder, a crispy fish sandwich, and curried red lentils. The list of local farms and purveyors represented on Dolly's menu is long, and the food is bar-none.

Guadalajara (2 Union St., Briarcliff Manor, 914/944-4380, www.guadalajarany.com, 4:30pm-9pm Tues.-Thurs., 1pm-10pm Fri.-Sat., 1pm-8pm Sun., $17-39) pours some of the best margaritas around at the bar in a mustard-yellow stucco building. Tile floors and bright colors complete the ambience inside. Order chiles rellenos, taquitos *al carbón*, tostadas, or *bistec*. Servers prepare guacamole at the table. Enjoy Mexican beers and occasional live music on the weekends.

Eastern Putnam County: Along I-84

You can't miss the red-and-white striped **Red Rooster Drive-In** (1566 Rte. 22, Brewster, 845/279-8046, www.redroosterdrivein.com, 10am-11pm Mon.-Wed., 10am-11:30pm Thurs., 10am-1am Fri.-Sat., 10am-midnight Sun., $3-13) when driving along Route 22 through Brewster. This place has loyal customers who've been coming for decades. Besides classic burgers, fries, onion rings, and fried chicken, there are malted shakes and egg creams. This also is the place to get your soft-serve/cherry-dip ice cream fix. Get ready to wait it out for a picnic table on the lawn and dig in.

★ **Tilly's Table** (100 Rte. 312, Brewster, 845/808-1840, www.tillystablerestaurant.com, 5pm-10pm Wed.-Sat., 11am-2:30pm and 5pm-9pm Sun., $17-44) serves farm-to-table dinners with main courses like prosciutto-stuffed Berkshire pork chops, rosemary roasted chicken, and New York strip steak. The Sunday brunch menu ($29.95 pp) features farm egg omelets and a crab cake Florentine. Summer concerts and comedy nights are popular events.

Cuisine doesn't get any more farm-to-table than the ★ **Clock Tower Bar & Grill** (512 Clock Tower Dr, Brewster, 845/582-0574, clocktowergrill.com, 4pm-9pm Tues.-Thurs., 4pm-10pm Fri.-Sat., $25-39). Owners Rich and Cassie got into the business to "fight the good fight in our broken food system." Within a few years, they had purchased a nearby farm and started raising their own Berkshire hogs, Dorper sheep, and Scottish Highland cattle. When dining here, you can start the evening with a Local Fashion (bourbon, brandied blackberries, and orange) or a glass of prosecco, then move on to the main event of venison loin, chicken pot pie, or sauerbraten beef stew. For sure, save a little room at the end for the tiramisu martini.

For an evening of house-cured gravlax, grilled antelope medallions, or honey-roasted duckling, head to The Arch (1292 Rte. 22, Brewster, 845/279-5011, www.archrestaurant.com, 5pm-9pm Wed.-Fri., 5pm-10pm Sat., 11:30am-7:30pm Sun., $25-45, price fixe Sun. brunch $48). For spicier fare, try Jaipore Royal Indian Cuisine (280 Rte. 22, Brewster, 845/277-3549, www.jaiporenyc.com, 11am-2:30pm and 5pm-9:30pm Wed.-Mon., $11-28), located in an 1856 mansion that was once a speakeasy in the 1920s. Known locally for its Sunday lunch and dinner buffets, the restaurant has several dining rooms, including an outdoor porch and patio.

Locals stop for burgers, hot dogs, and curly fries at Forrest's Sidestreet Café (6 Old Route 22, Pawling, 845/878-6571, 11am-3pm Thurs.-Sun. and Fri. nights in summer, $3-5, cash only), near Pawling and the Dutchess County line, where a friendly couple serves simple food from a converted truck on the west side of Route 22. This is a convenient place for a quick bite: hot dogs, sausages, burgers, grilled cheese, and chicken nuggets. The food truck usually closes during the winter months.

You'll find steamed littleneck clams, shrimp cocktail, and New England-style lobster rolls on the menu at Mahopac Seafood & Gourmet Market (545 Route 6, Mahopac, 845/621-2489, mahopacseafoodmarket.com, noon-8pm Tues.-Sat., 11:30am-3:30pm Sun., starters $12-24, mains $18-34).

Enjoy the views of Lake Mahopac when you dine at Lakehouse Restaurant and Bar (825 South Lake Blvd., Mahopac, 845/621-5200, lakehouserestaurantandbar.com, 11:30am-10pm Sun.-Thurs., 11:30am-11pm Fri.-Sat., $19-41). The menu has a little of everything, from clams and calamari to chicken Milanese and filet mignon.

If you're out for a ride on the Putnam County Trailway and need a bite to eat,

hold out for the ★ Freight House Café (609 Rte. 6, Mahopac, 845/628-1872, www.thefreighthousecafe.com, 9am-3pm Wed.-Mon., $5-15), located just off the bike path on the site of the first building constructed for the New York Central & Hudson River Railroad branch, in 1872. The menu includes house-made granola, smoothies, wraps, buffalo cauliflower, grass-fed beef burgers, and—wait for it—house-made dairy-free peanut butter cups.

ACCOMMODATIONS

Memorable accommodations are somewhat limited in tiny Putnam County; however, vacation rentals are a great option with the Airbnb and VRBO listing services. Happily, it's a short drive to more lodging choices in Orange and Dutchess Counties.

Under $100

Clean, friendly, and affordable, the Countryside Motel (3577 Rte. 9, Cold Spring, 845/265-2090, from $75) has 22 rooms with full- or queen-size beds and in-room AC units. Some rooms have kitchenettes; two are suites with whirlpool tubs. The location on busy Route 9 may be noisy at times, but the beds are decent and it's only five miles from the Metro-North station in Cold Spring. Plan on calling a ride-share if you arrive by train.

$150-300

One mile from Boscobel, the Cold Spring Hotel & Cafe (124 Main St., Cold Spring, 845/264-0824, www.coldspringhotelny.com, from $125) has nine cozy rooms above a ground floor café under the same ownership. Rooms have pine floors and carved mahogany queen beds with private tiled baths. Book one for the weekend, or the whole place for a special occasion. There is no elevator on the property.

The lobby of the three-story redbrick ★ Pig Hill Inn (73 Main St., Cold Spring, 845/265-9247, www.pighillinn.com, $160-260)

1: Pig Hill Inn 2: Hudson House River Inn

doubles as an antiques shop, and the effect is a cozy and historical feel. All nine rooms are individually appointed in Victorian decor and have private baths—some with marble tile and basins; several have poster beds, whirlpool tubs, and fireplaces or tiny woodstoves. After a comfortable night's sleep, enjoy breakfast made to order in the atrium. This is an ideal place for a peaceful and intimate getaway.

At the bottom of Cold Spring's Main Street, the 1832 **Hudson House River Inn** (2 Main St., Cold Spring, 845/265-9355, www.hudsonhouseinn.com, $190-285) has 11 simply furnished guest rooms and 2 suites. Lodging includes breakfast in the tavern on-site. Some rooms have balconies with views of the Hudson River, which is steps away from the building. Others have small terraces that face Main Street. You can walk to antiques shopping and more fine dining along Main Street, as well as the Metro-North train station. The rooms are fairly basic for the price, but a stay here is worth it for the convenient location, historical appeal, and the convenience of a good restaurant downstairs.

For a relaxing golf weekend or a Dia:Beacon getaway, the **Inn at The Garrison** (845/424-3604, thegarrison.com, $128-300) has seven guest rooms with wood floors, king beds, and white quilted bed covers.

Campgrounds

The best place to pitch a tent in Putnam County is the shores of Canopus Lake in **Clarence Fahnestock Memorial State Park** (1498 Rte. 301, Carmel, 845/225-7207, www.reserveamerica.com, $15-19 in-state, $20-24 out-of-state).

INFORMATION AND SERVICES

The **Putnam Visitors Bureau** (110 Old Rte. 6, Bldg. 3, Carmel, 800/470-4854 or 845/225-0381, www.visitputnam.org) is headquartered

in Carmel, and its website contains detailed information on major destinations and sights in the county. The **Brewster Chamber of Commerce** (16 Mount Ebo Rd. S., Suite 12A, 845/279-2477, www.brewsterchamber.com) is located near the Southeast Museum. You can pick up maps and brochures at the Cold Spring visitors center, located directly above the pedestrian train track crossing at the foot of Main Street.

GETTING THERE AND AROUND
Bus

Putnam Area Rapid Transit (PART, 845/878-7433, www.putnamcountyny.com, $2.50 one-way) covers major towns throughout the county with four lines, but the **Metro-North rail lines** are a more reliable way to get around. The Cold Spring Trolley (845/878-7433, $2) can get you from the train station to Boscobel and Manitoga. You can flag down the trolley anywhere you see one. Inquire at the Cold Spring visitors booth above the pedestrian train track crossing at the foot of Main Street.

Train

Two Metro-North rail lines serve Putnam County: The Hudson Line stops in Garrison and Cold Spring along the river, while the Harlem Line runs to Brewster on its way from Grand Central Station to Dover Plains in Dutchess County. Ride-shares and taxis generally are available from the stations to destinations across the county.

Car

The easiest way to see Putnam County is by car, and the fastest routes are I-84 and the Taconic State Parkway. On busy weekend days in Cold Spring, look for free parking in the large municipal lot on Fair Street, by Riverview Restaurant.

Mid-Hudson Valley and the Southern Catskills

North of the Hudson Highlands, the river wid-ens once again, and the surrounding terrain forms rolling hills, babbling brooks, and expansive orchards. Fenced horse farms, fields of wildflowers, and ranks of wood stacked for winter heat are common sightings along the back roads of Dutchess and Ulster Counties. The two counties share 40 miles of shoreline along this stretch of the Hudson, with four points of connection: the Newburgh-Beacon, Mid-Hudson, and Kingston-Rhinecliff Bridges—plus the Walkway Over the Hudson pedestrian park, which connects Highland in Ulster County to Poughkeepsie in Dutchess County. A vibrant arts scene and abundant opportunities for farm-to-table dining bring visitors for weekends and longer stays.

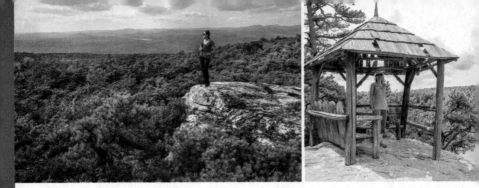

Highlights

Look for ★ to find recommended sights, activities, dining, and lodging.

© MOON.COM

★ **Beacon:** Contemporary art museum Dia:Beacon draws cultural aficionados here for getaways that include good eats, fun shopping, and hikes on Mount Beacon (page 127).

★ **Culinary Institute of America:** Set on a picturesque riverside campus, the CIA trains aspiring professionals and enthusiasts in the art of fine cuisine. Tour the grounds at sunset before eating in one of the five public restaurants on campus (page 136).

★ **Innisfree Garden:** This lush landscape applies Chinese and Japanese garden principles to local flora with Modernist and Romantic influences (page 139).

★ **Millerton:** Antiques, fine teas, organic farms, and the Harlem Valley Rail Trail are the top reasons to seek out this former railroad hub near the Connecticut state line (page 140).

★ **Historic Huguenot Street:** This historic street in New Paltz features stone dwellings now more than 300 years old, built by French immigrants who came here fleeing religious persecution (page 166).

★ **Minnewaska State Park Preserve:** Ulster County's gem of a park covers 12,000 acres of the Shawangunk Ridge with a sparkling glacial lake (page 167).

★ **Ski Belleayre Mountain:** Experience the highest skiable slopes in Ulster County, plus a cross country trail system for downhill mountain biking (page 172).

★ **Climb the Gunks:** Pack your climbing gear and head to the Shawangunk Cliffs, one of the top rock climbing destinations in the country (page 177).

Mid-Hudson Valley and the Southern Catskills

Cultural highlights in the Mid-Hudson region include the Frances Lehman Loeb Art Center at Vassar College, the Dia:Beacon museum, and the prestigious Culinary Institute of America (CIA). To complement the cuisine, a handful of wineries on both sides of the river produce award-winning chardonnay, pinot noir, merlot, and cabernet franc wines.

Several large state parks, including the southern region of the Catskill Forest Preserve and Minnewaska State Park Preserve, offer leaf-peepers a prime setting for viewing the annual display of fall colors. If you aren't afraid of heights, head to the Shawangunk Ridge in Ulster County for a day of rock-climbing. And if you are inclined to stay at sea level, there are miles of country roads to explore by bicycle and trails to wander by foot.

PLANNING YOUR TIME

By far the most popular destination in the region is the bustling college town of New Paltz and the surrounding countryside. You can walk the town center in a few hours, but to absorb the alternative vibe, you'll want at least a couple of days. Plan a hike or a bike ride and then grab a meal at one of the area's notable eateries. Rock climbers will want to spend the week scaling the ledges of the Gunks.

Poughkeepsie and Kingston, the largest cities in the area, are not destinations per se; however, you won't be wasting your time if you stop to stroll or dine along their historic waterfronts. History buffs may want to make a special trip to tour the many preserved sites.

In northern Dutchess County, a 60-mile loop begins at the train station in Poughkeepsie and follows Route 44 east to Millbrook, then Route 22 north to Millerton, and Route 199 west to the Hudson River. From there, Route 9 hugs the riverbank back

to Poughkeepsie. The drive should take two to three hours, depending on stops.

Ulster is a large county, and there are several options for scenic driving routes. One approach is to begin at the Mid-Hudson Bridge and follow Route 9D north to Kingston. Then take Route 28 west to Mount Tremper. A short loop along Route 212 heading northeast takes you through Woodstock and Saugerties and eventually back to Route 9W. Or you can continue along Route 28 to Belleayre Mountain and Delaware County beyond. Closer to Kingston, Route 209 south off Route 28 goes to New Paltz and Minnewaska State Park Preserve. Allow about half an hour to drive from New Paltz to Kingston on local roads, and an hour to cross the county from east to west.

Travelers who are visiting the area to explore options for higher education can take in several college campuses in a relatively short drive: Founded in 1861, **Vassar College** is a private liberal arts school with a beautiful campus on the edge of urban Poughkeepsie. On the Hudson River in Poughkeepsie, **Marist College** has a Catholic heritage but takes a nonsectarian approach to education today. Creative types are drawn to **Bard College,** a small liberal arts campus in Tivoli (Dutchess County), where fine arts and performing arts take center stage. Aspiring chefs and culinary artists, as well as those interested in food business and hospitality management, should not miss a tour of the flagship **Culinary Institute of America** campus in Hyde Park. **SUNY New Paltz** is a four-year public school offering degrees in business, education, liberal arts, science, and engineering. Student life is lively and fun here, with the town of New Paltz adjoining the campus.

Previous: hiking up Mount Beacon; Shawangunk Ridge; a shaded overlook at Lake Minnewaska.

Dutchess County

Scenic Dutchess County offers a telling mix of restored historic landmarks and nearly deserted manufacturing centers, bedroom communities, and progressive towns that attract weekenders by the thousands. A sampling of its historic riverside mansions should anchor every first-time visitor's itinerary. The county seat, Poughkeepsie, was designated the New York state capital in 1777, a distinction it held for about a decade. IBM set up shop in the 1950s, and despite the massive layoffs of the early 1990s and reorganizations in recent decades, the company remains a top employer.

Poughkeepsie and Dover Plains mark the northern ends of the Metro-North commuter lines. But while the southern half of Dutchess County has succumbed to the congestion of suburban sprawl, the northern part retains an idyllic charm.

ALONG THE RIVER: ROUTE 9

★ Beacon

Today it's hard to believe Beacon was a struggling manufacturing center just three decades ago. The town began to show signs of revival in the 1990s with the restoration of a stretch of East Main Street, now the city's antiques district. Its 14,000 residents live between Mount Beacon, a recent extension of the Hudson Highlands State Park, and the eastern bank of the Hudson. Today, nearly the entire 1.5-mile street has been developed, from Route 9D to Wappinger Creek—with only a few older buildings remaining in the middle stretch. More than 100 artists have opened studios in town, and plenty of galleries, cafés, shops, and restaurants followed. You won't regret an hour or two of browsing the boutiques and good eats that have popped up along Main Street.

Aside from the Dia:Beacon museum, which should lead any itinerary to this region, a few other sights may be worth a peek.

DIA:BEACON

A converted Nabisco box printing plant along the Hudson River holds the permanent collection of New York City-based Dia Center for the Arts, including works from the 1960s through the 2020s. Since its opening in 2003, **Dia:Beacon** (3 Beekman St., Beacon, 845/440-0100, www.diabeacon.org, 10am-5pm Fri.-Mon., adults $15, seniors and students $12, under 12 free, reservations required), has played a pivotal role in transforming the town of Beacon into a thriving artists' community. Spacious single-artist galleries are flooded with natural light to showcase paintings, sculptures, and installations. On long-term view, four works by Mary Corse reflect and refract light to create unique viewing experiences. A 2020 installation, "May amnesia never kiss us on the mouth" examines how individuals bear witness to experiences of violence, loss, displacement, and forced migration through performance. Outside, the West Garden presents sweeping river views. The bookshop and café are open 10am-5pm Friday-Monday.

MADAM BRETT HOMESTEAD

The 1709 **Madam Brett Homestead** (50 Van Nydeck Ave., Beacon, 845/831-6533, www.melzingahnsdar.org, tours 1pm-4pm 2nd Sat. each month May-Dec. or by appointment, adults $5, students $2), another George Washington haunt and Dutchess County's oldest dwelling. Walk through 17 rooms filled with antiques, artwork, and seven generations' worth of Brett family memorabilia.

HOWLAND CULTURAL CENTER

On the National Historic Register, the **Howland Cultural Center** (477 Main St., Beacon, 845/831-4988, www. howlandculturalcenter.org) hosts art exhibits, performances, and other events. Depending on the season, you could catch the Juilliard

Beacon

© MOON.COM

Memorial Park

WILKES ST

MAPLE ST

LINCOLN ST

KENT ST

CANNON ST

VERPLANCK AVE

OAK ST

WALNUT ST

CROSS ST

WILLOW ST

FOX ST

RALPH ST

NORTH AVE

VERPLANCK AVE

TOMPKINS AVE

COLONIAL RD

BANK ST

W MAIN ST

BEEKMAN ST

RED FLYNN SR

RAILROAD DR

HERBERT ST

ACKERMAN ST

VERPLANCK AVE

NORTH ST

FISHKILL AVE

CHURCH ST

HENRY ST

CATHERINE ST

CHESTNUT ST

S CHESTNUT ST

VINE ST

TELLER AVE

CHURCHILL ST

N WALNUT ST

MAIN ST

BRETT ST

ELM ST

DEWINDT ST

SOUTH AVE

CLIFF ST

BEACON ST

WOLCOTT AVE

ROMBOUT AVE

SUKHOTHAI

THE ROUNDHOUSE AT BEACON FALLS

BEACON HOTEL

HOWLAND CULTURAL CENTER

BEACON PANTRY

MADAM BRETT HOMESTEAD

MAX'S ON MAIN

HOMESPUN FOODS

ARTISAN WINE SHOP

BEACON INSTITUTE FOR RIVERS AND ESTUARIES

HUDSON BEACH GLASS

KITCHEN SINK FOOD AND DRINK

BEACON CREAMERY

BANK SQUARE COFFEEHOUSE

BOTSFORD BRIAR B&B

DIA:BEACON

TRAIN STATION

LONG DOCK BEACON

Hudson River

Riverfront Park

Dennings Point

Long Dock Park

Inset map

To Fishkill

NEWBURGH-BEACON BRIDGE

To Newburgh

52

9D

84

FISHKILL AVE

MT BEACON TRAILHEAD

To Cold Spring

9D

MAP AREA

MAIN ST

WOLCOTT AVE

NORTH AVE

Hudson River

0 0.5 mi
0 0.5 km

0 100 yds
0 100 m

String Quartet, Broadway in Beacon, the A-Y Dancers, or a Latin-American artist festival.

MOUNT BEACON

A sign and trail map at the south end of town mark the starting point for a hike up **Mount Beacon** (4.4 miles round-trip, 1,000 vertical feet). Prepare to experience one of the toughest stair workouts around, and then reward yourself with aerial views of the Beacon-Newburgh Bridge and surrounding countryside. Your destination is the ruins of an old casino, which patrons reached via the world's steepest incline railway. Park in the recently improved lot at the intersection of Wolcott Avenue (Rte. 9D) and Howland Avenue, across from Bob's Corner Store.

MOUNT GULIAN HISTORIC SITE

Farther north on Route 9D, the **Mount Gulian Historic Site** (145 Sterling St., Beacon, 845/831-8172, www.mountgulian. org, tours at noon, 1pm, and 2pm Fri. and Sun. Apr. 30-Oct. 24, adults $10, seniors $8, children $5; reservations required) appears at the end of a row of modern townhouses. The 18th-century Dutch stone barn and 44 acres of gardens descending to the riverbank belonged to the Verplanck family and served as the headquarters of influential Revolutionary War General Friedrich Wilhelm Augustus von Steuben, a German volunteer who led the Americans to a critical victory at Freehold, New Jersey, in 1778. This site also holds significance in Black history of the region: Master gardener James F. Brown kept a first-person diary of his years on the estate, and it has been preserved as one of very few written records by a Black person of the time.

CLEARWATER

Beacon has become a something of a hub of environmental activity too. The Hudson River sloop *Clearwater* offers a great way to see and learn about the river ecosystem up close. In 1966, folk singer Pete Seeger announced he planned to build a boat to save the river. It was to be a replica of the boats that sailed the Hudson centuries ago. Seeger wanted to bring awareness to the problem of pollution, research the state of the water, and educate the public. The organization that Seeger founded, Hudson River Sloop Clearwater (724 Wolcott Ave., Beacon, 845/265-8080, www.clearwater. org), continues to host educational sailing trips and the annual **Clearwater's Great Hudson River Revival,** a wildly popular music and environmental festival held each year in mid-June.

BEACON INSTITUTE FOR RIVERS AND ESTUARIES

The **Beacon Institute for Rivers and Estuaries** (199 Main St., Beacon, 845/838-1600, www.bire.org, open daily except holidays), an extension of Clarkson University, aims to study and protect rivers, estuaries, and watersheds. Its gallery displays rotating works by local artists, mostly focused on the river. The organization also hosts youth summer science camps and organizes clean-up days at Denning's Point.

LONG DOCK PARK

Scenic Hudson operates **Long Dock Park** (23 Long Dock Rd., dawn-dusk daily year-round), a green space on the waterfront with a kayak launch and restored barn for community events. You can rent kayaks and stand-up paddleboards ($20 for 1 hour) from **Mountain Tops Outfitters** (144 Main St., Beacon, 845/831-1997, www.mountaintopsoutfitters. com, 11am-6pm Mon.-Sat., 11am-5pm Sun.). Stop by the shop to reserve gear midweek or go directly to Long Dock Park on the weekends. Bikes ($15 per hour) can be reserved through **Cold Spring Rental & Tours** (Long Dock Park, 347/638-7707, www. coldspringbikerentaltours.com, 9am-7pm daily). The **Klara Sauer Trail** (1 mile, easy) connects the park to the Beacon train station and **Denning's Point State Park.**

Fishkill and Wappingers Falls

Two miles east of Beacon, the signature steeple of the **First Reformed Church**

(55 Main St., Fishkill, 845/896-9836, www. fishkillreformed.org) marks the village center of Fishkill (Fisherman's Creek), a major hub of wartime activity during the American Revolution. The church dates to 1731 and served as both a New York State government meeting place and a prison. Today, the town primarily hosts business travelers.

One mile south of town at the highway interchange of I-84 and Route 9, the **Van Wyck Homestead Museum** (504 Rte. 9, at I-84, Fishkill, 845/896-9560, 1pm-4pm Sat.-Sun. June-Oct., donation) stands out among the surrounding group of chain hotels. Army officers and heads of state convened here during the American Revolution. The barracks and blacksmith shop that once surrounded the home are lost to history, but the town historical society continues to restore the inside with original documents and period furnishings.

Stony Kill Farm Environmental Education Center (79 Farmstead Lane, Wappingers Falls, 845/831-1617, www. stonykill.org, grounds sunrise-sunset daily year-round, greenhouse and barn 11am-1pm Sat.-Sun. Feb.-Nov.), run by the New York Department of Environmental Conservation, is perfect for a picnic, easy nature walk, and greenhouse tour. Look for one of two entrances off Route 9D (exit 11 from I-84). A tree-lined driveway leads to the Manor House and surrounding gardens. Inside, a visitors center houses an extensive library with titles on every nature topic you can think of, from acid rain to wildlife management to environmental literature. Several easy walking trails, ranging from 0.5 to 2.5 miles long, meander through evergreen and hardwood forests, across fields, and around ponds. Brochures for self-guided tours are available at each trailhead. The center holds special events throughout the year, including maple sugaring demonstrations, wildflower walks, a butterfly exhibit, and programs for children.

1: Main Street in Beacon 2: Fishkill Falls

Poughkeepsie

Poughkeepsie suffered the fate of postindustrial contraction worse than most—and has taken the longest to recover among riverside communities. The majority of the city's middle-class residents fled the city center for the suburbs during the late 20th century, leaving once-beautiful homes boarded up and a six-lane arterial in their wake. When IBM slashed its workforce by two-thirds in the early 1990s, scores of small businesses went under, and the local economy never fully recovered. And yet, this city of 31,000 retains a few historical gems—like the Bardavon 1869 Opera House. Trendy restaurants come and go along once deserted Main Street, and the waterfront has come back to life. With the proximity of Vassar College and the Culinary Institute of America, it was only a matter of time.

Poughkeepsie's Main Street begins at Waryas Park under the Mid-Hudson Bridge and runs east-west between the two legs of the arterial (Rte. 44 and Rte. 55) until it reaches the town of Arlington. The Hudson River Sloop *Clearwater* and its sister vessel, *Mystic Whaler*, dock here when they are in the area, as Poughkeepsie is the headquarters for the nonprofit environmental organization that runs them. Modeled after the Dutch vessels that sailed the Hudson in the late 18th century, *Clearwater* was conceived in the 1960s as a call to action to clean up the river before it was too late. In a unique classroom setting, *Clearwater* volunteers educate local residents about the importance of environmental awareness and conservation. Since 1966, the watchdog organization has battled GE on the dumping of PCBs into the river, prosecuted Clean Water Act offenders, and pioneered the model of encouraging environmental advocacy through a hands-on sailing experience.

Moving away from the riverfront, a number of historic sites are clustered in the downtown area near Academy Street. Top among them is the **Bardavon 1869 Opera House** (35 Market St., Poughkeepsie, 845/473-5288, box office 845/338-6088, www.bardavon.

Poughkeepsie

org), which escaped demolition in the mid-1970s only to become listed on the National Register of Historic Places. With its original pipe organ (a 1928 Wurlitzer theater organ), and an interior dome that dates to 1920, the Bardavon is one of the oldest surviving theaters in the United States. Legendary performers from Mark Twain to Frank Sinatra have appeared on its stage. Today, the theater hosts the Hudson Valley Philharmonic and a full schedule of musical, dance, film, and theater productions by contemporary artists, as well as virtual performances and classic films. It also regularly presents at the Ulster Performing Arts Center in Kingston and Bethel Woods Center for the Arts.

Samuel B. Morse became a household name in the 1840s when he developed the first commercial telegraph, sending the famous words "What hath God wrought" across the line. With money earned from the venture, Morse bought **Locust Grove** (2683 South Rd., Poughkeepsie, 845/454-4500, www.lgny.org, 10am-5pm daily), a 100-acre property south of the Mid-Hudson Bridge that is now a national historic landmark. The Italianate villa houses an informative exhibit on telegraph technology, as well as American and European furniture and many of Morse's own paintings. But the surrounding woods and gardens are the real draw. In the tradition of 19th century landscape design, Morse had his estate sculpted to frame particular views, with carriage roads leading from one vista to the next. The original kitchen garden has been preserved as the Heritage Vegetable Garden for visitors to experience today. Tours are available Saturday and Sunday at 10:15am,

11:30am, 12:45pm, 2pm, and 3:15pm for $15 per person, or weekdays by appointment for $25 per person.

Walkway Over the Hudson State Historic Park

A 1.3-mile-long span connects downtown Poughkeepsie to Highland, more than 200 feet above the Hudson River. Formerly known as the 1889 Poughkeepsie-Highland Railroad Bridge, which was destroyed by a fire in 1974, the **Walkway Over the Hudson** (www.walkway.org, 7am-sunset daily, weather permitting) is the longest elevated pedestrian bridge in the world and connects to rail trails in both Dutchess and Ulster Counties. Wheelchairs can access the park from both sides, and visitors with mobility needs may use motorized scooters or power-assisted vehicles. On warm days, vendors may be selling frozen treats and kettle corn at either end.

To start at the east side, drive Route 9 to Route 9G north. Bear right onto Washington Street and continue for half a mile. Turn left on Route 9G/Parker Avenue and park at the lot on the left (61 Parker Ave., $5 for 4 hours). The west side parking lot is located at 87 Haviland Road, Highland.

Near the walkway on the Poughkeepsie side, the **Mid-Hudson Children's Museum** (75 N. Water St., Poughkeepsie, 845/471-0589, http://mhcm.org, 9:30am-5pm Tues.-Sat., 11am-5pm Sun., $9) brings art and science to life for the little ones. If you live anywhere close to the location, a membership here is well worth the cost. Renovations were ongoing in late 2021, with no estimated date of completion.

Vassar College

Between downtown Poughkeepsie and Arlington is the ivory tower of Vassar College, a top-ranked liberal arts school that draws students from across the country and around the world. Vassar's attractive campus is spread over 1,000 acres with some 200 varieties of trees interspersed among inviting lawns. English brewer Matthew Vassar founded the

college in 1861 in an effort to provide young women with courses in science, math, art history, and music to rival those of the best men's schools in the country. Vassar remained a women's college until 1969, when the first coed class was admitted.

Vassar prides itself on being first among U.S. colleges to have established its own art gallery. Today, the **Frances Lehman Loeb Art Center** (124 Raymond Ave., Poughkeepsie, 845/437-5632 or 845/437-5237, http://fllac.vassar.edu, 10am-5pm Tues.-Wed. and Fri.-Sun., 10am-7pm Thurs., free) holds a varied permanent collection, from ancient Egyptian sculptures of marble and red granite to contemporary American paintings. The museum stays open late on Thursday evenings. Enter the gallery near the main gate on Raymond Avenue.

East of Vassar College, where Route 55 meets the Taconic State Parkway, **James Baird State Park** (845/452-1489, www.nysparks.com, hours vary seasonally) has an 18-hole golf course, tennis courts, picnic areas, and hiking trails. Its wooded trails are popular with local runners, while families use the playground and attend programs at the nature center on summer weekends.

Back at the river's edge, Matthew Vassar's former home is now the **Springside National Historic Site** (185 Academy St., Poughkeepsie, 845/454-2060, www.springsidelandmark.org, dawn-dusk daily, no restrooms), preserved as the last standing design of landscape architect Andrew Jackson Downing. Most of the estate's 44 acres belong to a private condominium complex now, but visitors can view the restored gatehouse and wander along old carriage roads. Look for the entrance on Academy Street, on the west side of Route 9.

Hyde Park

If you love to study the past and travel to eat, Hyde Park is your town. Springwood, the **Home of Franklin D. Roosevelt National Historic Site** (Rte. 9, Hyde Park, 845/229-5320 or 800/337-8474, www.nps.gov/hofr, tour times vary, combined entry adults $20 for 2 days or single site $10, under age 16 free, grounds dawn-dusk daily, free), where the four-term president lived all his life, houses FDR's presidential library and museum. Exhibits inside chronicle the president's and first lady's achievements. Allow at least two hours to see this site. Plan another two hours for a tour of nearby **Top Cottage** (7097 Albany Post Rd./Rte. 9, Hyde Park, 845/229-5320, www.nps.gov/hofr, Wed.-Sun. May-Oct., $10), the hilltop retreat where FDR met with international heads of state. Trails on 300 acres lead to the river's edge.

Eleanor Roosevelt spent many quiet years at the unassuming Val-Kill Cottage after FDR's death. Today, the **Eleanor Roosevelt National Historic Site—Val-Kill** (Rte. 9G, Hyde Park, 845/229-9422, www.nps.gov/elro, 9am-5pm daily May-Oct., tours 1pm and 3pm Thurs.-Mon. Nov.-Apr., $10) welcomes visitors with guided home tours and 180 acres of beautifully landscaped grounds (8am-7pm daily).

Between Hyde Park and Rhinebeck along Route 9 stands a tribute to the Gilded Age: the former residence of Ogden Mills—a financier and philanthropist—and Ruth Livingston Mills, a descendent of the Livingston family, who first settled much of Columbia County. The home began as a 25-room Greek Revival in 1832. Subsequent renovations by the same architectural firm that built the Vanderbilt Estate turned it into a massive 65-room estate adorned with exquisite furnishings from Europe and Asia. The property was handed over to the State of New York in 1938 to become the **Staatsburgh State Historic Site** (Old Post Rd., Staatsburg, 845/889-8851, http://parks.ny.gov, 11am-4pm Sat.-Sun. Jan.-Mar., 11am-5pm Tues.-Sun. Apr.-Oct., call for Nov.-Dec. schedule, adults $6, seniors and students $4, under age 13 free).

Milea Estate Vineyard (40 Hollow Circle Rd., Staatsburg, 845/264-0403, www.mileaestatevineyard.com, noon-6pm Wed.-Thurs., noon-8pm Fri.-Sat., noon-6pm Sun.) entered the local wine scene in 2017 with an award-winning chardonnay as well as a well-received riesling and pinot noir. Also on the premises, **Valia's Wood-Fired Oven Pizza** ($20-25) serves the weekend crowd starting at 4:30pm on Fridays and from 12:30pm on Saturdays and Sundays. Outside food is not permitted at the winery.

Train enthusiasts, save time to visit the **Hyde Park Railroad Station** (34 River Rd., Hyde Park, 845/229-2338, www.hydeparkstation.com, 5pm-9pm Mon., noon-5pm Sat.-Sun. and holidays June-Sept., adults $5, children $4). Built in 1914, the station was restored by the Hudson Valley Railroad Society and holds a treasured place on the National Register of Historic Places. The first Monday of the month is Hobby Night (7pm-9pm), and on the second Monday, the Hudson Valley Railroad Society offers railroad history programs. Follow River Road from Route 9 in Hyde Park.

Vanderbilt Estate

Take yourself right back to the Gilded Age with a tour inside the **Vanderbilt Estate** (Rte. 9, Hyde Park, 845/229-7770, www.nps.gov/vama, 10am-3pm Fri.-Mon., adults $10, under age 15 $1). The 50-room home of Frederick and Louise Vanderbilt exhibits a variety of interior design influences, from Renaissance to rococo. Note the carved wooden ceiling in the formal dining room, one of many European antiques found by designer Stanford White.

Though they only spent a few weeks per year at the estate, the Vanderbilts enjoyed it as a place to entertain guests, who arrived by boat, rail, or private car. Thirteen rooms on the third floor were reserved as quarters for the maids of lady visitors. Outside, the property remains as beautiful today as it did a century ago. Local residents meet here on weekends to play Frisbee and picnic on the lawn. Contemporary artists often set up

1: view from the Walkway Over the Hudson
2: hors d'oeuvres served at the Culinary Institute of America 3: the remains of a casino atop Mount Beacon 4: the Vanderbilt Estate in Hyde Park

canvases to paint the river and surrounding landscape. The grounds are open 8am-7pm daily and there is no entry fee. The **Hyde Park Trail** system connects the Roosevelt and Vanderbilt estates along the river. Inquire at either of the sites for a trail map.

★ Culinary Institute of America

Since 1970, Hyde Park has claimed the oldest culinary college in the United States, the prestigious **Culinary Institute of America** (1946 Campus Dr., Hyde Park, 845/451-1588, www.ciachef.edu, tours at 2pm Wed. and Fri. when school is in session, $8, reservations required). Set on a picturesque riverside campus, formerly the site of a Jesuit seminary, the CIA trains aspiring professionals and enthusiasts in the art of fine cuisine. Its New York Campus facilities include 41 kitchens and the largest collection of culinary books and reference materials of any library in the country.

Tour the grounds on your own at sunset before dining in one of the five public restaurants on campus. Or book a guided tour led by a current CIA student. Better yet, enroll in one of the CIA's **Boot Camp** culinary vacation programs, which are multiday intensive courses geared toward cooking enthusiasts. Classes cover a variety of rotating topics, such as Flavors of the Hudson Valley, Italian Cuisine, and Pastries. Tuition runs $975 for two days and $2,250 for five days. Other one-day events open to the public include butchery demonstrations ($125), baking classes ($250), and wine-food pairings ($125).

The institute operates five restaurants on its New York campus: **American Bounty** (845/451-1011, www.americanbountyrestaurant.com, $22-31) has been the mainstay, with menus that showcase the local harvest. **The Bocuse** (845/451-1012, www.bocuserestaurant.com, $26-34, 3-course prix-fixe $42) brings contemporary French cuisine to life. More casual **Post Road Brew House** (845/451-1015, $14-22) serves pub fare and craft beers. **Ristorante Caterina de' Medici & Al Forno Trattoria** (845/451-1013,

www.ristorantecaterinademedici.com, $14-28) does a pretty good job at creating the ambience of a Tuscan villa. And the ever-popular **Apple Pie Bakery Café** (845/905-4500, www.applepiebakerycafe.com, $11-14) got a fresh coat of paint plus a new modern look in 2018—and most importantly, the makeover included the introduction of table service to alleviate long lines. Current information for all of these venues is published at www.ciarestaurantgroup.com.

Rhinebeck

Continuing north on Route 9, upscale Rhinebeck is a gathering place for second-home owners and weekend warriors in an otherwise rural region. Victorian, Colonial, and Greek Revival buildings line several blocks of boutique stores, country inns, and gourmet restaurants expanding out from the intersection of Routes 9 and 308. Route 9 is called Mill Street south of Route 308, and Montgomery Street north of Route 308; Route 308 is also called Market Street.

At the center of all the activity is the 1766 **Beekman Arms** (Rte. 9, Rhinebeck, 845/876-7077, www.beekmandelamaterinn.com), reportedly the oldest continuously operating inn in the United States. Colonial history and political intrigue rise from every creak in the floorboards. George Washington, Philip Schuyler, Benedict Arnold, and Alexander Hamilton are among the most famous overnight guests. Local townspeople gathered inside for safety while the British burned Kingston to the ground across the Hudson.

As Rhinebeck grew into a commercial crossroads, the inn became a popular venue for political and cultural discussion. FDR even delivered several victory speeches from the front porch. The inn has expanded over the years, but much of the original building remains intact, including the oak beams and pine plank floor. The place is worth a peek, whether or not you plan to stay the night.

Next door to the Beekman Arms, FDR oversaw construction of the **Rhinebeck Post**

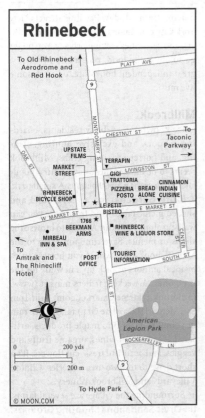

Rhinebeck

To Old Rhinebeck Aerodrome and Red Hook

PLATT AVE

9

MONTGOMERY ST

CHESTNUT ST

To Taconic Parkway →

OAK ST

UPSTATE FILMS

MARKET STREET

TERRAPIN

LIVINGSTON ST

GIGI ▼TRATTORIA

PIZZERIA BREAD INDIAN POSTO ALONE CUISINE

CINNAMON

RHINEBECK BICYCLE SHOP ■

LE PETIT BISTRO

E MARKET ST

W MARKET ST

1766 ★

BEEKMAN ARMS

■ RHINEBECK WINE & LIQUOR STORE

MIRBEAU INN & SPA

CENTER ST

To Amtrak and The Rhinecliff Hotel

POST OFFICE

TOURIST INFORMATION

SOUTH ST

MILL ST

American Legion Park

ROCKEFELLER LN

0   200 yds

0   200 m

9

To Hyde Park

© MOON.COM

---

dramatic landscape. With ties to the prominent Beekman and Livingston families, this fanciful Queen Anne country home began as an Italianate villa in the mid-19th century. Carefully planned trails, vistas, and lawns around the property reflect the Romantic-era aesthetic.

North of town, the **Dutchess County Fairgrounds** holds antique car shows and the annual **Dutchess County Fair.** Amtrak services the train station in Rhinecliff, three miles to the west.

Red Hook

The sleepy town of Red Hook received its name when early Dutch explorers ventured up the Hudson to find red sumac and Virginia creeper in full bloom. The Dutch called it Red Hoek (Red Peninsula), and the name has stuck ever since. A modern-day bedroom community, Red Hook encompasses the Village of Tivoli and the hamlet of Annandale-on-Hudson on the banks of the river, as well as Bard College and the Village of Red Hook to the east. A small commercial district fans out from the intersection of Routes 9 and 199, with a John Deere store, a CVS pharmacy, Stewarts, and a few casual eateries.

A rocker on the North Porch is the best seat in the house at **Montgomery Place** (River Rd., Annandale-on-Hudson, 845/758-5461, www.bard.edu, 10:30am-2:30pm Sat. May-Oct., adults $10, grounds free). Nestled among 434 acres of woodlands with views of the Catskill Mountains across the Hudson, Montgomery Place is a stunning riverside estate conceived in the Federal style. Located in Annandale-on-Hudson, the home has been restored with period furnishings and enchanting gardens. Fruit from the estate orchards is available in season at the Montgomery Place Orchards Farm Stand. Bard College acquired this property for $18 million from Historic Hudson Valley in 2016. The college has started hosting Salon Series events at Montgomery Place to facilitate discussions on climate change and sustainable agriculture, and its Fisher Center launched a free outdoor series

---

Office (6383 Mill St.) through the Works Progress Administration (WPA). The building was designed to commemorate the first house in Rhinebeck. Inside, a series of murals chronicle the town's history. The **Dutch Reformed Church** (16 Albany Post Rd., Hyde Park, 845/229-5354), across Route 9 from the post office, was built in 1808.

Idyllic family farms and grand country estates surround the town of Rhinebeck. **Wilderstein** (330 Morton Rd., Rhinebeck, 845/876-4818, www.wilderstein.org, noon-4pm Thurs.-Sun. May-Oct., noon-4pm Sat.-Sun. Dec., guided tours by reservation at 1pm, 2pm, and 3pm, adults $11, students and seniors $10, under age 12 free), a riverside mansion located south of town on Route 9, has a five-story round tower that juts upward from its center, offering views of an equally of film, music, and dance events on the lawn in fall 2018.

Many of the undergraduate students at **Bard College** (Rte. 9G, Annandale, 845/758-6822, www.bard.edu) have views of the Hudson and Catskill Mountains from their dorms. An affiliate of Columbia University, the liberal arts school recently doubled in size to encompass 1,000 acres of lawns and woodlands. A variety of music and performing arts programs are open to the public year-round. You can drop into the indoor pool and fitness center for a day pass fee (beware of ongoing petty theft issues in the locker rooms). Five minutes' drive from campus, **Tivoli** has a handful of restaurants frequented by college professors. Just over the border in Columbia County, **Germantown** has a small grocer, **Otto's Market** (215 Main St., Germantown, 518/537-7200, http://ottosmarket.com, 8am-7pm Thurs.-Tues.), and an outstanding destination restaurant, **Gaskins** (2 Church Ave., Germantown, 518/537-2107, http://gaskinsny.com, 5pm-9pm Thurs.-Sun.).

CENTRAL DUTCHESS COUNTY: ROUTES 44 AND 22

Pawling

Routes 22 and 55 meet at Pawling, in the southeastern corner of Dutchess County. Named after Colonel Henry Beekman's daughter, Catherine Pawling, the town has been a crossroads of commercial activity since colonial days. Pawling's early settlers were Quakers, as documented by the display of artifacts in the **Quaker Museum, Akin Free Library** (378 Old Quaker Hill Rd., Pawling, 607/684-3785, www.akinfreelibrary.org). The library hosts occasional book signings and film series. The 1764 **Oblong Friends Meeting House** (Meeting House Rd., Pawling, by appointment only) served as a temporary hospital for George Washington's troops in 1778, and Washington set up headquarters in the **John Kane House** (www.pawling-history.org). Inside is a replica of the village from the year 1948, complete with

moving trains. Today, Pawling attracts New York City commuters, Appalachian Trail hikers, and celebrities seeking privacy. You might go to enjoy the food, rent a bike, browse a great independent bookstore, or catch some live music.

Millbrook

Once known for celebrity residents, boarding schools, and exclusive hunting, fishing, and horseback riding clubs, Millbrook seems to be quieter these days, with a population of less than 1,500 people. A small park, **Tribute Gardens,** has a playground and shaded picnic tables, and from here you can walk up along Franklin Avenue to browse the shops or menus. Save time for a trip to the Merritt Bookstore, where you browse titles by local authors or pick up a new toy for the little ones. A weekly farmers market (www.millbrooknyfarmersmarket.com, 9am-1pm Sat. Memorial Day-late Oct.) takes place rain or shine. You can find maple products, artisanal breads, local wines, organic fruits and veggies, and beautiful fresh-cut flowers. It's a short drive to the two area wineries, Clinton Vineyards and Millbrook Winery.

Surrounding the village are several farms, the **Orvis Sandanona Shooting Grounds,** and the Millbrook Golf & Tennis Club (members only). Look for the historic **Nine Partners Meeting House and Cemetery,** a local landmark at the eastern edge of the golf course and the intersection of Route 343 and Church Street. The building is not open to the public, but its's neat to see a structure built in 1780 that's still used for Monthly Meetings today.

The scenic rural roads that surround Millbrook make for ideal running and cycling. A popular route is to follow the **Dutchess Wine Trail,** which isn't exactly a trail, but a joint marketing effort of two local vineyards: **Millbrook Vineyards & Winery** (26 Wing Rd., Millbrook, 845/677-8383, www.millbrookwine.com, noon-5pm Mon.-Thurs., noon-6pm Fri.-Sun., tastings $12.50, tasting and tour $15) introduced French hybrid grapes to the region and makes an outstanding chardonnay. The winery also hosts occasional jazz concerts and an October harvest party. A few miles away, **Clinton Vineyards** (450 Shultzville Rd., Clinton Corners, 845/266-5372, www.clintonvineyards.com, 1pm-5pm Sat.-Sun. Apr.-Dec.) is known for its seyval blanc and an estate-bottled pinot noir. Tastings are $18-40 pp.

The **Cary Institute of Ecosystem Studies** (Rte. 44 E., Millbrook, 845/677-5343, www.caryinstitute.org, Apr.-Oct.) maintains a 2,000-acre outdoor campus for field research, with some short trails open to the public. The **Cary Pines Trail** (1.3 miles) meanders across a meadow and through a stand of white pines, while the **Wappinger Creek Trail** (1.25 miles) leads through a grove of sugar maples. Both are easy routes to navigate and complete.

★ Innisfree Garden

Mist hangs over the pond on chilly mornings at the celebrated 200-acre **Innisfree Garden** (362 Tyrrell Rd., Millbrook, 845/677-8000, www.innisfreegarden.org, 10am-5pm Wed.-Sun. May-Oct., $10, cash only). Inspired by ancient Chinese and Japanese gardens, the property applies Eastern ideas of design and motion to a decidedly American landscape.

Harvard landscape architect Lester Collins is the mastermind behind the project, which started in the 1930s as an ambitious collaboration with local residents Walter and Marion Beck. Their collective vision resulted in a lush display of natural elements that has stood the test of time.

The largest rocks have names: Turtle, Dragon, Owl. And every stone, tree, and chair seems arranged with a purpose in mind—to frame a view or reveal a special flower. When the bugs aren't too bad, you can slip into an Adirondack chair and read a book or simply watch, listen, and think. Allow about 90 minutes to explore the entire park.

The Harlem Valley

Continuing northeast from Millbrook, Route 44 enters the scenic Harlem Valley, which follows the west side of the Taconic Range and the Connecticut border from Pawling to Pine Plains. The land here is sparsely populated, with only a few thousand residents per town, and much of it is permanently protected from development. Taconic State Park, Stissing Mountain Forest, and the Harlem Valley Rail Trail are among the largest wilderness areas.

From the west, Route 44 winds downhill to meet Route 22 at the rural town of Amenia and the historic **Troutbeck resort** (515 Leedsville Rd., Amenia, 845/789-1555,

MID-HUDSON VALLEY
DUTCHESS COUNTY

www.troutbeck.com). Named in 1765 for its counterpart in England, Troutbeck was founded by literary-minded farmers who knew the likes of Emerson and Thoreau. Sycamore trees and flower gardens surround the original stone house. In the early 20th century, Sinclair Lewis, Ernest Hemingway, and Theodore Roosevelt were frequent guests of Troutbeck's second owners, Joel and Amy Spingarn. Joel Spingarn was instrumental in the founding of the NAACP and served as the organization's second president. The inn modernized itself in 2017 to attract a new generation of romantics, locavores, adventurers, and creative types. Now it has 17 guest rooms and suites in the main house, with a separate four-bedroom cottage. The dining room serves farm-to-table food and is open to the public.

Perched high above the valley at 1,200 feet elevation, **Wethersfield** (noon-5pm Fri.-Sun. June-Sept., garden tour $10, house and garden $20) presents another opportunity to view a picturesque country estate from the early 20th century. The three-acre formal garden represents the classical Italian style, with sculptures and a topiary, terraces, and an extensive plant list. The Wilderness Garden encompasses a seven-acre forest with a carriage road

surrounding it. Reservations are required for guided tours. Hiking and horse trails (hikers $5, equestrians $20) stay open for a longer season (Apr.-Nov.).

South of Amenia on Route 22 is Wassaic and the terminus for the Harlem Valley Line of the Metro-North commuter rail. The ride to Grand Central Station takes about two hours, with a transfer in Southeast. If traveling by bike, you can pick up the **Harlem Valley Rail Trail** (10.7 miles paved with rolling hills) from the train station, heading over to Millerton.

The Crown Maple brand syrup you see in many gourmet food stores comes from a farm in this part of Dutchess County, **Crown Maple** (47 McCourt Rd., Dover Plains, 845/877-0640, www.crownmaple.com). Purists would argue their infused maple products stray too far from the real thing, but they certainly have captured the imagination and attention of the press. The farm opens to the public for occasional events; check Facebook for details.

★ Millerton

A scenic location in the Harlem Valley, close proximity to the Housatonic River in Connecticut, and a bevy of antiques stores

a row of Adirondack chairs on the lawn at Innisfree Garden

Millerton

© MOON.COM

have put Millerton into the spotlight. Founded in 1851, the town once served as a railroad hub for this part of New York State. Today, it's become a thriving center for cycling, farm-to-table experiences, and the arts.

At the entrance to the Harlem Valley Rail Trail stands a one-room schoolhouse, restored to hold the town's visitors center. Pop in to the **Irondale Schoolhouse** (16 Main St., Millerton, www.irondaleschoolhouse.org, 11am-4pm Sat.-Sun. May-mid Oct.) for maps and current event info. Then wander over to the much-loved **Harney & Sons Tea Shop & Tasting Room** (13 Main St., Millerton, 518/789-2121, www.harney.com, 10am-5pm Wed.-Sat., 11am-4pm Sun., $8-17), which occupies a prominent location next to a small town park. This is the site of the Saturday morning **Millerton Farmers' Market** (Millerton Methodist Church, Dutchess Ave.

and Main St., www.neccmillerton.org, 10am-2pm Sat. May-Dec., 2nd and 4th Sat. only Jan.-Apr.). While you're there, check out what's showing at **The UnGallery** (10am-noon Sat. May-Oct.), an informal outdoor space next to the market for local artists to present their work.

Catch a first-run indie film or live HD streaming of the Metropolitan Opera, Bolshoi Ballet, and National Theater Live at **The Moviehouse** (48 Main St., Millerton, 860/435-2897, www.themoviehouse.net, adults $11.50, under age 12 $7.50).

A self-guided walking tour of the village starts at the schoolhouse and takes in 26 sites, including The Moviehouse and North East-Millerton Library. Pick up a brochure with directions at Oblong Books & Music, Harney's Tea, Irondale Schoolhouse, or Irving Farm. In autumn, you might time a visit with the annual **Fall for Art** festival, when the entire village turns into one large gallery.

Beyond the village proper, you'll find several organic farms and the **Rudd Pond Area** in Taconic State Park (59 Rudd Dr., Millerton, 518/789-3059, http://parks.ny.gov, summer weekends and holidays $7). You can swim (8am-6pm daily summer) in the pond, or pick up food to go at McEnroe's Organic Farm and just enjoy a pond-side picnic. If you want to stay overnight, there are tent sites ($15-22).

About 13 miles west of Millerton (about 20 minutes' drive), **Stissing Mountain** has a fire tower with panoramic views, if you're willing to climb the stairs after a steep-ish two-mile hike from the parking lot near Thompson Pond Reserve (Lake Rd., Pine Plains). Note that the state Department of Environmental Conservation maintains a 590-acre multiple use area here that spans the towns of Milan, Pine Plains, and Stanford in Dutchess County, but you can't access the fire tower from the public land.

RECREATION
Winter Sports

Cross-country skiers have good options in Dutchess County if Mother Nature brings enough snow. The golf course at Baird Park (11 kilometers) has rolling hills for a good workout. Mills Norrie State Park has a variety of terrain on trails and old carriage roads. The Harlem Valley Rail Trail (10.7 miles) and Dutchess County Rail Trails are paved routes but not plowed in winter. In Pawling, head to Lakeside Park or The Great Swamp after a winter storm.

The **McCann Ice Arena** (Mid-Hudson Civic Center, 14 Civic Center Plaza, Poughkeepsie, 845/454-5800, www.midhudsonciviccenter.org, 10am-5:30pm Mon.-Fri., noon-4pm Sat.) offers public skating sessions year-round.

If the winter is cold and the ice thick, head to Tivoli Bay to see the local ice boating experts sail the river. The Hudson Valley has its very own **Ice Yacht Club**

(http://hudsonrivericeyachting.blogspot.com and www.hriyc.org, Jan.-Feb.).

Hiking

A 30-mile stretch of the **Appalachian Trail** (AT) passes through the hills of Dutchess County, connecting the towns of East Fishkill, Dover Plains, Beekman, and Pawling along the way. Several well-marked access areas have trailside parking. In Stormville, find one on Route 52, three miles east of the Taconic State Parkway. In Poughquag, the area is at the intersection of Routes 55 and 216 or Depot Hill Road, off Route 216. In Pawling, it's on Route 22, north of town. Note that mountain bikes are not allowed on the AT.

Many shorter hikes await across the county: **Pawling Nature Reserve** (Quaker Lake Rd., Pawling, 914/244-3271, www.nature.org), on 1,000 acres owned by the Nature Conservancy, has a few loops around Quaker Lake and the smaller French Lake. For example, the **Blue Trail** (2.2 miles) is an easy loop that stays clear of the AT. Short but steep, **Stissing Mountain** (2 miles round-trip) rewards hikers with views from a fire tower.

Scenic Hudson maintains a 1,000-acre park on **Fishkill Ridge** (Sunnyside Rd., Fishkill) with a network of well-marked trails that present dramatic views of the surrounding wilderness and Hudson River below. The **Overlook Trail** (1.75 miles) starts on Sunnyside Road in Fishkill and ascends the ridge in a series of steep switchbacks to meet the **White Trail** (4.6 miles), which starts on Pocket Road in Beacon. Another way to reach Fishkill Ridge is to start at the **Mount Beacon Trailhead** and take the Casino Trail to the Yellow Trail, which connects to the White Trail. The entire hike covers 7.7 miles; allow 5-6 hours for this challenge. All of these routes make for very strenuous hiking over rocky terrain. Detailed trail maps are available at www.scenichudson.org and http://hikethehudsonvalley.com.

1: the paved Harlem Valley Rail Trail **2:** the start of the Harlem Valley Rail Trail at the Wassaic train station **3:** the Housatonic River near Millerton

NO
MOTOR
VEHICLES

H V R T

PATROLLED
BY SHERIFFS
ON ATV'S

Start!
Walking
Path

ALL PETS
MUST BE
ON A LEASH

PLEASE CLEAN UP
AFTER YOUR PET

For a much easier urban stroll, try the **Walkway Loop Trail** (4.4 miles) in Poughkeepsie, which combines a walk across the pedestrian bridge with a second crossing over the Mid-Hudson Bridge to complete the loop. In Hyde Park at Val-Kill, **Eleanor's Walk** (1-mile loop) follows an old road around the lower part of the property, while the **Top Cottage Trail** (2 miles round-trip) climbs to the top of a hill for aerial views of the estate.

Cycling and Mountain Biking

Whether you are riding off-road or on pavement, Dutchess County presents terrain to suit all levels. The scenery alternates between rolling hills, village streets, and Hudson River vistas. The **Mid Hudson Bicycle Club** (http://midhudsonbicycleclub.org) organizes road rides in six levels according to pace and difficulty of the terrain. The **Dutchess County Rail Trail** (13 miles, www.dutchessrailtrail.com) is a paved path that begins at the former Hopewell Junction train depot and connects to the Walkway Over the Hudson (www.walkway.org). From the river, cyclists can continue another four miles into Ulster County. Road crossings are well marked, and there are several parking areas along the trail.

A 10-mile section of the more remote **Harlem Valley Rail Trail** (www.hvrt.org) begins at the Wassaic train station on Route 22 and reaches Millerton near the Harney & Sons tea shop. The path follows the tracks of the old New York and Harlem Railroad, through wooded forests, grassy meadows, and pastured farmland. It has fewer road crossings than the Dutchess County Rail Trail and is paved the entire way for foot and bike traffic.

The always busy **Bikeway** (1581 Rte. 376, Wappingers Falls, 845/463-7433, www.bikeway.com, 10am-8pm Mon., 10am-6pm Tues.-Wed. and Fri.-Sat., 11am-8pm Thurs.) is the biggest shop around and most convenient to the Dutchess County Rail Trail, but it does not have rentals. Farther north, **Rhinebeck Bicycle Shop** (10 Garden St., Rhinebeck, 845/876-4025, www.rhinebeckbicycleshop. com, 10am-5:30pm Tues.-Sat.) is a Fuji and Giant dealer, and offers repairs and rentals. It has a second location in Kingston called **The Famous Bike Brothers** (139 Boices Lane, 845/336-5581, www.bikebrosny.com).

Mountain biking continues to be a developing sport in this area. Pawling has the **Lakeside Mountain Bike Trail** with 8.4 miles of mostly intermediate level singletrack. Pleasant Valley has the **Taconic Hereford Multiple Use Area,** which locals call "909" because it's that many acres big. This trail system revolves around a four-mile-long dirt road with singletrack loops and connectors branching off, some of them quite technical, for a total of 22 miles. Park on Tyrell Road, off the Taconic Parkway.

Golf

Visiting golfers have a dozen or more public courses to choose from in Dutchess County. The best one for the money is **The Links at Union Vale** (153 N. Parliman Rd., LaGrangeville, 845/223-1000, http://luvgolf.com, 7am-7pm daily, $32-41 for 18 holes walking, $51-70 riding Mon.-Fri., $41-67 walking, $54-97 riding Sat.-Sun. and holidays). The **Harp & Eagle Pub** ($8-14) opens at 11am daily in summer and serves Irish Breakfast (7am-11am Sat.-Sun.).

The **Beekman Golf Course** (11 Country Club Rd., Hopewell Junction, 845/226-7700, www.beekmangolf.com, Sat.-Sun. $30-59, Mon.-Fri. $30-44) offers 27 holes, a driving range, and quick eats at the **Beekman Bar & Grill.**

To combine a round of golf with the historic sites in Hyde Park, check out **Casperkill Golf Club** (110 Golf Club Lane, Poughkeepsie, 845/463-0900, http://casperkillgolf.com, Mon.-Fri. $35, Sat.-Sun. $55, no denim). Built in 1944, the course runs along a creek in a residential area that is set back from the busy commercial corridor along Route 9 (South Rd.).

Vassar College has a basic nine-hole course on campus that plays first-come, first-serve: **Vassar Golf Course** (124 Raymond

Ave., Poughkeepsie, 845/473-9838, http://vassargolfcourse.com, $11-13 for 9 holes, no tee times).

Swimming and Boating

Kids love to slip and slide down the tubes at **SplashDown Beach Water Park** (16 Old Rte. 9, West Fishkill, 845/897-9600, www.splashdownbeach.com, 10am-6pm daily May-mid-June, 10am-7pm late June-Labor Day, adults $39, children under 42 inches and seniors $32). "Beach" is a misnomer, however; there is no water here aside from that in the park's own pools, and the place gets crazy crowded on weekends.

Kayakers can paddle lakes, ponds, creeks, and the Hudson River in Dutchess County. **The River Connection** (9 W. Market St., Hyde Park, 845/229-0595, www.the-river-connection.com) offers water sports instruction as well as equipment sales and rentals. Certified instructors lead trips from various launch points along the river, including Norrie Point (Staatsburg), Tivoli, Croton Point, and Poughkeepsie. The outfitter occasionally offers two-hour "Getaway" paddles as well.

The **Hyde Park Marina** (31 River Point Rd., Poughkeepsie, 845/473-8283, http://hydreparkmarina.com) offers temporary docking for bass boats in the spring striper fishing seasons for $80 per week. The shop is a good resource for info on local tides too.

Fishing and Hunting

Anglers will be hard-pressed to choose among the many streams, lakes, and ponds in Dutchess County—although many require a boat to get to the action. And of course, there's also the **Hudson River** itself, where striper fishing in the spring is the main draw. In winter, check conditions at **Sylvan Lake, Upton Lake,** or **Stissing Pond** for ice fishing opportunities.

The **Orvis Sandanona Shooting Grounds** (3047 Sharon Rd., Millbrook, 845/677-9701, www.orvis.com, 9am-5pm daily) offers fly-fishing lessons (Apr.-Oct.) and guided trips to nearby trout waters, including the Roeliff Jansen Kill, Wappingers Creek, and Housatonic River in Connecticut. The club also provides instruction in the English Churchill method of shooting clays (year-round). You can test your marksmanship at the annual Orvis Cup held in September each year.

Aviation

Private pilots and aviation enthusiasts, make sure to plan a weekend visit to the **Old Rhinebeck Aerodrome** (9 Norton Rd., Red Hook, 845/752-3200, www.oldrhinebeck.org, museum 10am-5pm daily May-Oct., adults $12). It hosts dazzling air shows (2pm-4pm Sat.-Sun.) every weekend during summer and fall, complete with vintage fashion shows. The museum's collection of antique aircraft includes working models dating back to the early 20th century. Book ahead to take a biplane ride.

Yoga and Spas

The Rhinebeck campus of the nationally known **Omega Institute for Holistic Studies** (150 Lake Dr., Rhinebeck, 845/266-4444, www.eomega.org) offers wellness weeks, yoga retreats, and spiritual programs throughout the year. A massage or body wrap at **Haven Spa** (6464 Montgomery St., Rhinebeck, 845/876-7369, www.havenrhinebeck.com, by appointment Wed.-Mon.) rejuvenates mind and body after a day of farm touring and wine-tasting.

The **Dutchess Inn and Spa** (151 Main St., Beacon, 845/205-2900, thedutchessinn.com) offers deep tissue, warm stone, and Swedish massages ranging $120-150 for 55 minutes. The **Beacon Yoga Center** (464 Main St., Beacon, 347/489-8406, http://beaconyogacenter.org, drop-in $21) offers daily classes in hatha, Vinyasa Flow, and restorative styles of yoga, plus occasional workshops in meditation and mindfulness.

ENTERTAINMENT AND EVENTS

Performing Arts

The 1869 **Bardavon Opera House** (35 Market St., Poughkeepsie, 845/473-2072, www.bardavon.org) holds distinction as not only one of the top performing arts venues in the county but also the oldest continuously operating theater in the state. It hosts the Hudson Valley Philharmonic, live HD broadcasts of the Metropolitan Opera, and a full schedule of musical, dance, film, and theater productions by contemporary artists.

At the other end of the architectural spectrum, the **Fisher Center for the Performing Arts** (Rte. 9G, Annandale, 845/758-7900, http://fishercenter.bard.edu, box office 10am-5pm Mon.-Fri.) occupies a modern stainless-steel building on the Bard College campus. Designed by Frank Gehry and opened in 2003, its shows include orchestra, chamber, and jazz music as well as modern theater, dance, and opera. The **Bard Music Festival** (Bard College, Rte. 9G, Annandale, 845/758-7900, http://fishercenter. bard.edu/bmf) focuses on a single composer each August.

The Rhinebeck Theatre Society and other local groups perform comedy, drama, and musicals at the **Center for the Performing Arts at Rhinebeck** (661 Rte. 308, Rhinebeck, 845/876-3080, www.centerforperformingarts. org). Indie films show regularly at **Upstate Films** (6415 Montgomery St., at Rte. 9, Rhinebeck, 845/876-2515, www.upstatefilms. org, $10, students and over age 62 $8, members $6). There is a second theater in Woodstock.

Bars and Nightlife

Beacon has more going on in the evenings these days than in years past. Under new ownership, **Carters Restaurant & Lounge** (424 Main St., Beacon, 845/743-6527, cartersrestaurantandlounge.com, 11am-10pm Mon.-Sat., 11am-8pm Sun.) has a full bar with lounge or patio seating. Beacon's oldest bar, **Max's on Main** (246 Main St., Beacon, 845/838-6297, www.maxsonmain.com, noon-10pm Mon.-Thurs., noon-11pm Fri.-Sat., noon-9pm Sun.), has margarita Mondays, trivia Tuesdays, and live music Friday-Saturday.

Inspired by the success of his TV show, *Live from Daryl's House,* musician Daryl Hall created a live music club in a historic building that was formerly the Towne Crier: **Daryl's House** (130 Rte. 22, Pawling, 845/289-0185, www.darylshouseclub.com, 3:30pm-11pm Wed., 11am-close Sat.-Sun.). Shows cover a lot of ground, from bluegrass and folk to eighties and a Bruce Springsteen tribute. Tickets range $20-40, and some events are free.

Poughkeepsie's proximity to New York City means that well-known performers come to town on a fairly regular basis. Most popular among the city's longest-running nightclubs is a former Vaudeville House now known as **The Chance Theater** (6 Crannell St., Poughkeepsie, 845/471-1966, www. thechancetheater.com). It has hosted many legendary artists over the years, including Pete Seeger, The Police, The Ramones, Bob Dylan, and David Bowie. Recently, concerts have featured the Voodoo Dolls and "Stolen" Temple Pilots. Concert-goers under age of 16 must attend with a parent, and you must be 18 or older to enter the nightclub per state law.

Mill House Brewing Company (289 Mill St., Poughkeepsie, www.millhousebrewing. com, 11am-9pm Sun.-Mon. and Thurs., 11am-10pm Fri.-Sat., $14-36) occupies a historic building in downtown Poughkeepsie. Tasty bar bites include deviled eggs, fried brussels sprouts, and mussels steamed in— of course—beer. **Mahoney's Irish Pub** (35 Main St., Poughkeepsie, 845/471-7026, www. mahoneysirishpub.com) in Poughkeepsie also has live music several nights a week.

In Rhinebeck, the wood-paneled Colonial **Tap Room** (6387 Mill St., Rhinebeck, 845/876-1766, www.beekmandelamaterinn. com) at the Beekman Arms offers a cozy and historic atmosphere for sipping cold draft beer. Alternatively, the **Rhinebeck Wine & Liquor Store** (41 E. Market St., Rhinebeck, 845/876-6264, www.rhinebeckwineandliquor. com, 9am-7pm Mon.-Sat., noon-7pm Sun.)

offers free tastings (4pm-7pm Fri.-Sat.). This is a great place to pick a local, organic, or kosher bottle.

Across the road from the FDR National Historic Site, the **Hyde Park Brewing Company** (4076 Albany Post Rd., Hyde Park, 845/229-8277, http://hydeparkbrewing.com, 4pm-10pm Wed.-Thurs., noon-10pm Fri.-Sat., noon-9pm Sun.) brews its own German-style ales and lagers on the premises.

Festivals

Summer in Dutchess County brings food, wine, auto, and art festivals, one after another. Kids get excited when the **Dutchess County Fair** (Dutchess County Fairgrounds, Rte. 9, Rhinebeck, 845/876-4000, www.dutchessfair.com) comes to town in August. One of the largest antique car shows in the Northeast is also held at the fairgrounds: The **Hudson River Valley Antique Auto Association's Annual Car Show & Swap Meet** (Dutchess County Fair Grounds, Rte. 9, 845/876-4001, www.rhinebeckcarshow.com) arrives in May.

Wineries, breweries, distilleries, and food trucks from all around the Hudson Valley gather at the fairgrounds the weekend after Labor Day to put on the **Hudson Valley Wine & Food Fest** (Dutchess County Fair Grounds, Rte. 9, 845/658-7181, www.hudsonvalleywinefest.com), a weekend of gourmet food, crafts, wine seminars, cooking demos, and live music.

The Beacon Arts Community Association organizes a monthly event, **Beacon Second Saturday** (845/546-6222, www.beaconarts.org), with gallery openings, artist receptions, food tastings, and later-than-usual hours.

Pawling hosts the annual **Pawling Triathlon** (2 Lakeside Dr., Pawling, 845/247-0271, http://pawlingrec.com) each June, drawing competitors from around the Tri-State area for a swim in Greenwood Mountain Lake, followed by a bike and a run. Strong swimmers may want to attempt the **Annual Great Newburgh to Beacon Swim** (www.riverpool.org, $75 entry), held in late July.

Kayaks will accompany you across the one-mile course.

Spectator Sports

For an evening of all-American fun, head to **Dutchess Stadium** (1500 Rte. 9D, Wappingers Falls, 845/838-0094, www.milb.com) to watch the Hudson Valley Renegades play minor league baseball. Tickets are easy to come by, and fireworks often follow the games.

SHOPPING

A busy commercial zone crowds Route 9 from Fishkill to Hyde Park, with one shopping mall after another. Head for the hills to avoid the chains.

If the art and hiking don't wear you out, wandering through all of Beacon's trendy boutiques likely will do the trick. Owned by a former apparel designer, **La Mere Clothing and Goods** (470 Main St., Beacon, 646/236-3908, http://lamereclothingandgoods.com, 11am-6pm Wed.-Sat., noon-5pm Sun.) is the place to find a cropped sweater, A-line blouse, velvet turtleneck, and many other current fashions. **Mountain Tops** (144 Main St., Beacon, 845/831-1997, www.mountaintopsoutfitters.com, 11am-6pm Mon.-Sat., 11am-5pm Sun.) can set you up with the right layers for a hike up Fishkill Ridge. The store carries Prana, Patagonia, Keen, and other outdoorsy brands. Next door, **Colorant** (146 Main St., Beacon, no phone, www.thisiscolorant.com) dyes silk, cotton, cashmere, and wool by hand and then fashions stylish apparel from the fabrics. Pop-up shops are starting to appear along Main Street in the fall, usually for just a weekend at a time.

Artist Yali Lewis of **Lewis & Pine** (133 Main St., Beacon, 845/689-4257, www.lewisandpine.com, 1pm-5pm Fri., 11am-6pm Sat.-Sun.) creates minimalist pieces of layered hardwood and metal in a Beacon studio and opened its retail space in 2018. Designers, artists, and glass-blowers collaborate to create modern lighting miracles at **Niche** (www.nichemodern.com). You can see and purchase beautiful hand-blown glass pendant lights at the studio in Beacon during the annual **Fall Factory Sale** (310 Fishkill Ave., Unit 11, Beacon, 212/777-2101), which takes place on a weekend on October.

Rhinebeck has a handful of imaginative shops. **Periwinkles** (24 E. Market St., Rhinebeck, 845/876-4014, www.periwinklesatrhinebeck.com, 11am-6pm Mon.-Thurs., 11am-9pm Fri.-Sat., 10am-6pm Sun.) sells Sally Spicer handbags, Yankee Candles, and the usual assortment of kitchen and bath accessories. A few doors closer to the intersection with Route 9, **Winter Sun & Summer Moon** (10-14 E. Market St., Rhinebeck, 845/876-3555, www.wintersunsummermoon.com, 10am-6pm Mon.-Sat., 11am-5pm Sun.) carries decorative candles, colorful pillows, and other accessories from around the world. Stop by **Cabin Fever Outfitters** (6406 Montgomery St., Rhinebeck, 845/876-6005, www.cabinfeveroutfitters.com, 11am-6pm Mon.-Sat., 11am-5pm Sun.) for any gear you left behind. The **Rhinebeck Bicycle Shop** (10 W. Garden St., 845/876-4025, 10am-5:30pm Tues.-Sat.) is on Garden Street.

The Corner Store (57 Broadway, Tivoli, 845/757-2100, http://hoteltivoli.org) at the Hotel Tivoli has one-of-a-kind jewelry pieces and ceramics by Caroline Wallner of Tivoli Tile Works.

Wine

Beacon's **Artisan Wine Shop** (180 Main St., Beacon, 845/440-6923, www.artisanwineshop.com, 10am-8pm Mon.-Sat., noon-6pm Sun.) has the chilled white wine you need for a riverside picnic after a Dia:Beacon visit. The **Rhinebeck Wine & Liquor Store** (41 E. Market St., Rhinebeck, 845/876-6264, www.rhinebeckwineandliquor.com, 10am-7pm Mon.-Sat., noon-7pm Sun.) carries labels from near and far and offers free tastings (4pm-7pm Fri.-Sat.). You can also purchase locally made wines at the individual winery tasting rooms.

Farm Stands and Local Products

The after-work stop for fresh-picked veggies at a local farm stand is a way of life for Dutchess County residents. True connoisseurs can tell from the first bite if their corn was picked in the morning or afternoon. You can often find these stands at major local intersections, such as at Routes 9 and 9G near Rhinebeck. If you have more time on your hands, pick your own produce at an orchard like **Fishkill Farms** (9 Fishkill Farm Rd., Hopewell Junction, 845/897-4377, www.fishkillfarms.com), which has been growing apples for over 75 years. At **Montgomery Place Orchards** (8 Davis Way, Red Hook, 845/758-6338, www.mporchards.com, 9am-6pm Wed.-Sun.), you can combine your picking with a tour of the historic Montgomery Place mansion.

New in 2017, the **Poughkeepsie Waterfront Market** (75 N. Water St., Poughkeepsie, http://mhcm.org, 3pm-6:30pm Mon. May-Oct.) was the brainchild of the Mid-Hudson Children's Museum. Vendors set up their booths along the riverbank, so you can wander through and find fresh produce, prepared foods, arts, and crafts.

Greig Farm (227 Pitcher Lane, Red Hook, 845/758-1234, www.greigfarm.com, 9am-7pm daily) has evolved from a standard apple- and pumpkin-picking operation to a year-round marketplace and bakery. You can browse local art, feed the goats, and stock up on produce for the week.

Walbridge Farm Market (538 Rte. 343, Millbrook, 845/677-6221, www.walbridgefarm.com, 10am-5pm Fri., 9am-5pm Sat., noon-5pm Sun.) has one of the best-stocked farm stores of anyone in the county. It's worth the short drive from town to pick up grass-fed beef, Ronnybrook yogurt, pastured eggs, and a selection of locally made treats. The farmers also host a popular festival in mid-July with hayrides, face painting, and live music. Say hello to the herd if you go.

Sawkill Farm (7782 Albany Post Rd., Red Hook, 845/514-4562, www.sawkillfarm.com, 10am-6pm Wed.-Sun.) stocks the freezers full

The Birth of American Art: The Hudson River School of Painters

In the early 19th century, America's first generation of artists began to discover and explore the wilderness of the Hudson River Valley, Catskills, and Adirondack Mountains. Inspired by what they saw—lush forests, cascading waterfalls, fall foliage, and 4,000-foot peaks—they began to paint a new kind of landscape.

Led by Thomas Cole (1801-1848), the movement found roots in European Romanticism and later became known as the Hudson River School. These painters, contemporaries of writers including Emerson, Thoreau, William Cullen Bryant, and Walt Whitman, shaped a young nation's first artistic movement, leading to the start of the Romantic era.

From his home and studio in Catskill, Cole painted Kaaterskill Falls, Catskill Creek, the Catskill Peaks, and other wilderness areas in the valley. Asher B. Durand (1796-1886), a contemporary and friend of Cole's, and Frederic Edwin Church, Cole's student, are also associated with the movement.

Today, you can view these works of art at the Frances Lehman Loeb Art Center at Vassar College in Poughkeepsie, the Olana State Historic Site (Church's home) near Hudson, and the Albany Institute of History and Art in Albany—as well as other museums and libraries in New York City and out of state.

Guided hikes from the Thomas Cole National Historic Site at Cedar Grove in the town of Catskill are another way to experience the works of these artists. You can hike to Kaaterskill Clove, the site of the famous Catskill Mountain House hotel, and Sunset Rock—places invite contemplation today just as they did two centuries ago.

of grass-fed beef, pasture-raised pork, lamb, and chicken. The fridge holds farm eggs and organic vegetables, all grown on-site. Naturally gray wool made from shearing of the resident sheep is about the most gorgeous sight around.

During the summer and fall harvest, at least a dozen farmers markets come to life, mostly on the weekends, although a few take place on weekday afternoons. Among the most popular events, the **Millbrook Farmers Market** (Front St. and Franklin Ave., Millbrook, www. millbrooknyfarmersmarket.com) happens 9am-1pm Saturdays May-October. **Beacon** (www.beaconfarmersmarket.org) has a market 10am-3pm Sunday. And you can find local produce, prepared foods, crafts, music, and more across from the town hall at **Hyde Park** (4390 Rte. 9, Hyde Park, 845/229-9336, hydepark.us, 9am-2pm Sat. June-Oct.). Other options include:

- **Fishkill** (Grand Union parking lot, Rte. 52, 845/897-4430, 9am-3pm Thurs. July-Oct.)

- **Millerton** (Dutchess Ave., just off Main St., Millerton, 518/789-4613, www. millertonfarmersmarket.org, 9am-1pm Sat. May-Sept.)

- **Pawling** (Charles Colman Blvd., next to the Pawling Chamber of Commerce Bldg., Pawling, 917/224-4801, www. pawlingfarmersmarket.org, 9am-1pm Sat. June-Sept.)

- **Rhinebeck** (municipal parking lot, 23 E. Market St., Rhinebeck, 845/876-7756, www. rhinebeckfarmersmarket.com, 10am-2pm Sun. May-Dec.)

Dykeman Farm (823 W. Dover Rd., Wingdale, 845/832-6068, www. dykemanfarm.com, 10am-5pm daily July-Labor Day, 10am-5pm daily Labor Day-Oct.) grows sweet corn and tomatoes and offers pick-your-own pumpkins in the fall. Northeast of Amenia, the **McEnroe Organic Farm Market** (5409 Rte. 22, Millerton,

518/789-4191, www.mcenroeorganicfarm. com, 9am-6pm Wed.-Sun.) offers organic produce in season, plus pick-your-own herbs and flowers, and a delightful café that serves organic soft-serve frozen yogurt.

Pick up fine teas and accessories for friends back home at the **Harney & Sons Tea Shop** (13 Main St., Railroad Plaza, Millerton, 518/789-2121, www.harney.com, 10am-5pm Wed.-Sat., 11am-4pm Sun.).

Three generations of the Baldwin family have milked cows in the same barn at **Shunpike Dairy** (1328 Shunpike Rd., Millbrook, 845/702-6224, http://shunpikedairy.com). This is one of very few dairies in the state licensed to sell raw milk. Serve yourself from a tank in the barn and leave cash in the box ($3 per half gallon). Pay a few dollars more if you need to use one of their jars. The farm sells eggs, yogurt, cheese, and maple syrup too.

Antiques and Galleries

Every town in Dutchess County has its share of antique treasures. Thirty such places are found under one art deco roof at Red Hook's **Annex Antiques Center** (23 E. Market St., Red Hook, 845/758-2843, 11am-5pm daily). The **Hyde Park Antiques Center** (4192 Albany Post Rd., Hyde Park, 845/229-8200, www.hydeparkantiques.net, 10am-5pm daily) represents more than 50 dealers with antiques that span the 18th-20th centuries. Allow plenty of time to wander through the maze of rooms, which contain vintage toys, jewelry, porcelain, pottery, and more. Best of all, there's something for every price point.

Millerton emerged on the scene a few years back with its own collection of sought-after treasures. **Jennings & Rohn Montage** (25 Main St., Millerton, 860/485-3387, www. montageantiques.com) formed as an off-shoot—and then replacement for—a long-time antiques business in Woodbury. The Millerton location now carries mid-century and country furniture, lighting, drawings, and "art from every period." Check the website for occasional pop-up shopping events.

Hudson Beach Glass (162 Main St., Beacon, 845/440-0068, www.hudson beachglass.com, 10am-6pm Mon.-Sat., 11am-6pm Sun.) carries jewelry, vases, bowls, and other glass works created by several local artists. It is one of the only glassworks galleries of its size in upstate New York.

Bookstores

Book lovers will find several independent shops to visit. For example, **Merritt Bookstore** (57 Front St., Millbrook, 845/677-5857, www.merrittbooks.com, 9am-5pm Mon.-Sat., 10am-4pm Sun.) has a fabulous children's collection and hosts frequent literary events. **The Book Cove** (22 Charles Colman Blvd., Pawling, 845/855-9590, www. pawlingbookcove.com, 11am-3pm Tues.-Fri. and Sun., 10am-3pm Sat.) also stocks a wonderful collection of literary fiction, travel books, and stationery. After a Harney & Sons tea tasting, you can browse the regional books, best-sellers, and signed copies at **Oblong Books & Music** (26 Main St., Millerton, 518/789-3797, www.oblongbooks. com, 10:30am-6pm daily).

FOOD

Dutchess County eateries range from classic diners and American bistros to game-inspired farm-fresh menus and the occasional international delight. New places open at a fast clip, and as elsewhere in the Hudson River Valley, farm-to-table dining experiences are among the most unique and memorable meals you'll find.

Along the River: Route 9
BEACON

The restaurant scene continues to mature in Beacon, thanks to the influx of Dia:Beacon visitors and a growing community of resident artists. Suggestions here are organized

---

1: veggies for sale at Shunpike Dairy **2:** canisters of looseleaf tea for sale at the Harney & Sons Tea Shop & Tasting Room **3:** silos and barns at Shunpike Dairy

roughly from west (near the river) to east (near Fishkill Creek) along Main Street.

Near the intersection of Main Street and Route 9D, **Bank Square Coffeehouse** (129 Main St., Beacon, 845/440-7165, www.banksquarecoffeehouse.com, 6am-9pm Mon.-Thurs., 6am-10pm Fri., 7am-10pm Sat., 7am-9pm Sun.) has a full menu of caffeinated drinks from beans roasted at Coffee Labs Roasters in Tarrytown, as well as pastries from a local bakery in Fishkill. If you like dark coffee, try the only-in-Beacon Mt. Beacon roast. Across the street, **The Beacon Creamery** (134 Main St., Beacon, 845/765-0444, www.janesicecream.com, 1pm-7pm daily) serves locally made Jane's Ice Cream, as well as house-based goods.

Across from Hudson Beach Glass, ★ **Kitchen Sink Food and Drink** (157 Main St., Beacon, 845/765-0240, http://kitchensinkny.com, 5pm-close Wed.-Mon., brunch from 11am Sun., $21-28) quickly became a hit for its Monday-night special: fried chicken (the only option on the menu that day). The rest of the week, you can try a sous-vide flank steak, ratatouille, or lamb gyro. Much of the produce served here comes from Truckload Farm in Hyde Park. Sunday brunch starts at 11am. You won't regret a juicy burger or crispy chicken sandwich with double cooked fries at **Meyer's Olde Dutch Food & Such** (184 Main St., Beacon, 845/440-6900, http://meyersoldedutch.com, 11:30am-9pm Sun.-Thurs., 11:30am-10pm Fri.-Sat., $6-13). It's run by the same chef-owner behind Kitchen Sink.

Stock up for a picnic or eat in the café at **Homespun Foods** (232 Main St., Beacon, 845/831-5096, http://homespunfoods.com, 10am-7pm Thurs.-Mon.). House-made pastries stand out most, but you also can order a simple tuna salad or turkey avocado sandwich. The café has opened a second location inside Dia:Beacon.

The kitchen at **Max's on Main** (246 Main St., Beacon, 845/838-6297, https://maxsonmain.com, noon-10pm Mon-Thurs., noon-11pm Fri.-Sat., noon-9pm Sun., $10-28) stays open late when most others have closed for the night. Creative comfort food is the theme, a la Firecracker Shrimp and Phamous Phish Tacos.

Beacon Pantry (382 Main St. Beacon, 845/440-8923, http://beaconpantry.com, café 10am-4pm Sat.-Sun., 11am-4pm Mon. and Thurs.-Fri., market 10am-6pm daily, $7-12) is a market and café that does cheese and charcuterie right. Grab a picnic basket and go!

For bistro fare like sautéed shrimp and rosemary garlic chicken, head to the recently designed **Carters Restaurant & Lounge** (424 Main St., Beacon, 845/743-6527, https://cartersrestaurantandlounge.com, 11am-10pm Mon.-Sat., 11am-8pm Sun., $16-24).

Beacon Falls Café (472 Main St., Beacon, 845/765-0172, http://beaconfallscafe.com, 10am-4pm Mon.-Tues. and Thurs., 10am-9pm Fri., 9am-9pm Sat., 9am-4pm Sun., $12-25) is run by a graduate of the Culinary Institute with pub-like dishes presented in a bistro setting.

In between gallery visits, stop for pad thai, green curry, or other Thai specialties at **Sukhothai** (516 Main St., Beacon, 845/790-5375, www.sukhothainy.com, 11:30am-9:30pm Sun.-Thurs., 11:30am-10:30pm Fri.-Sat., lunch $9, dinner $15-25). This restaurant serves the most authentic Thai cuisine in the area. There are a few sidewalk tables outside, and happily, an air-conditioned dining room inside.

After extensive renovations, a one-time textile mill and lawnmower factory transformed into **The Roundhouse at Beacon Falls** (2 E. Main St., Beacon, 845/765-8369, www.roundhousebeacon.com, 3pm-9pm Mon. and Thurs., 3pm-10pm Fri., 11:30am-10pm Sat., 11:30am-8pm Sun., $16-34). The views are great, but food and service still could be improved.

One More Bite (389 Main St., Beacon, 845/765-0648, www.onemorebitecc.com, noon-9pm Thurs.-Mon., $12-17) brings Korean fusion rice bowls to the Beacon dining scene. From *banh mi* to *bulgogi*, you'll find it all here.

FISHKILL AND WAPPINGERS FALLS

Meals at **Hudson's Ribs & Fish** (1099 Rte. 9, Fishkill, 845/297-5002, http://hudsonsribsandfish.com, 4pm-9pm Tues.-Thurs., 4pm-10pm Fri.-Sat., noon-9pm Sun., $21-32) come with a piping-hot popover on the side.

For midweek lunch at a welcoming pizzeria, head to **The Tomato Café** (1123 Main St., Fishkill, 845/896-7779, www.tomatocafeny.com, 11am-9pm Mon.-Sat., 9am-3pm Sun., $12-18). Gluten-free crust is an option. Look for a second location near Vassar College (15 Collegeview Ave., Poughkeepsie, 845/473-7779). **Red Line Diner** (588 Route 9, Fishkill, 845/765-8401, http://dineatredline.com, 24 hours daily, $12-16) takes the usual diner food up a notch or two with a four-cheese mac and cheese, fresh-baked biscuits, and spinach-artichoke dip. This place is part of a restaurant group that includes The Daily Planet in LaGrange and Table Top Diner in Poughkeepsie.

Aroma Osteria (114 Old Post Rd., Wappingers Falls, 845/298-6790, www.aromaosteriarestaurant.com, 5pm-9pm Tues.-Thurs., noon-2:30pm and 5pm-9:30pm Fri.-Sat., 4pm-8:30pm Sun., $23-33) is good enough to remind you of a trip to Italy. Start with the heirloom tomato salad in summer, and then try a pasta course of spaghetti with baby clams or mushroom ravioli in a creamy porcini sauce. Vegetarians and gluten-free eaters will find plenty of options too. Take advantage of the $35 prix fixe dinner special Tuesday-Thursday.

Newcomer **Heritage Food & Drink** (1379 Rte. 9, Wappingers Falls, 845/298-1555, www.heritagefooddrink.com, 11:30am-9:30pm Mon.-Thurs., 11:30am-10pm Fri., 11am-10pm Sat., 11am-9pm Sun., $16-31) serves Asian-inspired seasonal dishes including shrimp ceviche, summer vegetable tempura, and wood-charred octopus.

POUGHKEEPSIE

Brasserie 292 (292 Main St., Poughkeepsie, 845/473-0292, www.brasserie292.com, lunch 11am-4pm Tues.-Fri., dinner 4pm-9:30pm Tues.-Thurs., 5pm-10:30pm Fri., 2pm-9pm Sat., 11am-9pm Sun., mains $18-35) sources ingredients from nearby farms to create hearty dishes like braised rabbit, grilled pork tenderloin, and grilled brook trout.

The **River Station** (25 Main St. or 1 N. Water St., Poughkeepsie, 845/452-9207, http://riverstationrest.com, 11:30am-9pm Tues.-Sat., $18-32) serves dependable surf and turf on a pleasant outdoor terrace that overlooks the Hudson.

Nearby, overlooking the river, **Shadows** (176 Rinaldi Blvd., Poughkeepsie, 845/486-9500, www.shadowsonthehudson.com, 11:30am-9pm Sun.-Thurs., 11:30am-10pm Fri.-Sat., $21-36) is a mammoth brick dining and events complex. It caters to a business crowd during weekday lunch hours and turns into a trendy nightclub on weekends. You'll likely catch views of the Mid-Hudson Bridge from your table, but don't expect a cozy, romantic feel. Surf and turf defines the menu, and then there are the usual sandwiches and salads. Late-night snacks and cocktails are served until 10pm Monday-Thursday and until 2am Friday-Saturday.

Near the train station, shepherd's pie, corned beef and cabbage, and fish-and-chips are the tradition at **Mahoney's Irish Pub & Restaurant** (35 Main St., Poughkeepsie, 845/471-7026, www.mahoneysirishpub.com, lunch 11am-5pm daily, dinner 5pm-10:30pm Mon.-Fri., 5pm-11pm Sat., 5pm-9pm Sun., pub open late, $15-26).

Ask a group of locals to name the best diner in town and you'll spark a heated debate. Near Marist College, **The Palace Diner** (194 Washington St., Poughkeepsie, 854/473-1576, www.thepalacediner.com, 24 hours daily, $17-23) has the best food all around. But the **Daily Planet** (1202 Rte. 55, LaGrangeville, 845/452-0110, www.dailyplanetdiner.com, 8am-10pm daily, $12-23), near Arlington High School, kicks it up a notch with unexpected dishes like walnut-crusted salmon and chicken-and-shrimp jambalaya.

Saigon Cafe (6A LaGrange Ave., Poughkeepsie, 845/473-1392, http://saigoncafepok.com, 11:30am-3pm and 5pm-10pm Mon.-Fri., noon-10pm Sat., 5pm-9:30pm Sun., $7-10) serves passable Vietnamese *pho* in a small but air-conditioned space just off the Vassar College campus. The kitchen uses gluten-free noodles in all of its homemade dishes.

Trust **Rosticceria Rossi & Sons** (45 S. Clover St., Poughkeepsie, 845/471-0654, www.rossideli.com, 10:30am-6pm Mon.-Fri., 10:30am-5pm Sat., $9-13) to deliver a classic Italian deli experience. The lines are long, but the imported cured meats are authentic.

At the **Mill House Brewing Company** (289 Mill St., Poughkeepsie, www.millhousebrewing.com, 11am-9pm Sun.-Mon. and Thurs., 11am-10pm Fri.-Sat., $14-36), the chefs especially take pride in their hand-crafted sausages and fresh fish. Try the beef and jalapeño cheddar brat or a pulled-pork hot dog.

The menu at **Pete's Famous Restaurant** (618 Main St., Poughkeepsie, 845/471-3317, http://petesfamousrestaurant.com, 6am-3pm Mon.-Fri., 6am-2pm Sat., $7-13) covers a lot of ground, from breakfast platters and fluffy omelets to a long list of burgers and sandwiches.

HYDE PARK

CIA sophomores run the kitchens in five campus restaurants at the **Culinary Institute of America** (1946 Campus Dr., Hyde Park, www.ciachef.edu). All five are located on the campus, and you can park in a two-story structure in Anton Plaza. It's a toss-up to say which of the two formal dining restaurants is the best. **American Bounty** (845/451-1011, www.americanbountyrestaurant.com, 11:30am-12:45pm and 6pm-8pm Tues.-Sat., $22-31) is a white-tablecloth affair that aims to please the locavore audience with creative soups, garden-fresh salads, and entrées from land and sea. Named for the father of modern French cuisine, chef Paul Bocuse, **The Bocuse Restaurant** (845/451-1012, www.bocuserestaurant.com, 11am-12:45pm and

6pm-8pm Tues.-Sat., $26-34, 3-course prix-fixe $45) replaced the former Escoffier with a here-and-now approach to classic French fare. Think poached turbot, trilogy of lamb, and apple tarte tatin, and you'll have a good idea of the menu.

Also on the CIA campus, **Ristorante Caterina de' Medici** (Colavita Center for Italian Food and Wine, 845/451-1013, www.ristorantecaterinademedici.com, 11:30am-8:30pm Mon.-Sat., $14-28) serves regional Italian specialties under a Venetian chandelier. For a more casual dining experience, ask to be seated in the Al Forno Trattoria.

Casual and fairly priced, the CIA's ★ **Apple Pie Bakery Café** (Roth Hall, 845/905-4500, www.applepiebakerycafe.com, 8am-2pm Mon., 8am-2:30pm Tues.-Fri., $11-14) bakes strawberry almond scones, sticky buns, and salted caramel doughnuts. It has long been a favorite among the locals and offers table service too. At the **Post Road Brew House** (General Foods Nutrition Center, 845/451-1015, www.ciarestaurantgroup.com, $12-22) the students have fun pairing craft beers with upscale pub food.

When making reservations, note that CIA restaurants are only open when the school is in session. And if everything isn't just perfect, remember it's a training restaurant, after all.

Not on campus, but right across from FDR's home, **Hyde Park Brewing Company** (4076 Albany Post Rd., Hyde Park, 845/229-8277, http://hydeparkbrewing.com, 4pm-10pm Wed.-Thurs., noon-10pm Fri.-Sat., noon-9pm Sun.) practices traditional German brewing techniques to make unique lagers, pilsners, hefeweizen, and stouts. The menu features foods that pair well with craft beer: nachos, schnitzel, paninis, charcuterie, and the like. Naturally, the kitchen also includes house-made beers in many of its dishes.

RHINEBECK

★ **Le Petit Bistro** (8 E. Market St., Rhinebeck, 845/876-7400, www.lepetitbistro.com, 5pm-9:30pm Wed.-Thurs., 5pm-10pm Fri.-Sat., 10:30am-3pm and 5pm-9pm Sun.,

$15-35) rivals Bocuse among the top French restaurants in the entire Hudson River Valley. Whether you order today's oysters, escargot, duckling, steak frites, or veal *française*, the meal should come perfectly prepared.

Inside the former First Baptist Church, **Terrapin** (6426 Montgomery St., Rhinebeck, 845/876-3330, www.terrapinrestaurant.com, 5pm-9:30pm daily, $19-36) probably has the most unique setting in all of Rhinebeck. Chef Josh Kroner founded the restaurant two decades ago and is a recognized pioneer in the locavore movement. You can order tapas (*shishito* peppers, meatballs, oyster shooters), Thai lettuce pockets, creative quesadillas, and heartier entrées like the maple-brined double-thick pork chop. Vegetarian and gluten-free options are clearly marked on the menu. At the same location, its sister establishment, **Terrapin Red Bistro** (11:30am-midnight daily, $11-17), is a cozier place that's open for lunch and dinner.

★ **Bread Alone** (45 E. Market St., Rhinebeck, 845/876-3108, www.breadalone.com, 7am-5pm daily, $9-16) serves legendary breads, pastries, and sandwiches at four locations and several farmers markets. In Rhinebeck, it's a popular place for a quick coffee or midweek lunch, and you can grab a bar of Fruition chocolate at the counter. At the bakery's HQ in Boiceville, a carbon-neutral baking facility is in the works.

Thin-crust pizzas are practically a work of art at ★ **Pizzeria Posto** (43 E. Market St., Rhinebeck, 845/876-3500, http://postopizzeria.com, noon-8:30pm Mon., noon-9pm Wed.-Thurs., noon-9:30pm Fri.-Sat., noon-8:30pm Sun., $15-20). The ingredients are fresh and the wood-fired oven method is foolproof. One of a pair of Hudson River Valley restaurants, **Market Street** (19 W. Market St., Rhinebeck, 845/876-7200, www.marketstrhinebeck.com, 5pm-9:30pm Sun.-Thurs., 5pm-10pm Fri.-Sat., $18-34) also cranks out thin-crust pizzas from a wood-fired oven. Gluten-free pasta is an option. The chicken is free-range, and the beef is grass-fed. The owners also run Cucina in Woodstock.

Gigi Trattoria (6422 Montgomery St., Rhinebeck, 845/876-1007, www.gigihudsonvalley.com, noon-9pm Tues.-Thurs., 11:30am-10pm Fri.-Sat., 11:30am-8:30pm Sun., $15-30) prepares "skizzas"—its own interpretation of flatbread (gluten-free version also available), as well as fried calamari, *burrata* cheese, and lamb *merguez* (sausage) skewers.

When you're craving more exotic flavors, head to ★ **Cinnamon Indian Cuisine** (51 E. Market St., Rhinebeck, 845/876-7510, http://cinnamoncuisine.com, 11:30am-2:30pm and 4:30pm-10pm Mon. and Wed.-Fri., 11:30am-3pm and 4:30pm-10pm Sat.-Sun., $18-20). Besides the familiar northern Indian dishes, the kitchen prepares *boti* kebabs (lamb) as a starter, a fish curry from the region of Goa, and a Persian-influenced lamb *rogan josh* curry. You can learn a lot about the subcontinent in just one meal here. The Spice Room upstairs serves cocktails 4pm-1am Thursday-Saturday.

Matchbox Café (6242 Rte. 9, Rhinebeck, 845/876-3911, www.thematchboxcafe.com, 11am-8pm Wed.-Sun., $10-20) is a husband-wife partnership that began with a bakery in Manhattan and evolved into a Rhinebeck eatery where the motto is "fine dining on a paper plate." The veggie burger is a standout. Everything on the menu is served all day.

RED HOOK AND TIVOLI

Flatiron Steakhouse (7488 S. Broadway, Red Hook, 845/758-8260, http://flatironsteakhouse.com, 5pm-9pm Wed.-Sat., $20-34) cooks much more than the name suggests—grilled shrimp and grits, ham tortellini, and Asian barbecue pork cheeks, for example.

At the corner of Routes 9 and 199, across from the Merritt Bookstore, **J&J's Gourmet** (1 E. Market St., 845/758-9030, www.jandjgourmet.com, 9am-4pm Thurs.-Mon., $6-12) has a window display of old cans and tins from brands like Ritz crackers, Life Savers, Coca-Cola, Hershey's, and Maxwell House. Inside is a gourmet deli that makes

Hudson River Valley Wineries

Enterprising Hudson River Valley farmers planted the first French-American hybrid grapes in the 1970s. Unlike the hot, dry climate that nurtures California zinfandel, merlot, and cabernet sauvignon grapes, cooler temperatures in the Hudson River Valley are well suited for growing the types of grapes you find in Burgundy, Germany, and northern Italy: chardonnay, aligote, dornfelder, and pinot noir. The resulting wines are earthy, crisp, and clean, with a moderate alcohol content.

Today, the Hudson River Valley is the smallest of four major wine regions in New York State, with about 20 producers. (The others are Long Island, the Finger Lakes, and Great Lakes regions.) Dutchess, Ulster, and Columbia Counties have several wineries with tasting rooms. Millbrook Vineyards & Winery has one of the largest operations in the area.

homemade soups and sandwiches. And on the same block, farther east, **Brigitte Bistro** (61 E. Market St., 845/835-6230, www.brigittebistro61.com, 5pm-10pm Tues.-Sat., $23-41) brings seasonal dishes inspired by the south of France, including escargot, octopus, duck confit, and the all-classic onion soup.

Holy Cow (7270 S. Broadway, Red Hook, 845/758-5959, noon-9pm Tues.-Sun.) should fill the need for soft-serve, or any kind of ice cream.

At the northern edge of the county, Bard College professors frequent **Santa Fe** (52 Broadway, Tivoli, 845/757-4100, www.santafetivoli.com, 4pm-9pm Mon.-Sat., $15-19) for tacos and burritos, margaritas and mojitos. Chipotle ginger marinated steak skewers make for a tasty starter.

Part of the Hotel Tivoli, **The Corner** (53 Broadway, Tivoli, 845/757-2100, http://hoteltivoli.org/the-corner, 5:30pm-9pm Thurs.-Mon., $25-38) serves Mediterranean dishes that showcase farm-fresh ingredients—chicken *tajine,* Spanish branzino, steak frites.

Next to the post office, **Rojo Tapas and Wine Bar** (76 Broadway, Tivoli, 845/757-1102, http://rojotapasandwine.com, 5pm-9pm Thurs.-Sun., $8-14) has a Spanish tortilla, stuffed red peppers, and Basque-style sausage among the small plates on the menu. Wines by the glass ($9-15) come primarily from Europe, Argentina, and New Zealand.

Osaka (74 Broadway, Tivoli, 845/757-5055, http://osakasushitivoli.com, 11:30am-2:30pm and 4:30pm-8:30pm Mon. and Wed.-Sat.,

3pm-8:30pm Sun., $14-19) is a friendly Japanese eatery that serves sashimi à la carte and a variety of maki rolls, as well as traditional hot dishes like *gyoza,* shrimp tempura, *udon,* and teriyaki. There is a second location in Rhinebeck.

Central Dutchess County: Routes 44 and 22
PAWLING AND PATTERSON
Pawling residents know ★ **McKinney & Doyle** (10 Charles Colman Blvd., Pawling, 845/855-3875, www.mckinneyanddoyle.com, 4pm-8:30pm Tues.-Thurs., 4pm-9pm Fri.-Sat., 9:30am-2pm Sun., $12-35) as simply "the bakery." Enter through the bakery and try not to drool at all the treats behind the glass counter. Grab a booth or table in the adjoining air-conditioned restaurant, which has brick walls and worn wood floors. The wine list rotates often but always has a few unique labels from around the world. Dinner entrées feature duck breast, lamb chops, and brook trout. Tuesday is Pub Night (4pm-8:30pm), with a menu of crispy calamari, chicken wings, fajitas, and the like. The bakery and soda fountain-ice cream shop (7am-4pm Sun.-Mon., 7am-7pm Tues.-Sat.) are open daily. Old-fashioned sodas, egg creams, and ice cream sodas add a retro touch.

Karen's Diner (56 Rte. 22, Pawling, 845/878-6654, http://karensdiner.com, 8am-2pm daily, $7-12) draws a crowd for breakfast and lunch. Among the specialties are the Farmers Omelet, with corned beef hash and a waffle, or a French toast "grand slam" for breakfast; for lunch, try a meatloaf sandwich or a buffalo chicken wrap.

Gluten-free eaters will find lots of choices at **Iron & Wine** (3191 Route 22, Patterson, 845/878-6800, www.ironandwinerestaurant. com, 4pm-10pm Wed.-Sun. and noon-10pm Sat.-Sun., small plates $8-14, large plates $14-24). The menu follows a Mediterranean theme, with tapas like a mushroom quesadilla, crispy octopus, and chorizo mussels, and larger plates of shrimp scampi, short rib Bolognese, and a seafood bouillabaisse. Its happy hour features $3 tacos and $5 margaritas.

MILLBROOK

The flavors of Provence prevail on chef Hervé Bochard's menu at ★ **Café Les Baux** (152 Church St., Millbrook, 845/677-8166, www. cafelesbaux.com, lunch noon-2:30pm Thurs.-Sun., dinner 5pm-9pm Thurs.-Mon., 5pm-10pm Fri.-Sat., $13-33). "The Baux," as it's known affectionately among locals, serves consistently tasty French-style salads (endive salad with roquefort cheese and walnuts), *croque monsieur* and *madame* sandwiches, steamed mussels, and steak frites.

Order a chicken salad sandwich at tiny **Babbett's Kitchen** (3293 Franklin Ave., Millbrook, 845/677-8602, www. babetteskitchen.com, 7am-4pm Wed.-Fri., 7am-5pm Sat., 8am-3pm Sun., $4-12) after a walk around Innisfree Garden. The café-bakery makes muffins, scones, and buttermilk biscuits daily. Beer and wine by the glass are the newest additions to the menu.

Slammin' Salmon (3267 Franklin Ave., Millbrook, 845/677-5400, www.slammin-salmon.com, 10am-5pm Mon.-Wed., 10am-6pm Thurs.-Sat., $8-12) gets fresh seafood deliveries on Tuesday and Friday, and the inventory sells out fast. Fresh-picked veggies from local farms arrive daily. The fridge holds organic eggs and dairy from Ronnybrook and Hudson River Valley Fresh. Shelves in the center of the shop hold the essentials for a picnic lunch or gourmet dinner. Behind the counter, the same ingredients appear in a variety

of salads and prepared dishes. Order a salmon sandwich to eat at a patio table outside, or take it to go.

Canoe Hill (3264 Franklin Ave., Millbrook, 845/605-1570, http://canoehillny. com, 8pm-8pm Mon.-Sat., noon-6pm Sun.) is a tiny place that serves $1 oysters 4pm-6pm daily. After that, you can order mussels, gnocchi, and other small plates to complete the meal.

Family-run **Maura's Kitchen** (18 Alden Place, Millbrook, 845/605-1620, www. mauraskitchenofmillbrook.com, noon-8pm Tues.-Thurs., noon-9pm Fri.-Sat., $17-30) makes soups, salads, and comfort food like porterhouse steak, coconut shrimp, and spaghetti with meatballs.

Just outside town, **Charlotte's** (4258 Rte. 44, Millbrook, 845/677-5888, www. charlottesny.com, 5pm-8:30pm Wed.-Thurs., 5pm-10pm Fri., 4:30pm-10pm Sat., 11:30am-8pm Sun., $20-28) delights even the most discerning of diners with a New American menu that changes daily. The converted 200-year-old church is a romantic venue for celebrating anniversaries and other special occasions.

Continuing up the Taconic State Parkway, the **Fireside BBQ and Grill** (1920 Salt Point Turnpike, Salt Point, 845/266-3440, www. firesidebbqgrill.com, 4pm-9pm Wed.-Sat., noon-8pm Sun., $9-22) serves 25-ounce beers in frosted mugs. It has been around for generations and has a friendly staff that serves tasty baby back ribs, barbecue, tri-tip, and prime rib on weekends.

MILLERTON

After a walk on the Harlem Valley Rail Trail, taste the latest imported teas along with lunch at the **Harney & Sons Tea Tasting Room** (13 Main St., Millerton, 518/789-2121, www. harney.com, 10am-5pm Wed.-Sat., 11am-4pm Sun., $8-17). Especially popular with the pour-over and cold brew crowds, ★ **Irving Farm Coffee House** (44 Main St., Millerton, 518/789-2020, www.irvingfarm.com, 8am-3pm Mon.-Fri., 8am-4pm Sat.-Sun.) is a Manhattan institution that serves specialty coffee made from single-origin beans that are roasted in a converted 19th-century carriage house just a mile away. You can also order wine, beer, and light snacks besides the usual menu of espresso drinks.

52 Main (52 Main St., Millerton, 518/789-0252, www.52main.com, 4pm-8pm Tues.-Thurs., 4pm-9pm Fri.-Sat., $10-27) is an eclectic small-plates venue. Only the serrano ham and paella hint of a true tapas menu. The **Oakhurst Diner** (19 Main St., Millerton, 518/592-1313, www.oakhurst-diner.com, 8am-8pm Thurs.-Mon., $10-20) is a contemporary diner that does best with breakfast fare, which it serves until 5pm daily.

You can eat and stay at **The Millerton Inn** (53 Main St., Millerton, 518/592-1900, http://themillertoninn.com, 11am-9pm Sun.-Thurs., 11am-10pm Fri.-Sat., $15-33). Starters include clam chowder and lamb lollipops. Choose from entrée options such as the market fish, steak au poivre, squash risotto, or beet and leek linguini.

Amy and Jessica at the **Rookie Farm Bakery** (24 Main St., Millerton, 518/821-3811, www.rookiefarmbakery.com, 10am-4pm Thurs.-Sat.) invented a new kind of pastry that they call the cookie tart. Try all six flavors, made from scratch in the on-site kitchen.

ACCOMMODATIONS

Business travelers congregate around corporate headquarters in southern Dutchess County, while the more distinctive inns—mostly of the bed-and-breakfast variety—are found in the northeastern part of the county. Book early around major events. The most popular hotels fill up as far as a year in advance.

$100-150

These days, the best options at this price point are listed as vacation rentals on **Airbnb** (www.airbnb.com). For example, small cottages, writer's retreats, and barn studios rent for around $120 and up per night. Rates do not include cleaning fees or service charges.

Much loved by Hudson Valley travelers, the ★ **Roosevelt Inn at Hyde Park** (4360 Albany Post Rd., Hyde Park, 845/229-2443, $90-120) is a practical motel-style choice close to all the historic attractions in this area. It has two room types: "deluxe" are in a modern building, while its "rustic" rooms in the original inn are more in keeping with the old-time Catskills vibe.

The **Inn at Pine Plains** (3036 Church St., Pine Plains, 518/771-3117, www.innatpineplains.com, $140-270) has four

coffee from Irving Farm Coffee House

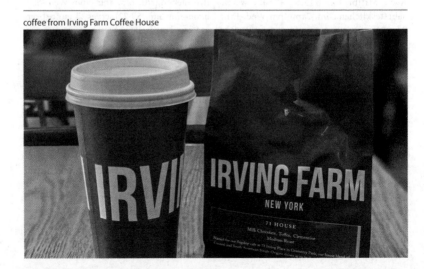

rooms, two suites, and a couple of two-bedroom options. The suites have kitchenettes and sleeper sofas for additional guests. Perks include locally roasted coffee and breads from a local bakery.

Le Chambord at Curry Estate (2737 Rte. 52, Hopewell Junction, 845/221-1941, www.lechambord.com, $150) is a historic property that's now managed by a family of six sisters. There are 9 rooms in the main building and 16 more in a newer wing—all fairly large, with high ceilings and white tiled baths. The current chef prepares American Continental fare for dinner ($24-48) Wednesday through Sunday, as well as Sunday brunch.

$150-200

Botsford Briar B&B (19 High St., Beacon, 845/831-6099, www.botsfordbriar.com, $185-225) has wicker furniture on the front porch, original hardwood floors, lace curtains, English faucets, and antique furnishings. The top-floor room has a river view and enclosed porch; the downstairs Gentleman's Parlor has a cozy fireplace for winter getaways. The owner is a needle-arts pro who once hosted quilting retreats in this 1889 Victorian. It's located across Route 9D from Main Street, near the Beacon train station.

Spotless and welcoming, the **Journey Inn** (1 Sherwood Place, Hyde Park, 845/229-8972, www.journeyinn.com, $160-260) is a bed-and-breakfast with seven rooms located across from the Vanderbilt Estate. Innkeepers Valerie and Eric Miller have partnered with the Culinary Institute and Omega Institute to offer special room rates to students of these programs. As a guest, you'll start your day with a multicourse breakfast of fruit, waffles, homemade sausage, and freshly baked treats. European soaps add a fine touch, and wireless internet is available throughout.

Two air-conditioned rooms appointed in country style come with a three-course breakfast of pastry, fruit, and something hot. Cozy and quiet, **Inn the Woods** (32 Howard Blvd. Extension, Hyde Park, 845/229-9331, www.innthewoods.com, $165-220) has a Tree Top Suite with a spiral staircase to the second floor, a king bed, and a kitchenette for preparing simple meals. Alternatively, the Cliffside Room also has a king bed, but not a kitchenette.

Carefully restored and reopened in 2017, **The Millerton Inn** (53 Main St., Millerton, 518/592-1900, http://themillertoninn.com, $179-309) has a variety of guest rooms, ranging from standard doubles to a king suite. Floors are wood, the decor is antiques, and the paint is fresh. Book a table in the dining room and taste the pan-seared feta, made on the innkeepers' own goat farm outside town.

At the edge of the village, the **Millbrook Country House** (3244 Sharon Turnpike, Millbrook, 845/677-9570, www.millbrookcountryhouse.com, $175-275) blends American Colonial architecture with 18th-century Italian decor. Journalist Lorraine Alexander and her husband, Giancarlo Grisi, moved from a Mediterranean town in Italy to open the bed-and-breakfast in 2002. The elegant furnishings and linens in their four guest rooms reflect the tastes of experienced world travelers. Behind the house is a white-picket-fenced flower and herb garden. This is a great launching point for a tour of Innisfree Garden, winery visits, or a day at Orvis Sandanona.

Ten minutes from the village, ★ **The Millbrook Inn** (3 Gifford Rd., Millbrook, 845/605-1120, www.themillbrookinn.com, $190-290) has eight rooms in a turn-of-the-century building that was once part of Hope Farm School. Neutral colors and dark wood accent the rooms; there are no floral prints here. For breakfast the innkeeper serves farm eggs and bacon, fresh fruit, and yogurt. This inn makes a convenient home base for a weekend of leaf-peeping and wine-tasting.

Over $200

Built in 1841, the nine-room **Red Hook Country Inn** (7460 S. Broadway, Red Hook, 845/758-8445, $210) is close to Bard College. Lace curtains let in plenty of natural light. Hardwood floors, antique furnishings, and floral bedspreads complete the look. The building and two of its guest rooms are wheelchair accessible. While you're there, enjoy a pot of tea and an Irish scone in **Maggie's RoyalTea** (11:30am-3:30pm Fri.-Sun.), run by the innkeeper and chef.

One of the newest boutique properties in the area, the ★ **The Dutchess Inn & Spa** (151 Main St., Beacon, 845/205-2900, http://thedutchessinn.com, from $250) makes for a delightful getaway to Beacon. Twelve rooms of varying sizes are spread across four floors; a couple of the rooms are dog-friendly, too. The midweek two-night special is a good deal in the off-season.

History buffs should plan an overnight stay at the 1766 **Beekman Arms and Delamater Inn** (6387 Mill St., Rhinebeck, 845/876-7077, www.beekmandelamaterinn.com, $229-279). Ask for one of the 13 rooms in the main house, where oak-beamed ceilings are low and wide-plank floors creak with every step. Soundproof it is not. It has been more than a decade since the last major renovations, and some travelers complain of peeling paint, rust, and a musty smell. For somewhat more updated accommodations, ask to stay in the Delamater part of the inn. Skip the included breakfast and try one of the reputable eateries in town. Securing a reservation for when the auto shows come to town may be futile. Repeat visitors reserve every room on the premises more than a year in advance.

For more secluded lodging on a working farm, check out ★ **WhistleWood Farm Bed and Breakfast** (52 Pells Rd., Rhinebeck, 845/876-6838, www. whistlewood.com, $200-325). It has four rooms in the main house and three more in a renovated barn. Oak and pine furnishings, gas fireplace stoves, and accents that include an elk-horn chandelier create a rustic feel. Some rooms have a four-poster bed, a whirlpool, and a private patio; all have air-conditioning and Wi-Fi. The owners serve a hearty farmers' breakfast. Afternoon coffee, tea, pie, and cake are included with your stay. Best of all, you'll be lovingly surrounded by horses, cows, donkeys, chickens, and a few dogs on the property.

Mirbeau Inn & Spa (46 W. Market St., Rhinebeck, 877/647-2328, www.rhinebeck. mirbeau.com, from $410) has a central location walking distance to most of Rhinebeck's shops and restaurants. Its modern rooms have fireplaces and soaking tubs, and there are accessible rooms with either a king or two queen beds. Wellness is the theme here, and you won't want to leave without experiencing the cedar wood sauna, eucalyptus steam room, and a massage or facial treatment.

★ **The Beacon Hotel** (424 Main St., Beacon, 845/765-2208, http://cartersrestaurantandlounge.com/the-hotel, $235) has a dozen modern guest rooms ranging from a spacious king suite to the Hiker's Haven, a room with four custom-built bunk beds. Once known as Dibble House, this property goes way back in Beacon history, to the 1870s, well before the Beacon Incline came on the scene.

Just six miles from the CIA campus, travel industry pros Nancy and Eric Norberg operate the ★ **Inn at Twaalfskill** (144 Vineyard Ave., Highland, 845/691-3605, https://innattwaalfskill.com, $210-235). It has three beautiful guest rooms, each with a number of special touches, and an inviting breakfast room that gets plenty of morning light. Luxury linens, air conditioning, and working windows are a plus for a building that dates back to the early 20th century.

Campgrounds

Ideal for a family car-camping trip, **Wilcox Memorial Park** (Rte. 199, Milan, 845/758-6100, http://co.dutchess.ny.us, May-Sept., nonresidents $35) has two small lakes with fishing, boat rentals, and swimming Memorial Day-Labor Day. Kids can safely explore miles of trails by foot or on bikes.

You're in for a glamping-style adventure at ★ **Malouf's Mountain Sunset Campground** (www.maloufmountain.com, Apr.-Oct., $48-80). All you have to do is hike in and out; the staff provides the rest—a tent, wood, cooking equipment, meals, and even a modern bathhouse with blow-dryers.

INFORMATION AND SERVICES

The **Dutchess County Tourism Promotion Agency** (3 Neptune Rd., Suite Q-17, Poughkeepsie, 845/463-4000, www. dutchesstourism.com) can provide a wealth of information on places to see across the county. Several of the smaller towns have visitors centers as well: **Rhinebeck Chamber of Commerce** (23F E. Market St., Rhinebeck, 845/876-5904, www.rhinebeckchamber. com) and **Red Hook Area Chamber of Commerce** (845/758-0824, www. redhookchamber.org).

GETTING THERE AND AROUND
Bus

Shortline Bus (800/631-8405, www. coachusa.com) provides daily service to Poughkeepsie, Hyde Park, and Rhinebeck from New York City (adults $45-52 round-trip), Long Island, and New Jersey. The **Dutchess County Public Transit System** (14 Commerce St., Poughkeepsie,

845/485-4690, www.dutchessny.gov) covers major destinations, including Dutchess County Community College, Marist College, and the Poughkeepsie Train Station.

Train

Amtrak and Metro-North offer frequent connections to the Poughkeepsie Train Station, and ride-share drivers are never far away. On weekdays, the parking lot overflows with commuters' vehicles. Amtrak also stops in Rhinecliff to the north. The Metro-North Hudson Line stops in Beacon, while the Harlem Line services Pawling, Dover Plains, and Wassaic.

Car

The most direct routes through Dutchess County are the Taconic State Parkway and Route 22. Route 9 follows the Hudson River through the most densely populated areas of the county. I-84 runs east-west, connecting motorists to I-87, the New York State Thruway. Avis and Hertz have rental car offices off Route 9, near the IBM complex in Poughkeepsie. Budget, Enterprise, and Sears also have rental facilities in the area. Each major town in the county has at least one taxi service.

Ulster County

The Esopus people were the first to settle mountainous Ulster County. European invasion began with a Dutch trading post in 1614, and a series of battles with the Native American population ensued for the next few decades. A group of French Huguenots arrived in 1663, fleeing religious persecution on the continent. One hundred years later came the British, who would burn the county seat of Kingston to the ground during the Revolutionary War.

Ulster's early industries were the production of cement and bluestone; its communities also prospered as the terminus for the Delaware and Ulster Canal, which delivered

coal from mines in Pennsylvania to the Eastern Seaboard.

Covering more than a thousand square miles of riverfront, foothills, and two distinct mountain ranges, modern-day Ulster County is a haven for hikers, rock climbers, organic farmers, foodies, and lovers of nature. The state university at New Paltz and nearby Minnewaska State Park Preserve attract a young and active crowd that supports an abundance of cafés, bookstores, restaurants, and gear shops. Farther west are bohemian Woodstock, the Esopus Creek, and a few of the summer boarding houses that were popular in the 1960s.

Ulster boasts the highest peak in the Catskills: Slide Mountain, which rises 4,180 feet above the town of Oliverea. The Ashokan Reservoir, completed in 1917 in a major engineering feat, supplies more than half of New York City's water.

ALONG THE RIVER: ROUTE 9W

One of the oldest and prettiest spans across the Hudson, the Mid-Hudson Bridge connects southern Ulster County to downtown Poughkeepsie. To the north of the auto bridge, a long-abandoned railroad bridge opened in 2009 as a pedestrian park, known as **Walkway Over the Hudson** (www.walkway. org). The span is 1.3 miles long and connects the town of Highland to Poughkeepsie's waterfront. There is parking at both ends of the span. To get to the west side of the walkway, follow Havelin Drive off Route 9W to a small park that connects to the bridge.

Ten miles south of the Mid-Hudson Bridge, **Gomez Mill House** (11 Millhouse Rd., Marlboro, 845/236-3126, www.gomez.org, 10am-4pm Wed.-Sun. mid-Apr.-early Nov., adults $8, seniors $6, students and children $3) boasts a multicultural past that reaches all the way back to the time of the Spanish Inquisition. Luis Moises Gomez, a Sephardi, or descendant of the Jews who settled Spain and Portugal in the Middle Ages, fled persecution in the early 18th century and built a trading post in Marlboro in 1714. Subsequent owners of the fieldstone home were Patriots of the American Revolution, farmers, writers, artisans, and environmentalists. Today, the building is the oldest surviving Jewish homestead in North America, and tours of the inside (10:30am, 1:15pm, and 2:45pm Wed.-Sat.) are available. The museum holds cultural events and lectures through the summer season.

Slabsides and John Burroughs Nature Sanctuary

Naturalist John Burroughs wrote hundreds of essays over the span of his career, many of them from a log cabin tucked away in the woods near present-day West Park. A student of Whitman and Thoreau, Burroughs treasured the simple things in life: books, friends, and above all, nature. Of a summer hike in the southern Catskills, he wrote, "An ideal trout brook was this, now hurrying, now loitering, now deepening around a great boulder, now gliding evenly over a pavement of green-gray stone and pebbles; no sediment or stain of any kind, but white and sparkling as snow-water, and nearly as cool."

A visit to the Burroughs retreat, called **Slabsides** (261 Floyd Ackert Rd., West Park, 845/384-6320, www. johnburroughsassociation.org), will bring out the nature writer in any traveler. The John Burroughs Association, formed soon after Burroughs died in 1921, maintains the grounds of the 180-acre **John Burroughs Nature Sanctuary** and opens the 1895 cabin to the public twice each year, on the third Saturday in May and the first Saturday in October. You can hike on four miles of easy to moderate trails (dawn-dusk daily). Allow about 20 minutes to walk from the parking lot to the cabin.

Kingston

As the third most important Dutch trading post (after New Amsterdam-Manhattan and Fort Orange-Albany), Kingston played a pivotal role in the establishment of New York State. But early settlers paid dearly for their independence: During the American Revolution, the British retaliated against the colonists by burning the city to the ground. The tragedy left its mark, and no story is repeated more often as one tours the Hudson River Valley's historic sights.

Like Saugerties to its north, Kingston developed around a strategic watershed: where the Rondout Creek meets the Hudson River. Settlers traded cement, bricks, and bluestone, and Kingston served as a transportation hub during the steam and rail eras. Today, greater Kingston (pop. 23,000) is a sea of huge retail stores with some interesting pockets of culture

Kingston

and history. A variety of architectural styles have been preserved, from Federal, Georgian, and Greek Revival to Romanesque, Italianate, neoclassical, and art deco. Two areas are of interest to the traveler: the Stockade District and the revitalized Rondout Village.

Colorful brick facades of mauve, orange, and lima-bean green line Wall Street inside the old stockade, originally built to keep Native Americans out. Many of the homes in this district are private residences, but a few are open to the public. A gorgeous Federal home at the corner of Main and Wall Streets was saved in the late 1930s by **Fred J. Johnston** (63 Main St., Kingston, 11am-4pm Fri.-Sat. May-Oct., adults $10), an antique and restoration specialist. Johnston deeded the home and collection of 18th- and 19th-century furnishings to a local nonprofit

organization, and the building is open to visitors thanks to Friends of Historic Kingston (845/339-0720, www.fohk.org).

Up the street stands the **Old Dutch Church** (272 Wall St., Kingston, 845/338-6759, www.olddutchchurch.org), dating to the 18th century. George Clinton, the first governor of New York and vice president to Jefferson and Madison, is buried here. Hoffman House, at the north end of Front Street, is a Dutch Colonial structure dating to 1679. A pair of entrepreneurs renovated the building in the mid-1970s and turned it into **Hoffman House Restaurant & Tavern** (94 N. Front St., Kingston, 845/338-2626, www.hoffmanhousetavern.com, 11:30am-7pm Tues.-Thurs., 11:30am-8pm Fri.-Sat., 3pm-7pm Sun., $21-27).

In 1777, a group of local political leaders

gathered in Kingston to draft the New York State constitution. The first senate convened at 296 Fair Street, now the **Senate House State Historic Site** (845/338-2786, http://senatehousekingston.org, 10am-5pm Wed.-Sat., 1pm-5pm Sun., adults $7, seniors $5, under age 12 free). A historical exhibit contains paintings by Kingston's own John Vanderlyn.

For a guided **Walking Tour** (1pm 1st Sat. of the month July-Oct., or by appointment) of the 1658 Stockade National Historic District or the Rondout National Historic District, contact **Friends of Historic Kingston** (63 Main St., 845/339-0720, www.fohk.org, adults $10, children $5). Stop by the **Tourism Information Caboose** (Washington Ave., 800/331-1518, www.kingston-ny.gov) to pick up a self-guided brochure. Take New York State Thruway exit 19 to reach downtown Kingston.

When you leave the Stockade District, follow Broadway to its end at **Rondout Landing,** where a handful of eateries and boutiques continue to bring new life and energy to this creekside village. In summer, you can have dinner on the patio and finish the evening with a stroll along the Rondout Creek.

The **Hudson River Maritime Museum** (50 Rondout Landing, 845/338-0071, www.hrmm.org, 11am-5pm Thurs.-Sun. May-Oct., adults $9, seniors and children $6) opens here each spring. A restored 1898 steam tug named *Mathilda* takes up most of the museum's yard. Inside are a 100-year-old shad boat and a number of model ships. A collection of paintings, prints, photos, blueprints, and artifacts document the maritime history of the river—from sloops and iceboats to steam engines and tugs—and the industries it has supported through the years. The museum offers a boat school program for local enthusiasts to learn about the craft of making wooden boats. It also teaches sailing classes to promote enjoyment of the river.

For a taste of life during the railroad era, visit the **Trolley Museum of New York** (89 E. Strand St., 845/331-3399, www.tmny.org, noon-5pm Sat.-Sun. May-Oct., adults $10, seniors and ages 5-12 $8, under age 5 free) at Rondout Landing and take a short ride along the original tracks of the Delaware & Ulster Railroad. The trolley stops at Kingston Point Park on the Hudson River. Exhibits inside the museum trace the history of rail transportation, and visitors can watch restorations in progress in the workshop below.

The **Catskill Mountain Railroad** (149 Aaron Court, Kingston, 845/332-4854, www.catskillmountainrailroad.com) runs themed train rides on a historic line to Hurley Mountain and back. Not to be missed around the holidays, the Polar Express event recreates the classic children' story on board an actual rail car.

Saugerties

The Esopus Creek empties into the Hudson at Saugerties. Water rushing out of the mountains once powered a mill that led the town to the forefront of the paper industry. Recognition on the National Register of Historic Places put Saugerties back on the map, with an eight-block stretch of 18th- and 19th-century homes, antiques shops, and top-notch restaurants that appeal to collectors and food travelers.

The restored **Saugerties Lighthouse** (168 Lighthouse Dr., off Mynderse St., 845/247-0656, www.saugertieslighthouse.com), built in 1869, stands at the mouth of the Esopus Creek. Access is via a 0.5-mile-long walk along a nature path that can be flooded at high tide, or by personal boat. Now a two-room bed-and-breakfast, the house is furnished in 1920s style. Guided tours (noon-3pm Sun. Memorial Day-Labor Day, adults $5, children $3) are available. Plan a picnic along the shoreline and enjoy the secluded river views.

Tucked away on a narrow country lane between Saugerties and Woodstock is a vestige of the bluestone era. Over four decades, sculpture artist Harvey Fite turned an abandoned quarry behind his house and studio into a six-acre sculpture garden that's open to the public

Saugerties

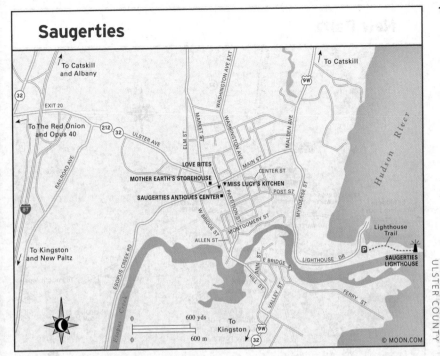

on weekends throughout the summer. A small gallery on-site holds a collection of quarryman's tools. Look for the turnoff to **Opus 40** (50 Fite Rd., Saugerties, 845/246-3400, www.opus40.org, 10am-5pm Thurs.-Sun. and holiday Mon. Memorial Day weekend-Columbus Day weekend, adults $11, students and seniors $9) from Route 212.

NEW PALTZ AND SURROUNDINGS

More than any other community in the Hudson River Valley, New Paltz offers travelers a vibrant alternative culture. Within walking distance from the town center, the State University of New York (SUNY) New Paltz campus fosters a lively student community.

New Paltz has deep roots in protecting groups who face discrimination. The town owes its name to a group of French Huguenots from Mannheim, Germany—part of a region called Die Pfalz—who came to the New World in 1677 to escape religious persecution. These early settlers built homes above the Wallkill River on present-day Huguenot Street.

A short walk uphill from Huguenot Street puts you on Main Street in striking distance of most of the shops and restaurants in town. The **Wallkill Valley Rail Trail** (22 miles, www.wvrta.org) crosses Main Street just below Route 32, making this an ideal stopover for walkers or cyclists following the 12.2-mile section from Wallkill to Rosendale. Drivers should take exit 18 from the New York State Thruway to reach New Paltz. Parking is available at the Huguenot Historical Society's lot (18 Broadhead Ave., 2 blocks north of Rte. 299/Main St.), as well as the Village of New Paltz municipal parking lot (off Huguenot St., north of Rte. 299/Main St.). Expect traffic jams and difficult parking on summer weekends.

Now affiliated with Locust Grove in Poughkeepsie, **Locust Lawn Farm and the Terwilliger House** (436 S. Rte. 32, Gardiner, 845/454-4500, www.lgny.org) make up yet

New Paltz

another historic homestead. This one, on the banks of the Plattekill Creek, was formerly occupied by five generations of the Hasbrouck family. On the estate are an 1814 Federal mansion with a collection of family memorabilia on display inside, and the colonial-era Dutch stone Terwilliger House. Sixty-minute guided tours (minimum 2 people, $15 pp weekends, $25 pp weekdays) can be arranged by appointment May-October.

Robibero Family Vineyards (714 Albany Post Rd., New Paltz, 845/255-9463, www. rnewyorkwine.com, 11am-6pm daily, tasting $20) got started in 2010 and has expanded its line-up of original blends over the years. Bring a blanket or chair to enjoy the lawn while you sip on a glass of white Traminette or red Rabbits Foot. Live music plays on weekend afternoons too.

★ Historic Huguenot Street

Several of the six original stone buildings on this street have survived more than three centuries of evolution in the community. The original structures of the Bevier-Elting, Jean Hasbrouck, and Abraham Hasbrouck Houses were built in the 1680s, and these homes are preserved as they would have looked in the 18th century. The 1799 LeFevre House was built in the Federal style, and the museum has furnished it with 19th-century accoutrements. The Deyo House is designed to portray an 1890s aesthetic, while the Colonial Freer House was remodeled in the 1940s.

You can download a free walking tour app from the Huguenot Historical Society website (www.huguenotstreet.org). The group also runs guided one-hour tours every day except for Wednesday at 10:30, noon, and 2:30pm, departing from the **DuBois Fort Visitor Center** (18 Broadhead Ave., New Paltz, 845/255-1660, Thurs.-Tues. June-Oct., adults $12, seniors and under 13 $10, under 6 free).

Keep an eye out for special events, some educational and some purely festive. In September, the Fall Harvest Celebration includes a farm-to-table dinner, while October brings cider tastings at the Reformed Church and spooky Halloween decorations all along the historic district.

The Shawangunk Ridge

Between New Paltz and the Catskill Mountains lies another mountain range with its own geologic history, the Shawangunk Ridge. The result of a continental collision, the exposed sedimentary rock of the Shawangunks offers amateur and professional geologists an accessible living laboratory to study the formation of the Appalachian Mountains—an eroded range that once stretched as high as the Himalayas.

The Shawangunk Ridge runs from the town of Rosendale all the way to New Jersey and Pennsylvania. From the spotted salamander to the black bear, it supports a delicate habitat for dozens of endangered plants and animals, among them the dwarf pitch pine, which grows on bedrock, and the peregrine falcon, made famous in the children's book *My Side of the Mountain*. Shale cliffs and dramatic overhangs also form ideal pitches for serious rock climbers, who know the area as "the Gunks." Climbers arrive by the hundreds on clear summer days, with their ropes, harnesses, and chalk in tow.

Three protected wilderness areas cover a large portion of the Shawangunk Ridge: Minnewaska State Park Preserve, the Mohonk Preserve, and Sam's Point Preserve.

★ Minnewaska State Park Preserve

Acquired by New York State in 1987, **Minnewaska State Park Preserve** (5281 Rte. 44/55, New Paltz, 845/255-0752, http://parks.ny.gov, day-use year-round, $10 per

vehicle) encompasses 12,000 acres with a main entrance at **Lake Minnewaska,** off Route 44/55. Though the elevation here is about 2,000 feet, the scrubby pines, precipitous cliffs, and sparkling water might trick you into thinking you are above 10,000 feet.

Swimming normally is permitted in the lake, but it has been known to close in years past for problems with leeches. Hikers have a full menu of options within Minnewaska, from easy 2-mile routes to challenging 10-mile loops. You can actually follow the ridgeline by foot from the Appalachian Trail at the New Jersey state line all the way to Wurtsboro and the Basha Kill preserve, in Sullivan County. Climbers will want to head to the Peter's Kill escarpment, a good alternative to the crowds at the Mohonk Preserve. Bicycles are allowed on the carriage paths only, not on the trails.

In addition to the Lake Minnewaska parking lot, Minnewaska has parking and trailheads at Peter's Kill to the east and Awosting to the west. A word of caution: To protect the fragile ecosystem, the park service limits the number of visitors allowed in Minnewaska at once. On summer weekends, the lots often fill immediately after opening. It's a good idea to arrive with a backup plan in mind, such as exploring the Wallkill Valley Rail Trail. Minnewaska is a day-use-only park; there are no overnight accommodations, and visitors must pack out all trash.

South of Minnewaska is the 4,600-acre **Sam's Point Area** (Sam's Point Rd., Cragsmoor, 845/647-7989, http://parks.ny.gov, 9am-7pm Thurs.-Mon., vehicles $10) of Minnewaska, created in 1997 to protect the rare ridgetop dwarf pine barrens that define the landscape. Trails lead to numerous valley vistas, and the moderately strenuous hike to **Verkeerderkill Falls** (7.6 miles) takes about five hours round-trip. Follow Route 52 to Cragsmoor.

Mohonk Preserve

Adjoining Minnewaska to the north is the **Mohonk Preserve** (3197 Rte. 44/55, New Paltz, 845/255-0919, www.mohonkpreserve.org, hikers $15, climbers, cyclists, and horseback riders $20), set aside by the environmentally aware Smiley family. Climbers flock here to choose from 1,000 different routes through world-class crags and crevices. Hikers have 65 miles of trails to explore. Follow Route 199 from New Paltz to find the Mohonk visitors center. Climbers will want to continue past the center to the West Trapps trailhead. Parking lots fill quickly on weekend mornings.

At the intersection of Minnewaska and Mohonk lies the fairytale **Mohonk Mountain House** (1000 Mountain Rest Rd., New Paltz, 855/883-3798, www.mohonk.com), whose story begins with 280 acres of land, a 10-room inn, and a pair of Quaker twins. In the late 19th century, Albert and Alfred Smiley built rival country inns on the ridgeline, which grew to accommodate hundreds of guests at a time. A network of carriage paths connected the properties and provided the ideal setting for quiet contemplation. One of the original buildings burned down, but to this day, the historic Mohonk Mountain House, on the shores of Lake Mohonk, is owned and run by descendants of the Smiley family.

In its heyday, this sprawling hotel entertained a slew of famous guests, among them John Burroughs, Andrew Carnegie, and Theodore Roosevelt. Mohonk is no longer the remote and elegant wilderness getaway it was in the 19th century, but the property remains as beautiful as ever and continues to draw a steady crowd of visitors. Today, it serves as a popular venue for weddings and corporate events. Be a guest for just a day—to golf, dine, or get a spa treatment—or stay longer in one of the rooms, suites, or cottages.

Rosendale

Surrounding New Paltz are several smaller but equally charming towns: Route 32 north takes you to Rosendale, home of the internationally acclaimed Rosendale Cement Company (www.rosendalecement.net), whose "natural cement" limestone was patented in 1798

and used in nearly every major construction project undertaken in the 19th century: Rosendale cement found its way into the Brooklyn Bridge, the wings of the U.S. Capitol, the pedestal of the Statue of Liberty, the Washington Monument, Grand Central Terminal, and even the Panama Canal. The company continued producing until 1970, when the last of the original mines shut down. In 2004, Edison Coatings in Connecticut initiated production of the cement for the purposes of restoring historic structures.

Geologists head to Rosendale's abandoned mines for clues about the past. The **Widow Jane Mine** (688 Rte. 213, 845/658-9900, www.centuryhouse.org, 1pm-4pm Sun. May 8-Sept. 25 or by appointment, adults $5, children $1), run by the Century House Historical Society, is a rare horizontal mine that is open to the public. Since its operational days ended, the mine has been used to grow mushrooms and trout, and as a venue for musical performances.

The society also operates the former estate of farmer-turned-businessman A. J. Snyder, an 1809 home that's listed on the National Register of Historic Places. A tour of the **Snyder Estate** (668 Rte. 213, 845/658-9900, www.centuryhouse.org, 1pm-4pm Sun. May 8-Sept. 25 or by appointment, adults $5, children $1) covers the house and mine, as well as a visit to the Delaware and Hudson Canal and a look at the old cement kilns.

High Falls

Hidden in the Shawangunk Mountains, on the south shore of the swift-flowing Rondout Creek, High Falls has found a niche in accommodating the spillover of weekenders from New Paltz. Many residents here started as weekenders, evolved into part-time commuters, and eventually moved in for good.

1: Lake Minnewaska **2:** clay pots on display in the Huguenot Street historic district **3:** wooden footbridge at Minnewaska State Park Preserve **4:** Mohonk Mountain House

A two-block stretch of businesses includes a handful of boutique stores and ever-changing eateries.

It was a cold January day in 1825 when the founders of the Delaware and Hudson Canal Company began their company's public offering with a show-and-tell on Wall Street: the burning of anthracite coal. In the midst of the War of 1812, the country faced its first energy crisis and needed an alternative to bituminous coal, which the British had been supplying. Pennsylvania coal offered an alternative; the challenge was getting it from inland hills to coastal settlements.

The offering succeeded and thus began the construction of the Delaware and Hudson Canal. Built by Irish immigrants on the heels of the Erie Canal (by the same architect), it measured 108 miles long, 4 feet deep, and 32 feet wide. Along the way, the canal passed through 108 locks and 137 bridges. At its terminus, it had to drop 70 feet to sea level in Rondout Creek—a series of five locks did the trick.

The **D&H Canal Museum** (1315 NY 213, High Falls, 845/687-2000, www.canalmuseum.org, 10am-4:30pm Sat.-Sun. May-Oct., adults $5, children $3), formerly housed in the St. John's Episcopal Church, has moved to a new location at the Mid Hudson Visitor Center at the former Depuy Canal House. Exhibits trace the history of canal and railroad transportation.

Traveling Route 209 from High Falls toward Kingston, you'll pass through Marbletown, where the Ulster County Historical Society maintains the **Bevier House Museum** (2682 Rte. 209, Marbletown, 845/377-1040, www.ulstercountyhs.org, 11am-5pm Sat.-Sun. May-Oct., adults $10, seniors $5, ages 5-12 $4, under age 5 free). The building is a stone farmhouse with an exhibit of 18th- and 19th-century furniture and farming tools. Five generations of Davenports have farmed the land in neighboring Stone Ridge. Today, the family's farm market, greenhouse, and pick-your-own crops at **Davenport Farms** (3411 Rte. 209, Stone Ridge, 845/687-0051, www.davenportfarms.com) are a favorite local supply station.

SOUTHERN CATSKILL MOUNTAINS: ROUTE 28
Ashokan Reservoir

Route 28 west from Kingston leads to the Ashokan ("Place of Fish") Reservoir, the southern Catskill Mountains, and many of the old resorts that made the region world-famous. Completed in 1915, the second-oldest reservoir in the New York City watershed (Croton is the oldest) was formed by damming the Esopus Creek. Nine villages were flooded in its making, and an entire cemetery of Revolutionary War graves were dug up and relocated. The Ashokan holds 122.9 billion gallons in an artificially constructed lake that covers 8,315 acres. The Dividing Weir separates the upper and lower basins of the reservoir.

Fish populations are healthy, but boaters and anglers require a free New York City Department of Environmental Protection (www.nyc.gov) permit to access the water. Woodstock-based **Overlook Bicycles** (1 Mountain Rd., Shokan, 845/657-4001, https://overlookbicycles.com) rents bikes for pedaling along the Ashokan Rail Trail.

Woodstock

Follow the turnoff for Route 375 to reach the mountain town of Woodstock, an artists' colony with deep roots in folk and rock music. (Bob Dylan was a longtime resident.) Unlike some of the Hudson Valley's river towns, Woodstock has not reinvented itself overnight to appeal to a new demographic. Its busy cafés and art galleries give the impression of a genuine place with a passion for the arts.

Present-day Woodstock attracts a creative and outdoor-oriented crowd, including many New York City escapees. Woodstock is also one of the few towns in the region that have inviting accommodations within walking distance of shops and restaurants.

A popular day hike from Woodstock is the **Overlook Mountain Fire Tower** (34

Wardwell Lane, 845/679-2580) at 3,150 feet elevation. On clear days, the summit rewards hikers with a sweeping view of the Hudson River to the east. The trail (2.4 miles one-way, moderate) passes the remains of the Overlook Mountain House, another of the Catskills' 19th-century inns. Listen for the rattle of the endangered timber rattlesnake along the way. To reach the trailhead from Woodstock, follow Rock City Road from Route 212 and cross Route 33, where the name changes to Meads Mountain Road. The trailhead is about 1.5 miles up the mountain.

Across from the trailhead, one of Woodstock's old inns, the former Mead Mountain House, is now a Tibetan Buddhist monastery called the **Karma Triyana Dharmachakra** (335 Meads Mountain Rd., 845/679-5906, www.kagyu.org, public access 8:30am-5:30pm daily, guided tours 1pm Sat.-Sun.). It may be the only monastery in the world located in a 19th-century farmhouse. Visitors can tour the main shrine room, which contains one of the largest Shakyamuni Buddha statues in North America. A library and bookstore (9am-5pm daily) are also open to the public. If you plan to walk or bike from town, it's 2.5 miles, and all uphill.

Beyond the Ashokan Reservoir and just minutes from Woodstock, a cluster of newish buildings along the Esopus Creek are the **Emerson Resort & Spa** (5340 Rte. 28, Mt. Tremper, 845/688-2828, www.emersonresort. com), with a landmark kaleidoscope and associated shops and restaurants.

Phoenicia

Keep going along Route 28 to understated Phoenicia, where you can float the Esopus by inner tube in summer and ski your way across the valley in winter. The Catskill Mountain Railroad no longer runs here, but you might try your legs at a pedal-powered rail vehicle with **Rail Explorers** (70 Lower High St., Phoenicia, 877/833-8588, www. railexplorers.net, $90 tandem). Picture a paddle boat on the water, except you'll be cruising along tracks next to the Esopus.

The eight-mile guided trip takes about two hours to complete.

Train aficionados will want to check out the **Empire State Railway Museum** (70 Lower High St., Phoenicia, 845/688-7501, www.esrm.com, 10am-4pm Sat.-Sun.), which celebrated its 60th anniversary in 2020. The historic Phoenicia station has been renovated in recent years. Engine #23, stored in the car barn, is up next for refurbishing.

Follow the moderately strenuous, red-blazed Phoenicia Trail up to the **Tremper Mountain Fire Tower** (3.4 miles one-way) for views of the Devil's Path and surrounding cloves and hollows. Park in the small lot along Route 40 (http://catskillcenter.org). Keep a look out for timber rattlesnakes in the rocky areas.

Slide Mountain

A few miles past Phoenicia in the town of Shandaken, Route 42 turns north to Greene County. Soon after, in Big Indian, comes the turn for Route 47, or Oliverea Slide Mountain Road. This road leads to Frost Valley and the base of Slide Mountain. It's an eight-mile drive along Route 47 to the historic and private Winnisook Club (1837 Oliverea Rd., Big Indian) and the Slide Mountain parking lot.

Naturalist John Burroughs spent long hours contemplating the highest peak in the Catskills. In an essay about the southern Catskills, he wrote that the peak looked like the back and shoulders of a gigantic horse. Burroughs spent many years fishing the streams that drained the mountain and camping on all sides of the peak before he attempted a summit. On approaching Slide at last from a spruce grove on the north side, he wrote, "The mountain rose like a huge, rock-bound fortress from this plain-like expanse. It was ledge upon ledge, precipice upon precipice, up which and over which we made our way slowly and with great labor, now pulling ourselves up by our hands, then cautiously finding niches for our feet and zigzagging right and left from shelf to shelf."

It's much easier to access Slide Mountain

today, but the hike remains one of the most difficult in the Catskill Forest Preserve. A strenuous five-mile route from the parking lot leads to the top. There are no views from the summit proper, but from a ridge that connects Slide to neighboring Wittenberg Mountain, you can see all but one of the thirty-four Catskill High Peaks that rise above 3,500 feet (Thomas Cole peak is obscured by Hunter Mountain). Allow four or five hours to complete the hike.

At the base of Slide Mountain, **Woodland Valley Campground** (1319 Woodland Valley Rd., Phoenicia, 845/688-7647, http://dec.ny.gov, camping $20 residents, $25 out-of-state) has well maintained campsites and good fishing in the creek. This is a great base camp for the Slide Wittenberg Trail or the Woodland Valley-Denning Trail.

★ Belleayre Mountain

Past the turnoff for Oliverea, Route 28 begins to climb until it reaches the base of the **Belleayre Mountain Ski Center** (181 Galli Curci Rd., Highmount, 845/254-5600, www.belleayre.com, 7am-6pm Mon.-Fri., 7am-7:30pm Sat.-Sun. Nov.-Mar.). With ideal terrain for intermediate skiers, Belleayre is located within the Catskill Forest Preserve. Skiers began carving turns down its slopes as early as the 1930s, and in 1949, the New York State Department of Environmental Conservation cleared a network of trails and opened the area to the public.

In summer, the resort has added **downhill mountain biking** and **Belleayre Beach at Pine Hill Lake** (33 Friendship Manor Rd., Pine Hill, 845/254-6195, vehicles $15, walk-in $5), a small lake suitable for swimming, fishing, and paddle boarding. Rentals are available on-site.

Shawangunk Wine Trail

Ulster County has several small wineries producing white and red varietals, many of them unique to the region. A few have teamed up to map out a wine trail along backroads connecting the New York State Thruway, I-84, and Highway 17 between New Paltz and Warwick in Orange County.

Head south from New Paltz to start at **Robibero Family Vineyards** (714 Albany Post Rd., New Paltz, 845/255-9463, www.rnewyorkwine.com, 11am-6pm daily, tasting $20), then make your way to **Whitecliff Vineyard & Winery** (331 McKinstry Rd., Gardiner, 845/255-4613, www.whitecliffwine.com, noon-5:30pm Mon.-Thurs., 11am-5:30pm Fri.-Sun. June-Nov.; 11:30am-5:30pm Thurs.-Mon. Feb.-May and Dec.; 11:30am-5pm Sat.-Sun. Jan.) to sample the award-winning vidal blanc. This winery has opened a second tasting room at its vineyard in Hudson, across the river in Columbia County.

Continue on to Pine Bush, where you can visit **Baldwin Vineyards** (176 Hardenburgh Rd., Pine Bush, 845/744-2226, http://baldwinvineyards.com, noon-5pm Thurs.-Fri. and Sun.-Mon., noon-8pm Sat.)—known for its chardonnay, strawberry wines, and live music on Saturdays—and **Brimstone Hill Vineyard & Winery** (61 Brimstone Hill Rd., Pine Bush, 845/744-2231, www.brimstonehillwinery.com, 11:30am-5:30pm Fri.-Mon.), where the vin rouge and noiret stand out.

Next, it's time to head east toward Marlboro, where the grapes grow closer to the Hudson River. **Benmarl Winery** (156 Highland Ave., Marlboro, 845/236-4265, http://benmarl.com, 11am-6pm daily, 4-wine tasting $15, reservations required) has been around the longest, having received the first farm wine license in the state. It's also one of the rare tasting rooms to stay open year-round, with à la carte food served on the weekends. Seek out a taste of the cabernet franc and seyval blanc estate bottles. This winery has B&B-style accommodations ($300 d) listed through Airbnb, and tastings are included with your stay!

If there's time, head over to the tasting rooms of two more Marlboro wineries: **Stoutridge Vineyard** (10 Ann Kaley Lane, Marlboro, 845/236-7620, www.stoutridge.com, 11am-6pm Thurs.-Sun., tasting $15)

Snow Stats: Belleayre Mountain

- Base: 2,025 feet
- Summit: 3,429 feet
- Vertical: 1,404 feet
- Trails: 50
- Lifts: 8
- Skiable acres: 174
- Snowmaking: 96 percent
- Snow report: 800/942-6904

4:30pm-7pm and on the weekends 1:30pm-4:30pm. The winery has added a farm-to-table menu from a local chef, but you are welcome to bring your own food as well. Picnicking is encouraged here.

A map of all these locations (845-256-8456, www.shawangunkwinetrail.com) is available online and at any of the member wineries.

RECREATION
Winter Sports

With the highest skiable peak in the Catskills, **Belleayre** (181 Galli Curci Rd., Highmount, 845/254-5600, www.belleayre.com, 9am-4pm daily Nov.-Mar., adults $95) is a fun ski hill for cross-country, downhill, and snowboarding. Families especially love the mountain for its varied terrain and range of instructional programs. Little ones can start on the Magic Carpet and progress all the way up to a competitive team. In this era of unpredictable winters, snowmaking covers 96 percent of the terrain. Belleayre also grooms 9.2 kilometers of cross-country ski trails. Multiday discounts and substantial discounts for advance purchase are available online.

In the shadow of Slide Mountain, the **Frost Valley YMCA** (2000 Frost Valley Rd., Claryville, 845/985-2291, http://frostvalley.

is both a winery and a distillery, so you can taste some of both when you visit. The winery follows sustainable winemaking processes, using gravity instead of pumps and filters, and skipping the sulfites and other additives. See if you can taste the difference. At nearby **Glorie Farm Winery** (40 Mountain Rd., Marlboro, 845/236-3265, http://gloriewine.com, 2pm-7:30pm Fri., 11am-5:30pm Sat.-Sun. and holiday Mondays, tasting $20), making wine became an extension of a longtime fruit farm business. Catch the live music every Friday

top of a ski trail at Belleayre Mountain

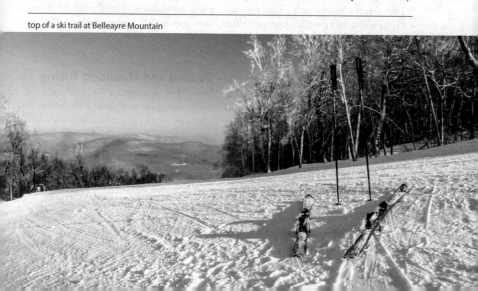

org, 9:30am-4:30pm Sat., 9:30am-12:30pm Sun. Dec.-Mar., full-day $40, half-day $25, includes lunch) provides access to 25 kilometers of cross-country ski trails, including several cable bridge crossings. Strung high above a swift-flowing creek, these "bridges" are made of three single cables in an inverted triangle: one for your feet and the other two for your hands. Choose a different route if you are at all afraid of heights. Ideal for groups, Frost Valley has cabins on the premises with hot showers and flush toilets. Some are in better shape than others. Meals are included with your stay, and reservations are required.

For the most extensive network of cross-country ski trails (35 kilometers), head to Minnewaska State Park Preserve. Grooming is spotty on the beginner and intermediate trails. Skiers with backcountry gear may enjoy the loop around Lake Awosting. In winter months, the carriage roads around Mohonk also invite Nordic skiing. Some are groomed for skate skiing only. Rent your gear on the way in at **Rock & Snow** (44 Main St., New Paltz, 845/255-1311, www.rocksnow.com, 9am-6pm Mon.-Thurs., 9am-8pm Fri., 8am-8pm Sat., 8am-7pm Sun.).

Hiking

Ulster County hikers can't go wrong with endless miles of beautiful terrain in the Shawangunks and southern Catskills. Here are some of the perennial favorites and a few lesser known routes:

You need to purchase a hiking pass (www.mohonk.com, adults $30, under 13 $25) to explore the 85 miles of private trails around the Mohonk Mountain House. For most, a trip through the **Labyrinth and Lemon Squeeze** (5.6-mile loop, difficult) is well worth the investment. You'll scramble over rocks, squeeze through cracks, and climb ladders—all for views of the Catskills and bragging rights for making it to the other side.

For a less challenging day hike near Woodstock, head to the base of **Overlook Mountain** (5 miles round-trip, moderate), on Meads Mountain Road (www.catskillcenter.

org) and walk the gravel road up to the fire tower and the ruins of the Overlook Mountain House. Overflow parking is available on MacDaniel Road, about 0.5 miles from the trailhead. For serious climbers, **Wittenberg Mountain** presents one of the toughest hikes in the Catskills (7.2 miles round-trip and 2,600 feet of elevation gain). This is a full-day hike that starts at the Woodland Valley Campground in Phoenicia. See http://hikethehudsonvalley.com for route details.

Near Saugerties, **Huckleberry Point** (4.5 miles round-trip) is a local favorite for great views that don't require scaling a 3,000-foot peak (you'll drive much of the elevation gain instead). Plan for moderately challenging terrain and weather that can change moment to moment.

Trails in the **John Burroughs Nature Sanctuary** (261 Floyd Ackert Rd., West Park, 845/384-6320, www.johnburroughsassociation.org) meander through four miles of forests and ferns, around a pond, and through a swamp, creating opportunities for wildflower and bird sightings. The **Ridge Trail** (0.9 mile one-way, moderate) is the longest in the park. Back at the river's edge, **Black Creek Preserve** (Winding Brook Acres Rd., off Route 9W, 7.6 miles north of the Mid-Hudson Bridge, dawn-dusk year-round) has two miles of trails on a 130-acre property managed by Scenic Hudson.

Cycling and Mountain Biking

New Paltz is a mecca for avid cyclists. Surrounding country roads have terrain to match all levels: flat fields, rolling hills, and steep climbs. Stop by the **Bicycle Depot** (15 Main St., New Paltz, 845/255-3859, www.bicycledepot.com, noon-5pm Wed.-Sat., 11am-4pm Sun., $40 per day, after 2pm $27) at the bottom of Main Street for route advice or to rent mountain bikes for tours of Minnewaska, Mohonk, or the local rail trails. **TRT Bicycles** (1066 Rte. 32, Rosendale, 845/658-7832, www.trtbicycles.com, 11am-5pm Mon. and Wed.-Fri., 11am-4pm Sat.)

rents Trek mountain and road bikes for $20 per hour or $40-50 per day. The **Wallkill Valley Rail Trail** is a favorite route for trail riding, jogging, and walking. This 12-mile trail connects the towns of New Paltz, Rosendale, and Gardiner. All trail signs have maps on the back.

For riding near Woodstock, try **Overlook Mountain Bikes** (93 Tinker St., Woodstock, 845/679-2122, www.overlookmountainbikes. com, 11am-5pm Thurs.-Mon.). Belleayre recently added downhill riding (10am-6pm daily July-Aug.) to its lineup of summer activities. The mountain provides tours, gondola access ($30), and rentals ($49). This store has an outpost in Shokan (1 Mountain Rd., Shokan, 845/657-4001), for those who'd like to rent a bike to explore the Ashokan Rail Trail.

Conveniently located on the 22-mile Wallkill Valley Rail Trail, **Happy Trails Bike Rental** (310 River Road Ext., New Paltz, 917/443-3600, http://happytrailsbikerental. com, daily by appointment, $15 per hour or $50 all day) has Biria brand cruiser bikes in two sizes. Your ride begins and ends at the popular **Rail Trail Café** (Stone Mtn. Farm, 310 River Road Ext., New Paltz). On this ride, the **Rosendale Trestle Bridge** is a fun spot for a selfie.

Golf

More than a dozen golf courses are scattered along the base of the Shawangunks in Ulster County. One of the prettiest, **Apple Greens Golf** (161 South St., Highland, 845/883-5500, www.applegreens.com, $30-70), is set on an apple orchard. The formerly private club **Wiltwyck** (404 Steward Lane, Kingston, 845/331-0700, http://wiltwyck.org, $28-50) has opened its championship course to the public in recent years.

Swimming and Boating

Ulster County offers access to several unusual water sports: A day of drifting along the Esopus Creek is practically a mandatory activity for anyone who lives within a day's drive of Phoenicia. Time your visit on the one

day a month when the water is released, and you'll be in for a real whitewater adventure. **Town Tinker Tube Rental** (10 Bridge St., Phoenicia, 845/688-5553, www.towntinker. com, 9am-6pm daily, $40 per day full gear rental) offers tubing courses for beginners and experts. It takes about two hours to travel 2.5 miles along the river.

Planning a trip to the Caribbean and need to get certified to dive? Spend two weekends with **Deep-Six Underwater Systems** (14 Deerpath Dr., New Paltz, 845/255-7446, www.deep-six.com) and you'll be good to go. Training dives take place at Diver's Cove in Lake Minnewaska, where the Mid-Hudson Diving Association has set up a bench and drying racks for fellow divers.

Lake Minnewaska is hands-down the most beautiful place to swim in Ulster County. In summer, the surface temperature climbs to a refreshing 75°F. Visibility is not as good as it once was (10-12 feet on average), but underwater cliffs and a maximum depth of 72 feet make for an interesting dive in a safe environment. Expect a thermocline at about 30 feet.

Hudson River Cruises (Rondout Landing, Kingston, 845/251-4021, www. hudsonrivercruises.com, 2:30pm Mon.-Fri., 11:30am and 2:30pm Sat.-Sun., adults $33, seniors $30, ages 4-11 $22) offers tours aboard the *Rip Van Winkle* from Rondout Landing. Passengers are able to see the historic Rondout and Esopus lighthouses and the Vanderbilt, Staatsburg, and Wilderstein estates from the shaded deck in spring, summer, and fall. The boat turns around at Hyde Park. This is a unique way to experience the fall colors. Inquire about dinner/sunset and brunch cruises.

Fishing

Anglers primarily use nymphs and streamers to fish the lower **Esopus Creek,** since it gets less water pressure than the Delaware, Willowemoc, and Beaver Kill. As a tailwater, the Esopus offers the best conditions late in the season. Access the stream near Boiceville.

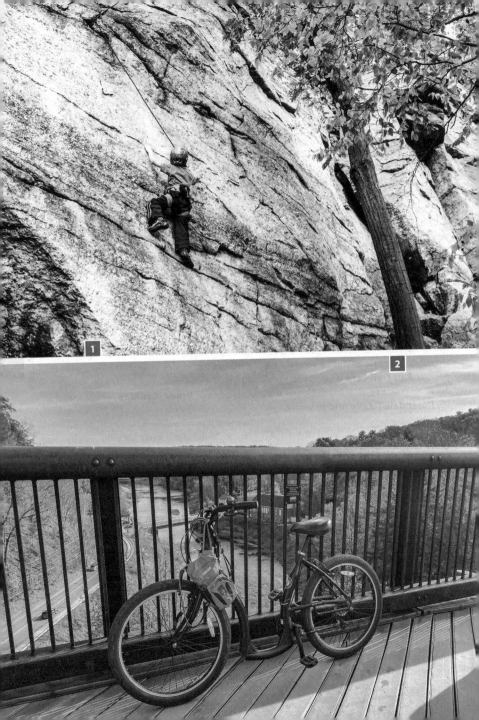

Contact **Fly-fishing with Bert Darrow** (P.O. Box 153, Rosendale, 845/658-9784, www. flyfishwithbert.com) for professional instruction and guiding services on the Catskills' trout streams in May, June, and September. He is a recognized expert in dry fly techniques and offers a two-day intensive program for $575.

The **Ashokan and Rondout Reservoirs** hold healthy populations of brown trout, smallmouth bass, and rock bass.

Aviation

Learn to glide at the **Mountain Wings Hang Gliding Center** (77 Hang Glider Rd., Ellenville, 845/647-3377, www.mtnwings. com), where an introductory program costs $180 per person. The course is certified by the United States Hang Gliding Association (USHGA) and includes four hours of training with videos and a simulator, followed by supervised flights.

You can jump from 13,500 feet and free-fall to 6,000 feet with **Skydive the Ranch** (55 Sandhill Rd., Gardiner, 845/255-4033, www.skydivetheranch.com, $225 per tandem jump including gear, plus $129 for a video of the dive). Repeat visitors can complete all 13 levels of the Instructor-Assisted Freefall (IAF) skydiver training program.

★ Rock Climbing

When the weather cooperates, climbers flock to the Shawangunk Cliffs, known locally as "the Gunks," to scale several of the 1,000 world-class pitches in the area. Climbers first discovered the Gunks in the mid-1930s, and today, most of the signature climbs are located within the **Mohonk Preserve** (West Trapps Trailhead, Rte. 44, Gardiner, $10). Fall is the best season to go because the rocks are more likely to be dry and the bugs are few. Visiting climbers congregate at The Trapps and The Near Trapps, while locals favor some of the more difficult to access routes. There are one-, two-, and three-pitch climbs for all levels of experience. If you're lead climbing, consider dropping a grade or two from your usual comfort zone—the routes here are notoriously more challenging than they appear at first.

A good alternative to climbing in the Mohonk Preserve is the **Peter's Kill Area** (Rte. 44/55, New Paltz, 845/255-0752, www. nysparks.com, from 9am daily, $10) in nearby Minnewaska State Park. Located five miles west of the junction of Routes 299 and 44/55, and one mile east of the main park entrance, Peter's Kill boasts some of the best bouldering anywhere in the northeast. You'll climb on quartz conglomerate cliffs found a 0.5-mile walk from the parking lot. A range of single-pitch climbs will suit various levels. The area has a daily limit of 70 climbers.

Before you go, pick up a helmet, shoes, chalk, and a climbing harness at **Rock & Snow** (44 Main St., New Paltz, 845/255-1311, www.rocksnow.com, 9am-6pm Mon.-Thurs., 9am-8pm Fri., 8am-8pm Sat., 8am-7pm Sun.). Brush up on your skills at **BC's New Paltz Climbing Gym** (formerly The Inner Wall, 234 Main St., New Paltz, 845/255-7625, http:// bcclimbinggym.com, 5pm-9pm Mon., 2pm-9pm Tues.-Sat., day pass $15, belay course $15, private one-hour lesson $60). Under new ownership in 2018, the space was being redesigned to attract more seasoned climbers with top-rope climbing, bouldering, and auto-belay routes.

HighXposure Adventures (800/777-2546, www.high-xposure.com) offers a range of classes and guided trips, including programs for women, lead training, and transition courses from indoor to outdoor environments. Locals also recommend **Mountain Skills** (845/853-5450, www. mountainskills.biz) for rock climbing as well as ice climbing instruction (full-day rates for single climber $295, two climbers $195 pp, three climbers $165 pp, four climbers $150 pp).

You can also rent climbing shoes and camping equipment at **The Gunks Climbing**

1: climbing in the Gunks 2: Wallkill Valley Rail Trail at the Rosendale Trestle Bridge

School (3124 Rte. 44/55, Gardiner, 800/310-4504, www.emsoutdoors.com, 8:30am-4:30pm daily), run by Eastern Mountain Sports, at the intersection of Routes 299 and 44/55. Unlike other EMS locations, this one is a designated Climbing Specialty Store that offers classes, rental gear, and repair services. Note that the center does not rent harnesses, helmets, ropes, or protective gear—however, you will be provided these items if you enroll in a class with EMS.

Yoga and Spa Treatments

Buttermilk Falls Inn & Spa (220 North Rd., Milton, 845/795-1310, www.buttermilkfallsinn.com) offers all kinds of relaxing spa treatments in a natural setting with river views. You can order lunch to eat beside a small indoor swimming pool, which also has a steam room and a dry sauna. Herbal tea and light snacks are provided in the welcome area. A one-hour massage costs $120-150. Choose from Swedish-style, hot stone, shiatsu, or reflexology. Follow it up with a facial or pedicure before dinner at Henry's Restaurant.

A 30,000-square-foot spa and wellness center at the **Mohonk Mountain House** (877/877-2664, www.mohonk.com, $160-215 for 60 minutes) has 200 windows overlooking Lake Mohonk and the hotel's 2,200-acre mountaintop estate. The spa was built with environmental conservation in mind: Excavated stone was recycled into walls and fireplaces, a geothermal system regulates temperature inside, and a 2,000-square-foot garden terrace functions as a green roof. Choose from a menu of 50 treatments, including the *gua sha* facial, Mohonk Red massage, which incorporates indigenous Mohonk Red witch hazel into the treatment, or the Shawangunk Grit exfoliation, which involves fine quartz grains from the surrounding cliffs. The private couples treatment room has a fireplace. Guests can take a gentle Yin Yoga or Aqua Yoga class or more energizing flow-style classes during a stay at the resort.

Near Phoenicia, you might pamper yourself at the **Emerson Resort and Spa** (5340 Rte. 28, Mt. Tremper, 845/688-2828, www.emersonresort.com, 10am-5pm Thurs.-Mon., 9am-1pm Tues., $135-155 for 60 minutes) near Woodstock, or pop in for a Vinyasa Flow yoga class ($17).

ENTERTAINMENT AND EVENTS
Performing Arts

The **Ulster Performing Arts Center** (601 Broadway, Kingston, 845/339-6088, www.bardavon.org) is managed by the Bardavon Theater in Poughkeepsie, across the river. It is the home of the Hudson Valley Philharmonic, as well as the Ulster Ballet Company and the Catskill Ballet.

Bars and Nightlife

New Paltz and Kingston's Rondout Landing have the most variety for nightlife. Woodstock has a few venues for live music as well. About a dozen bars line a short stretch of Main Street in New Paltz, a town that allows its watering holes to stay open until 4am. Many, though by no means all, of them are student hangouts. **Bacchus** (4 S. Chestnut St., New Paltz, 845/255-8636, www.bacchusnewpaltz.com, noon-10pm Wed.-Sun.), near the corner of Main and Chestnut Streets, keeps 300 beers on hand to accompany an equally extensive late-night menu of pizzas, burgers, wings, and the like. Buffalo wings and a dozen TVs are a hit at **McGillicuddy's Restaurant & Tap House** (84 Main St., New Paltz, 845/256-9289, www.cuddysny.com, 3pm-midnight Mon.-Thurs., 3pm-4am Fri., noon-4am Sat., noon-midnight Sun., cover charge Fri.-Sat. night $3-5), which also has a pool table and dance floor. Nightly drink specials start at 9pm, from $6 Bud Light pitchers on Mondays to $4 Bacardi drinks on Saturdays.

P&G Restaurant (91 Main St., New Paltz, 845/255-6161, www.pandgs.com, 11am-9pm Sun.-Tues and Thurs.-Fri., 11am-10pm Sat.), affectionately known as "Pigs," is a New Paltz institution among students and alumni. It started out as a dance club in the year 1900.

Nightly specials include 2 for 1 Tuesdays and college night on Thursdays.

In the Water Street Market plaza, **Jar'd Wine Pub** (10 Main St., Suite 305, New Paltz, 845/255-8466, https://jardwinepub.com, 3pm-9pm Mon.-Fri., noon-10pm Sat., noon-7pm Sun.) pours interesting wines by the glass, representing everywhere from the Finger Lakes to Germany and Croatia. Try the Cava Kombucha Cocktail for something different.

The Colony (22 Rock City Rd., Woodstock, 845/679-7625, www.colonywoodstock.com, 4pm-11pm Mon. and Wed.-Fri., 11am-11pm Sat.-Sun., $9-15) has been reimagined as a contemporary live music venue, with English pub-style eats. Reserve tickets for classic country, folk music, and other events (8pm, $10-20). At the legendary **Country Inn** (1380 County Road 2, Krumville, 845/657-8956, www.krumville.com), in a southern Catskill hamlet, choose from hundreds of beers among a crowd of locals and travelers.

Festivals

The **Belleayre Music Festival** (181 Galli Curci Rd., Highmount, 845/254-6094) draws a large crowd of music lovers to the Catskills each summer. Popular with kids in October is the **Headless Horseman Hayrides & Haunted Houses** (778 Broadway, Ulster Park, 845/339-2666, www.headlesshorseman. com) on Route 9W between Highland and Kingston. The attraction is open during the last two weekends in September and every weekend in October. Reservations are required.

The **Ulster County Fair** (249 Libertyville Rd., 845/255-1380, www.ulstercountyfair. com, $17), which began in 1886, takes place in August each year, with music, amusement rides, and fireworks. The fairgrounds are located two miles outside New Paltz. Each October, the **Woodstock Film Festival** (845/810-0131, www.woodstockfilmfestival. com) draws a group of leading filmmakers, critics, and local enthusiasts to watch some of the industry's newest and boldest independent films.

Hardneck garlic is indigenous to the Saugerties area; July is the harvest season. Some say it's bitterer than what you buy at the grocery store; others disagree. See for yourself during the last weekend in September, when Saugerties hosts the wildly popular **Hudson Valley Garlic Festival** (Pavilion St., Saugerties, 845/246-3090, www.hvgf.org, adults $10, under age 12 free, cash only). Local musicians, guest chefs, and a long list of food vendors all participate.

SHOPPING
Clothing

The **Groovy Blueberry** (1 Water St. and 57 Main St., New Paltz, 845/256-0873, www. groovyblueberry.com) is a one-of-a-kind shop for locally made tie-dye T-shirts and hoodies. The **Emerson Country Stores** (5340 Rte. 28, at Mt. Pleasant Rd., Mt. Tremper, 845/688-5800, www.emersonresort.com, 10am-5pm Thurs.-Fri. and Sun.-Mon., 10am-6pm Sat.) include half a dozen shops selling everything from kaleidoscopes to games and toys to men's and women's apparel.

Farm Stands

Davenport Farms (3411 Rte. 209, Stone Ridge, 845/687-0051, www.davenportfarms. com, 7am-6pm daily) operates a popular farmers market, greenhouse, and pick-your-own field on Route 209 in Stone Ridge. To pick your own strawberries, apples, pumpkins, or flowers, head to **Kelder's Farm** (5755 Rte. 209, Kerhonkson, 845/626-7137, https:// keldersfarm.com, 10am-6pm Mon.-Tues. and Thurs.-Sun.) in early June.

With three locations, in Kingston (300 Kings Mall Court), Saugerties (249 Main St.), and Poughkeepsie (1955 South Rd.), **Mother Earth's Storehouse** (www. motherearthstorehouse.com) organic grocer is a sight for sore eyes after a long search for healthy food. At the Kingston location, the deli counter packs a crowd at lunchtime, and the staff really know their stuff. Inexpensive it is not.

Not really a farm, but locally made just the

A Wave of Farm Distilleries

In 2008, New York State passed the Farm Distillery Bill, allowing the sale of distilled products on-site for the first time since Prohibition, provided the makers source 70 percent of their materials from the state's agricultural market. The Hudson River Valley was a major grower of barley and rye in the 19th century, and more than 1,000 farms produced regional whiskey and gin. After a long dry spell, a growing group of microdistilleries has captured the imaginations of farmers, restaurants, travelers, and aficionados. With copper stills and on-site malt houses, at least a dozen distilleries are open for tours, tastings, and retail sales across the region.

Tuthilltown Spirits Distillery/Hudson Whiskey (14 Grist Mill Lane, Gardiner, 845/255-1527, www.hudsonwhiskey.com, noon-6pm Sun.-Mon. and Thurs.-Fri., noon-8pm Sat.) was the first of its kind in New York State. Besides the signature lineup of bourbon and rye, the company makes an apple vodka, cacao liqueur, and its own bitters.

Hillrock Estate Distillery (408 Pooles Hill Rd., Ancram, 518/329-1023, www.hillrockdistillery.com) is the creation of the former head distiller of Maker's Mark, who is experimenting with the Solera system of aging whiskey to get the complex flavors that connoisseurs desire. The spirit is then finished in 20-year-old oloroso sherry casks to add the final touch. Barley for the bourbon is grown on the farm, and the entire production process takes place here as well.

Albany Distilling Company (78 Montgomery St., Albany, 518/621-7191, www.albanydistilling.com, tours and tastings 4pm-8pm Tues.-Fri., noon-5pm Sat.) is a small operation in downtown Albany, producing one batch of spirits at a time. Products include the Ironweed whiskey and Quackenbush Still House rum labels. It is the first licensed distillery in Albany since Prohibition.

Although some local malting facilities have opened recently, the founders of **Coppersea Distilling** (1592 Broadway, Rte. 9W, West Park, 845/444-1044, www.coppersea.com) prefer to malt their own grain seeds.

The **Warwick Valley Winery & Distillery** (114 Little York Rd., Warwick, 845/258-4858, www.wvwinery.com, 11am-6pm daily) makes a rustic gin as well as apple and pear brandies.

Orange County Distillery (286 Maple Ave., New Hampton, 845/374-2011, http://orangecountydistillery.com, 4pm-9pm Thurs., 3pm-10pm Fri., noon-10pm Sat., noon-7pm Sun.) is a small operation that hosts tastings, tours, and frequent music events.

Taconic Distillery (179 Bowen Rd., Stanfordville, 845/393-4583, www.taconicdistillery.com) has award-winning bourbon and rye whiskies that you can sample in the tasting room (noon-6pm Sat.).

Hudson Valley Distillers (1727 Rte. 9, Claremont, 518/537-6820, www.hudsondistillers.com, noon-6pm Sun.-Mon. and Thurs.-Fri., noon-8pm Sat.) makes vodka from local apples and gin distilled from local wines. Shop its beverage market or order a drink at the Cocktail Grove.

Dennings Point Distillery (10 N. Chestnut St., Beacon, 845/476-8413, www.denningspointdistillery.com, 2pm-8pm Fri.-Sat., 2pm-6pm Sun.) offers tours on Saturday only. With hints of wildflowers and honey, Maid of the Meadow is one of the unique spirits on the tasting list.

same, **Fruition Chocolate Works** (3091 Rte. 28, Shokan, 845/657-6717, www.tastefruition.com, noon-5pm Fri.-Sun.) makes small batches of specialty bars that wow even the most seasoned tasters. Try the award-winning Cinnamon Maple Bourbon bar, or the 100 percent if you dare. Chocolatier Bryan Graham is a graduate of the Culinary Institute and former sous chef of the Apple Pie Bakery Café. Fair Trade beans come from Peru, and everything else happens in the workshop in Shokan.

Antiques and Galleries

There are dozens of antiques shops and art galleries across Ulster County, many of them clustered around Saugerties and Rosendale. The **Woodstock School of Art** (2470

Rte. 212, Woodstock, 845/679-2388, www. woodstockschoolofart.org) holds auctions and exhibitions during summer months, as well as classes and workshops year-round. The **Center for Photography at Woodstock** (59 Tinker St., Woodstock, 845/679-9957, www.cpw.org, noon-4pm Sat.) shows contemporary works in a small gallery. It also runs workshops, auctions, and lectures.

Most of the 30 antiques shops in Saugerties are located within the eight-block commercial area on Main, Market, and Partition Streets. **Saugerties Antiques Center** (220 Main St., Saugerties, 845/246-8234, 11am-5pm daily) has friendly staff, great selection, and the occasional good deal.

Outdated: An Antique Café (314 Wall St., Kingston, 845/331-0030, www.outdatedcafe.com, 10am-5pm Fri.-Mon.) brings shopping together with food in a trendy café atmosphere. The food ($5-12) is local, organic, and vegetarian. You might find a vintage globe, a funky chair, or one-of-a-kind linens.

Bookstores

Across from the Bread Alone Bakery, **Mirabai Books** (23 Mill Hill Rd., Woodstock, 845/679-2100, www.mirabai.com, 11am-6pm daily) stocks a unique collection of metaphysical books, music, and jewelry, all related to inspiring, transforming, and healing. The owners have added a two-room apartment ($195-495) above the shop, so you can absorb the good vibes all night long.

FOOD

Ulster County holds some culinary surprises, as well as a number of mainstay establishments.

Along the River: Route 9W

A CIA grad oversees the surf-and-turf menu at ★ **Ship to Shore** (15 W. Strand St., Rondout Landing, Kingston, 845/334-8887, www.shiptoshorehudsonvalley.com, noon-10pm Mon.-Sat., 11am-9pm Sun., $23-38). You could eat an entire meal from the appetizers alone: shrimp spring rolls, stuffed calamari, and Hudson Valley foie gras. Or save room for crab meat ravioli or baked Chatham codfish. Or go all out for a surf-and-turf combo. Enjoy live jazz on Saturday evenings. In a brick building a few doors up the hill from the waterfront, **Dolce** (27 Broadway, Kingston, 845/339-0921, www.dolcekingston.com, 9am-2pm Thurs.-Sun., $8-15) serves crepes (order a house combo or build your own, gluten-free available too), paninis, and a dependable selection of coffee and tea to warm you on a rainy day.

In Kingston's Stockade District, pop into **Jane's Homemade Ice Cream** (307 Wall St., Kingston, 845/338-1801, www.janesicecream.com, hours vary) for a milk shake or quick lunch. For fine dining in this area, ★ **Le Canard Enchaine** (276 Fair St., Kingston, 845/339-2003, www.le-canardenchaine.com, noon-9:30pm Mon., 5pm-9:30pm Tues., noon-9:30pm Thurs., noon-10pm Fri.-Sat., $30-35) is an authentic French bistro serving classics like Long Island duck, trout almandine, and filet mignon bordelaise.

In Saugerties, **Love Bites Cafe** (85 Partition St., Saugerties, 845/246-1795, http://lovebites.cafe, 11am-4pm Mon. and Fri., 9am-4pm Sat.-Sun., $11-18) serves breakfast (green toast, gluten-free corned beef hash bowl, or build your own omelet) and creative sandwiches (bohemian club, cauliflower "wings") for lunch. **Miss Lucy's Kitchen** (90 Partition St., Saugerties, 845/246-9240, www.misslucyskitchen.com, lunch noon-3pm Wed.-Fri., 11am-3pm Sat.-Sun., dinner 5pm-9pm Wed.-Thurs. and Sun., 5pm-10pm Fri.-Sat., $20-25) takes farm-to-table more seriously than most and works with a very long list of local purveyors. Entrées include grilled hanger steak, slow-roasted pork shoulder, and house-made pappardelle.

ImmuneSchein Ginger Elixirs & Tea Haus (1776 Rte. 212, Saugerties, 845/389-3497, http://immune-schein.com, 10am-6pm Thurs.-Mon., $3) is the place to catch up with a friend over a cup of loose-leaf English Breakfast or Turmeric Ginger tea. Make sure

Five Places for a Summer Picnic

- **Boscobel House and Gardens:** Picnic among the roses on the grounds of an 18th-century Federal-style mansion in the Hudson Highlands.

- **Lake Minnewaska:** Put on your hiking shoes and spread a blanket along the rocky shoreline of Lake Minnewaska. Bring your own drinking water and pack out your trash.

- **Kaaterskill Falls:** Bring a sketch pad—and your lunch—to the place that inspired Thomas Cole and the Hudson River School of painters.

- **Storm King Art Center:** What goes better together than art and food? Stroll the expansive grounds of this outdoor museum and enjoy a quiet picnic on the lawn, or order from the on-site café.

- **Saratoga Performing Arts Center:** Bring a lawn chair and settle in for a concert, ballet, or symphony performance in this outdoor amphitheater.

to allow enough time to browse the gift shop for tea-ware, elixirs, and chocolate.

Located in an 1830s farmhouse between Saugerties and Woodstock, **The Red Onion** (1654 Rte. 212, Saugerties, 845/679-1223, www.redonionrestaurant.com, 5pm-9pm Mon.-Tues and Thurs.-Sun., $17-38) serves international fare and a Sunday brunch at half a dozen tables arranged around a cozy bar. Thai-style mussels have been a longstanding special on the appetizer menu. Entrées usually range from basic grilled fish to roasted duck breast to sautéed calf's liver.

New Paltz and Surroundings

New Paltz just about has it all when it comes to food: sushi, Mediterranean, haute cuisine, frozen yogurt, and artisanal cheese. For breakfast or a quick bite to eat at lunchtime, head to **The Bakery** (13A N. Front St., New Paltz, 845/255-8840, www.ilovethebakery.com, 8am-6pm daily, $5-10)—which also is a café and restaurant. Soups and sandwiches change daily, and there are a handful of tables in a courtyard outside. Service can be slow, but the baked goods are worth the wait.

★ **Garvan's Gastropub** (215 Huguenot St., New Paltz, 845/255-7888, www.garvans. com, noon-9pm Tues.-Sun., $18-29) has been delighting New Paltz locals since it opened with gorgonzola sliders, braised short ribs,

and truffle fries. The setting is historic, but the menus are quite contemporary. The best Italian cuisine west of the Hudson these days comes from the kitchen at **A Tavola Trattoria** (46 Main St., 845/255-1426, www. atavolany.com, 5:30pm-10pm Thurs.-Mon., $14-34). In summer, local tomato gazpacho and slow-roasted beets appear on the antipasti menu. Lemon ricotta gnocchi, pork loin saltimbocca, or fish of the day give a hint of the main dishes.

At the end of Main Street, the **Clemson Bros. Brewery** (3 Main St., Rte. 299, New Paltz, 845/256-1700, clemsonbrewing.com, 11am-10pm Sun.-Thurs., 11am-midnight Fri.-Sat., $14-20) has munchies to refuel after a bike ride and freshly brewed beers to wash them down. Beer-infused pizza and Shawangunk Jambalaya also stand out. **Gadaleto's Seafood** (246 Main St., Cherry Hill Shopping Center, New Paltz, 845/255-1717, www. gadaletos.com, 11am-6:30pm Mon.-Sat., $10-28) is a local institution that supplies many area restaurants with their fresh catch. Sample the shellfish at the raw bar or place an order for fish-and-chips or crab cakes. Be prepared to wait; the casual restaurant can get crowded, and service tends to take a while.

A gathering place in the Water Street Market plaza, the ★ **Mudd Puddle Café** (10 Main St., Ste. 312, New Paltz, 845/255-3436, www.muddpuddlecoffee.com, 9am-6pm daily, $5-12) roasts its own coffee, makes a decent chai latte from real black tea leaves and spices, and serves breakfast/lunch from 9am until 2pm Thursday through Monday; drinks and pastries are available all day, every day. Try the Italian panini or turkey Reuben for a filling lunch after pedaling the rail trail. On the upper level of the same plaza, **The Parish Restaurant** (10 Main St. #327, 845/255-4205, https://theparishrestaurant.com, $15-26) has a lovely view and New Orleans-themed food. Mixologist Matthew Sweeney keeps the cocktail menu fresh and exciting with, for example, the Rock and Rye Manhattan featuring chocolate hazelnut-infused bourbon and a Sour Cherry Gimlet made from Luxardo sour cherry gin. Soft-serve ice cream is the main attraction at **The Udder Place** (10 Main St., New Paltz, 11am-6pm daily, $3.75/scoop), but the menu also features a few dairy-free flavors.

Nearby, **The Station** (5 Main St., New Paltz, 845/256-9447, www.thestation77.com, 11:30am-10:30pm Mon.-Tues. and Thurs., 11:30am-11pm Fri.-Sat., 1pm-10:30pm Sun., $17-37) takes its name from the train station it converted into an eatery. The menu consists of reasonably priced standard Italian fare.

The Chinese/Japanese menu at **Asian Fusion** (215 Main St., New Paltz, 845/255-3333, http://asianfusionnp.com, 11am-10pm Mon.-Sat., noon-10pm Sun., $12-22) starts with appetizers like spring rolls, scallion pancakes, and miso soup, then moves along to feature a variety of dumplings, teriyaki dishes, udon, sushi rolls, and more. Gluten-free *mei fun* noodles are an option with several of the noodle dishes.

Apizza! (121 Main St., New Paltz, 845/419-2744, www.coalovenpizza.org, 3pm-11pm Mon. and Thurs., noon-11pm Fri.-Sun., $12-18) opened on Main Street in 2021 to serve red- and white-sauce pizzas. Among the long list of specialty toppings are Moroccan dry cured olives, capers, sopressata, and white truffle oil. The gluten-free crust is housemade, and dairy-free cheese is available.

Tucked away in the woods beside the Wallkill Valley Rail Trail near Rosendale, the ★ **Rail Trail Café** (Stone Mtn. Farm, 310 River Road Ext., New Paltz, 845/389-7714, www.railtrailcaferosendale.com, 9am-7:30pm Fri.-Sun. spring-fall, noon-7pm Thurs. summer only, $10-18) has pizzas, salads, burritos, and other snacks to fuel your bike ride. Enjoy the live music in a rustic outdoor setting.

Grass-fed empanadas, pan-seared trout, and the pulled pork sandwich stand out on the dinner menu at **The Egg's Nest Saloon** (Rte. 213, High Falls, 845/687-7255, www.theeggsnest.com, 5pm-9pm Mon. and Thurs.-Fri., 10am-9pm Sat., 10am-8pm Sun., $16-26). Plan your hunger for 5-6pm weekdays to take advantage of "Magic Hour" food and drink specials.

Mountain Brauhaus (3123 Rte. 44, Gardiner, 845/255-9766, www.mountainbrauhaus.com, 2pm-7pm Wed.-Thurs., noon-8pm Fri.-Sat., noon-7:30pm Sun., $18-28) is an informal restaurant that welcomes hikers from The Gunks. Sauerbraten, schnitzels, and Swabian rostbraten all are prepared in traditional German fashion. The difference is the produce is mostly organic, eggs come from nearby Feather Farm, and deep-frying is done with oil free of trans fats. Don't forget to order the spaetzle on the side. This is a great place to sample some German beer and wine too.

Southern Catskill Mountains: Route 28

For a casual meal and a memorable experience, try a homemade muffin at ★ **Bread Alone** (22 Mill Hill Rd., Woodstock, 845/679-2108, www.breadalone.com, 7am-5pm daily, $5-15), a European-style organic bakery and café with additional locations in Kingston, Rhinebeck, and Boiceville. The owner, Daniel Leader, is a CIA graduate who traveled from Paris to the Pyrenees to learn what gives European breads their hearty flavor. He now produces 15 tons of fresh bread per week from twin ovens that were custom-built by a Parisian oven mason. At headquarters in Boiceville, you can take an impromptu tour of

the bakery while you sip a frothy cappuccino; a state-of-the-art carbon-neutral baking facility is in the works here, too.

Oriole 9 (17 Tinker St., Woodstock, 845/679-5763, www.oriole9.com, 9am-8pm Mon.-Tues. and Fri.-Sat., 9am-3pm Sun., $7-18) is a slow food kind of place where you can order Feather Ridge eggs, tofu hash, a prosciutto and brie press, or falafel. Another breakfast mainstay, famous for its variety of supersize pancakes and equally tasty French toast, lies farther west in Phoenicia.

For a Middle Eastern-style meal with accents from around the world, try ★ **Joshua's Café** (51 Tinker St., Woodstock, 845/679-5533, www.joshuaswoodstock.com, noon-8pm Wed.-Thurs. and Sun., noon-9pm Fri.-Sat., $22-32), a local institution now run by the daughter of the original chef. Three-course entrées includes a tasting plate, warm pita, and a side salad.

Locals drive from near and far to experience the farm-to-table dining at ★ **Peekamoose Restaurant & Tap Room** (8373 State Rte. 28, Big Indian, 845/254-6500, www.peekamooserestaurant.com, 4pm-9pm Thurs. and Sun.-Mon., 4pm-10pm Fri.-Sat., $26-35), where the owners bring a little bit of Brooklyn to the Catskills. Choose the fisherman stew or roasted beet "tartare." Then move on to pan-seared Beaverkill Hatchery rainbow trout or slow-braised short ribs with roasted celery root.

Try the crispy squid appetizer and pork filet scaloppini in a farmhouse setting at **Cucina** (109 Mill Hill Rd., Woodstock, 845/679-9800, www.cucinawoodstock.com, 5pm-10pm Mon.-Thurs., 4pm-10pm Fri.-Sun., $19-29).

ACCOMMODATIONS

Ulster accommodations conjure images of historical mountain houses, rustic country inns, and wooded campgrounds. There are surprisingly few places to stay in downtown

New Paltz, but many bed-and-breakfast inns dot the surrounding countryside, and the number of Airbnb properties is growing by the month, many of them managed by highly regarded "superhosts."

Under $100

True to its reputation as a university town, New Paltz has one of the few hostel accommodations in the Hudson River Valley. Stay from one night to two weeks at the **New Paltz Hostel** (145 Main St., New Paltz, 845/255-6676, www.newpaltzhostel.com, coed dorm $40), within walking distance to public transportation, university buildings, and stores and restaurants of downtown New Paltz. The hostel closes during the day, 10am-4pm. In addition to the coed dorm room, there are three private rooms ($70-80) that can accommodate small groups of travelers.

$100-150

On Airbnb, you can find rustic cabins and cottages starting around $120. For example, a cozy one-bedroom cabin in Olivebridge is $125, or the Woodstock Treescape Cottage goes for $156/night.

$150-200

★ **The Woodstock Inn on the Millstream** (48 Tannery Brook Rd., Woodstock, 845/679-8211, www.woodstock-inn-ny.com, $169-375) oozes good vibes spread by longtime innkeeper Karen Pignataro. She offers 18 well-appointed rooms and studios in three buildings beside a creek that are walking distance from town, yet comfortably removed from the daily bustle on Tinker Street. Guests can relax in hammocks or deck chairs on the lawn or in the shade of the maple trees by the Millstream.

A picturesque stream meanders through the property at **CS Coach House** (913 Rte. 213, High Falls, 845/687-7946, www.cscoachhouse.com, $225-235). The inn is a 1760 stone house; four guest rooms are located on two floors of the carriage house. Relax on your private balcony and scan the forest for

1: Rail Trail Café 2: bread at Bread Alone bakery 3: Buttermilk Falls Inn & Spa wildlife, or listen to the stream from the comfort of a four-poster bed.

Minnewaska Lodge (3116 Rte. 44/55, Gardiner, 845/255-1110, www.minnewaskalodge.com, $225-350) has 26 modern but cozy rooms with a fitness center and ground-floor breakfast room. Walls are on the thin side, but trails lead right from the back porch, and the restaurants and shops of New Paltz are just six miles away.

★ **Twin Gables** (73 Tinker St., Woodstock, 845/679-9479, www.twingableswoodstockny.com, $149-239) has been open as a boutique hotel since 1926 and went through a major transformation in 2020 that put artwork back at the center of the guest experience. The inn has ten beautifully designed king- and queen-sized rooms; some have private baths, while others share.

In Marlboro, **Danskammer House** (5 West St., Marlboro, 845/236-9836, https://danskammerhouse.com, $190-245) dates back to 1870 and now has five guest suites with modern, private bathrooms. The innkeepers, an anthropologist and a linguist, expressly welcome guests of all backgrounds, origins, and orientations.

Over $200

★ **Hasbrouck House** (3805 Main St., Stone Ridge, 845/687-0736, www.hasbrouckhouseny.com, from $245) has been meticulously restored and is part of a small boutique hospitality group based in Brooklyn. The original building is a three-story 18th-century Dutch Colonial, with additional rooms and suites in the Carriage House and Stable House. The modern color palette is neutral and cool. Savor a farm-to-table dinner at **Butterfield** (845/687-0887, www.butterfieldstoneridge.com, 5pm-8:30pm Wed.-Sun., $26-42), or a more casual meal under the tent on the bluestone patio at **Butcher & Bar** (4pm-10pm Mon.-Fri., 10am-10pm Sat.-Sun., closed in winter).

Weekend reservations are difficult to secure at the unusual two-room **Saugerties Lighthouse** (168 Lighthouse Dr., off Mynderse St., Saugerties, 845/247-0656, www.saugertieslighthouse.com, $525 for up to 4 people, breakfast included). Accommodations are rustic, with a shared bath, composting toilet, and limited electricity—but you can't beat the views.

The historic and all-inclusive **Mohonk Mountain House** (1000 Mountain Rest Rd., New Paltz, 845/255-1000, www.mohonk.com, from $655) is quite the opposite of the lighthouse B&B. Rates include buffet-style breakfast and lunch and a four-course dinner, as well as afternoon tea and cookies. Rooms, suites, and cottages represent a variety of styles. Some create the feeling of a cozy mountain lodge, while others feature elaborate Victorian fabrics. Optional extras include balconies, fireplaces, or views.

Once a 17th-century trading post, **Buttermilk Falls Inn & Spa** (220 North Rd., Milton, 845/795-1310, www.buttermilkfallsinn.com, $300-375) now caters to a discerning kind of traveler: Thirteen individually decorated guest rooms in three carriage houses have fireplaces, private baths, cable TV, high-speed internet, and air-conditioning. Most important, all have river, garden, or pond and field views. The owners maintain 70 acres of riverside trails that meander through woods, fields, and gardens. Breakfast includes such treats as freshly baked croissants, and guests may also enjoy afternoon tea service. Spa packages are available.

The **Emerson Resort and Spa** (146 Mt. Pleasant Rd., Mt. Tremper, 845/688-2828, www.emersonresort.com, $275-494) has 26 guest rooms and suites, some of them pet-friendly. Accommodations in the lodge are most rustic, with log walls and framed drawings of fish over the beds. Rooms in the main building look and feel more contemporary. All have soaking tubs, flat-screen TVs, in-room wine fridges, private decks, and fireplaces. Also in the Mt. Tremper complex are a full spa (10am-5pm Thurs.-Mon., 9am-1pm Tues.), country store, and Woodnotes Grill ($11-30). Yoga and fitness classes (drop-in $17) are open to nonguests.

Bohemian **Hotel Dylan** (320 Maverick Rd., Woodstock, 845/684-5422, http://thehoteldylan.com, $269) has a colorful Ikea-esque look. Borrow a board game or an antique vinyl record from the front desk and enjoy your stay.

The ★ **ElmRock Inn** (4496 Rte. 209, Stone Ridge, 845/687-4492, www.elmrockinn.com, $200-320) sits just off busy Route 209 among a stand of black locust trees, 15 minutes from downtown New Paltz. The 1770 brick Colonial farmhouse was renovated in 2012 when it changed hands. Five cozy—and immaculate—guest rooms have air-conditioning as well as high-quality linens and down comforters for winter. When the weather cooperates, chef Mark serves breakfast on the bluestone patio next to the organic herb garden.

Campgrounds

Campers have all kinds of options in Ulster County. **Yogi Bear's Jellystone Park/Lazy River** (50 Bevier Rd., Gardiner, 848/255-5193, www.lazyriverny.com, Apr. 28-early Oct., $52-63) is a large but well-run operation. Amenities include canoe rentals, showers, and swimming pools.

INFORMATION AND SERVICES

The **Kingston Heritage Area Visitors Center** (20 Broadway, Kingston, 845/331-7517, www.kingston-ny.gov, 8:30am-4:30pm daily Sept.-June, 9am-4pm daily July-Aug.) can provide information about Kingston's past and present. This is the place to pick up brochures, maps, and schedules of events.

Alternatively, look for the **Kingston Tourism Caboose** (800/331-1518) in the traffic circle off I-87 exit 19. The Saugerties Chamber of Commerce building on Partition Street has visitor info and opens at noon Friday-Sunday (www.discoversaugerties.com). A tourist information center at **Belleayre Mountain** (845/254-5600, www.belleayre.com) also has a wealth of information for travelers.

GETTING THERE AND AROUND
Bus

Ulster County Area Transit (845/340-3333) serves major towns and rural areas across the county. Routes and schedules are available online at ulstercountyny.gov). In addition, **Adirondack Trailways** (800/858-8555, www.trailwaysny.com) runs connector services to and from other destinations in the region.

Kingston has its own reliable public transportation system, called **CiTiBus** (845/331-3725, www.kingston-ny.gov, $1), with three city routes. The closest train station is at Rhinecliff (Hutton St. and Charles St.) directly across the Hudson River.

Car

Car rentals can be found at the Stewart and Albany airports. Ride-share services and taxis also are available at the airports, bus terminals, and at the Rhinecliff train station. Kingston gets congested, by Ulster County standards, and the narrow streets downtown can be disorienting. But with a little patience, it's easy enough to find your way around.

Western Catskills to the Delaware River

In the days before air-conditioning, the promise of lively entertainment, kosher food, and a cool mountain breeze lured hundreds of thousands of families out of the sweltering New York City heat and into the perennial weekend traffic jam on slow and winding Route 17. Their destination was the western Catskills, where a handful of grand resorts delivered wholesome family fun.

During the 1950s and 1960s, dozens of stand-up comedians launched their careers in this land of bungalows and boarding houses. George Burns, Rodney Dangerfield, and Don Rickles all performed in the Borscht Belt—at places like Grossinger's, The Concord, The Nevele, and Kutsher's. But just as these resorts had reached their prime, affordable jet travel intervened, and travelers

Highlights

Look for ★ to find recommended sights, activities, dining, and lodging.

★ **Bethel Woods Center for the Arts:** Relive Woodstock and the 1960s at this museum and performing arts center on the site of the original Woodstock Music Festival (page 193).

★ **Catskill Fly Fishing Center and Museum:** Located in the heart of some of the country's best fly-fishing, the museum celebrates the art and sport of the catch (page 194).

★ **Roscoe:** They call it Trout Town USA for a good reason. A haven for anglers and outdoor enthusiasts of all kinds, Roscoe lies at the junction of the Beaver Kill river and Willowemoc Creek, on land that provoked many a battle between the Iroquois and Algonquin nations (page 196).

★ **Upper Delaware Scenic and Recreational River:** This winding stretch of Route 97 begins near the Orange-Sullivan county line and leads to breathtaking views of New York, Pennsylvania, and the Delaware River (page 197).

★ **Callicoon:** Anglers and leaf peepers congregate in Callicoon along the Delaware River, a stone's throw from Pennsylvania and the Delaware County line (page 198).

★ **Roxbury:** Financier Jay Gould and naturalist John Burroughs both hailed from this lively town in the far Western Catskills (page 211).

★ **Stone & Thistle Farm:** Roll up your sleeves and help the chores get done during a farm stay with the Warren family in East Meredith (page 213).

Western Catskills to the Delaware River

© MOON.COM

began to skip the Catskills in favor of more exotic destinations.

It's been a few decades since Grossinger's resort closed its doors. At its peak, the 1,200-acre resort served 150,000 guests a year. All that remains of the original property today is a golf course. Meanwhile, the last of the family-owned resorts, Kutsher's, was leveled in 2014 to make way for a new wellness resort.

And yet, even as the old guard fades quietly into history, a new wave of visitors has arrived to take its place. After several decades of neglect and decline, the Catskills are once again in vogue. The market for second homes is booming, and once-forgotten towns like Andes and Livingston Manor are getting makeovers seemingly overnight as artists, chefs, and other creative types make their way north to enjoy a simpler, more sustainable way of life. They come for the hiking and the fly-fishing, real food and yoga retreats. The heady days of the Borscht Belt may never happen again, but a new era of food-inspired travel is taking shape. Farmers are opening one-of-a-kind eateries and tiny inns to help people get connected to the sources of their food.

PLANNING YOUR TIME

Although sleepy Sullivan and Delaware Counties do not directly border the Hudson River, they make a natural extension to many Hudson River Valley itineraries. The busiest seasons in the western Catskills correspond to peak fishing conditions: April-June and September-October. In July and August, many inns fill with parents visiting their children at local summer camps. Hunters arrive in November, and most towns are quiet January-March.

It takes less than an hour to drive the length of the Quickway (Rte. 17) from Wurtsboro to Rockland, but there are many back roads to explore along the way. A weekend stay allows time for both sightseeing and recreation. Most Sullivan County itineraries center on a specific activity, such as fishing, yoga, or antiques shopping. Head here to enjoy the serenity of a quiet morning on the Beaver Kill or to visit a selection of the three dozen shops along the Sullivan County Antiques Trail.

Popular itineraries in Delaware County include self-guided barn and farm-stand tours, daylong bike rides, and multiday hikes and canoe trips. No major highways cross the county, and it takes about three hours to drive the perimeter. Add a half-day stop to pick your own fresh berries or bid on rare antiques in a country auction.

Sullivan County

Home to many of the family resorts that made the Catskills famous during the early to mid-20th century, Sullivan County stretches from the Orange and Ulster county lines in the east to the Delaware River and state of Pennsylvania to the west, covering a total area of about 1,000 square miles. The northern part of Sullivan County lies within the Catskill Preserve, but the terrain is more hilly than mountainous, with many of the same exposed rock ledges that characterize other parts of the Catskill region.

With a low population density (though not as low as Delaware County), Sullivan County supports a diverse ecosystem, including a growing number of bald eagles that make an annual winter appearance. Abundant trout in two famous rivers, the Willowemoc and Beaver Kill, attract diehard fly-fishers, while two large reservoirs at Neversink and

Previous: Upper Delaware Scenic and Recreational River; fall in the Catskills; Bethel Woods Center for the Arts.

Rondout send freshwater to New York City, 90 miles southeast. Despite its outdoor treasures, Sullivan County is best known as the site of the original 1969 Woodstock Music Festival, a three-day extravaganza that took place in the town of Bethel.

Sullivan County separated from Ulster County in 1809, borrowing its name from the controversial Revolutionary War General John Sullivan. In 1779, Sullivan led a devastating attack against the remaining Native American settlements in New York and Pennsylvania. He later became the first governor of New Hampshire.

Early Dutch settlers in Sullivan County built tanneries, bluestone quarries, sawmills, and gristmills to compensate for the lack of arable land. Irish and German immigrants later arrived to build a canal and two railroads connecting Pennsylvania and its stores of natural resources to New York City. Novelist and local resident Stephen Crane popularized Sullivan County in the 1890s with a series of *Sullivan County Sketches*. Around 1900 the Jewish Agricultural Society began to encourage Jewish farmers to move to Sullivan County from New York City. But when the new residents found the land difficult to farm, they supplemented their income by turning their farmhouses into boarding houses. Thus began the Borsch Belt and its history of famous resort hotels, most of which are lost to history.

Today, Sullivan County consists of 15 townships and no large cities. Monticello is the county seat.

ALONG THE QUICKWAY
Wurtsboro

Wurtsboro moves at the comfortably slow pace of a rural community. A string of inviting shops and cafés lines a two-block stretch of Sullivan Street, off Route 209.

Aviation enthusiasts will want to meet the pilots at the family-run **Wurtsboro Airport** (Rte. 209, 845/888-2791, www.wurtsboroairport.com, flights available 10am-4pm daily), one of the oldest soaring sites in the country. A low ridge of the Catskills passes through the town, creating the ideal updraft for flying sans motor. In fact, pilots have soared as far as Georgia in one day from this tiny airstrip. A sailplane ride begins with an exhilarating tow on the runway. Most flights pass over the **Basha Kill Wildlife Management Area** (Rte. 209 S., Wurtsboro, 845/754-0743, www.thebashakill.org) outside town, a prime location for viewing bald eagles. The airport is located on Route 209, two miles north of town. Call to schedule a tour or lesson.

Monticello

Sullivan County's largest township and government headquarters, Monticello is the next major stop on the Quickway. Many of the storefronts along Broadway are showing signs of age and neglect, but the imposing **Sullivan County Courthouse** (414 Broadway), made of sandstone in 1909, is a notable exception.

Resorts World Catskills (888 Resorts World Dr., Monticello, 833/586-9358, http://rwcatskills.com) is a casino and destination resort with an 18-story hotel, two swimming pools, and fitness centers, all surrounded by a Vegas-style entertainment complex. The resort has 10 restaurants, the Crystal Life Spa, an indoor water park, and the state's first Topgolf Swing Suite simulator (11am-2am Fri.-Sat., $20 per person/hour).

Monticello's newest attraction, **The Kartrite Resort & Indoor Waterpark** (555 Resorts World Dr., Monticello, 845/513-8855, www.thekartrite.com, 11am-7pm daily) has several waterslides, a lazy river, and a Flowrider standing wave. Day passes are spendy at $99, but they are included with the cost of an overnight stay.

Kiamesha Lake and Fallsburg

Follow Route 42 northeast out of Monticello to reach Kiamesha Lake, a popular fishing destination, where smallmouth bass, perch, and panfish are the most common catches. Continuing along Route 42, the weathered buildings that line the streets of Fallsburg were once rows of pristine stucco hotels drawing visitors all the way from the Atlantic coast. Tough times have lingered in the area since the advent of air-conditioning and airplane travel, and the largest employers are now three county prisons in neighboring Woodbourne. That said, local residents are taking steps to revive their quiet town. Long-abandoned hotels and bungalows are disappearing from sight. And an overlook at the Neversink River offers visitors a place to enjoy the falls that provided waterpower for the mills and tanneries that sustained the town in its earlier days.

Sivananda Ashram Yoga Ranch

Every Friday after work, a group of harried city dwellers gather at a busy yoga center in Manhattan for a ride to a weekend escape at the **Sivananda Ashram Yoga Ranch** (500 Budd Rd., Woodbourne, 845/436-6492, https://sivanandayogaranch.org) in northern Sullivan County. A getaway here promises ample time for relaxing and rejuvenating.

Located 12 miles north of Monticello in Woodbourne, the yoga center occupies 77 acres of secluded countryside. Wooded areas surround open lawns and a pond. Guests can participate in a single class, a weekend retreat, or a monthlong residential program. The day begins with breathing and meditation exercises. Asana sessions take place at 8am and 4pm daily. After yoga practice, guests can walk the nature trails or enjoy the wood-fired sauna. Volunteers prepare meals from a large organic garden and greenhouse. Accommodations ($70-130 pp) are shared rooms in either a turn-of-the-20th-century farmhouse or a 1920s-era hotel. Camping is also allowed. Call ahead for transportation from the bus terminal in Woodbourne. Classes cost $50 for a full day, $25 half day, and $12 for one class.

Hurleyville

Route 104 out of Monticello leads to Hurleyville, where you can take a walk through history at the **Sullivan County**

Historical Society Museum (265 Main St., Hurleyville, 845/434-8044, www. sullivancountyhistory.org, 10am-4:30pm Tues.-Sat., 1pm-4:30pm Sun., free). Built in 1912, the building housed the Hurleyville Schoolhouse until 1945. Exhibits include a vintage general store and post office as well as a collection of textiles from the turn of the 20th century.

TOP EXPERIENCE

★ Bethel Woods Center for the Arts

Dairy farmer Max Yasgur put the unassuming town of Bethel in the global spotlight when he agreed to host the 1969 Woodstock Music Festival—a soggy three-day extravaganza that turned green pastures to slop, private homes into soup kitchens, and schools into makeshift hospitals.

The idea for a rock concert near Bob Dylan's home in Woodstock began as a late-night conversation in a Manhattan apartment and became, within a few short months, the most notable music event in history. Hundreds of thousands attended, among them Ken Kesey and the Merry Pranksters. They grooved to the hottest sounds of the day, including Jefferson Airplane, Creedence Clearwater Revival, The Who, The Grateful Dead, and the closing act, Jimi Hendrix. Cars en route to Bethel jammed the New York State Thruway and created a 10-mile backup a full day before the event began.

Cable TV executive Alan Gerry purchased the former Yasgur Farm in the late 1990s and announced plans to invest $46 million to create the **Bethel Woods Center for the Arts** (200 Hurd Rd., Bethel, 866/781-2922, www. bethelwoodscenter.org). Today, the center has a 4,800-seat copper-roofed pavilion, a 7,500-square-foot stage, and lawn seating for 12,000. Performances span a range of genres, from rock and pop to classical, jazz, opera, and country music.

Over the years, Bethel Woods has expanded to include the interactive **Museum** at Bethel Woods (Apr.-Dec., hours vary seasonally, adults $18, seniors $15, ages 6-18 $10, under age 5 free; all ages $5 for special exhibit only) and an arts education program. The museum's main exhibit, *Woodstock and the Sixties,* uses film, photos, articles, music, and personal narratives to show how the ideals of the era are relevant today. Special exhibits have honored the 50th anniversary of the Civil Rights Act of 1964 and the 50th anniversary of the Beatles' arrival in the United States. Highlights in 2021 included performances by Pitbull and Chris Stapleton, and a special visual exhibit, "Lights, Color, Fashion: Psychedelic Posters and Patterns of 1960s San Francisco."

Students can get involved too, through creative writing workshops on Saturdays in the fall, or summer musical theater, jazz, or opera classes. Bethel Woods manages to serve as both a reminder of a key moment in history and a community-building engine today.

Liberty to Livingston Manor

Back on the Quickway, **Liberty**'s town center has a few antiques shops and a Greek Revival Methodist church. To the east, the **Neversink Reservoir** (Rte. 16, Neversink, daily), completed in 1953, holds 34.9 billion gallons of water and covers 93 square miles in the northeastern corner of Sullivan County. Its northern section lies within the Catskill Park. The reservoir is open to fishing for brown trout, smallmouth bass, pickerel, panfish, and landlocked salmon. Follow Route 16 east from the Quickway.

Beyond Neversink, the privately owned **Grahamsville Historic District** (Rte. 55, Grahamsville) on Route 55 consists of six Gothic Revival, Italianate, and Greek Revival structures (viewable from the exterior) on 200 acres. Outside town, the **Kalonymus Escarpment,** a National Natural Landmark created by glacial activity, may pique the interest of amateur geologists. The **Rondout Reservoir** in Grahamsville is an observation point for bald eagles.

East of the Quickway along Route 82 lies the hamlet of DeBruce, where New York State operates one of its 12 fish hatcheries. The **Catskill Hatchery** (Mongaup Rd., Livingston Manor, 845/439-4328, www.dec. ny.gov, 8am-4pm Mon.-Fri., 8am-noon Sat.-Sun.) specializes in raising brown trout. Some 115,000 pounds of fingerlings and yearlings leave the hatchery each year, from a base of two million eggs. The state places the trout in rivers, streams, lakes, and ponds to support recreational fishing and to restore native species to damaged environments.

Livingston Manor might still be the kind of place where the milk arrives daily at your doorstep. During the railroad era, the town once known as Purvis had the only Y-shaped track in the area for turning trains around. The town became a transportation hub as a result. A pair of wagon wheels marks the beginning of Main Street, and the swift-flowing Willowemoc Creek runs parallel to it, with an attractive schoolhouse on the opposite shore. Fly-fishing conditions are just about ideal here, and every other storefront sells fishing gear.

The reopening of a historic property, **The DeBruce** (www.thedebruce.com), as an upscale restaurant and inn has brought new life to this sleepy town.

★ Catskill Fly Fishing Center and Museum

A few miles farther up the Willowemoc is the **Catskill Fly Fishing Center and Museum** (1031 Old Rte. 17, Livingston Manor, 845/439-4810, http://cffcm.com, 10am-4pm Fri.-Mon., free), a beautiful facility on 55 acres. A one-lane wooden bridge leads to the parking lot, and you can often see fly-fishers casting right in front of the museum.

These waters were the stomping ground of the late Lee Wulff, celebrated angler, conservationist, and writer. His words appear on a plaque inside the museum: "Over my

1: monument at the site of the 1969 Woodstock Festival in Bethel **2:** Catskill Fly Fishing Center and Museum

The New York City Watershed

New York City consumes nearly 1 billion gallons of water a day, and most of it comes from reservoirs in the Catskill region. The massive watershed is the largest unfiltered surface water supply anywhere in the world.

Reservoir	Capacity (billion gallons)
Ashokan Reservoir (1915)	22.9
Cannonsville Reservoir (1964)	95.7
Croton System (1842)	86.6
Neversink Reservoir (1954)	34.9
Pepacton Reservoir (1955)	140.2
Rondout Reservoir (1950)	9.6
Schoharie Reservoir (1928)	17.6

Reservoir permits are free but required in order to fish. Rowboats are allowed, but motorboats are not. Camping is also not allowed.

many years of fishing, I have learned that angling's problems are never solved. They rise anew with each new pool and each new day. Fishing, especially fly fishing, has problems, solutions, challenges and rewards, which have always captured my imagination and stimulated my creativity." His wife, Joan Wulff, continues to run the **Wulff School of Fly Fishing** (7 Main St., Livingston Manor, 800/328-3638, www.royalwulff.com) nearby in Roscoe.

The exhibits in this well-funded museum will interest most outdoors enthusiasts, whether or not they care to learn how to tie a fly. Vintage rods and reels depict the sport in its early days. A wall of materials used in tying flies includes fox hair and a rare feather that comes from specially bred chickens. An old-fashioned Cortland line-braiding machine in the back corner still works.

Watch the pros tie their delicate flies on Saturday April-October. The center offers courses on stream ecology and angling, fly tying, and rod building. The gift shop has a wonderful collection of books, plus a series of colorful Catskills River Maps for $13 each. A blue sign on the west side of Old Route 17 marks the entrance to the center.

Covered Bridges

Most visitors enjoy crossing Sullivan County's rivers, even if they don't want to catch the fish that live in them. Early settlers in the area constructed bridges over the Beaver Kill and Willowemoc using native hemlock trees, and three historic covered bridges have survived to the present day: **Covered Bridge State Park** (Livingston Manor) outside of Livingston Manor, **Beaverkill Campground** (792 Berrybrook Rd. Spur, Roscoe, 845/439-4281, www.dec.ny.gov) in Lewbeach (Rte. 154), and **Willowemoc** (Rte. 84).

★ Roscoe

The land around Roscoe, at the western edge of Sullivan County, once marked the disputed border between the Iroquois and Algonquin nations. Today the town is better known as a haven for anglers and outdoors enthusiasts, and store owners kindly ask patrons to leave their studded wading shoes at the door. The Beaver Kill and Willowemoc Creek meet in Roscoe, aka Trout Town USA, at a place called Junction Pool, which is recognized as the birthplace of dry fly casting. Opening day of trout season (Apr. 1) draws a crowd of fishing enthusiasts each year, from distinguished instructors and fly-tiers to renowned New York City chefs. The DEC stocks brown trout each spring; any brooks you catch are wild.

More developed than the surrounding hamlets, Roscoe has a number of reputable tackle shops, inns, and restaurants, most of them in a row along Stewart Street. **Shortline Bus** (800/631-8405, www.coachusa.com, adults $38 one-way) offers weekend packages to Roscoe from Port Authority in New York City.

ALONG THE DELAWARE: ROUTE 97
★ Upper Delaware Scenic and Recreational River

Exit 53 off I-84 puts you at the intersection of Route 97 and the start of the **Upper Delaware Scenic and Recreational River** (Rte. 97, 845/252-7414, www.upperdelaware. com or www.nps.gov), a national park that extends 73 miles from the New York-New Jersey state line through Sullivan County and into the southern part of Delaware County. It takes about three hours to drive the length of the park.

Conceived in the early 1930s as a scenic and commercial route, Route 97 connects Port Jervis in Orange County to Hancock in Delaware County, with the majority of the highway running through Sullivan County. This winding road is New York's equivalent to the West Coast's Highway 1. It climbs over hills and crosses ravines, featuring many turnouts and picnic areas along the way. Route 97 enters Sullivan County at Mongaup, just after the Hawk's Nest section of the road in Orange County. Brown "Scenic Byway" signs depict a river and road with green on both sides.

At 410 miles in length, the Delaware is the longest free-flowing river in the northeast. Its East Branch originates in the natural springs of the Catskills, while the West Branch begins in Schoharie County, near Pennsylvania. The rocky terrain of the western Catskills forms Class I and Class II rapids along some stretches. Before the era of rail travel, the Delaware and Hudson Canal

served as a vital connection between the two commercial rivers. For anglers, the Delaware is home to scores of trout, bass, walleye, eel, and shad.

Take a detour from Route 97 at the town of Pond Eddy (Rte. 41), about five miles past the Hawk's Nest, to head north to Glen Spey and the **St. Volodymyr Ukrainian Orthodox Cathedral** (Glen Spey, 845/856-5500). Like its counterpart in Greene County, this architectural wonder was built without a single nail.

Mongaup Valley Wildlife Management Area

An 11,000-acre expanse of forested hills, streams, and rivers connects the towns of Bethel, Lumberland, Forestburgh, and Highland in Sullivan County and extends to Deer Park in Orange County. The juncture of the Mongaup and Delaware Rivers is prime bald eagle habitat, but you may also see white-tailed deer, wild turkeys, grouse, coyotes, fox, porcupines, and black bear. Keep an eye out for other migrating raptors, owls, and wetland birds. The water supports many different kinds of fish, including smallmouth bass, largemouth bass, crappie, panfish, and stocked and wild trout. There are two blinds for viewing eagles—one on Route 43 and the other on Plank Road. Hiking, biking, snowshoeing, cross-country skiing, fishing, and hunting all are permitted.

The Eagle Institute

Although winter is not the most popular season to visit the Delaware River, it is the best time to catch once-endangered bald eagles in action. A small group of eagles are year-round residents along the Delaware, while a larger population migrates from Canada, spending mid-December through mid-March in the warmer climate.

The nonprofit **Eagle Institute** (Rte. 97, Barryville, 845/557-6162, www.eagleinstitute. org), based in Barryville, runs guided field trips and other educational programs. Popular observation points include **Mongaup Falls Reservoir** (Forestburgh), off Route 42 (not to be confused with Mongaup Pond in north-eastern Sullivan County) and **Rio Reservoir** in Forestburgh. The institute has a winter field office just across the Roebling Bridge from Minisink Ford (176 Scenic Dr., Lackawaxen, PA, 570/685-5960).

Novelist Stephen Crane reportedly penned *The Red Badge of Courage* from his cabin in nearby Forestburgh.

Minisink Ford

Sullivan County's only Revolutionary War skirmish took place at Minisink Ford in July 1779, when a group of 120 colonists were defeated by a combined force of Native American and Tory soldiers. Today, the site is listed on the National Register of Historic Places. **Minisink Battleground Park** (County Rd. 168, Minisink Ford, 845/807-0261, from 8am daily) encompasses 57 acres of woodlands, with walking trails and an interpretive center that recounts both the political and the natural history of the site.

Also at Minisink Ford is the oldest suspension bridge in the country, the Delaware Aqueduct or **Roebling Bridge.** Built by John A. Roebling, the same engineer who designed the Brooklyn Bridge, this historic bridge dates to 1848, when it was constructed to support the Delaware and Hudson Canal. Though the bridge has been converted to carry cars instead of coal, the original cables still hold it in place.

Narrowsburg

The Delaware River reaches its deepest point, 113 feet, at Narrowsburg, where the earliest colonial settlers arrived in the 1770s, during the French and Indian War. The **Fort Delaware Museum** (6615 Rte. 97, Narrowsburg, 845/807-0261 Sept.-Apr., 845/252-6660 May-Aug., https://sullivanny. us, 10am-5pm Fri.-Mon., noon-5pm Sun. Memorial Day-Labor Day), run by the New York State Department of Education, recreates the pioneers' way of life and is a popular destination for local schoolchildren. Over the years, Narrowsburg has developed a vibrant

community of artists and a number of cultural attractions. Several art galleries and theaters draw year-round visitors.

From Narrowsburg, Route 52 leads away from the river toward Cochecton Center, Kenoza Lake, Jeffersonville, and eventually Liberty. Along the way is a historical bridge made of stone instead of timber. While many covered bridges have been preserved, the only original stone bridge with three arches remaining in the United States crosses the Callicoon Creek in the town of Kenoza Lake. It was built in 1872 and is now known as **Stone Arch Bridge Historical Park** (Rte. 52 and Rte. 52A, Kenoza Lake, 845/807-0261, http://sullivanny.us).

★ Callicoon

If you stay on Route 97 and continue north toward Delaware County, you'll reach the hamlet of Callicoon (Wild Turkey), where the only remaining single-screen movie theater in Sullivan County is still open for business. Built in 1948, the 380-seat **Callicoon Theater** (30 Upper Main St., Callicoon, 845/887-4460, www.callicoontheater.com) screens current releases year-round as well as alternative and foreign films September-June. Although it was first settled in the 1600s, no building in Callicoon predates 1888 because of a fire that leveled the town. The theater is in the process of transitioning to a nonprofit organization. It received a grant in 2021 for repairs and renovations, which will include building a stage for live performances.

RECREATION
Winter Sports

Sullivan County has one small downhill ski area that's ideal for youngsters, or anyone who's just starting to get the hang of the sport. **Holiday Mountain** (99 Holiday Mountain Rd., Monticello, 845/796-3161, www. holidaymtn.com, 3pm-9pm Tues.-Thurs., noon-9pm Fri., 9am-9pm Sat., 9am-5pm Sun.

1: old trains in Roscoe **2:** Upper Delaware Scenic and Recreational River

Dec.-Feb.) in Monticello has snowmaking facilities to cover all 14 of its trails.

For Nordic skiers, many of Sullivan County's hotels and inns maintain their own trails. The towns of Fallsburg and Thompson open trails to the public. **Morningside Park** (11 Morningside Park Rd., Fallsburg, 845/434-5877, www.townoffallsburg.com, dawn-dusk daily) allows skiers to enjoy 2.5 miles of parkland. **Thompson Park** (179 Town Park Rd., Monticello, 845/794-5280, dawn-dusk daily) features 150 acres of parkland for cross-country skiers.

Hiking

For many years, the 108-mile-long **Delaware and Hudson Canal** carried coal, cement, bluestone, and other industrial materials from Honesdale, Pennsylvania, to Kingston, New York, for the Albany and New York City markets. Built by Irish and German immigrants over the course of three years, the canal played an instrumental role in the growth and development of the Atlantic Seaboard. It had 108 locks and 22 aqueducts, and 136 bridges, 22 reservoirs, and 16 dams along its length. The advent of the steam train retired the canal from service, but today you can walk, bike, or ski some 20 miles of it. The restored sections, however, are not yet all connected. The canal runs mainly through Orange and Ulster Counties, but in Sullivan County, a 3.5-mile segment connects the towns of Wurtsboro with the hamlet of Phillipsport. Canoeing and fishing are also permitted along this stretch.

Willowemoc Wild Forest, in the southwest corner of the Catskill Forest Preserve, is another good place to get away from it all. Located 18 miles north of Liberty and nine miles northeast of Livingston Manor, its 14,800 "forever wild" acres include trails maintained for hiking, skiing, biking, and snowmobiling. About 15 miles of paths are reserved for hikers only. The terrain is gentle, with rolling hills instead of tall peaks. Four trailheads departing from Neversink and Rockland have parking nearby. Campfires

and primitive camping are allowed, but there are no facilities.

Privately run **Eldred Preserve** (1040 Rte. 55, Eldred, 845/557-8316, http://theeldredpreserve.com) is a year-round fishing and hunting resort on 3,000 acres off Route 55. Facilities include three stocked fishing ponds and a sporting-clay range, and the resort runs fishing tournaments in summer. Services include guided trips, corporate events, a pro shop, and motel-style accommodations in log-cabin buildings.

The National Park Service maintains the challenging **Tusten Mountain Trail** (3-mile loop, Rte. 97, www.tusten.org, 8:30am-6pm daily), between Barryville and Narrowsburg near the Ten Mile River. The route leads to the mountain summit, reaching 1,100 feet at its highest point.

Stock up on hiking gear and supplies at **Morgan Outdoors** (46 Main St., Livingston Manor, 845/439-5507, www.morgan-outdoors.com, 10am-6pm Mon. and Thurs.-Sat., 10am-4pm Sun.). Rent gear for camping or snowshoeing, or pick up hand-drawn maps of the area. This store also functions as an information center for visitors who want to explore the nearby Catskill Park. Inquire about guided hikes on the calendar.

Cycling and Mountain Biking

Pearson Park (Walnut Mountain, Liberty, 845/292-7690, 8am-dusk daily May-Sept.), on Walnut Mountain, has 265 acres of novice to expert terrain, including challenging single-track riding.

Golf

Sullivan County offers several championship golf courses with moderate greens fees and inspiring views of the Catskills. **Tennanah Lake Golf and Tennis Club** (100 Fairway View Dr., Roscoe, 888/561-3935 or 607/498-5502, www.tennanah.com, $28-48) bills itself as "Sullivan County's Oldest Golf Course" and features daily specials that include meals at The Grille restaurant or discount rates for twosomes and foursomes. Serious golfers can

American Ginseng

The Chinese weren't the only ones to discover the healthful effects of wild ginseng. Native Americans discovered the plant in the Catskills long before the Dutch settlers arrived, and local residents have been consuming it in teas, lotions, and tonics ever since.

In Chinese medicine, ginseng root is believed to energize and rejuvenate the body and enhance immunity. Although most of the world's supply is now cultivated in China and Korea, the highest-quality ginseng grows wild under the shade of deciduous trees like the sugar maple.

In the mid-1990s, Bob Beyfuss at the Cornell Cooperative Extension of Greene County began an experiment—to teach local farmers how to simulate the wild growth of ginseng in their own backyards, the Catskill Mountains. Earning a price of $500 or more per pound, the root offered struggling farmers a way to supplement their meager income.

Wild ginseng is difficult to find and identify. Few who know it well are willing to share their secrets. But those who care to sustain its presence in the Catskills spread the seeds of a plant before they harvest its root. The plant is protected by law in New York State and may only be picked September-November.

stay at the club's Inn at Tennanah or Wood Lake Country Estates.

Swimming and Boating

Mongaup Pond is a 12-acre lake, the largest body of water inside the Catskill Park that is not a New York City reservoir. A variety of fish live in the lake, and visitors can swim, fish, and paddle in its refreshing waters. Boat rentals are available through the **Mongaup Pond Campground** (231 Mongaup Pond Rd., Livingston Manor, 845/439-4233, www.dec.ny.gov, $22). Camping is permitted mid-May through Columbus Day.

Mongaup Pond has a swimming beach with lifeguard supervision. Rowboats and canoes are allowed on the lake (rentals available), but not motorboats. For a day at the beach, head to 1,400-acre **Lake Superior State Park** (Rte. 55, Bethel, 845/794-3000, www.nysparks.com, dawn-dusk mid-May-Sept.).

Several outfitters run trips along the Delaware: **Kittatinny Canoes** (3854 Rte. 97, Barryville, 800/356-2852, www.kittatinny.com, 9am-5pm Mon.-Thurs., 9am-11pm Fri.-Sun.) has canoes, rafts, kayaks, and tubes for trips ranging from calm to white water. **Whitewater Willie's** (37 S. Maple Ave., Port Jervis, 845/856-7055 or 800/724-8342, www.silvercanoe.com, Apr.-Sept.) has joined forces

with Silver Canoe and is another reputable operation with reasonable prices.

Lander's River Trips (5961 Rte. 97, Narrowsburg, 800/252-3925, www.landersrivertrips.com, rentals $40-50), family-run since 1954, runs 10 bases along the Upper Delaware River, with rafts, canoes, and kayaks for rent. Camping and packages are available.

Fishing and Hunting

Fly-fishing was first introduced to the United States in Sullivan County, and the tradition draws a majority of Sullivan County visitors today. You can learn to tie flies at one of several area schools, such as the renowned **Wulff School of Fly Fishing** (7 Main St., Livingston Manor, 800/328-3638, www.royalwulff.com). Or drop in for a workshop at the **Catskill Museum of Fly Fishing** (1031 Old Rte. 17, Livingston Manor, 845/439-4810, http://ccfm.org, 10am-4pm Fri.-Mon.). Trout season opens April 1, and the shad run peaks in May on the Delaware River. In addition, the county and state stock hundreds of lakes and streams. The **Beaverkill Angler** (52 Stewart Ave., Roscoe, 607/498-5194, www.beaverkillangler.com, 9am-5pm daily in season) has everything you need for a day of casting in the river. Leave your studded shoes at the door.

Guides and gear are available at a number of additional operations in Trout Town USA. **Catskill Flies Fly Shop & Fishing Adventures** (6 Stewart Ave., Roscoe, 607/498-6146, www.catskillflies.com, 8am-5pm daily) leads trips and rents equipment. You can sleep and fish with **Baxter House B&B and River Outfitters** (Old Rte. 17, Roscoe, 607/290-4022 or 607/348-7497, www.baxterhouse.net). A half day of wade fishing runs $350 for one or two people, full day $499. Drift boat trips are $499 full day and $375 evening hatch float. Modest accommodations are available in six recently renovated rooms ($65-125).

Local fisherman Anthony Ritter runs drift boat trips along the Upper Delaware River through **Gone Fishing Guide Service** (20 Lake St., Narrowsburg, 845/252-3657, www.gonefishingguideservice.com, daily Apr.-Nov.). Catches include shad, trout, smallmouth bass, and walleye. Half-day trips for one or two people run $300, full-day trips $400.

Other local guides include Stefan Spoerri (845/252-7309) at Narrowsburg. Stop in at the **Catskill Delaware Outdoor Store** (34A Dorrer Dr., Callicoon, 845/887-4800, 8am-6pm daily) for fishing and hunting supplies and licenses, as well as current river conditions.

Aviation

Learn to fly (with or without an engine) or just take an aerial tour at the private **Wurtsboro Airport** (Rte. 209, Wurtsboro, 845/888-2791, www.wurtsboroairport.com, flights available 10am-4pm daily). There are grass and paved runways. Taxi service is available for rides into town ($5-6). Other local facilities include **Sullivan County International Airport** (MSV, Bethel, 845/807-0326).

Yoga and Spas

Sat Nam Yoga Spa (333 Mount Cliff Rd., Hurleyville, 845/866-3063, www.satnamyogaspa.com) offers walk-in kundalini yoga and meditation classes, flotation therapy, massage treatments, and wellness packages. The studio is also a bed-and-breakfast inn with rooms in a converted barn.

In 2018, Resorts World Catskills opened the **Crystal Life Spa** (845/428-7200, http://rwcatskills.com) in Monticello, with all the essentials for a day of pampering.

ENTERTAINMENT AND EVENTS

Performing Arts

The **Bethel Woods Center for the Arts** (200 Hurd Rd., Bethel, 866/781-2922, www.bethelwoodscenter.org) produces first-rate concerts that draw crowds from all over the Hudson River Valley area. ACDC, John Mayer, Natalie Merchant, and the Dave Matthews Band all have performed here, as have Tim McGraw, Rosanne Cash, and Arlo Guthrie.

The **Forestburgh Playhouse** (39 Forestburgh Rd., Forestburgh, 845/794-1194, www.fbplayhouse.org) is the oldest professional summer theater in New York State. Productions include Broadway musicals, comedies, and cabarets before and after the shows. The playhouse also has a tavern and children's theater on-site.

Bars and Nightlife

The biggest entertainment venue in Sullivan County is the expansive **Resorts World Catskills** (888 Resorts World Dr., Monticello, http://rwcatskills.com) and adjoining business. **Doubletop Bar & Grill** (6pm-2pm Fri.-Sat.) is a sports bar with a small stage for live bands. The **Empire Lounge** (noon-midnight Sun.-Thurs., noon-2am Fri.-Sat.) takes its cue from the speakeasy era with a menu of Prohibition-themed cocktails.

Festivals and Events

The ultimate place to celebrate opening day of the trout season is the Junction Pool in Roscoe. Crowds of locals and fly-fishing enthusiasts gather on the often icy rocks to watch celebrity "first casters" kick off the season. The annual **Two-Headed Trout Dinner**

Sullivan County Farmers Markets

Farmers markets are a way of life in the Western Catskills. More than a place to stock up on fresh produce, they bring communities together to celebrate the season's harvest with heirloom fruits and vegetables, heritage meats, gourmet foods, and unique crafts. In eight locations across the county, you'll find fresh-picked produce as well as a variety of plants, flowers, soaps, pottery, candles, jewelry, and other crafts—all made by local artisans. Local farmers also bring their cheese, yogurt, jam, wine, maple syrup, eggs, fish, and meat to sell. You can easily consume a meal at the market and leave with ingredients for another feast at home. To learn more about Sullivan County's markets, visit http://homegrownwithheart. com. These are some of the best:

honey for sale at the Callicoon farmers market

- **Bethel** (Bethel Woods, 200 Hurd Dr., 11am-4pm Sun. late Aug.-early Oct.)

- **Callicoon** (Callicoon Creek Park, A. Dorrer Dr., near the bridge over Delaware River to Pennsylvania, 11am-2pm Sun. year-round; Holiday Market in early Dec.)

- **Roscoe** (1978 Old Rte. 17, Niforatos Field, 10am-2pm Sun. May-Oct.)

is held Saturday night at the Rockland House (www.roscoeny.com).

Morgan Outdoors (46 Main St., Livingston Manor, 845/439-5507, www.morgan-outdoors.com, 10am-6pm Mon. and Thurs.-Sat., 10am-4pm Sun.) hosts occasional events for outdoor enthusiasts. Recent talks have focused on Exploring the Catskill Forest, Geocaching, and Native Plants.

During the boiling season (Feb.-Mar.), **Muthig Farm** (681 Muthig Rd., Parksville, free) welcomes visitors to see the old-fashioned way of turning hard maple tree sap into pure maple syrup: with a wood-fired evaporator. The farm is located near the Neversink Reservoir.

SHOPPING

Sullivan County shops carry antiques and a wide variety of handmade country goods, from marmalade to greeting cards. **Canal Towne Emporium** (169 Sullivan St., Wurtsboro, 845/888-2100, www.canaltowne. com, 10am-5pm daily) is a cavernous gift shop filled with gourmet foods (some locally produced and some from afar), as well as candles, bath products, and other country accents for the home.

Antiques

Turning the old into something new is a popular pastime in Sullivan County, and at least a dozen towns hold an antiques shop or two. Here are some of the best:

Browse collections of clothing, pottery, Depression-era glass, prints, mirrors, and more at the **Antique Center of Callicoon** (26 Upper Main St., Callicoon, 845/887-5918, 11am-4pm Mon. and Thurs.-Sat., 11am-3pm Sun. July-Aug., call for hours Sept.-June). Look for a three-story building across from the train station.

In business for more than 25 years, **Antique Palace Emporium** (300 Chestnut St., Liberty, 845/292-2270, www. antiquepalaceemporium.com, call for hours) restores and reupholsters vintage American furniture dating from the late 1800s to the early 1900s. The store is open year-round, but hours vary.

Across from the Catskill Distilling Company, owners Monte Sachs and Stacy Cohen also run the **Stray Cat Gallery & The Next Door Store** (2032 Rte. 17B, Bethel, 845/796-8643, www.straycatgallery. com, 11am-6pm Fri.-Sun. or by appointment) in a restored Victorian home. A permanent exhibit of nature photographs by Jerry Cohen is displayed upstairs, with rotating works by other local artists on the lower level. The annex sells jewelry, crafts, antiques, and other collectibles.

Farm Stands and Local Products

In this land of dairy farms and boutique growers, it's difficult to narrow the list of farm stands to manageable length. Callicoon's **Apple Pond Farm** (80 Hahn Rd., Callicoon Center, 845/482-4764, www.applepondfarm. com) is one of the standouts. **Silver Heights Farm** (216 Eggler Rd., Jeffersonville, 845/482-3608, www.silverheightsfarm.com) grows heirloom vegetables, herbs, and flowering plants.

At the **Callicoon Farmers' Market** (Callicoon Creek Park, A. Dorrer Dr., 11am-2pm Sun. year-round), be sure to seek out **Channery Hill Farm,** makers of a delicious garlic scape relish among other farm goods, and **Eminence Road Farm Winery** (www. eminenceroad.com), experts at organic and sustainable methods of producing excellent riesling, chardonnay, and pinot noir wines.

FOOD

While not as sophisticated as the cuisine found closer to the Hudson, Sullivan County has a few good standbys for hearty country cooking.

Along the Quickway

You don't have to stay overnight to savor the food at ★ **The DeBruce** (982 DeBruce Rd., Livingston Manor, 845/439-3900, www. thedebruce.com, 6pm-9pm Wed.-Sun., prix fixe tasting menu $225 pp) in Livingston Manor. The multi-course tasting menu is offered Wednesday, Thursday, Saturday, and Sunday, while the less formal à la carte menu is served Wednesday through Sunday. Reservations are required for either of these dining experiences.

The signature restaurant at Resorts World Catskills is **Cellaio** (888 Resorts World Dr., Monticello, 845/428-7497, http://rwcatskills. com, 5pm-10pm Wed.-Sun., $27-48), specializing in steaks, chilled seafood, and housemade pasta. Also in the complex, **Lotus** (845/428-7496, 5pm-10pm Sun.-Tues., 5pm-11pm Fri.-Sat., $22-45) is a good choice when you're in the mood for upscale Chinese food.

Along the Delaware: Route 97

A CIA-trained chef and his wife are the team behind ★ **The Heron** (40 Main St., Narrowsburg, 845/252-3333, http:// theheronrestaurant.com, noon-8pm Thurs.-Sat., 11am-4pm Sun., $15-30), loved by locals for its focus on sustainably grown food. The menu features homemade buttermilk biscuits, roasted bone marrow, and baked Blue Point oysters.

Villa Roma (356 Villa Roma Rd., Callicoon, 845/887-4880 or 800/533-6767, www.villaroma.com, $10-20) is primarily an all-inclusive resort, but it has several dining options that are also open to resort nonguests. In the main dining room, a CIA graduate prepares Italian American cuisine, including rich pasta dishes and hearty meat entrées such as prime rib and roasted duck. The seasonal Beechwoods Restaurant & Grill offers a more varied menu.

Benji and Jakes (5 Horseshoe Lake Rd., White Lake, 845/583-4031, www. benjiandjakes.com, hours vary seasonally, $15-25) tosses a reliable thin-crust pizza.

1: the silo and barn at Channery Hill Farm
2: Apple Pond Farm

Special pies include an eggplant parmesan and super spicy Death by Pizza.

Concertgoers have several food options at Bethel Woods. Inside the museum and open during museum hours, **Yasgur's Farm Café** (200 Hurd Rd., Bethel, 866/781-2922, www.bethelwoodscenter.org, 10:30am-5pm daily Apr.-Dec., $7-12) serves bagels, burgers, paninis, and salads. A preconcert buffet dinner is offered before select shows at **The Market Shed,** also on the concert grounds.

ACCOMMODATIONS

Sullivan County lodging consists mainly of rustic country inns with a few B&B gems in the mix. Middletown has a handful of chain hotels, including a Courtyard by Marriott, Hampton Inn, and Best Western. Plan ahead in summer, as any of these places sell out on summer camp parent weekends and when there's a big concert playing at Bethel Woods.

$100-150

The Reynolds House (1934 Old Rte. 17, Roscoe, 607/498-4422, www.reynoldshouseinn.com, $95-250) is a value option for no-frills accommodations in a central location. Each room in this cheerful three-story inn has a private bath with a very small shower. Dark wood and floral prints define the look and feel. The breakfast room has a fireplace and kitchenette. The inn caters to hunters and anglers, as well as parents of children at local summer camps.

Bass' Hancock House Hotel (137 E. Front St., Hancock, 607/637-7100, www.hancockhousehotel.com, $130-215) is a modern building that's intended to keep the past alive. The site of the original Hancock Hotel, located two blocks away, hosted celebrities and world leaders in the first half of the 20th century. The new hotel, run by Lynn and Russell Bass, has 32 clean rooms with two queen beds in each. The hotel also has a taproom and restaurant on the main floor. Rooms fill up during summer camp parent weekends.

Resorts World Catskills (888 Resorts World Dr., Monticello, 833/586-9358, http://rwcatskills.com, from $197) has modern king and queen suites with an on-site spa and casino. For more of a boutique experience, The Alder (from $129) is an extension of the main casino.

$150-200

Villa Roma (356 Villa Roma Rd., Callicoon, 877/256-7506, www.villaroma.com, Apr.-Dec., $163), a resort and conference center, manages to blend some of the old-fashioned Catskill resort flavor with a host of modern amenities. A variety of vacation packages include meals and entertainment as well as accommodations.

The **Sat Nam Inn** (333 Mount Cliff Rd., Hurleyville, 845/866-3063, www.satnamyogaspa.com, $175) is part of a yoga center and wellness retreat located near the Sivananda ashram. Rates include accommodations in a renovated barn and breakfast. Visitors are welcome to take yoga classes, schedule flotation therapy sessions, and book massage treatments. Vacation rentals are also available for longer stays.

In Liberty, **Lazy Pond Bed and Breakfast** (79 Old Loomis Rd., Liberty, 845/292-2362, $175-225) caters to families and parents of summer camp kids with 25 guest rooms on a six-acre property. Rooms are basic but very clean. The property came under new ownership in 2021 and some enhancements are in the works.

Over $200

The ★ **Bradstan Country Hotel** (1561 Rte. 17B, White Lake, 845/583-4114, www.bradstancountryhotel.com, May-Nov., from $350) has the best accommodations close to the Bethel Woods Center for the Arts. The main house, a white building with three gables and a wide front porch, has two large rooms, a small suite, and two large suites. Several rooms have views of the lake across the street. Two separate cottages each have a large bedroom with a queen bed and additional twin bed, as well as a full galley kitchen. All rooms have air-conditioning and ceiling fans. Owners Scott and Eddie attend to guests and serve a tasty hot breakfast, included in the room rates. There is a two-night minimum on summer weekends.

Enjoy a peaceful retreat beside a 250-acre private lake at the ★ Inn at Lake Joseph (162 St. Joseph Rd., Forestburgh, 845/791-9506, www.lakejoseph.com, from $300). Its gorgeous Redwood room has 18-foot ceilings, and the Tudor room has high ceilings and a deck with over 700 square feet of living space. There is a full-service fitness center and spa nearby, but chances are you won't want to leave the property.

Start with a hundred-year-old building on the bank of the Willowemoc inside the Catskill Forest Preserve. Then add city-style sophistication: newly tiled marble floors, fine linens, haute cuisine—and you have the makings of a new culinary destination in a once sleepy town. ★ The DeBruce (982 DeBruce Rd., Livingston Manor, 845/439-3900, www. thedebruce.com, from $525) underwent a thorough makeover and visitors are applauding the results. Nightly rates include breakfast and a multicourse dinner for two.

The Kartrite Resort & Indoor Waterpark (555 Resorts World Dr., Monticello, 845/513-8855, www.thekartrite. com, from $340) has modern and cheery suites that are designed for families. Some rooms have bunkbeds and patios. All reservations include entry for four people to the hotel's indoor waterpark.

Campgrounds

Beaverkill Campground (792 Berrybrook Rd. Spur, Roscoe, 845/439-4281 or 845/256-3099, www.dec.ny.gov, mid-May-Labor Day, $20-25) has 108 sites along the Beaver Kill with hot showers. On the Delaware, Indianhead Campground (Barryville, 800/874-2628, www.indianheadcanoes.com, $10-15 pp) has wooded campsites with fire rings, right next to the river. Berentsen's Campground (266 Roose Gap Rd., Bloomingburg, 845/733-4984, www.berentsencampground.com, tent sites $35-50) has a stream winding through the property and a swimming pool that's popular with families. Full hookups are available, and pets are welcome.

INFORMATION AND SERVICES

The Sullivan County Visitors Association (100 North St., Monticello, 845/794-3000, www.scva.net) operates information booths at Rock Hill, Livingston Manor, and Roscoe during the busy fishing season. Look for the red caboose off Route 17 at DeBruce Road.

GETTING THERE AND AROUND

Sullivan County is easily accessible from Stewart International Airport (SWF, 1180 1st St., New Windsor, 845/564-7200, www. panynj.gov) and New York City transportation hubs. Shortline Bus (800/631-8405, www.coachusa.com, adults $32 one-way, discounts for seniors, students, and children) provides service from Port Authority in New York City to Monticello, with frequent express service and connections to smaller towns like Roscoe. Many resorts provide shuttle transportation from Monticello.

Taxi and rideshare services in Monticello and Bloomingburg serve all major airports.

Delaware County

It's hard to imagine two worlds more opposed than the exclusive Hamptons of Long Island and the fertile hills of rural Delaware County. And yet, scores of former beachgoers have traded their ocean view for a fixer-upper and a pair of cross-country skis.

The reason? Property that's beautiful, affordable, and within a three-hour drive of New York City. Roughly the size of Rhode Island, Delaware County is the third largest in New York State and has the lowest population density (33 people per square mile) of any county in the Hudson River Valley and Catskill region—a figure that almost triples in summer. Encompassing the headwaters of the Delaware River, the area is known for an abundance of freshwater and unparalleled hunting and fishing. Lately, heirloom vegetables and heritage livestock farming are on the rise as well.

Early European settlers arrived in present-day Delaware County in the 1780s by traveling the Catskill Turnpike. This first route to the western frontier was a dirt road with periodic tollgates that connected the Village of Catskill in Greene County to the Susquehanna River in Unadilla.

New York State recognized Delaware County as a separate county in 1797. Lumbering and stonecutting sustained the local economy at first, followed by agriculture. In the 1840s, Delaware County became a focal point of the Anti-Rent Wars, during which poor farmers across the country began to protest the feudal system that prevented them from owning the land they farmed.

Holstein and Jersey cows still graze the hillsides here, and you'll find a sampling of barns in every shape, style, and condition—from those that are barely still standing to others that have been restored as inviting markets, homes, and bookstores.

ALONG ROUTE 28

Fleischmanns

A 40-mile drive from Kingston along Route 28 leads to Fleischmanns, at the eastern edge of Delaware County. Initially known as Griffin Corners in the early 19th century, the town is named for Charles F. Fleischmann (think yeast and whiskey). Fleischmann had emigrated from Austria-Hungary to Cincinnati in the 1860s and started the Vienna Bakery, which would make him world famous. Already a successful businessman, he bought property in Delaware County in 1883 and began spending summers in the mountain air.

Soon an entire community of summer residents, mostly well-to-do families, was building lavish Victorian homes along Wagner Avenue, many of which are standing today. Dozens of resorts opened in the surrounding area, but only a handful remain in business.

At the center of Main Street stands the handsome **Skene Memorial Library** (1017 Main St., Fleischmanns, 845/254-4581, www.skenelib.org, 10am-2pm Tues. and Sat., 1pm-5pm Wed.-Fri.), founded with a $5,000 grant from Andrew Carnegie and completed in 1901. An old carriage barn behind the library houses the **Fleischmanns Museum of Memories** (1017 Main St., Fleischmanns, 845/254-5514, 11am-3pm Sat. Memorial Day weekend-June and Sept.-Columbus Day weekend, 11am-3pm Thurs.-Sat. July-Aug., free), with exhibits that document the town's history as a thriving summer resort.

Arkville

One of the most scenic railroad lines in the east connected Kingston on the Hudson to Oneonta at the western boundary of Delaware County. Over the course of its hundred-year history, the Delaware & Ulster Railroad transported lumber, bluestone, livestock, produce, coal, and tourists across 107 miles of mountains and valleys. Two stretches of the original route have been restored for visitor enjoyment: the Trolley Museum of New York in Kingston and the **Delaware & Ulster Railroad** (43510 Rte. 28, 845/586-3877, www.durr.org) in Arkville.

The depot is the most visible attraction around, on the south side of the street as you enter Arkville on Route 28. Tours leave twice daily (Sat.-Sun. May-June and Sept.-Oct., Thurs.-Sun. July-Aug.). A round-trip tour to Roxbury takes less than two hours (one hour round-trip to Halcottsville). Dogs are welcome aboard the D&U.

Margaretville and the Pepacton Reservoir

Delaware County sustained $20 million in flood damage when the Blizzard of 1996 was followed by unseasonably warm temperatures and heavy rains. Margaretville's Bridge Street, along the banks of the East Branch of the Delaware, suffered some of the most severe damage from the disaster, and nine buildings were ultimately condemned.

In the years since, town officials succeeded in turning the natural disaster into an economic opportunity. With a sizable disaster-relief grant from New York State, Margaretville constructed a new waterfront park and river walk, along with new sidewalks and landscaping along Main Street. The result is an attractive downtown, with several restaurants, shops, and inns—all of which are close to boundless areas for fishing, hiking, and cycling.

A scenic detour from Route 28 leads to the Pepacton Reservoir, formed by a dam at the beginning of the East Branch of the Delaware River. The reservoir is named for one of the four towns it flooded when construction was completed in 1955, and one gets the feeling that more than a few locals are still bitter over the loss.

With a capacity of 140.2 billion gallons of water, the Pepacton is the largest reservoir in the New York City Watershed and provides about 25 percent of the total supply. The artificially constructed lake covers 15 miles and 7,500 acres, supporting a healthy population of brown trout. Fish taken from these waters average about five pounds, with record-setters exceeding 20 pounds. Fishing and rowboats are allowed with a free permit. Several outfitters supply gear and lead trips on the reservoir. No swimming or motorboats are allowed.

At the western end of the reservoir on Route 30 is the village of Downsville and the **Downsville Covered Bridge,** at the intersection of Route 206. This 174-foot bridge was closed for restoration and repairs in 2021.

Andes

Northeast of the Peptacon Reservoir lies the upland village of Andes, where in 1845 Moses Earle and a group of local farmers refused to pay overdue rents to protest the feudal system of land ownership. Sheriff Osman Steele intervened in the dispute and was killed by the protesters, drawing national attention to the issue. President Abraham Lincoln signed the National Homestead Act into law 15 years later, in 1862, distributing hundreds of millions of acres of land into private hands.

One of the oldest buildings in town is the 1840s **Hunting Tavern Museum** (Rte. 28, 845/676-3775, call before visiting), named for its first proprietor, Ephraim Hunting. Sheriff Steele reportedly downed his last drink here and uttered the now-famous words, "Lead cannot penetrate Steele," shortly before he was shot. Today, the tavern hosts local art exhibits, dance performances, and period dinners.

Proximity to the reservoir and a handful of businesses make Andes a popular stop on the Delaware County loop. The **Andes Hotel and Restaurant** kicks off the visitor experience, with lodging, live music, a cozy tavern, and a menu that features locally caught wild trout, along with seasonal produce. Galleries and antiques shops invite exploration along

Main Street. Admire rare 19th-century furniture, photography, and taxidermy at **Kabinett & Kammer** (7 Main St., Andes, 845/676-4242, www.kabinettandkammer. com, hours vary). Owner Sean Scherer personally finds and curates every item in the store. The aesthetic is unabashedly masculine.

Between Andres and DeLancy, the Kaufman family runs **Catskill Mountain Maple** (65 Charlie Wood Rd., DeLancey, 607/746-6215, https://catskillmountainmaple.com) saphouse and showroom during the sugaring season and an online store year-round for maple and honey products. Their annual Maple Weekend in late March is a popular event.

In winter, snowmobilers gather on Main Street at **Hogan's General Store** (103 Main St., Andes, 845/676-3470) to refuel. The **Trailways Bus Line** (703/691-3052, www. trailways.com) passes through town.

Bovina

Scenic Route 6 connects Margaretville to Bovina, where actors Brad Pitt and Jennifer Aniston were residents until their split in 2005. Bovina Center is a blink-and-you'll-miss-it kind of place with a general store and some pockets of farm-to-table activity. For example, **Brushland Eating House** (1927 County Rd. 6, Bovina, 607/832-4861, www. brushlandeatinghouse.com, $10-26) keeps it simple, with classics like pork schnitzel, hand-rolled pasta, and a "one-flip burger." **Russell's** (2099 Main St., Bovina, 607/832-4242, www.russellsgeneral.com, 9:30am-2pm Sat.-Sun.), a general store run from a building that's been a store since 1823, is now owned by the Bovina Historical Society. Pop in to refuel your car or yourself.

★ Roxbury

In an unlikely pairing, financier Jay Gould and naturalist John Burroughs share the town of Roxbury as their birthplace and family homesteads. When Gould left home to invest in railroads, Burroughs remained in the Catskills writing volumes about the natural wonders around him.

A line from "The Heart of the Southern Catskills" captures Burroughs' worldview: "Only the sea and the mountain forest brook are pure, all between is contaminated more or less by the work of man." **Woodchuck Lodge** (1633 Burroughs Memorial Rd., Roxbury, no phone, http://jbwoodchucklodge. org), the Burroughs family farmhouse, is now a national historic landmark. It's located on Burroughs Memorial Road, off Hardscrabble Road, three miles north of Roxbury. Free guided tours are offered the first weekend of the month, 11am-3pm Saturday-Sunday, May-October.

The Gould family left behind a legacy of architectural splendor. St. Lawrence marble and Tiffany stained glass windows adorn the **Jay Gould Reformed Church** (53873 Rte. 30, Roxbury, 607/326-7101, www.gouldchurch. org). Helen Gould Shephard, daughter of Jay Gould, built the 1911 classic Greek Revival building that has housed the **Roxbury Arts Group** (5025 Vega Mountain Rd., Roxbury, 607/326-7610, www.roxburyartsgroup.org) since 1988. Recently restored **Kirkside Park** (Rte. 30, Main St., Roxbury, 607/326-3722, www.roxburyny.com) and the **Shephard Hills Golf Course** (Golf Course Rd. off Bridge St., Roxbury, 607/326-7121, www. shephardhills.com, greens fees $30-39, cart included) were also part of her original estate. Today, Roxbury is an attractive town of 2,500 residents, many of them retirees and second-home owners who enjoy the variety of outdoor activities within reach.

Roxbury also boasts its own ski area, **Plattekill Mountain** (Plattekill Mountain Rd., Roxbury, 607/326-3500, www.plattekill.com).

Delhi

In the center of Delaware County, where Route 10 meets Route 28, is Delhi (DEL-high), the largest and most commercially developed municipality in the region. As the county seat,

---

1: sunset on the Pepacton Reservoir **2:** a vintage locomotive at the Delaware & Ulster Railroad depot in Arkville this town of 50,000 centers on the historic **Delaware County Courthouse Square** (3 Court St.), now an open green space bounded by 2nd, Church, Main, and Court Streets. The striking 19th-century brick facade on the courthouse is now home to county offices.

The State University of New York (SUNY) College of Technology at Delhi opened in 1913 as the State School of Agriculture and Domestic Science and currently enrolls about 3,500 students per year. Also in town are headquarters for several regional newspapers and radio stations, a few restaurants, and a couple of banks.

The **Delaware County Historical Association** (46549 Rte. 10, Delhi, 607/746-3849, www.dcha-ny.org, 11am-4pm Tues.-Sun. Memorial Day-mid-Oct., adults $5, children $1.50) maintains seven historic buildings on a property located 2.5 miles north of Delhi on Route 10. Among the restored buildings are a tollgate house from the Catskill Turnpike and the 1797 Frisbee House and barn. The museum displays rotating exhibits in its two galleries, from war memorabilia to quilt shows.

Hamden Covered Bridge

The Hamden Covered Bridge spans the West Branch of the Delaware River, along Route 10 between Delhi and Walton. Built in 1859 in the long truss style, the 125-foot bridge was refurbished in 2000. Look for a dirt pullout with a visitor sign just north of the bridge, on the west side of Route 10. On a sunny day, bring lunch to the picnic table on the west side of the bridge and watch the tractors roll by.

Route 10 heads south from Delhi along the West Branch of the Delaware River, passing through the quiet towns of Hamden, Walton, and Deposit along the way.

ALONG ROUTE 23
Catskill Scenic Trail

If you follow Route 23 west from Greene County, you'll reach the town of Grand Gorge just over the Delaware County line. The East Branch of the Delaware River begins here, and you can pick up the **Catskill Scenic Trail** (Rte. 23, Grand Gorge, 845/586-2929, www.catskillscenictrail.org), which sits on top of the old railroad tracks of the Ulster & Delaware Railroad and runs 19 miles to Bloomville. The hard-packed trail is well suited for biking, jogging, horseback riding, and cross-country skiing, and it offers access to several fishing spots along the river. The railroad track foundation keeps the trail at a gentle grade, so visitors of all ages and physical conditioning can enjoy the hike. The trail may be accessed from many towns along the way; parking lots are available in Bloomville at Route 10 and Route 33. No overnight camping is available.

At the intersection of Routes 23 and 10 lies Stamford and Mount Utsayantha (Beautiful Spring). The West Branch of the Delaware originates at this 3,214-foot peak, and it's one of the few Catskill summits that you can reach by car. A one-mile gravel road leads to the top and a view of four states on clear days. On the way to the summit is the recognized gravesite of a Mohawk woman who drowned herself in a nearby lake in grief over the loss of her son.

Stamford evolved from a distribution center for butter to a thriving resort town at the turn of the 20th century, and its 20-acre mountaintop park lured visitors from across the country. Today, the walking paths are overgrown, and the abandoned observation tower shows signs of neglect. The Utsayantha Flyers Organization has built several launch ramps for hang gliders and keeps a watchful eye on the property.

Hanford Mills Museum

Turn off Route 23 onto Route 12 to reach East Meredith and the working sawmill and gristmill at the **Hanford Mills Museum** (73 County Rd. 12, East Meredith, 607/278-5744 or 800/295-4992, www.hanfordmills.org, 10am-5pm Wed.-Sun. and holiday Mon. mid-May-mid-Oct., adults $9, seniors $7, under age 12 free). Listed on the National Register of Historic Places, the museum offers a chance to see how a water-powered sawmill worked

Snow Stats: Plattekill Mountain

- Base: 2,150 feet
- Summit: 3,500 feet
- Vertical: 1,100 feet
- Trails: 38
- Lifts: 4
- Longest trail: 2 miles
- Skiable acres: 75
- Snowmaking: 75 percent
- Snow report: 607/326-3500

in the 19th century. Vintage woodworking equipment gives young and old a glimpse into the past. Seasonal demonstrations, such as the February ice harvest, are especially interesting.

★ Stone & Thistle Farm

Learn how a sustainable farm works and help get the day's chores done at **Stone & Thistle Farm** (1211 Kelso Rd., East Meredith, 607/278-5800, www.stoneandthistlefarm. com). Take a tour of the pastures and Kortright Creek Creamery operations, meet the grass-fed and pastured animals, or pick up meat, eggs, dairy, maple syrup, jam, and homemade goodies at the farm store, which is open by appointment only. For a longer visit, sleep over in the creek-side farm cabin or enjoy a bed-and-breakfast stay in the guest suite. Call ahead to join a Saturday evening dinner or Sunday brunch.

RECREATION
Winter Sports

You have to be one of the first 2,000 skiers to get fresh tracks at **Plattekill Mountain** (469 Plattekill Rd., Roxbury, 607/326-3500, www.plattekill.com, 8:45am-4:15pm Fri.-Sun., adults $45-85, under age 7 free) on a powder day. Normally open three days a

week, the mom-and-pop mountain sells $25 tickets and runs the T-bar to expert terrain on days of 12 inches or more. But the owners stop selling tickets when they reach the 2,000 mark. Plattekill can get upward of 200 inches of snow a year—more natural snow than even the Catskill High Peaks typically get. Besides the downhill slopes, Plattekill has a terrain park and a snowtubing hill.

The **Delhi College Golf Course** (Rte. 28, Delhi, 607/746-4653, golfcourse.delhi. edu) is open to the public all winter long for cross-country skiing and snowshoeing. Snowmobilers congregate in the town of Andes, often to have lunch at the **Andes Hotel** (110 Main St., Andes, 845/676-3980, www.andeshotel.com, 3pm-9pm Tues.-Sat., 3pm-8pm Sun.).

Hiking

Mount Utsayantha (1-mile dirt road) has an easily accessible fire tower at 3,200 feet elevation. Park on Mountain Avenue in Stamford. The **Andes Rail Trail** (0.9 mile one-way, Rte. 28, Andes) offers an easy walk along an old railroad bed, with the option to add an additional 1.1 miles up to the old depot on the **Bullet Hole Spur Trail.** The total distance of this easy hike would be 4 miles.

A stretch of the 552-mile **Finger Lakes Trail System** (https://fingerlakestrail.org) connecting the New York-Pennsylvania border with the Long Path in the Catskills crosses Delaware County with several good places to camp overnight, including Beale Pond at **Oquaga Creek State Park** (Rte. 20, Masonville, 607/467-4160, parks.ny.gov). Contact **Finger Lakes Trail Conference Service Center** (www.fltconference.org) for a current trail map and information about access points and routes.

Near Andes, the **Delaware Wild Forest** in the Catskill Forest Preserve has 33 miles of trails to explore. An easy loop is the **Little Pond Trail** (1.5 miles) with yellow markers. It connects to the more challenging red-blazed **Touch-Me-Not Trail** (6.5 miles one-way), which climbs over Cabot Mountain.

Cycling and Mountain Biking

Whether you want to log 15 miles or 100, Delaware County has some of the best terrain around for cycling. Plan a route to tour the county's covered bridges. Avid cyclists won't want to miss the annual **Tour of the Catskills** (www.tourofthecatskills. com), which bills itself as "America's Largest Pro-Am Stage Race."

In summer, the **Plattekill Bike Park** (Plattekill Mountain Rd., Roxbury, 607/326-3500, www.plattekill.com) opens its lifts (10am-5pm Sat.-Sun. early May-early Nov.) to serve 60 miles of trails. Wednesday through Friday, you can access the trails, but the lifts won't be running. Bike rentals ($50 for 2 hours, $110-150 for 2 days) are available. Tickets for all-day lift and trail access cost $35; the trails-only rate is $15 per day. A single lift ride with your bike is $10. A SkyRide, sans bike, is $7. Shuttle service is offered to the Catskill Scenic Rail Trail in nearby Roxbury. RV and tent camping ($10) is permitted at the base of the mountain.

Golf

Hanah Mountain Resort and Country Club (576 W. Hubbell Hill Rd., Margaretville, 800/752-6494, www.hanahcountryresort. com, greens fees $45-65) has a USGA-rated course that's known as the Terminator. Inquire about combined room and greens fee packages.

Swimming and Boating

Paddlers head for the Delaware and Susquehanna Rivers or the Pepacton Reservoir for adventure. Located near the Pepacton Reservoir, **Al's Sport Store** (Rte. 30 and Rte. 206, Downsville, 607/363-7740, www.alssportstore.com, 7:30am-5pm Mon.-Fri., 7am-6pm Sat., 7am-5pm Sun.) offers day or overnight camping trips on the Delaware River. Shuttle service is available.

Fishing

Delaware County offers hundreds of miles of some of the top fishing streams, rivers, and reservoirs in the country. The season begins each April with the hatching of the blue-winged olive fly. For freestone stream fishing, the **Willowemoc Creek** and **Beaver Kill** are legendary. The **Pepacton Reservoir** offers still-water anglers plentiful opportunities for catching bass and occasionally huge brown trout.

ENTERTAINMENT AND EVENTS
Performing Arts

The **West Kortright Centre** (49 W. Kortright Church Rd., East Meredith, 607/278-5454, www.westkc.org) is one of the premier performance venues in Delaware County. Housed in a restored Greek Revival church on Turnpike Road in West Kortright, it has hosted world-famous composers, poets, musicians, and other artists since the 1970s. A series of musical performances takes place throughout the summer season, as well as gallery exhibits.

Set in a historic building in downtown Franklin, the **Franklin Stage Company at Chapel Hall** (25 Institute St., Franklin, 607/829-3700, www.franklinstagecompany. org) produces a mix of modern and classical theater. The company's free admission policy sets a fun and irreverent tone.

Bars and Nightlife

In Roxbury, **The Old Mill** (2318 County Rd. 41, Roxbury, 607/326-6090, www. oldmillroxbury.com, 5pm-11pm Mon.-Thurs., 5pm-midnight Fri.-Sat., 5pm-10pm Sun.) was planning to open across the street from The Roxbury motel. Stop in for a cold beer, fun cocktails, or glass of fine wine.

Union Grove Distillery (43311 Rte. 28, Arkville, http://uniongrovedistillery.com, 3pm-9pm Fri.-Sat., 1pm-5pm Sun.) has a Vly Creek Vodka made of local apples and wheat. Catskill maple syrup finds its way into some of the spirits too. Enjoy a tasting, and then grab a bottle to go.

1: checking for trout in a mountain stream
2: the Hamden Covered Bridge

Festivals

Maple Shade Farm (2066 Rte. 18, Delhi, 607/746-8866, www.mapleshadefarmny.com) hosts the **Taste of the Catskills** event in October—a family-friendly weekend that celebrates local food, beer, and crafts.

SHOPPING

If you love to buy and sell goods on eBay, try the offline equivalent at one of Delaware County's professional auction houses. At **McIntosh Auction Service** (Bovina Center, 607/832-4829 or 607/832-4241, www.mcintoshauction.com), Chuck McIntosh has been in the business for 30 years. After you've won the farm, you can sample the local bounty at the **Pakatakan Farmers Market** (Kelly Round Barn, Rte. 30, Halcottsville, 845/586-3326, www.roundbarnmarket.org, 10am-1pm Sat.).

Lucky Dog Organic Farm Store (35796 Rte. 10, Hamden, 607/746-8383, www.luckydogorganic.com, 8am-5pm Mon.-Fri., $5-10) is a combination farm stand, eatery, and boutique that grows much of its own produce on a 160-acre farm. It also carries meat, dairy, eggs, and prepared foods from other local farms, as well as candles, soaps, and other gifts.

Shaver Hill Maple Country Gift Shop (450 Shaver Rd., Harpersfield, 607/652-6792, www.shaverhillfarm.com, 9am-5pm Sat.-Mon.) sells an creative assortment of maple-themed goods, including pancake mix, maple cotton candy, maple flavored popcorn, and cinnamon granulated maple sugar—and of course, jugs of pure New York maple syrup.

FOOD
Along Route 28

The **Arkville Bread and Breakfast** (43285 Rte. 28, Arkville, 845/586-1122, 7am-2pm Wed.-Mon., $9) serves omelets, home fries, bacon, and a rotating list of sandwiches in a casual setting. Real maple syrup is available for an extra charge. **Oakley's** (44681 Rte. 28, Arkville, 845/586-3474, www.oakleyswoodfirepizzaandgrill.com, 4pm-9pm Wed.-Thurs., noon-10pm Fri.-Sat., noon-9pm Sun., $11-19) created quite a stir when the new owners added wood-fired pizza to the menu. This is a great place to enjoy a cold beer outside on the deck, where dogs are welcome, too.

Kid-friendly American fare comes out of the kitchen at **The Inn Between Restaurant** (42377 Rte. 28, Margaretville, 845/586-4265, 4pm-9pm Wed.-Sat., $15-35), making it a

historic round barn, home of the Pakatakan Farmers Market

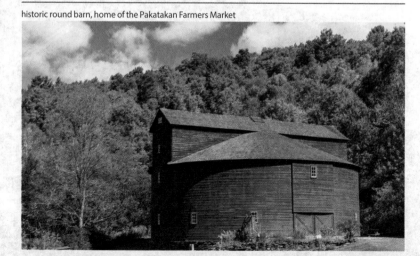

good choice after a day on the ski hill. **Crazy River Café** (42287 Rte. 28, Margaretville, 845/586-6266, 8am-3pm Thurs.-Tues., $5-10) gets high marks among locals for its soups and sandwiches.

Downsville has the **Old Schoolhouse Inn** (28218 Rte. 28, Downsville, 607/363-7814, www.oldschoolhouseinn.com, 11:30am-9pm Wed.-Thurs. and Sun., 11:30am-9pm Fri.-Sat., $10-35). The menu includes lobster, prime rib, and trout dishes, and you'll dine under a large collection of stuffed hunting trophies.

The Andes Hotel (110 Main St., Andes, 845/676-3980, www.theandeshotel.com, 3pm-9pm Tues.-Sat., 3pm-8pm Sun., $17-28) is just a restaurant these days. The kitchen uses farm-fresh ingredients to make chicken pot pie, Maryland crab cakes, steak dinners, and other hearty fare. Pop in for Taco Tuesday or for the weekly entrée specials.

A couple from Brooklyn opened ★ **Brushland Eating House** (1927 County Rd. 6, Bovina Center, 607/832-4861, www. brushlandeatinghouse.com, 6pm seating Thurs.-Sat., prix fixe $75 pp) to focus on simple foods for supper. Seasonal ingredients such as carrots and beets and cuts of meat from locally raised livestock define the menu. Try whatever cheese they are serving that night. Aside from one Long Island white, wines by the glass come from Europe. Four Airbnbs near the restaurant can be home for the weekend or longer.

Roxbury also has a gourmet food truck called ★ **Ate O Ate** (607/326-3392, www. ateoatecatering.com, $8-16). Check the website for the truck's whereabouts, and then you can order and pay online before you go. The menu sometimes features themes such as Spanish tapas or Hawaiian luau. Also keep an eye out for prix fixe dinners at the Union Grove Distillery.

Chappie's (53535 State Rte. 28, Roxbury, 607/326-7020, noon-8pm Mon.-Thurs., noon-9pm Fri., 11am-9pm Sat.-Sun., $15-24) offers a simple menu of artisanal pizzas, steak frites, and a locally sourced beef burger, with a rotating wine list.

Along Route 23

A dinner at ★ **Stone & Thistle Farm's Fable** (1211 Kelso Rd., East Meredith, 607/278-5800, www.stoneandthistlefarm. com, $55 pp) will change how fresh you thought farm-to-table food could be. On select Saturdays June through October, this sustainable farm offers a tour at 6:30pm followed by dinner at 7pm in an 1863 Greek Revival farmhouse. The menu is prix fixe and features the farm's own meats, dairy, and produce, plus locally grown fruits and artisanal cheeses. Families are welcome, and children may be allowed to pet the animals and help collect eggs. Stone & Thistle's cattle, sheep, and goats are exclusively grass-fed; pigs, poultry, and rabbits eat a small amount of local grains as a supplement. Reservations are required for brunch or dinner. A separate cabin by the creek and private suite in the farmhouse are available for overnight accommodations.

ACCOMMODATIONS

Accommodations are hit-or-miss in rural Delaware County. Small country inns range from musty and neglected to positively charming. The good news is that even the best are relatively affordable. The Plattekill ski and mountain biking area (www.plattekill. com) has listings of local house rentals as an alternative to the standard B&B or motel lodging. Based in Margaretville, **Pine Hollow Lodging** (845/586-1433, www. pinehollowlodging.com) also manages a number of vacation rentals, and of course there's always the now ubiquitous Airbnb.

Under $100

Popular with fishing enthusiasts, ★ **Smith's Colonial Motel** (23085 Rte. 97, Hancock, 607/637-2989, www.smithscolonialmotel.com, $75-130) is walking distance to the Delaware River. This well-kept property has an impressive list of amenities for the price, including cable TV with HBO and high-speed internet. Guest room walls are paneled in knotty pine, and minimal furnishings accent scenic views of the river below.

Adjoining Al's Sports Store, the **Downsville Motel** (6964 River Rd., Downsville, 607/363-7575, https://www.alssportstore.com, $79-89) is a small, two-story motel with several guest rooms and a second-story apartment ($120/night for 2 people, $15 per additional guest) with two bedrooms and a full kitchen.

Set in a Victorian home on a hill above the town, the **Margaretville Mountain Inn** (1478 Margaretville Mountain Rd., Margaretville, 845/586-3933, www.margaretvilleinn.com, from $95) has several floral rooms with brass bed frames. Some rooms share a bath. Views from the porch are a highlight, and breakfast is included with an overnight stay. For modern accommodations and a more convenient location, request one of the two-room units in the newer Village Suites building in town. Inquire about ski and stay packages.

$100-150

Want to help out on a family farm, or simply take in the scenery and the food? **Stone & Thistle Farm** (1211 Kelso Rd., East Meredith, 607/278-5800, www.stoneandthistlefarm.com, $125-160) has a private suite in the main farmhouse and a rustic cabin by the creek. The cabin has electricity and a fridge, a hot plate, a microwave, and an outdoor grill. A solar shower, a sink, and a composting toilet are outside. Guests can participate in farm chores through a farm stay program or relax on the stone patio with a book. Horses are welcome to stay in the horse barn ($25 per night).

★ **Brushland Eating House** (1927 County Rd. 6, Bovina Center, 607/832-4861, www.brushlandeatinghouse.com) is primarily a restaurant, but it has four vacation rentals that appeal to artists, writers, and anyone in search of a quiet retreat: **Above Brushland** ($144) has good natural light, hardwood floors, pine cabinets, exposed beams, and white walls. Best of all, a good meal is just a flight of stairs away. Furnishings are simple, like the menu. Across the road, **The White House** ($189) is a restored 1884 farmhouse

that sleeps six people in three bedrooms. On top of Bramley Mountain, **Owl Nest** ($239) is a two-bedroom cabin that sleeps up to five people. **Behind Brushland** ($145) is another two-bedroom.

The Old Schoolhouse Inn & Restaurant (28218 State Hwy. 206, Downsville, 607/363-7814, www.oldschoolhouseinn.com, $105-200) has four cozy guest rooms, plus a honeymoon suite.

$150-200

Hanah Mountain Resort and Country Club (576 W. Hubbell Hill Rd., Margaretville, 800/752-6494, www.hanahcountryresort.com, $140-310) provides standard chain hotel-style accommodations, but the resort offers enough activities to keep you out and about the entire day. Take the free shuttle to Plattekill Mountain for some downhill mountain biking, or head out to face the Terminator golf course. A golf school on-site will help tune up your game. The resort offers numerous golf, ski, and mountain biking packages.

At **Harmony Hill Lodging and Retreat Center** (694 McKee Hill Rd., East Meredith, 607/278-6609, www.harmonyhillretreat.com, $150-265), a stay begins with a walk around the fieldstone labyrinth. Two treehouse yurts are available May-October. For a small group, choose the Mountain Chalet, a 1,200-square-foot cabin that sleeps up to six adults. Set on 70 acres of meadow and woods, the property has its own trails and a creek. Guided meditation and yoga instruction can be scheduled during your stay.

For a motel with a pop-culture twist, try ★ **The Roxbury** (2258 County Rd. 41, Roxbury, 607/326-7200, www.theroxburymotel.com, $138-404). Its rooms combine technology, style, and simplicity to redefine the motel experience around the concept of creativity. A few of its signature rooms take bold use of color to the extreme, with mosaic quilts, zebra stripes, and psychedelic swirls. Some have kitchenettes as well. Amenities include Wi-Fi and flat-screen TVs, as well as high-end linens and bath products.

Service is exceptionally attentive. Best of all, access to the on-site Shimmer Spa facilities (for guests only) costs just $20 per person per stay.

South Kortright has a couple of additional options for memorable Airbnb stays: **Table Earth House** ($260) and **Table Studio** ($267) both are hosted by Inez, a former restaurateur in the area.

Campgrounds

Peaceful Valley Campsite (485 Banker Rd., Downsville, 607/363-2211, www.nypeacefulvalley.com, $15 pp) is the place to pitch your tent. You can also rent a room in a cottage or cabin ($30 and up). Canoe rentals are available by the day or by the week. An alternative is the **Little Pond Campground** (549 Little Pond State Campground Rd., Andes, 845/439-5480, www.dec.ny.gov, $22-27). From Route 30 in Margaretville, go south about six miles to New York City Road and then to Barkaboom Road, and the campground is on the right.

INFORMATION AND SERVICES

The **Delaware County Chamber of Commerce** (5½ Main St., Delhi, 607/746-2281, www.delawarecounty.org) maintains an informative website.

GETTING THERE AND AROUND

It's easier to rent a canoe than a car in outdoor-oriented Delaware County, but you'll need wheels to get around this rural county, as public transportation is virtually nonexistent. **Albany International Airport** (ALB, 518/242-2200, www.albanyairport.com) is the best bet for a rental. Some of the national rental companies also have outposts in Kingston over in Ulster County.

Upper Hudson Valley and the Northern Catskills

The Catskill and Berkshire Mountains frame the upper—and most rugged—section of the Hudson River Valley. In between, small lakes and dense hardwood forests alternate with rolling hills and cultivated fields. Rural communities dot the landscape, welcoming visitors with historic sights, heirloom vegetables, antiques shops, and the promise of outdoor adventure.

Striking in any season, the Upper Hudson Valley makes an exceptionally enjoyable winter getaway, when every inn has a wood fire burning and hearty meals warm you from the inside out. Greene and Columbia Counties' many lodges, bed-and-breakfasts, and country inns create that cozy feeling the Austrians call *gemütlichkeit*. Cross-country skiers can explore varied terrain on private and public lands,

Highlights

Look for ★ to find recommended sights, activities, dining, and lodging.

★ **Kaaterskill Falls:** A new and safe viewing platform overlooks the upper falls, with a well-marked trail down to the bottom of the 180-foot falls that inspired many a Hudson River School painter (page 228).

★ **The Escarpment Trail:** Plan a three-day backpacking trip to hike this 23.9-mile trail that begins near Windham, crosses seven summits higher than 3,000 feet, and ends at Haines Falls (page 229).

★ **Windham Mountain Resort:** This long-time ski resort has stepped it up with friendly policies for uphill skiing in winter and lift-access mountain biking trails in summer (page 231).

★ **Olana State Historic Site:** The former estate of Hudson River School painter Frederic Church overlooks the Rip Van Winkle Bridge (page 248).

★ **Taconic State Park:** This expansive green space encompasses 5,000 acres at the base of the Taconic Range, near the Massachusetts and Connecticut state lines (page 252).

★ **Mount Lebanon Shaker Village:** This remarkable collection of artifacts offers an informative introduction to the Shaker way of life (page 253).

while downhill skiers and riders can find steeps and parks for all levels at the Windham, Hunter, Belleayre, and Catamount resorts. And for those who don't measure fun in vertical feet, snowmobiles, snowshoes, and ice skates provide a few more alternatives.

In August 2011, Tropical Storm Irene struck the Catskills with heavy rainfall, high winds, and severe flooding. It was the most severe storm in the area in at least a century. The Windham and Hunter ski areas sustained the greatest damage. Although some businesses were able to reopen within days, many were forced to close at least temporarily, and some never recovered. The aftermath is still visible in the form of slides along Route 23A near Haines Falls and on Twin Mountain. Many of the creeks have been permanently widened and filled with debris.

If you're the kind of person who travels to eat, the Upper Hudson Valley also holds a few surprises. Gaskins in Germantown, Local 111 in Philmont, and Wm Farmer & Sons in Hudson could top any gourmet's must-try list.

And there's another way to sample the fruits of the land: by rolling up your sleeves and picking what's in season. There is at least one farmers market, roadside stand, or pick-your-own orchard in just about every town in Columbia and Greene Counties.

PLANNING YOUR TIME

With a selective itinerary, you can easily tour Greene or Columbia in a day of scenic driving. (It takes less than an hour to drive the length of either one.) But you'll need a long weekend to take in a few of the historic sights and outdoor activities these counties offer. Allow an hour for the round-trip hike to Kaaterskill Falls or a day to summit one of the High Peaks. Tours of Clermont and Olana last about an hour, plus time to walk the grounds and contemplate the views. Serious antiques shoppers can spend a full day or more in downtown Hudson.

Many visitors to the Upper Hudson Valley plan weekend getaways around a farm visit, local festival, or bed-and-breakfast inn. Others choose to take in a history tour or special meal en route between New York City and New England or western New York State.

In Greene County, the loop along Routes 23 and 23A covers about 40 miles and takes less than an hour to complete by car with no stops. An out-and-back excursion to Coxsackie along Route 385 and the Hudson River adds another hour round-trip. Columbia County has three parallel routes running north to south: Route 9G follows the river's edge, the Taconic State Parkway is the fastest, and Route 22 runs along the foot of the Taconic Hills in the eastern part of the county.

Starting at the southern border with Dutchess County, take a favorite scenic drive that follows Route 9G about 30 minutes north to the city of Hudson, then meander on local roads up to Kinderhook and Chatham. From there, you can zip back to your starting point along the Taconic Parkway, or continue east and take Route 22 south through Hillsdale and Copake. The entire loop should take 2-3 hours with no stops.

Previous: Olana State Historic Site; a Greene County flower garden; the top of Kaaterskill Falls.

Upper Hudson Valley and the Northern Catskills

© MOON.COM

Greene County

In the days before New York City residents could hop a flight to Bermuda for the weekend, they vacationed in the Catskills. If you had the means to vacation in remote Greene County during the early to mid-19th century, you might have stayed at the world-famous Catskill Mountain House—along with Alexander Graham Bell, Henry James, Oscar Wilde, Ulysses S. Grant, Mark Twain, and their contemporaries. A one-day journey from New York City began with a steamboat ride to Catskill Landing and concluded with a harrowing 12-mile, four-hour stagecoach ride to the eastern edge of the High Peaks region.

Between the Kaaterskill Creek and Sleepy Hollow, a steep and narrow road climbed to the top of a rocky plateau called Pine Orchard. Here, the classical Mountain House stood with its 13 Corinthian columns, painted stark white against a backdrop of hemlock and white pines and surrounded by hundreds of square miles of untamed forest. In the words of author Roland Van Zandt, the hotel offered the "ideal combination of wilderness and luxury" and symbolized "a nation's young wealth, leisure, and cultural attainments."

Modern rail and jet travel changed Greene County forever, sending would-be visitors to more exotic destinations. In 1963, the New York State Department of Conservation declared the long-abandoned hotel a danger to hikers and burned what remained of the building to the ground one winter morning. Visitors today can only imagine the imposing white structure and the famous people who stayed in it, but the setting remains as enchanting as two centuries ago.

Located on the west side of the Hudson, with Albany County to the north and Ulster County to the south, Greene County has 20 miles of riverfront, several bustling valley and mountain towns, and Kaaterskill Falls—at 260 feet, the highest waterfall in the east. The magical surroundings inspired American literary master Washington Irving to write the tale of Rip Van Winkle, the hen-pecked husband who wandered into the mountains and fell into a 20-year sleep.

Named after Revolutionary War General Nathanael Greene of Rhode Island, the original Greene County consisted of four towns: Catskill and Coxsackie on the river, Freehold in the valley, and Windham on the mountaintop. Agriculture, forestry, and a few dozen tanneries drove the local economy in the early days. But the opening of the Erie Canal in 1825 diverted ships and manufactured goods from Catskill to Troy, sending the once-prosperous county into a tailspin—until a group of Romantic Era writers and painters, including Thomas Cole, popularized the region for its natural beauty.

Dairy farms and orchards came next, along with German and Irish immigrants and summer residents. From the polka dancers at the Mountain Brauhaus to the International Celtic Festival at Hunter Mountain, the county retains much of its immigrant influence today.

After a steady decline during the mid-20th century, Greene County is quietly capturing the imagination of travelers, writers, and outdoor enthusiasts again. Author Allegra Goodman chose the valley as the setting for her first novel, *Kaaterskill Falls* (Delta, 1999), which intertwines the stories of three Orthodox Jewish families from New York City who spend summers in the area. On the mountaintop, an effort has been underway to revive Hunter Village with a focus on art and cultural events.

Members of the Catskill 3500 Club visit Greene County to climb many of the highest peaks in the range, including Blackhead, Black Dome, and Thomas Cole mountains. The county also supports two destination ski resorts—Hunter Mountain and Windham Mountain—which offer city dwellers a convenient alternative to driving four hours to New England resorts or traveling by plane to the Rockies.

Note that the weather is often cooler, windier, and wetter on the mountaintop than at the river's edge. Bring layers, regardless of the season.

ALONG THE RIVER: ROUTE 385
Rip Van Winkle Bridge

The Rip Van Winkle Bridge spans the Hudson at mile 112, counting from the south. If you approach the crossing from Routes 9G or 82, both in Columbia County, the first sight of the Catskills' purple-gray peaks may catch you off guard. For generations, the bridge has stood as a divider between civilization and wilderness, or what many locals call "up country." The range's cluster of High Peaks rises to 4,000 feet, just 12 miles west of the sea-level river.

Begin your tour of Greene County with a walk along the mile-long span of the bridge. Built during the Great Depression at a cost of $2.4 million and opened in 1935, the bridge connects the small cities of Catskill and Hudson, ushering visitors into the forever-wild lands of the Catskill Preserve (car toll $1.50, eastbound only). The New York State

Bridge Authority has preserved the look of the original Dutch colonial toll plaza so as not to alter the view from the Olana State Historic Site directly across the river.

Park in the small lot near the toll plaza on the Catskill side of the bridge. It's pedestrians only on the sidewalk; bikes must use the narrow traffic lanes. Pause at the middle of the span to take in the 360-degree views. The river below is tidal freshwater. To the north, Stockport Middle Ground Island is one of four sites belonging to the National Estuarine Research Reserve System. The Hudson-Athens Lighthouse, on a smaller island to the northwest, was established in 1874 and had a live-in keeper until 1949. The gentle hills of Columbia County rise in the east behind the waterfront city of Hudson. And the clay-tiled rooftop of Olana, the Persian-style castle of painter Frederic Church, stands above the trees to the southeast. Turn back west, and the Catskill Mountains beckon.

Hudson River Skywalk

The **Hudson River Skywalk** (www.hudsonriverskywalk.org) is a relatively new path that connects the Thomas Cole National Historic Site in Catskill with Olana State Historic Site estate in Columbia County, via

Rip Van Winkle Bridge

Catskill

To Athens

BRIDGE APPROACH

THOMAS COLE NATIONAL HISTORIC SITE

S WASHINGTON ST

23

HUDSON RIVER SKYWALK
RIP VAN WINKLE BRIDGE

River

Hudson

CEDAR ST

HIGH ST

GRACE ST

WOODLAND AVE

SPRING ST

DAY ST

NEW ST

THOMPSON ST

LA CONCA D'ORO

HiLo CATSKILL

GARDEN GATE CAFÉ

385

9

CONE E ISLAND

RIVER BASIN SPORTS

To Catskill Park and New York Zipline Adventure Tours at Hunter Mountain

W BRIDGE ST

WATER ST

MAIN ST

GREENE COUNTY COUNCIL ON THE ARTS

394 MAIN WINE BAR

MAGPIE BOOKSHOP

WILLIAM ST

CATSKILL PUBLIC LIBRARY

PROSPECT AVE

GREENE COUNTY COURTHOUSE

VERDIGRIS TEA & CHOCOLATE BAR

W MAIN ST

GREENE ST

BROAD ST

MAIN ST

CATSKILL MARINA

Elliot Park

CREEKSIDE RESTAURANT

RIVER ST

DUTCHMAN'S LANDING

CATSKILL POINT

GRANDVIEW AVE

RAMSHORN-LIVINGSTON SANCTUARY

FRANK GUIDO'S PORT OF CALL

To Hudson and Olana State Historic Site

0   0.25 mi
0   0.25 km

© MOON.COM

the Rip Van Winkle bridge. The pedestrian walkway covers six miles round-trip, and you can start from either side.

Catskill

Historian Henry Brace wrote in 1876 that early Dutch settlers purchased the village of Catskill in 1684 for "a gun, two shirts, a kettle, two kegs of beer, and, as usual, a little rum." For more than two centuries, the village thrived as an agricultural crossroads and a gateway to the mountains. But the building of the Rip Van Winkle Bridge marked the beginning of a long decline. These days, the town is dreadfully quiet in winter; come summer, however, the waterfront awakens with boating, outdoor dining, and an open-air market. The flurry of development taking place across the river in Hudson has somewhat spilled over to Main Street in Catskill over the years, with

a few new restaurants, cafés, and gift shops opening each season.

Catskill's Main Street runs parallel to Catskill Creek, which widens and empties into the Hudson just past the center of town. There is a municipal parking lot off Main. Two-story row houses line both sides of the street, many of them housing attorneys' offices, as Catskill is the county seat. The **Greene County Courthouse,** at the intersection of Main and Bridge Street (Rte. 385), is a white neoclassical structure that towers over its neighbors. Behind it is the **Catskill Public Library** (1 Franklin St., 518/943-4230, www. catskillpubliclibrary.org, 9am-noon Mon., 11am-5pm Tues. and Fri., 11am-7pm Thurs., 10am-1pm Sat.), in another neoclassical building. The library has a local history collection with many books about the steamboats of the Hudson.

Main Street takes a sharp turn to the left as you approach the mouth of the Catskill Creek. Follow West Main to its end to reach Catskill Point, Dutchman's Landing, and Frank Guido's Port of Call restaurant. Many community activities take place here during the summer months.

RamsHorn-Livingston Sanctuary (Grandview Ave., 518/678-3248, www. scenichudson.org, dawn-dusk daily) is the largest tidal swamp forest along the Hudson. Paddlers can rent boats and explore some 480 acres via 3.5 miles of waterways that lead out to the river itself. Heron, waterfowl, and other birds feed here, and American shad and bass come in spring to spawn. Open year-round, the sanctuary is jointly owned and operated by the Scenic Hudson Land Trust and the **National Audubon Society** (P.O. Box 1, Craryville, 518/325-5203, http://ny.audubon. org).

Cedar Grove

Around the time that the Romantic Era began to take hold in America, a young artist named Thomas Cole ventured up the river from New York City in search of inspiration for a series of sketches. The canvases and exhibition that followed put him in the national spotlight and helped to make the Catskills world-famous.

Cole spent most of his adult years at Cedar Grove in the town of Catskill, now the **Thomas Cole National Historic Site** (218 Spring St., Catskill, 518/943-7465, www. thomascole.org, 10am-5pm Wed.-Sun. May-Oct., indoor guided tour adults $10, seniors and students $9, under age 13 free). He painted landscapes and taught students, including Frederic Church, who later established his own residence on a hillside across the river. With a shared interest in painting mountain peaks and waterfalls instead of portraits, Cole and his students became known collectively as the Hudson River School of painting.

Today, the pale-yellow house sits on the outskirts of town, close to a busy traffic light and a Mobil gas station. Despite the encroaching surroundings, the views continue to inspire awe. On display inside the house and studios are a few of Cole's paintings, as well as furniture and family memorabilia. The **Hudson River School Art Trail** (http:// hudsonriverschool.org) is a collaborative project that includes organized hikes and paddles to experience the settings that inspired the artistic movement.

Athens

Head north on County Road 385 (Spring St.) from Catskill about four miles and you'll come to the much smaller village of Athens. The Dutch arrived here in 1686, and the town was a landing point for the Athens-Hudson ferry service, which dates to the late 1770s. Built into a hillside, with a splash of color on some of its old Victorian homes, the town hints of San Francisco, except for the two industrial plants that frame its borders. A few restaurants are popping up, and the town has a wonderful branch of the county library system, the **D. R. Evarts Public Library** (80 2nd St., Athens, https://drevartslibrary.org).

It's rare to find many cars in the **Cohotate Preserve** (Rte. 385, www.gcswcd.com, free), south of town, but the site is worth a visit for its river views and environmental information. The parking lot is well marked with a large sign on Route 385. A gravel road leads to the river, and from there, an interpretive trail describes the habitats of local plants, animals, and fish, leading to spectacular river views. The Greene County Environmental Education Center recently added a pond to attract and support a greater variety of wildlife for nature walkers. Students of Columbia-Greene Community College take environmental classes in a new lab on the premises. For those who want to get on the water, there is a well-maintained boat ramp with parking for 25 cars just north of town.

Coxsackie

Continuing north along Route 385 brings you to Coxsackie (cook-SAK-ee), borrowed from an Algonquin expression meaning "owl hoot" or "place of wild geese." Reed's Landing was once a busy center for shipbuilding and transportation, and today the town retains an industrial feel. The remains of a Hudson River freighter called the *Storm King* rest in shallow water near the town's River Park.

When the icehouses of the Hudson became obsolete, creative entrepreneurs discovered they were ideal for growing mushrooms. The Greene County Historical Society has estimated that by the late 1930s, Coxsackie-based Knaust Brothers controlled about 85 percent of the country's mushroom business as a supplier to companies like Heinz and Campbell's.

One mile south of the Coxsackie boat launch is the **Hudson River Islands State Park** (518/732-0187, www.nysparks.com), on the islands of Gay's Point and Stockport Middle Ground. Accessible only by boat, the park protects many rare and endangered species and allows picnics, fishing, and camping Memorial Day-Columbus Day.

Moving away from the river, the main attraction in Coxsackie is the oldest surviving dwelling in upstate New York, a 1663 stone house now known as the **Bronck Museum** (90 County Rd. 42, 518/731-6490, www. gchistory.org, noon-4pm Wed.-Fri., 10am-4pm Sat. and holiday Mon., 1pm-4pm Sun. Memorial Day weekend-mid-Oct., adults $7, ages 12-15 $3, ages 5-11 $2, under age 5 free). In 1662, Pieter Bronck, a Dutchman who lived in Albany, received a land patent from the British government to settle in modern-day Coxsackie. He built a one-room structure in 1663 and expanded it 20 years later to include a loft with an Indian lookout. In 1738, Bronck's grandson added a new brick house to the property.

The museum consists of these two homes—furnished with period art, linens, ceramics, and silver—and several Dutch colonial barns. The Victorian Horse Barn contains a model of the famous Catskill Mountain House and other Greene County memorabilia. A single center pole supports the roof of the Thirteen-Sided Barn. The Dutch Barn has its original wood floor, made of pegged oak planks three inches thick. The Greene County Historical Society runs the museum and holds special events throughout the year; check www. gchistory.org for a current calendar.

Unless you are continuing to Albany via Route 9W or the New York State Thruway, now is a good time to retrace your steps to Catskill and head west on Route 23 or 23A toward the mountaintop.

ALONG ROUTE 23A
Catskill Park

The 700,000-acre Catskill Park is a vast wilderness area made of both private and public land. It spans four counties and is managed in part by the state of New York's Department of Environmental Conservation (DEC). Within this area, the state operates the Catskill Forest Preserve, which includes a network of trails and a number of campgrounds that are open to the public. This preserved wilderness includes all but two of the 35 Catskill High Peaks.

★ KAATERSKILL FALLS

Asher B. Durand, another of the Hudson River painters, spent many summers in **Palenville** and established one of America's first artist colonies here in the 1840s. This quiet town sits at the base of the High Peaks and the edge of the Catskill Park. Washington Irving's Rip Van Winkle fell into his 20-year slumber above Palenville in the Kaaterskill Clove.

Leaving town, you enter the Catskill Park, and the road becomes narrow and steep, with retaining walls and hairpin turns. Ice-climbers scale the frozen waterfalls in winter, while hikers take to the trails in spring, summer, and fall. Look for the lower trailhead to **Kaaterskill Falls** about a mile into the ascent.

With the old tanneries and hotels long gone, the falls are more pristine today than they were a hundred years ago. An hour-long walk from the lower trailhead (2 miles round-trip) on a well-marked but very steep trail brings you to the base of the falls and back. Parking for the trailhead is on the left side of Route 23A, about 0.3 miles uphill from the hairpin turn, where you'll see smaller Bastion Falls. You'll have to cross the highway and walk along the shoulder of the road to get back down to the trailhead.

To avoid the dangerous highway crossing and a strenuous hike, drive up to the new overlook reached via Laurel House Road, off Route 218. From the **Kaaterskill Falls Viewing Platform,** you can view the upper falls safely and embark on a longer hike from the upper trailhead (4.7 miles round-trip, moderate) out to Inspiration Point or down to the lower falls (just be sure your legs can handle the 181 stairs you'll have to climb back up). This area is safe to hike only if you stay on marked trails and observe all warning signs; sadly, fatalities have occurred here with alarming frequency when people get too close to the edge and slip on the wet rocks. Do not leave the trail under any circumstances. Visit http://hikethehudsonvalley.com for turn-by-turn directions and more route advice.

Both the lower and upper parking lots fill to capacity on weekends, even in the late fall. Observe all "No Parking" signs and make a back-up plan in case the lots are full.

★ THE ESCARPMENT TRAIL

Backpackers, mountaineers, and ultra-distance trail runners love this 23.9-mile trail that begins near Windham, crosses seven summits higher than 3,000 feet, and ends at Haines Falls. Strong hikers can complete the point-to-point route in a weekend, assuming you've arranged a shuttle pickup. However, three days is more realistic to conquer all the ups and downs the trail will throw at you. The northern section of the trail has two options for lean-to shelters. Water is scarce when you get up high, so be sure to filter and refill at the various springs when you descend into the valleys.

If you only have time for a day hike, start at the **North-South Lake Campground** on Schutt Road and first take a short walk from the beach to the site of the **Catskill Mountain House** (0.25 mile each way).

Then hike to **Sunset Rock** (1.75 miles each way), **Boulder Rock** (4 miles each way), or **Artists Rock** (5.25 miles each way). Views of the valley get better and better the farther you go. The terrain is moderately challenging for these hikes.

A small green hut before the turnoff to North Lake in Haines Falls has visitor information. Gas, groceries, and banking services all are located along Main Street (Rte. 23A), and several places in town rent snowmobiles and mountain bikes. Turn right on County Road 18 (North Lake Rd.) to reach the campground, lakes, and trails described above.

Tannersville

Tannersville bears the responsibility of reminding locals and visitors of an unfortunate episode in Catskill history. Around the turn of the 19th century, the business of manufacturing leather became lucrative for those who were willing to endure the labor-intensive process. When mountaintop tanners discovered that hemlock bark served as an effective tanning agent, they began to strip the virgin forest of its trees, peeling the bark away and leaving the trunks to rot on the forest floor. By 1855, the forest had been stripped of almost every hemlock tree, and the mountaintop had to reinvent itself.

Tannersville didn't actually incorporate until after the tannery boom had passed, but the centrally located **Mountain Top Arboretum** (Rte. 23C, 518/589-3903, www.mtarboretum.org, year-round, $5 donation) seems to make amends for the past. Stop by for a lesson in native and exotic trees and shrubs. You can wander across seven acres in a guided or self-led tour, or join one of many horticultural education programs. This is a great place to park for access to the **Kaaterskill Rail Trail** (easy, 3 miles one-way), which connects the Mountain Top Historical Society in Haines Falls to the Kaaterskill Falls viewing platform off Laurel House Road.

Hunter Mountain Ski Bowl

As soon as temperatures dip below freezing,

Catskill Mountain House

site of the historic Catskill Mountain House

By virtue of its remote setting within a day's journey from thriving New York City, the antebellum **Catskill Mountain House** became one of America's first luxury resorts. Under the direction of Charles L. Beach, son of a stagecoach operator, the inn drew influential artists, designers, businesspeople, and politicians from the entire Atlantic corridor for more than 50 years. Some guests stayed a week, while others spent the full summer in the cool mountain air. Beach expanded the original Greek-style building rapidly to keep up with demand, growing from 10 rooms in 1824 to more than 300 by the 1880s.

The Catskill Mountain House remained a focal point of the American Romantic Movement until the advent of modern rail and auto transportation diverted visitors away from the region. By 1950, the building stood in ruins. Today, it is lost to history. The view, however, continues to astound first-time visitors. On a clear day, you can see five states from the edge of the escarpment.

the 1,100 snow guns at **Hunter Mountain** (Rte. 23A, 518/263-4223, www.huntermtn. com, 8:30am-4pm daily) begin to paint the mountain white. A winter destination since 1960, Hunter still attracts diehard skiers from all over the Tri-State area. Its snowmaking operation proudly covers 100 percent of the mountain in corduroy snow, top to bottom. The leaf-peeping is pretty epic up here in the fall, too.

You can walk to the sleepy town of Hunter from the parking lot, as long as you aren't wearing ski boots. Many of the buildings on Main Street flooded during Hurricane Irene in 2011; those who could afford to rebuild did so over the next few years. The Catskill Mountain Foundation (CMF) has set up shop in Hunter Village. It is a nonprofit organization dedicated to revitalizing the mountaintop with cultural events and programs. Look for its free *Catskill Mountain Guide,* which has a detailed calendar of events.

New York Zipline Canopy Tours

The most exciting summer attraction at Hunter Mountain is a 4.6-mile zip line that opened in 2010 as the longest and highest course in North America, **New York Zipline Canopy Tours** (Hunter Mountain, Rte. 23A, 518/263-4388, www.ziplinenewyork.com, 8am-4pm Wed.-Sun.). The family-friendly

Mid-Mountain ($99) canopy tour is designed for all levels, while the SkyRider tour ($139) sends the adrenaline rushing as you reach a height of 600 feet and have to complete segments up to 3,200 feet long. This is an extreme sport, and you may reach speeds of 50 mph on the first line. Allow three hours to complete the entire course.

Leaving Hunter on Route 23A, you pass Route 296, a shortcut to Windham. An alternative and more scenic route, however, is to continue west until County Road 17, the turn-off to Jewett, which winds its way through orchards and historical homes up to Maplecrest, just outside of Windham.

If you skip the scenic drive and head toward Lexington, you'll soon pass the Baroque-style lanterns of the **St. John the Baptist Ukrainian Catholic Church** (518/263-3862, www.brama.com, mass 9am daily and 10am Sun., shop noon-4pm Tues.-Fri., 10am-2pm and 6pm-8pm Sat., 11:30am-2pm Sun.). Built of cedar logs imported from British Columbia, the church serves as a spiritual and cultural center for Ukrainians living in the United States and represents the traditional architecture and wood carvings of the Carpathian highland people. The church hosts art exhibits and a folk-art store in a separate community center.

Prattsville

Route 23A meets up with Route 23 out of Windham in an open field at the Batavia Kill crossing. From there, it is a mile into Prattsville, another mountaintop village. You can't drive through Prattsville without learning a thing or two about its founder, the eccentric Colonel Zadock Pratt. For some 13 years in the early 19th century, Pratt ran one of the world's largest and most successful tanneries, and he used the profits to build present-day Prattsville. According to local lore, he completed the building of a new tannery dam in November 1824, as the first layer of ice was forming on the Schoharie Creek, and then celebrated by swimming the length of the dam.

Despite his role in destroying a large chunk

of the Catskill forest, Zadock was well liked by his community, as his generosity far outweighed his shameless self-promotion. His life's achievements are depicted in a bas-relief sculpture on a large, flat rock at the outskirts of town. Called Pratt Rock, the stone carving includes the tannery, a hemlock tree, and many of Pratt's family members.

In the center of town, Pratt's former residence is now the **Zadock Pratt Museum** (1450 Main St., Prattsville, 518/299-3258, https://zadockprattmuseum.org, 10am-5pm Fri.-Mon.). It contains period furnishings, a Steinway piano, photographs of Pratt, and a model of his tannery.

ALONG ROUTE 23
★ Windham Mountain Resort

From the intersection of Routes 23 and 23A, it is a nine-mile drive along the Batavia Kill to **Windham Mountain Resort** (19 Resort Dr., Windham, 518/734-4300, www.windhammountain.com). With a base elevation of 1,500 feet and a summit of 3,100 feet, Windham attracts New York City day-trippers by the busload. Mogul experts head for the bumps on Wheelchair and Wedel, while speed demons let loose on Wolverine. Intermediate skiers enjoy the two-mile-long Wrap Around trail, and a run through the terrain park ends with an enormous gap jump at the bottom.

In summer months, the resort has transformed itself into a mountain biking destination. **Windham Mountain Bike Park** boasts the longest jump trail on the east coast. Lifts (9am-5pm Sat.-Sun.) run, so you skip the uphill climb. Check the UCI World Cup schedule and you might catch a professional race during your stay.

Windham village is about a mile from the ski resort parking lot, too far to walk in winter weather. Along Main Street, contemporary art galleries alternate with skier-friendly eateries. A few of the ski shops rent mountain bikes in summer. From Windham, the Mohican Trail (Rte. 23) begins to descend back down to the valley floor, and the peaks of Blackhead and Black Dome come into view. The Escarpment

Trail-Windham Trailhead (Rte. 23, East Windham) begins here, at the edge of the Elm Ridge Wild Forest.

East Durham

Irish immigrants were among the first settlers on the north side of Route 23. Stone walls mark old boundaries along County Road 31, and every sign in Durham and East Durham has a shamrock, or at least green lettering. A visit to **Guaranteed Irish** (2220 Rte. 145, East Durham, 518/634-2392, 10am-5pm daily), at the corner of County Road 31 and Route 145, will put you in the proper frame of mind to enjoy this town. An enormous retail space has an overwhelming selection of Irish-made goods.

The **Zoom Flume Water Park** (Shady Glen Rd. off Rte. 145, East Durham, 800/888-3586, www.zoomflume.com, 10am-6pm daily June-Sept., some weekends until 7pm, adults $36, under age 8 $29, under age 3 free) is a popular attraction for families on hot summer days. Lazy River is a gentle tube ride, while Black Vortex shoots you through a completely dark tunnel, and the Canyon Plunge is just about vertical. There is a short open tube run for the littlest thrill seekers and a zip line for the older set. Stay-and-play packages are available at **The Country Place Resort** (56 Shady Glen Rd., East Durham, 518/239-4559, www.thecountryplace.com, $99-139), adjacent to the park.

On the same road, **Hull-O Farms** (10 Cochrane Rd., Durham, 518/239-6950, www.hull-o.com), founded in 1779, is a working dairy farm that allows overnight "farm stay" guests to participate in everyday activities. Accommodations are provided in one of three separate guest houses (from $175 pp, including meals).

Freehold and Greenville

The best reason to divert to Freehold when traveling along Route 23 is to try the French-inspired menu at **Ruby's Hotel** (3689 Rte. 67, Freehold, 518/634-7790, www.rubyshotel.com, 5pm-9pm Thurs., 5pm-10pm Fri.-Sat. summer, 5pm-10pm Fri.-Sat. fall-spring, $18-29). Nearby, the **Freehold Airport** (4000 Rte. 67, Freehold, www.freeholdaviation.com, 9am-6:30pm daily Apr.-Dec.) has a ground and flight school and general aviation services. The restaurant is about a 10-minute walk from the runway.

A few miles up the road from Freehold on Route 32, William Vanderbilt constructed a Queen Anne-style home in 1889. Today, the white two-story building is a county inn set on six acres of manicured lawns and decorated in Victorian and country accents. In summer, the **Greenville Arms 1889 Inn** (11135 Rte. 32, Greenville, 888/665-0044, www.greenvillearms.com, $125-235) hosts a series of Hudson River Valley Art Workshops in its Carriage House Studio.

Cairo

Once the center of a booming Greene County poultry business and a major producer of fresh fruits, Cairo (CARE-o) is a good place to stop for services. You'll find groceries at Hannaford's supermarket, gas at Cumberland Farm, a liquor store with great wine selections, and a True Value hardware. Decorative streetlights and new-ish concrete sidewalks line Main Street, but the town could use a few more interesting restaurants.

The primary colors of the **Mahayana Buddhist Temple** (700 Ira Vail Rd., 518/622-3619, https://en.mahayana.us, 8:30am-5:30pm daily, donation) look oddly out of place in South Cairo, 2.5 miles from Route 23B. Members of the New York City-based Eastern States Buddhist Temple of America retreat to the woods here for quiet contemplation. A red-and-yellow arch leads the way down a steep driveway to the temple, set on two small ponds. Visitors are welcome to explore the site.

Don't leave Cairo without wandering through the hamlets of Purling and Round Top. Newly built log cabins alternate here

---

1: Kaaterskill Falls 2: the zip line at the Zoom Flume Water Park 3: view from the top of Kaaterskill Falls with 150-year-old farmhouses, and fields have grown up around abandoned farm equipment. Leaving Cairo on Mountain Avenue (County Rd. 24), you'll pass the Purling post office, Shinglekill Falls, and a roller rink that has been open more or less continuously since the 1950s.

RECREATION
Winter Sports

You haven't "Skied the East" until you've endured subzero temperatures, frostbite warnings, and the wet blast of artificial snow in your face. The après-ski whirlpool tub (there are many options) becomes an all-important finish to the day. **Hunter Mountain Ski Bowl** (Rte. 23A, Hunter, 800/367-7669, www.huntermtn.com, 8:30am-4pm Sat.-Sun. and holidays, 9am-4pm Mon.-Fri. mid-Nov.-Apr., from $70, discounts for advance purchase online) has three mountains that can handle 15,000 skiers per hour; however, the lift lines still can run up to an hour on busy weekends. A new six-person chair opened for the 2018-2019 season, increasing the mountain's skiable terrain by a third. Hunter is now part of the Epic pass network managed by Vail.

Windham Mountain Resort (19 Resort Dr., Windham, 800/754-9463, www.windhammountain.com, 8am-4pm Sat.-Sun., 9am-4pm Mon.-Fri. mid-Nov.-mid-Apr., $50-144) is open as long as the weather cooperates. You can also ski at night (4pm-10pm Fri.-Sat. and some holidays Dec.-Mar.). Pick up Route 23 West at New York State Thruway exit 21. Book lift tickets and rental equipment, or listen to the snow report updated daily, at www.windhammountain.com. The mountain welcomes uphill skiers for a nominal day pass fee.

Several areas on the mountaintop offer varied terrain for cross country skiers: The **Mountain Trails Cross Country Ski Center** (Rte. 23A, Tannersville, 518/589-5361, www.mtntrails.com, 9am-4:30pm Sat.-Sun., full-day adults $20, $18 after 2pm, teens $18, juniors $10, full-day rental $20) has 35 kilometers of groomed, patrolled trails with rentals, sales, a lodge, lessons, and a snack bar

on-site. Daily hours vary according to snow conditions. You also can rent snowshoes here.

In the valley, the **Winter Clove Inn Nordic Skiing Area** (557 Winter Clove Rd., Round Top, 518/622-3267, www.winterclove.com) opens 400 acres to the public, with rentals available. Expert trails climb into the hills, while the easier trails follow a streambed.

The trails at **Colgate Lake** (off Rte. 78, East Jewett) run through an open meadow with great views of the Blackhead Mountain Range. Take Route 23A to Tannersville, and turn onto Route 23C, and then right onto Route 78 by the post office. Hunter Mountain and Windham Mountain both have 4- to 12-lane snow tubing runs with lift access.

Hiking

Hikers can't get enough of the northern Catskills in summer and fall. They hit the trails in search of tasty wild blueberries, geological wonders, or simply a view and a breath of fresh air. Trailhead parking lots fill early on sunny weekends, but with a little determination, it's still possible to escape the crowds. Although the most popular trails are well maintained, it's not uncommon to encounter some bushwhacking on many hikes. It's a good idea to carry water, topographical maps, and a compass or GPS, no matter how far you plan to go. *Catskill Trails: A Ranger's Guide to the High Peaks, Book One,* by Edward G. Henry (Black Dome Press, 2000), covers more than 20 hikes in the area, including the trails to Kaaterskill Falls and the escarpment.

With 9,000 feet of elevation gain over 23 miles, the **Devil's Path** earns its moniker as the toughest hike in the Catskills. You can hike a moderate portion of it in a day trip up **Indian Head** and **Twin Mountain** (6 miles round-trip) from Tannersville, and reward yourself with spectacular views at the top. Start at the trailhead on Prediger Road in Elka Park.

To see what inspired the romantic

1: skier at Windham Mountain Resort 2: mountain biking on the Round Top Trail Network

landscapes of the Hudson River School painters, hike a portion of the almost-as-difficult **Escarpment Trail** (23.9 miles), which connects Route 23 in East Windham with the North-South Lake Campground in Haines Falls. Dramatic elevation changes make for challenging terrain, so plan to take it slow. Camping is not restricted below 3,500 feet, but it's best to set up camp in designated areas to minimize the impact on the forest. You can fill water bottles at numerous natural springs along the trail.

For a guided hike, the **Mountain Top Historical Society** (Haines Falls, 518/589-6657, www.mths.org) leads summer and fall trips. There is no charge to join, but the organization asks participants to complete a registration form in advance. The site links to online versions of area topographical maps on Maptech.com.

Back at the river's edge, the Scenic Hudson Land Trust has rescued a seven-acre stretch of shoreline from development and created **Four-Mile Point Preserve** (Four-Mile Point Rd., Coxsackie, 845/473-4440, www.scenichudson.org, dawn-dusk daily), which features a short nature trail that leads to an overlook 60 feet above the river. From the Rip Van Winkle Bridge, follow Route 385 almost eight miles north to Four-Mile Point Road.

Cycling and Mountain Biking

Cyclists in Greene County can find miles of traffic-free roads to pedal, but be prepared to climb. The **Tour of the Catskills** (www.tourofthecatskills.com) is a three-day cycling race that takes place in August each year. Part of the event is a 77-mile *gran fondo* ride around the Route 23A-Route 23-Route 32 loop. Along the way, you'll gain 5,538 feet of elevation.

Many old logging roads offer scenic and challenging mountain biking terrain, and community groups are leading development of singletrack trail systems around the county. For a first-rate downhill riding experience, head to **Windham Mountain Bike Park** (19 Resort Dr., Windham, 800/754-9463, www.

windhammountain.com, 9am-5pm Sat.-Sun. June and Sept., 10am-6pm Mon. and Thurs.-Fri., 9am-5pm Sat.-Sun. Jul.-Aug.). Test yourself in the skills park, which has berms, tabletops, and the obligatory rock garden. Or ride the high-speed quad to access trails like Wilderness Roll (4.6 kilometers) and Batavia Skill (4.7 kilometers). You can rent bikes at the resort, or check out **Windham Mountain Outfitters** (61 Rte. 296, Windham, 518/734-4700, www.windhamoutfitters.com).

Elm Ridge Wild Forest has several loops of singletrack. The red markers indicate beginner and intermediate level terrain. **The Escarpment Trail** (blue markers) requires more technical skills to maneuver around the many roots and loose rocks. The **Round Top Trail Network** centers around Riedlbauers (57 Ravine Dr., Round Top, 518/965-0487) and connects several resorts in the area. Trails are maintained by the Round Top Mountain Biking Association.

Golf

Greene County has 10 golf courses with scenic views of the surrounding countryside. Most are open April through November. The **Blackhead Mountain Lodge & Country Club** (Blackhead Mountain Rd., 518/622-3157, www.blackheadmtn.com, 18 holes with cart Sat.-Sun. $50, Mon.-Fri. $35) maintains a challenging 18-hole par-72 course with stunning views of the High Peaks. **Christman's Windham House Country Inn and Golf Resort** (5742 Rte. 23, Windham, 518/734-4230, www.windhamhouse.com, Mon.-Fri. $45, Sat.-Sun. $65) operates two courses—an 18-hole and a 9-hole—with four sets of tees. Tannersville has two 9-hole par 35 courses that are open to the public: **Colonial Country Club** (6245 Main St., Tannersville, 518/589-9807, http://colonialccny.com, $20-30) and the **Rip Van Winkle Country Club** (3200 Rte. 23A, Tannersville, 518/678-9779, www.rvwcc.com, 18 holes Sat.-Sun. and holidays $25, Mon.-Fri. $20, cart extra). The **Windham Country Club** (Rte. 296, Windham, 518/734-9910, www.windhamcountryclub.com,

Mon.-Fri. $25, Sat.-Sun. $47) is a challenging 18-hole public course with a five-acre driving range and pro shop on-site.

Swimming and Boating

Dips in mountain lakes and paddles along the river are the water sports of choice in Greene County. **North Lake** (County Rd. 18, Haines Falls, 518/589-5058, www.dec.ny.gov) offers swimming and nonmotorized boating, and lifeguards are on duty Memorial Day-Labor Day. Farther west, **Dolan's Lake** (Ski Bowl Rd., Hunter, 518/263-4020) has a picnic area and lifeguard on duty in summer months.

Several marinas offer boaters convenient access to the Hudson. Part of the New York State Parks system, the **Athens Boat Launch** (Rte. 385, Athens, 518/732-0187) has a hard surface ramp and parking for 25 cars. The **Coxsackie Boat Launch** (Reed St., Coxsackie, 518/731-2718), also a state facility, has a hard surface ramp and parking for 36 cars and trailers.

In Catskill, turn right at the bend in Main Street onto Greene Street to get to the full-service **Catskill Marina** (10 Greene St., 518/943-4170, www.catskillmarina.net), which has gasoline, 85 boat slips (maximum 150 feet), showers, restrooms, laundry, and even a heated pool. **Riverview** (103 Main St., Catskill, 518/943-5311, www.riverviewmarineservices.com) rents kayaks, rowboats, and canoes. **Dutchman's Landing** (Lower Main St., 518/943-3830) has four boat ramps, picnic tables, and barbecues.

The **Hudson River Watertrail Association** (www.hrwa.org) sponsors numerous outings and operates facilities for river-goers. The group is lobbying to develop a water trail from the mouth of the Hudson to the Great Lakes.

Fishing and Hunting

Whether you want to catch shad, bass, or trout, **River Basin Sport Shop** (66 W. Bridge St., Catskill, 518/943-2111, 9:30am-5pm Thurs.-Sat.) will provide all the tackle and advice you need for fishing in the area.

North Lake can provide a strong pickerel bite in addition to good bass fishing. For pickerel, try the point that connects North Lake to South Lake. Bass fishing can be excellent on warmer days. Try fishing with a Senko (rubber worm) in and around brush piles, fallen trees and rocks. In the lower sections of **Catskill Creek**, you can find stocked brown trout. The **Batavia Kill** near Prattsville is a mecca for fly fishing. **Green Lake** near Athens is a fun place to bring the kids for an hour or two of spin casting.

Licensed hunters may take grouse, pheasant, turkey, deer, black bear, and small game from public wilderness areas or private clubs during specified seasons. For regulations and information, contact the **New York State Department of Environmental Conservation** (866/933-2257, www.dec.ny.gov).

Yoga and Spas

The Mountain Club Spa inside the Kaatskill Mountain Club at Hunter Mountain (62 Liftside Dr., Hunter, 800/486-8376, ext. 3017, www.mountainclubspa.genbook.com) sets the mood for a relaxing and rejuvenating weekend. Massage therapy services (50 minutes, $100-125) include aromatherapy, reflexology, and hot stones. Facials, body wraps, and nail services are also available.

Alpine Spa (11 Resort Dr., Windham, 518/734-4300, www.windhammountain.com) at Windham Mountain Resort is a winter-only operation. In town, **The Windham Spa** (16 Mitchell Hollow Rd., Windham, 518/734-9617, www.thewindhamspa.com, 10am-6pm Thurs.-Sat., 10am-5pm Sun.-Mon.) uses Eminence Organic skin-care products. Facials start at $145 for 55 minutes.

Nicole at **Mountain Breeze Yoga** (11111 Rte. 23, Windham, 518/588-3195, www.mountainbreezeyoga.com, $16 drop-in cash or PayPal) teaches a rejuvenating 90-minute *vinyasa* blend class on Sunday mornings and other classes and workshops throughout the week. The Tibetan singing bowls are a popular treat.

ENTERTAINMENT AND EVENTS

Bars and Nightlife

The German theme continues all year long in Round Top, where the **Mountain Brauhaus** (430 Winter Clove Rd., Round Top, 800/999-7376, www.crystalbrook.com) pours Dinkelacker beer by the stein. Polka dancers take the floor on weekend nights.

Van Winkles at the Kaatskill Mountain Club (62 Liftside Dr., Hunter, 518/263-5580, www.kaatskillmountainclub.com) is a quieter alternative to the main **Hunter Mountain Bar** (518/263-4223). Take advantage of happy hour drink prices 4pm-6pm daily.

Après-ski options at Windham include the **Taphouse Grille** (5359 Rte. 23/ Main St., Windham, 518/734-9090, www.taphousegrillewindham.com, 4pm till late Mon.-Fri., noon till late Sat.-Sun.) for a round of local craft beers and bar eats like breaded wings, tempura, and truffle fries. Windham Mountain now manages the lively **Tavern 23** at the Winwood Inn (5220 Main St., Windham, 518/734-4055, www.windhammountain.com, 5pm-10pm Tues.-Sun.), which serves seasonal drinks like the Mountain Mule, Ski Country (maple bourbon), and Windham Spritz (prosecco).

For live music and dancing, check out **The Avalon Lounge** (29 Church St., Catskill, www.theavalonlounge.com, 5pm-midnight Wed.-Thurs., 5pm-2am Fri.-Sat., 4pm-10pm or 11pm Sun., tickets $15-25) which has a bar, lounge, and performance space. The kitchen (5pm-10pm Wed.-Sat. and 4pm-9pm Sun.) offers Korean-themed bar food.

Tucked behind the post office, **Ze Windham Wine Bar** (5369 Main St., Windham, 518/734-9200, www.zewinebar.com, 2pm-8pm Fri., noon-8pm Sat.) is a cozy place with an extensive wine list, perfect for a glass or two. Charcuterie plates and cheese spreads take the edge off until dinner. The

outdoor Ice Wine Bar has fire pits, comfy couches, and a pop-up boutique shop. Weekly "Wine School" tasting events are popular with the local crowd on Tuesdays.

Festivals and Events

Bass tournaments draw large crowds to Catskill in spring, when the striped bass are running. Anglers should head to **River Basin Sport Shop** (66 W. Bridge St., Catskill, 518/943-2111, 9:30am-5pm Thurs.-Sat.) for dates and details. For longtime Catskill residents, the run of the American shad heralds the arrival of summer.

For 27 years, the **Michael J. Quill Irish Cultural & Sports Centre** (2267 Rte. 145, 518/634-2286, https://eastdurhamirishfestival.com) has hosted the **East Durham Irish Festival,** drawing participants from across the Hudson River Valley with Irish music performances and a one-acre "map" of Ireland, decorated with flags of the country's provinces and counties.

The Catskill Mountain Foundation theater shows a mix of independent and Hollywood films. In summer, a series of Hunter Mountain Festivals draws large crowds, with the **International Celtic Festival** and **Oktoberfest** among the most popular events. A calendar is available at www.huntermtn.com.

In summer, beginner and experienced artists can enroll in a series of **Hudson River Valley Art Workshops** (South St., Greenville, 518/966-5219, www.artworkshops.com) at the Greenville Arms 1889 Inn. Weekend and weeklong programs cover watercolor, oil, acrylic, pastel, drawing, or collage.

SHOPPING

Antiques, crafts, and locally made foods are among the best finds in Greene County. Loved by locals for carrying Carhartt work pants, all manner of scarves and wraps for women, and fun stocking stuffers around the holidays, **The Westerner** (11305 Rte. 32, Greenville, 518/966-8700, https://www.westernerny.com,

1: antique fly rod on display at River Basin Sport Shop 2: catching bluegill on Green Lake 3: Ze Windham Wine Bar

10am-6pm daily) has a friendly staff and artfully curated merchandise.

Farm Stands and Local Products

Local farmers bring produce to the **Catskill Farmers Market** (Dutchman's Landing Park, Catskill, 518/622-9820, 4pm-7pm Fri., June-Oct.). In summer, stop by **Black Horse Farms** (10094 Rte. 9W, Athens, 518/943-9324, www.blackhorsefarms.com, 10am-6pm Mon.-Sat., 10am-5pm Sun.) for fresh-picked corn on the cob and other seasonal produce. The family-run store also sells baked goods, plants, maple syrup, and honey.

At the corner of Routes 23A and 32 outside Catskill, **Story Farms** (4640 Rte. 32, Catskill, 518/678-9716, www.storyfarms.org, 9am-5pm Tues.-Sun.) is one of the most popular stands in the area. Locals stop for corn, tomatoes, peppers, onions, squash, apples, pears, plums, peaches, and whatever else has been picked that day.

On the mountaintop, the **Catskill Mountain Country Store & Restaurant** (5504 Rte. 23, Windham, 518/734-3387, www.catskillmtncountrystore.com, 9am-5pm Mon.-Thurs., 9am-6pm Fri., 8am-6pm Sat., 8am-5pm Sun.) has a great selection of housemade preserves you can bring home. Pickled beets, relish, and jams all are made using locally grown produce. The back of the store has home goods, candles, and a few books and games for children.

Pop into **Traphagen's Honey and Gourmet Shop** (Lexington Rd./Rte. 23A, Hunter, 518/263-4150, 9am-5pm Fri.-Mon.) on the way out of Hunter to satisfy a craving for sugar.

Antiques and Eclectic

At the offbeat **Last Chance Antiques and Cheese Café** (6009 Main St., Tannersville, 518/589-6424, www.lastchanceonline.com, 11am-8:30pm Mon.-Thurs., 11am-9pm Fri.-Sun.), what began as a way of luring antiques shoppers in the door has evolved into a full-fledged gourmet food store and restaurant.

The store is covered floor to ceiling in antique instruments and Victorian-era accessories. Enjoy an unusual brew (there are 300 to choose from), a cheese platter, or a rich chocolate fondue.

With support from the Hunter Foundation, **Tannersville Antique & Artisan Center** (6045 Main St., Tannersville, 518/589-5600, www.tannersvilleantiques.com, 11am-5pm Sun.-Tues. and Thurs., 11am-7pm Fri.-Sat.) represents 80 different artists and vendors, including photographer Francis X. Driscoll, whose work captures striking images of the Catskill Forest Preserve.

Guaranteed Irish (2220 Rte. 145, East Durham, 518/634-2392, 10am-5pm Sat.-Thurs., 10am-6pm Fri.), at the corner of County Roads 31 and 145, contains a wide variety of Irish-made goods, including handcrafted jewelry, tweed jackets, and Celtic music. With 5,000 square feet of space, Guaranteed Irish bills itself as America's largest Irish import store.

Magpie Bookshop (392 Main St., Catskill, 518/303-6035, www.magpiebookshop.com, 11am-5pm Tues.-Sat.) is the place to browse nature books and other good reads on a rainy day. The former Catskill Mountain Foundation Shop has moved from Hunter to Tannersville and now operates as the **Kaaterskill Shoppe** (6042 Main St, Tannersville, 518/589-7500, https://kaatart.square.site, 11am-6pm Fri.-Sun.). This is a great place to look for that one-of-a-kind gift. Everything is sourced with sustainability in mind. **Mahalo Gifts** (397 Main St., 518/943-7467, https://mahalo-gifts-inc.shoplightspeed.com, 10am-5pm Sun.-Fri., 10am-6pm Sat.) sells an eclectic variety of gifts with an emphasis on "made in the USA" and eco-conscious options.

Opportunities for shopping in Windham trend toward country kitsch. **Carole's Gift Emporium** (5335 Main St./Rte. 23, Windham, 518/734-3387, www.carolesgiftemporium.com, 10am-6pm Mon.-Sat., 10am-5pm Sun.) has Yankee Candles, toys and games, and seasonal decor to browse.

Apples to Apples

New York State produces 30 million bushels of apples each year, and almost a quarter of those come from orchards in the Hudson River Valley. These are small operations that sell their harvest at farm stands, farmers markets, and as you-pick activities.

Growing conditions favor many varieties of the fruit, from best sellers like McIntosh, Empire, and Gala to heirlooms like the Esopus Spitzenburg and Cox's Orange Pippin. Flavors vary widely from sweet to tart.

Farming techniques have changed in recent years to dense plantings with built-in irrigation and trellises to support heavy branches. Dwarf trees make picking much more efficient.

In the late summer through fall, apples appear on many local menus. When no longer fresh and crisp, they can be baked into pies, mashed into sauce, dried, cooked down into apple butter, or distilled into cider and liquor. The possibilities are endless. Seek out an orchard or two as you roam about the farmland.

Local artist **Alec Alberti** (822 Mitchell Hollow Rd., Windham, 518/734-4689) carves wooden bears, moose, tables, and other pieces in a workshop in his home. He doesn't maintain a dedicated website for his business, but you can find him on Facebook.

FOOD
Along the River: Route 385
394 Main Wine Bar (394 Main St., Catskill, 518/947-4774, www.394mainstreet.com, noon-9pm Wed.-Thurs. and Sun., noon-midnight Fri.-Sat., $7-15) has a brewpub vibe, with small plates like shrimp tacos. Larger entrées include the Italian-style Meal in a Heel (aka a sandwich made of the ends of a loaf of bread).

Verdigris Tea & Chocolate Bar (291 Main St., Catskill, 518/943-2601, www. verdigristea.com, 9am-5pm Mon.-Sat.) has the widest selection of fine teas anywhere other than Harney & Sons, and many of them are organic. Taste the First Flush Darjeeling, one of the fragrant chai teas, or a healing herbal tea like the Aladdin's Lamp Turmeric. You can order a frothy matcha latte. Non-tea drinkers may prefer the Mexican hot chocolate or a simple vanilla steamer, with a locally sourced dark chocolate bar on the side.

★ **HiLo Catskill** (365 Main St., Catskill, www.hilocatskill.com, 7am-4pm daily, $5-14) serves coffee drinks, pastries, and light eats to start your day. Besides a full menu of espresso creations, you can have a golden turmeric latte, kombucha, or CBD seltzer, along with a bagel, frittata, granola, or salad.

The **Garden Gate Café** (424 Main St., Catskill, 518/943-1994, 6:30am-3pm Mon.-Fri., $5) serves breakfast and lunch with a menu covering everything from omelets to burgers. A couple of tables are set up on the sidewalk for alfresco dining. Up the street a bit, **La Conca D'Oro** (440 Main St., Catskill, 518/943-3549, https://www. laconcadoroonline.com, 4pm-9pm Thurs.-Mon., $15-36), a small brick building with green awnings, serves dependable Italian-American fare to a local clientele.

River views are the main reason to go to **Frank Guido's Port of Call** (7 Main St., Catskill, 518/943-5088, http:// frankguidosportofcall.com, 3pm-8pm Tues.-Thurs., noon-9pm Fri.-Sat., noon-8pm Sun., closed winter, $14-47) at Catskill Point. The menu puts seafood in the spotlight with steamed littleneck clams, lobster salad, ahi tuna, and the like. The owners also operate a popular restaurant in Kingston, Mariner's Harbor. At the Hop-O-Nose marina, **Creek Side Restaurant** (160 W. Main St., Catskill, 518/943-6522, 11:30am-9pm Mon. and Thurs.-Fri., 11:30am-10pm Sat., 11:30am-8pm Sun., $15-30) is an unexpected delight with everything from pasta and chicken dishes to surf and turf.

Destination Dining: Damon Baehrel

One of the Hudson River Valley's most unusual culinary personalities tends a 12-acre property on a country road a few miles west of Coxsackie. Owner, chef, and author Damon Baehrel is the ultimate forager. Most of the food that ends up on your plate comes from a 12-acre property that Baehrel tends by hand. Forest, farm, and restaurant have been a one-man show since 1990, when he opened the restaurant as a showcase for his former catering business, Sagecrest Catering. His prix fixe menu features at least a dozen courses—sometimes as many as 30, and there is always an element of surprise to the evening. The coffee table-worthy book *Native Harvest* captures his philosophy and introduces many of the plants that define his cuisine.

The eponymous restaurant **Damon Baehrel** (776 Rte. 45, Earlton, www.damonbaehrel. com, seating times vary, $365 pp) currently has a multiyear waiting list, with guests from around the world hoping to take in the four-hour-plus experience. Reservations must be made by email: reservationrequests@damonbaehrel.com.

★ **Cone-E-Island** (8 W. Bridge St., Catskill, 518/943-1979, noon-10pm daily summer, 3pm-8pm Mon.-Thurs., 3pm-9pm Fri., 1pm-9pm Sat., 1pm-8pm Sun. spring and fall) has soft-serve and a long list of other desserts, with outdoor tables overlooking the Catskill Creek.

Along Route 23A

Whatever time of day you pass through town, chances are you'll find something to eat in Tannersville, where new restaurants and cafés seem to be opening all the time. Under the leadership of chef Corwin Kave, the **Deer Mountain Inn** (790 County Rd. 25, Tannersville, 518/589-6268, www. deermountaininn.com, 5pm-9pm Thurs.-Sun., $12-36) has become a destination restaurant. The kitchen prepares a nightly menu featuring local ingredients such as sourdough focaccia, New York steelhead trout, crab salad, and creative cocktails, such as the Hudson Duster and Evergreen Collins. You can stay the night ($275) if a room is available.

★ **Circle W** (3328 Rte. 23A, Palenville, 518/678-3250, https://www.circlewmarket. com, 8am-5pm Thurs.-Mon., $4-12) has hot cocoa and light eats to warm you up after a hike to Huckleberry Point. It's also a general store with a variety of organic and local foods on the shelves.

The **Last Chance Antiques and Cheese Café** (6009 Main St., Tannersville, 518/589-6424, www.lastchanceonline.com, 11am-8:30pm Mon.-Thurs., 11am-9pm Fri.-Sun., $11-27) is known as much for its comfort food as its antiques. French dip, meatloaf, a tuna melt, or the chicken potpie won't disappoint. **Maggie's Krooked Café & Juice Bar** (Main St., Tannersville, 518/589-6101, www. krookedcafe.com, 7am-7pm daily, $9-19) pours a reliable cup of coffee, bakes delicious homemade muffins, and cooks up hearty breakfast fare.

Pancho Villa's Mexican Restaurant (3087 Main St., Tannersville, 518/589-5134, www.panchovillamex.com, 4pm-9:30pm Mon. and Wed.-Thurs., 4pm-10pm Fri., noon-10pm Sat., noon-9pm Sun., $15-20) will satisfy a craving for south-of-the-border cuisine.

Aside from fast food in the lodge, dining options at Hunter Mountain include **Van Winkles** (62 Liftside Dr., Hunter, 518/263-5580, www.kaatskillmountainclub.com, 5pm-9pm Sun.-Thurs., 5pm-10pm Fri.-Sat., $10-25) at the Kaatskill Mountain Club, where chef Tim Lang is a Catskill native and Culinary Institute of America graduate. In addition to hearty pub fare, he offers vegetarian and gluten-free dishes, such as a goat cheese salad

1: the menu at Messina's La Griglia in Windham
2: soft-serve ice cream at Cone-E-Island in Catskill
3: waiting for Cone-E-Island ice cream beside the Catskill Creek

1 Specials
SOUP
NE CLAM CHOWDER
APPETIZERS
MUSSELS BIANCO
Baked clams
CLASSICO
ENTREE'S

2 Joy

3

and salmon with veggies. The restaurant also serves breakfast and lunch on the weekends.

Along Route 23

★ **Mountain View Brasserie** (10697 Rte. 32, Greenville, 518/966-5522, www.mountainviewbrasserie.com, 4pm-9pm Wed.-Thurs., noon-3pm and 4pm-9pm Fri.-Sat., 3pm-9pm Sun., $20-39) occupies a large, cozy dining room, and the menu includes a classic French onion soup, an outstanding cut of prime rib, traditional seafood bouillabaisse, and some unusual wines, including a sauvignon blanc from New Zealand. This is a lovely place to try for a holiday lunch.

Ruby's Hotel (3689 Rte. 67, Freehold, 518/634-7790, www.rubyshotel.com, 5pm-9pm Fri.-Sat. summer and winter, $18-29) serves French-influenced cuisine, including duck confit and coq au vin, as well as steaks and seafood. The restaurant has a bar and soda fountain in the front and a formal dining room in the back. Outdoor seating is available in the summer.

Locals adore the ★ **Bavarian Manor** (866 Mountain Ave., Purling, 518/622-3261, www.bavarianmanor.com, 5pm-9pm Thurs.-Sat., 1pm-8pm Sun., $18-25) in Purling. The business has hosted German Americans (and those who wish they were) since 1865. The decidedly old-world restaurant serves all the requisite dishes—schnitzel, sauerbraten, spaetzle, rouladen, and bratwurst—as well as seafood and wild game. Locals gather in the attached bar, where you can order from the full menu. The restaurant was temporarily closed in late 2021, with reopening plans to be announced.

Maassmann's Restaurant (Blackhead Mountain Rd., Round Top, 518/622-3157, http://www.blackheadmtn.com, 5pm-8:30pm Fri.-Sun. May-Oct., $12-31), at the Blackhead Mountain Golf Course, is popular with locals for special occasions like Easter dinner. On the menu are American and German dishes. Call ahead to reserve the Stammtisch Corner, which seats 5-7 people.

The Alpine Pork Store (Rte. 23B, South Cairo, 518/622-3056, www.alpineporkstore.

com, 9am-4pm Fri., 9am-3pm Sat.), in South Cairo, supplies local restaurants with German-style sausages or wursts. There also is a full menu of fresh meats cut to order. This is a good place to stop on the way to a ski condo at Windham Mountain.

The smell of fresh-baked bread wafts out of ★ **Bistro Brie & Bordeaux** (5386 Rte. 23, Windham, 518/734-4911, www.bistrobrieandbordeaux.com, 5pm-8pm Fri.-Sun., $17-35) in the afternoon as the kitchen prepares for the evening meal. This is an unusual find on the mountaintop—real French country food, from a baked brie tart to PEI mussels and fries. Dine on the heated front porch or choose a table inside.

The **Catskill Mountain Country Store & Restaurant** (5504 Rte. 23, Windham, 518/734-3387, www.catskillmtncountrystore.com, 9am-3pm Mon. and Thurs.-Fri., 8am-4pm Sat., 8am-3pm Sun.) serves breakfast all day with entrées made from organic eggs and milk. An adjoining gift shop has a wide selection of house-made preserves, pickles, and mustards, as well as New York maple syrup. The refrigerator has smoked trout, Cowbella milk and yogurt, and hard salami. Pies are baked following the owner's grandfather's recipes. The maple pecan fudge is a sinful treat.

Messina's La Griglia (5658 Rte. 23, Windham, 518/734-4499, www.messinasitalianrestaurant.com, 4pm-9pm Thurs.-Mon., $16-28) has been in business for a quarter century making Italian standards with a local flair, such as filet mignon entrée with Dijon mustard, shallots, herbs, and mushrooms in a burgundy wine demi-glace. The casual setting features views of the ski slopes.

ACCOMMODATIONS

Country inns with a colonial ambience are the theme for places to stay in Greene County. You can find a few modern hotels near the ski resorts and budget motels along the highways, but the accommodations with the most character include a hearty breakfast and a friendly chat with the innkeeper.

$100-150

The ★ **Winter Clove Inn** (Winter Clove Rd., Round Top, 518/622-3267, www.winterclove. com, $115-150 pp, including all meals) is a great choice for value and hospitality in a historical setting. It rests on 400 acres at the base of North Mountain, bordering the Catskill Forest Preserve. A creek meanders through the property, and when the winter storms roll in, guests can ski on 15 kilometers of marked cross-country trails. Inside, guest rooms feature colonial decor, with hardwood floors, four-poster beds, and lacy white linens. The hotel attracts more suburban families than city folk. Its amenities include heated indoor and outdoor swimming pools and a nine-hole golf course. The old carriage house was converted into a bowling alley and soda fountain in the 1950s. Repeat visitors to the bowling alley quickly learn to use the warp in the floor to their advantage.

Winwood Inn (Main St., Windham, 518/734-3000, www.winwoodinn.com, $99-254) offers free transportation to Windham from the train station in Hudson, 40 minutes away. Its 55 modern rooms are painted in earthy tones and are minimally furnished. Ask for a mountain view, or you may end up facing the courtyard instead. Amenities include an indoor fitness center and a movie theater.

The combination of antique furnishings and original contemporary art at the **Greenville Arms 1889 Inn** (11135 Rte. 32, Greenville, 888/665-0044, www. greenvillearms.com, $125-235) gives the place a unique feel. Some rooms in the main house of this country inn feature canopied or four-poster beds and private porches or balconies. Owners Eliot and Letitia Dalton also offer two rooms in a Victorian cottage on the grounds. Rates include breakfast and afternoon tea.

Family-run **Albergo Allegria** (43 Rte. 296, Windham, 518/734-5560, www.albergousa. com, $99-229) operates a bed-and-breakfast inn in an 1892 Victorian, as well as a separate cottage on Main Street and a farmhouse on Maplecrest Road. Rooms in the inn range from small and cozy to spacious and private. Guests rave about the frittatas, and best of all, the kitchen stays open 24 hours daily.

Next to the Kaaterskill Creek, the cozy ★ **Brookside Bed and Breakfast** (North Lake Rd., Haines Falls, 518/589-6049, $100-135) serves its guests a full country-style breakfast to fuel the day's outdoor activities. Two queen rooms have access to a hallway bath, and the king suite has its own private bath and a small sitting area that looks out onto the garden.

$150-200

The owners of **Glen Falls House** (230 Winter Clove Rd., Round Top, 518/622-9363, www. glenfallshouse.com, $169-305) have renovated an 1881 farm property with contemporary flair. The main farmhouse has 17 beautiful guest rooms, plus cozier rooms in a separate cottage, and two motel-style buildings currently under ongoing a similar makeover. The inn has opened its refinished outdoor pool to the local community. Trotwood Restaurant ($12-24) on-site serves slow braised pork belly, farm fresh duck breast, and burgers using ingredients from local farms.

A mile from the slopes, on the road that connects Windham to Hunter, is the modern ★ **Hotel Vienna** (107 Rte. 296, Windham, 518/734-5300, www.thehotelvienna.com, $120-190). Straight out of the Austrian Alps, rooms have beamed ceilings, cherry furniture, lace curtains, and tiled balconies. Amenities include cable TV, phones, and air-conditioning as well as an indoor pool and whirlpool tub. For those returning from the slopes, the innkeeper serves afternoon cookies and tea by the breakfast-room fireplace. Midweek specials and ski packages are available.

Built in the 1940s and renovated in 2008, the ★ **Mountain Brook Inn** (57 Rte. 23C/Hill St., Tannersville, 518/589-6740, www. hotelmountainbrook.com, $175-395) suits travelers in search of modern comforts and country quiet in a classic Adirondack lodge setting. You'll have three choices for accommodations. Rooms in the main lodge have queen beds and mountain views. The east lodge is a separate building with some larger rooms and more mountain views. Pets are allowed in this building, but not in the main lodge. Private cabins have king beds, fireplaces, and private porches. All rates include a full breakfast with choices such as eggs any style, buttermilk pancakes, bread pudding French toast, or a breakfast skillet. The innkeepers help make any stay here special and memorable.

Family-owned **Crystal Brook Resort** (430 Winter Clove Rd., Round Top, 800/999-7376, www.crystalbrook.com, $96-300 pp/night) retains its German-American heritage in lodging and the adjoining Mountain Brauhaus restaurant, where the menu features Dinkelacker, Hofbräu, and *hefe weisse* beers, as well as schnitzel, goulash, and bratwurst to eat.

Over $200

The Kaatskill Mountain Club (518/263-5580, www.huntermtn.com, $250 and up) at Hunter Mountain has everything you need for an indulgent winter getaway: ski-in/ski-out suites, a heated outdoor swimming pool, a spa, its own bar and restaurant, a video arcade for the kids, and massage services for parents. Accommodations are studios or suites with up to three bedrooms. Packages are offered for the zip line in summer and ski lift tickets in winter.

Sunny Hill Resort & Golf Course (352 Sunny Hill Rd., Greenville, 518/634-7642, www.sunnyhill.com, $140-230 pp d, including all meals) is popular with golfers and families. The resort has 100 basic motel-style rooms in seven different buildings gathered around the 18-hole golf course. Some rooms have balconies and mountain views.

Scribner's Catskill Lodge (13 Scribner Hollow Rd., Hunter, 518/628-5150, www.scribnerslodge.com, $236-395) updated its rooms and common areas in 2016 for a more airy and contemporary feel. Its restaurant, **Prospect at Scribner's** (518/628-5150, www.

scribnersprospect.com), has huge picture windows with a large deck and fire pit.

Blackhead Mountain Lodge & Country Club (67 Crows Nest Rd., Round Top, www.blackheadmtn.com, $150-340) offers 22 basic rooms in a motel layout, with stay-and-play golf packages. Locals frequent Maassmann's Restaurant on the property.

Tumblin' Falls House (44 Falls View Lane, Purling, 518/965-0536, www.tumblinfalls.com) was run as a B&B for a few years, but recently converted to a five-bedroom vacation rental ($648) listed on Airbnb. The Victorian house is located across Route 24 from the retro roller rink and set back from the road overlooking Shinglekill Falls. Bedrooms have mountain and forest views. There is a fireplace inside and a hot tub on the deck.

Campgrounds

Greene County has two state campgrounds and more than a dozen private campgrounds to choose from. **North-South Lake Campground** (N. Lake Rd., Haines Falls, 518/589-5058, www.dec.ny.gov, early May-Oct., $22-27) has 200 tent and RV sites, plus picnic areas, hot showers, flush toilets, and a boat launch. **Devil's Tombstone State Campground** (Rte. 214, Hunter, 845/688-7160, www.dec.ny.gov, mid-May-Aug., $16-21) has 24 sites, picnic tables, and a playground.

You can also set up camp at the long-standing **Whip-O-Will** (3835 County Rd. 31, Purling, 518/622-3277, www.whip-o-will.com, Apr.-mid-Oct., $35-120).

INFORMATION AND SERVICES

Visitor information is available at exit 21 off the New York State Thruway (I-87). The **Greene County Tourism office** (700 Rte. 23B, Leeds, 518/943-3223, www.greatnortherncatskills.com, 9am-4pm daily year-round, longer hours in summer) will answer questions through its website. After hours, an outdoor kiosk provides information on local sights and accommodations.

The **Greene County Council on the Arts** (398 Main St., Catskill, 518/943-3400, www.greenearts.org, 10am-5pm Wed.-Sat.) keeps a calendar of countywide gallery exhibits, performances, lectures, and related events.

GETTING THERE AND AROUND
Bus
Trailways of New York (800/858-8555, trailwaysny.com) offers daily service year-round from the Port Authority Terminal in New York City. Stops include Catskill, Palenville, Hunter, and Windham, and you can walk to town from the bus stops or inquire about hotel and resort shuttles.

Train
Greene County does not have its own rail service, but **Amtrak** (800/872-7245, www. amtrak.com) stops in Hudson, across the river, about eight miles from Catskill Village. You can get a ride share or taxi from the station, and some area hotels also run free shuttles.

Car
The New York State Thruway (I-87) and Route 9W are the primary north-south arteries through Greene County. Exit the thruway at exit 21 for the most direct approach to the mountaintop. Routes 23 and 23A traverse the county from the Rip Van Winkle Bridge to the border with Delaware County. **Enterprise Rent-a-Car** (78 Green St., 518/828-5492, www.enterprise.com) has a location in Hudson. **Charlies Carstar** (4524 Rte. 32, Catskill, 518/678-3237) is an auto body shop and Hertz rental location.

Columbia County

Framed by the Hudson River to the west and the Berkshire Mountains to the east, the landscape of Columbia County features rolling hills, green pastures, and extensive woodlands. Many longtime farmers in Columbia County have converted their struggling dairy operations into niche organic businesses that cater to local restaurants and residents who join community-supported agriculture programs. The transition has allowed many local growers to keep their connection to the land while earning an almost satisfactory living. The historic city of Hudson got its start as a center for whaling and shipping in the early 19th century and later became a center for iron ore production. An industrial past continues to haunt the city.

Named after Christopher Columbus, Columbia County's history is closely tied to that of the powerful Livingston family. In the late 17th century, Scottish entrepreneur Robert Livingston began buying land along both sides of the Hudson from Native American tribes. In the early 1700s, King George I deeded him a large tract of land covering most of present-day Columbia County. He became the first lord of Livingston Manor, which served as the county seat, with its own representation in the New York State legislature. Six more generations of Livingstons held prominent political and economic positions in the area until the mid-20th century, when the family's riverside property, Clermont, was handed over to the state.

ALONG THE HUDSON: ROUTE 9G
Clermont State Historic Site
Wild turkeys roam the grounds at Clermont (Clear Mountain, in French), the former riverside estate of Robert Livingston Jr., who is also known as Robert of Clermont, or simply as the Chancellor. Robert Jr. served as New York State chancellor, signed the Declaration of Independence, and later became ambassador to France. In 1728, he inherited 13,000 acres of present-day Columbia County from his father, the first lord of Livingston Manor,

and built a Georgian-style riverside home between 1730 and 1750. The house was designed to catch stunning views of the Catskill Mountains across the river.

The British burned this first home to the ground during the Revolutionary War as punishment for Livingston's support of colonial independence. Margaret Beekman Livingston, who managed the estate during the war, escaped with a grandfather clock that remains in the foyer today. She promptly rebuilt the home in time to host George and Martha Washington in 1782.

When he wasn't involved in national affairs, Robert of Clermont turned his attention to entrepreneurial projects. For example, he introduced merino sheep from France and partnered with Robert Fulton to build the first steamship to cruise the Hudson.

Frozen in time since the start of the Great Depression, the manor reflects the tastes of the seven generations that lived in it. A crystal chandelier in the drawing room came from 19th-century France, and the library contains books from the 17th century. The dining room, which was restored in January 2004, has a marble fireplace mantel. And the original house telephone sits on a table outside the dining room (the telephone number was 3). A frieze over the fireplace in the study depicts Alice Livingston and her two daughters, the last residents of the estate. Oddly, an entire room upstairs is dedicated to pets of the family.

Today, the beautifully landscaped grounds of the 500-acre **Clermont State Historic Site** (1 Clermont Ave., Germantown, 518/537-4240, http://parks.ny.gov and www.friendsofclermont.org, 11am-4pm Wed.-Sun. and holiday Mon. Apr.-Oct., 11am-3pm Sat.-Sun. Nov.-Dec. 20, vehicles $5) are open to the public year-round. A popular time to visit is mid-May, when the lilacs are in bloom. The mansion was closed in late 2021 due to restoration work; however, the grounds remain open.

The visitors center, located in the old carriage house, stocks a good selection of local interest books. A reference library in the house is open by appointment. Nearby Germantown has gas stations, ATMs, and the obligatory Stewart's Shop.

★ Olana State Historic Site

Ten miles north of Germantown stands another historic residence, in every way quite the opposite of Clermont. Landscape painter Frederic Edwin Church began his career in 1846 under the tutelage of Thomas Cole and went on to earn worldwide recognition. At age 24, he became the youngest artist ever elected to the National Academy of Design. As a painter who also grasped the power of marketing, Church learned how to generate hype and income for his paintings. He often showed a single painting at a time and charged admission for anyone who wished to view it.

Though he traveled extensively during his lifetime, Church held a strong connection to the Hudson River Valley and chose to settle on 126 acres just south of the present-day Rip Van Winkle Bridge. Following a trip to the Middle East, he designed a sprawling Persian-style residence on top of a hill overlooking the Hudson and landscaped the grounds as if he were composing one of his romantic paintings. New York State rescued the home in 1966 from the nephew of Church's daughter-in-law, who intended to sell all of its furnishings in a Sotheby's auction. On display are a few of Church's own works, as well as many of the paintings, sculptures, and furnishings he collected from his travels to South America and the Middle East.

Olana (5720 Rte. 9G, Hudson, 518/828-0135, www.olana.org, 8am-sunset daily) is open with guided tours on the hour. House Tours cost $12 adults; Historic Landscape Tours are $25-35. Book your tickets in advance, as the events often sell out early. Visitors are welcome to walk the trails in summer, which sometimes feature art installations, or to snowshoe and cross-country ski in winter.

Hudson

If you looked down Hudson's Warren Street for the first time and thought you had landed

Hudson

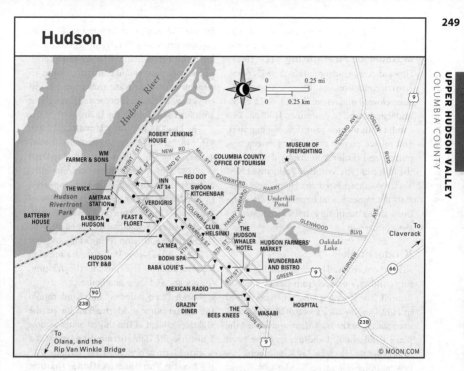

in an Atlantic Seaboard beach town, you wouldn't be far from the truth. The city still reflects its heritage as a whaling port in the early 19th century.

Fearing a British retaliation after the American Revolution, a group of Nantucket whalers moved inland to the Hudson River shoreline and incorporated a city in 1785. With a strategic location and carefully planned grid of streets, Claverack Landing, later renamed Hudson, became a center for shipbuilding and whale-oil production. By the mid-19th century, the city was firmly established as the economic and political center of Columbia County.

As the city declined in the early 20th century, it earned a reputation for its active red-light district. Author Bruce Hall revisits this aspect of Hudson's history in a book called *Diamond Street: The Story of the Little Town with the Big Red Light District* (Black Dome Press, 1994). Today, antiques shops have replaced the brothels and sparked a long-lasting

economic boom. Rows of restored Greek Revival and Federal townhouses line both sides of historic Warren Street for several blocks, extending from the town square to the river. New York City designers flock to dozens of antiques shops, which carry everything from Tibetan tapestries to Russian furniture. Hudson today gives city escapees some of the comforts of home and rural residents a place to experience a blossoming arts and culture scene.

In the 100 block is the **Robert Jenkins House & Museum** (113 Warren St., 518/828-9764, https://hudson-dar.org, 1pm-4pm Sat.-Sun. July-Oct., or by appointment, $4 suggested donation), an 1811 Federal-style building with whaling and military exhibits that document the city's colorful past. A promenade at the end of Warren Street offers river views, and the city has developed the area surrounding the train station into a green space called the **Henry Hudson Riverfront Park.**

The Firemen's Association of the State of New York (FASNY) operates the **Museum of Firefighting** (117 Harry Howard Ave., Hudson, 518/822-1875, www.fasnyfiremuseum.com, 10am-4:30pm Wed.-Sun., closed holidays, adults $10, children $5, under age 3 free) in downtown Hudson. Two exhibit halls include paintings, photographs, and related memorabilia. The fire engines, pumps, and clothing on display date back to the 18th and 19th centuries. Residents of New York's Volunteer Fireman's Home, next door, staff the museum and happily answer questions about the history and current state of their profession.

Kinderhook

Kinderhook received its name, which is Dutch for "children's point," from Henry Hudson himself. The story goes that when he arrived in 1609, Hudson saw a group of Mohican children staring at the *Half Moon* and named the place Kinderhook Landing, now the town of Stuyvesant. Present-day Kinderhook lies several miles inland, on Kinderhook Creek. Numerous restored homes and historical sites make this town one of the most interesting destinations in northern Columbia County. The village hosted several notable guests during the Revolutionary War: Colonel Henry Knox passed through on his way to deliver a shipment of artillery from Fort Ticonderoga to Boston, and Colonel Benedict Arnold spent the night to recover after the victory of Bemis Heights.

Washington Irving reportedly wrote "Rip Van Winkle" during a stay in Kinderhook, and he based "The Legend of Sleepy Hollow" on local residents, though the story took place in Tarrytown. The **Columbia County Museum** (5 Albany Ave., Kinderhook, 518/758-9265, www.cchsny.org, 10am-4pm Thurs.-Sun.), run by the Columbia County Historical Society, has extensive collections of paintings and artifacts from around the county.

Take a tour of a Federal-style mansion at the **James Vanderpoel House** (16 Broad St., 518/758-9265, www.cchsny.org, $7.50, by appointment only). This restored brick building is the former home of James Vanderpoel, a prominent lawyer and politician. Inside, an elegant, curved staircase rises from a grand entryway. The home is decorated throughout with furnishings from the 1820s.

The **Luykas Van Alen House** (2589 Rte. 9H, 518/758-9625, www.cchsny.org, noon-4pm Fri. and Sun., 10am-4pm Sat. May-Oct.) is a 1737 Dutch farmhouse with mid-18th-century furnishings. The site appeared in Martin Scorsese's 1993 film *The Age of Innocence*. On the property is the white 1920 Ichabod Crane Schoolhouse, named after the teacher in Washington Irving's famous story "The Legend of Sleepy Hollow." An admission fee ($10, students free) includes the museum, the houses, and the schoolhouse.

Located two miles outside Kinderhook, the former home of Martin Van Buren, the eighth president of the United States, is now a historic site. The surrounding land was a working farm of over 200 acres. Built in 1797, the **Martin Van Buren National Historic Site** (1013 Old Post Rd., 518/758-9689, www.nps.gov/mava, 9am-4pm daily mid-May-Oct., free) is a Federal-style home that was remodeled in 1849, and Van Buren spared no expense: Brussels carpets and 51 elaborate wallpaper panels that form a hunting mural are on display inside.

ALONG THE TACONIC STATE PARKWAY

Lake Taghkanic State Park

During sticky summer heat waves, **Lake Taghkanic State Park** (1528 Rte. 82, Taghkanic, 518/851-3631, http://parks.ny.gov, vehicles $10) is a popular day trip for Mid-Hudson Valley residents. The clean and refreshing lake has two beaches with lifeguard supervision and a boat launch. Overnight accommodations include tent and RV campsites, as well as cabins and cottages (reserve

---

1: Olana State Historic Site **2:** Clermont State Historic Site **3:** Lake Taghkanic State Park

1

2

3

at www.reserveamerica.com, May-Oct. only). The park service maintains trails for hiking and biking. In winter, it allows cross-country skiing, snowmobiles, and ice-skating when the lake freezes. Hunters can take deer and turkey in season.

Claverack

Continuing north on the Taconic State Parkway, you arrive at the intersection of Route 23, an old canon route from the Revolutionary War that connects Hillsdale to Hudson. Equidistant between Hudson and the Taconic is the hamlet of Claverack, best known for its 1786 stone courthouse, where Alexander Hamilton tried a famous libel case involving a Hudson newspaper publisher and President Thomas Jefferson.

The name Claverack derives from the Dutch for clover field. Historians believe Henry Hudson chose the name for the fields of white clover he saw when he first arrived. The 1727 Reformed Protestant Dutch Church stands as a testament to the town's first settlers, and Dutch architecture populates this stretch of Route 23.

Several pick-your-own berry farms and orchards are nearby, including **Philip Orchards** (270 Rte. 9H, Claverack, 518/851-6351, https://philiporchardsny.com, 9am-5pm Fri.-Mon., Labor Day-Oct.) for apples and pears. Contemporary writer Leila Philip wrote a memoir of her family's long-standing connection to Claverack entitled *A Family Place: A Hudson Valley Farm, Three Centuries, Five Wars, One Family* (Viking, 2001).

Chatham and Ghent

Though it is technically part of Columbia County, Chatham marks the unofficial gateway to southern New England and the Berkshires. There are actually several Chathams: At the commercial center is the town of Chatham, Route 203 off the Taconic State Parkway. The Village of Chatham, founded in 1795, has dozens of historical markers and claims one of the country's last operational one-room schoolhouses,

now home to the **Riders Mills Historical Association** (at the intersection of Riders Mills Rd. and Drowne Rd., 518/794-7146, www.ridersmillsschoolhouse.org). Quiet North Chatham lies on the Valatie Kill and the Rensselaer County line, while East Chatham offers a treasure trove for book lovers: a secondhand bookstore called **Librarium** (126 Black Bridge Rd. II, 518/392-5209, www.thelibrarium.com).

Art Omi (1405 County Rd. 22, Ghent, www.artomi.org) offers an artist-in-residence program on 120 acres of farmland. The Sculpture & Architecture Park is open to the public, with works by more than 60 artists from all over the world. Bring your hiking boots, snowshoes, or cross-country skis to get around. The Charles B. Benenson Visitors Center has an indoor gallery and a café for additional exhibitions.

ALONG ROUTE 22
★ Taconic State Park

Just east of Route 22, at the intersection of the New York, Massachusetts, and Connecticut state lines, lies a hidden outdoor gem: the 6,000-acre **Taconic State Park** (Rte. 344, off Rte. 22, Copake Falls, 518/329-3993, http://parks.ny.gov, year-round, vehicles $8). The park encompasses an 11-mile stretch of the Taconic Range—the vestiges of a mountain range that geologists believe stood taller than the Himalayas during the Ordovician time period, 450 million years ago.

The state has developed two areas for year-round use—Copake Falls and Rudd Pond—with extensive hiking, biking, and nature trails, as well as fishing, swimming, and camping. In winter, the trails belong to cross-country skiers and snowmobiles. The **Copake Falls Area** (518/329-3993) is located on Route 344 or Valley View Road. To find the **Rudd Pond Area** (59 Rudd Pond Rd., Millerton, 518/789-3059, year-round), turn off Route 22 at Route 62 in Millerton, and head two miles north.

The highlight of this wilderness area is **Bash Bish Falls,** at 80 feet, the tallest single-drop waterfall in Massachusetts (the falls are located just over the state line). Beginning about a mile upstream from the town of Copake Falls, an easy hike (1.5 miles round-trip) through a hemlock and hardwood forest takes you to the base of the falls. (For a shorter but steeper route, park in the lot on the Massachusetts side.) The water cascades over a sheer granite cliff, landing in a pristine mountain pool. Cold temperature and strong currents discourage most hikers from taking a dip. The ecosystem supports a diverse population, including coyotes, red foxes, and brook trout. After the falls, the Bash Bish Brook winds its way through the Mid-Hudson Valley and empties into the Hudson River. Plan to get here before 10am to enjoy the view before the crowds.

South of the state park, Columbia and Dutchess Counties have teamed up to convert a 43-mile stretch of the old New York and Harlem Railroad into a pathway for walking, running, and cycling. A five-mile section of the **Harlem Valley Rail Trail** (518/789-9591, www.hvrt.org) connects Under Mountain Road in Ancram to the Orphan Farm Road in Copake, and the Taconic State Park entrance in Copake Falls. Lined in spots with weathered split-rail fencing, the paved trail traverses the base of the Taconic Mountains. In several clearings, you can see the Catskill Mountains to the west. More sections are in the early stages of development and not yet open to the public.

According to local residents, Mohican arrowheads, spears, and axes can still occasionally be found in the vicinity of Copake. A tall clock and a Vietnam Veterans War Memorial at the intersection of Routes 22 and 7A mark the center of town, but there's not much reason to stop.

Hillsdale and Catamount

When Hillsdale residents speak of "the mountains," they mean the Berkshires, not the Catskills. Located at the Massachusetts state line, the town is part sleepy Hudson River Valley, part upscale New England.

Catamount Ski & Snowboarding Area (3290 Rte. 23, Hillsdale, 518/325-3200, www.catamountski.com, 9am-4pm Mon.-Fri., 8:30am-4pm Sat.-Sun. and holidays, Mon.-Fri. $20, Sat.-Sun. and holidays $68), at the Massachusetts state line, is a great mountain to hit on a midweek snow day. With 33 trails, seven lifts, and a fun terrain park, the area draws families from across the Hudson River Valley. The minimal lodge has stacks of blue lockers and cafeteria-style lunch fare. A heated tent next to the lodge houses a small gift shop with winter wear. In spring, summer, and fall, the **Catamount Aerial Adventure Park** (3290 Rte. 23, Hillsdale, 518/325-3200, https://catamountski.com, 9am-5:30pm daily spring-summer, 9am-5:30pm Sat.-Sun. fall, adults $58, youth $52) opens 11 zip-line courses and 162 platforms above the trees to riders of all levels age 7 and up. Two of the runs are 2,000 feet long.

Austerlitz

The sale of abundant fresh blueberries helped early settlers pay their taxes in rural Austerlitz. Today, an annual Blueberry Festival commemorates the town's heritage. The **Austerlitz Historical Society** (518/392-0062, www.oldausterlitz.org) completed the creation of Old Austerlitz, a museum site at the intersection of Route 22 and Harvey Mountain Road that collects and restores buildings, artifacts, and related town memorabilia. To date, the site includes a blacksmith shop; the 1794 Morey-Devereaux House from Nassau, New York; the 1790 Harvey House from northeastern Connecticut; an 1840 granary from Stillwater, New York; a one-room schoolhouse from 1818; and an 1850s church. The society sponsors events and workshops year-round.

★ Mount Lebanon Shaker Village

In 1772, an Englishwoman named Ann Lee rose to the forefront of a radical dissident movement and led a small group of Shaking Quakers—so named for their tendency to break out in violent shakes during their worship services—to the New World to escape religious persecution. The United Society of Believers eventually established a leadership center in New Lebanon, New York, and grew to include some 6,000 members in 19 communities by the mid-19th century. The Shaker community evolved considerably over the years, but two ideals underpinned the religion: simplicity and celibacy. Above all, members strove to live a selfless and communal existence. Industrialization during the 19th century gradually eroded the once thriving Shaker community (along with other utopian social experiments like it), and the few remaining followers withdrew from society, leaving only traces of the culture.

Mount Lebanon Shaker Village (202 Shaker Rd., New Lebanon, 518/794-9100, www.shakermuseumandlibrary.org, guided tour $10) is a national historic landmark located in the northeast corner of Columbia County. Eight families once farmed and lived here on 6,000 acres of rolling hills, forests, and fields. More than two dozen of the original buildings have been preserved. The museum contains one of the largest collections of Shaker artifacts and offers an informative introduction to the Shaker way of life. Among other values, the culture emphasizes high quality, precision, hospitality, invention, and systematic thinking. As a result, the industrious Shakers made fine furniture, tools, farm produce, and clothes. The museum has Shaker stoves, a washing machine, chairs, and textiles for display.

Visitors are welcome June-October. Once on-site, you can view the original beams and chutes of the granary and the drying racks in the washhouse, as well as cemeteries, aqueducts, and the remains of several old mills. The site is a short drive from the Hancock Shaker Village, across the Massachusetts state line in the Berkshires.

Snow Stats: Catamount

- Base: 1,000 feet
- Summit: 2,000 feet
- Vertical drop: 1,000 feet
- Trails: 36
- Lifts: 7, including 3 magic carpets
- Skiable acres: 110
- Longest run: 1.75 miles
- Snowmaking: 98 percent of skiable terrain
- Snow report: 800/342-1840

RECREATION
Winter Sports
Catamount Ski & Snowboarding Area (3290 Rte. 23, Hillsdale, 518/325-3200, www.catamountski.com, 8:30am-4pm Sat.-Sun. and holidays, 9am-4pm Mon.-Fri., adults $68, $20 Mon.-Fri.) also offers night skiing (3pm-9pm Wed., 3pm-10pm Fri.-Sat.) on 15 of its trails.

Nordic skiers will find more than 15 wilderness areas with groomed and ungroomed trails across Columbia County. **Clermont** (1 Clermont Ave., Germantown, 518/537-4240, www.friendsofclermont.org) opens its trails and grounds free to cross-country skiers. Or explore the carriage roads and six miles of trails on the grounds of **Olana State Historic Site** (5720 Rte. 9G, Hudson, 518/828-0135, www.olana.org). **Lake Taghkanic State Park** (1528 Rte. 82, Taghkanic, 518/851-2060, http://parks.ny.gov) has trails around the lake. **Taconic State Park** (Rte. 344, off Rte. 22, Copake Falls, 518/329-3993) has extensive trails in both developed areas, Copake Falls and Rudd Pond. Two cottages for rent

1: Copake Falls in Taconic State Park 2: main dwelling house of the Mount Lebanon Shaker Village

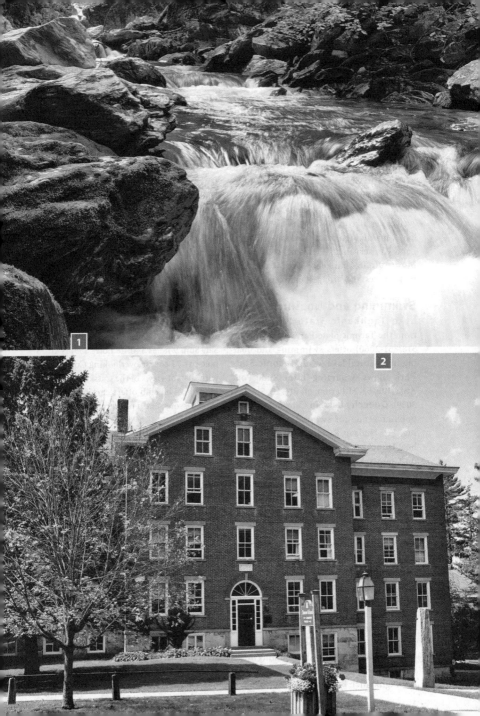

year-round each have a fridge, a stove, a microwave, dishes and utensils, a bath with shower, and oil heat.

Hiking

Hikers can explore state forests, historic sites, and wildlife preserves in Columbia County. Olana, Clermont, and Martin Van Buren National Historic Site have well-maintained trails for nature walks and scenic views. To get farther away from civilization, head to **Beebe Hill State Forest** (County Rd. 5, Austerlitz) and hike to the fire tower (2 miles round-trip, easy). Or stop in Philmont for an even easier hike to view **High Falls** (1.5-mile loop), maintained by the Columbia County Land Conservancy. A summit of **Alander Mountain** (5.4-mile loop) in Taconic State Park will test the strongest of hikers.

Swimming and Boating

Lake Taghkanic State Park (access from the Taconic State Parkway or Rte. 82, 518/851-2060) offers swimming and boating in a natural lake, while **Taconic State Park** allows swimming in the Rudd Pond Area (Rte. 62, Millerton, off Rte. 22, 518/789-3059). **Queechy Lake** in Canaan is another popular venue for swimming and canoeing. For Hudson River access, head to the boat launches on Front Street in Hudson or on County Road 35A (Northern Blvd.) in Germantown.

Fishing and Hunting

The New York State Department of Environmental Conservation stocks **Kinderhook Creek, Claverack Creek, Roeliff Jansen Creek,** and the unfortunately named **Ore Pit Pond** in Taconic State Park with trout. Fly fishers head to the **Taghkanic Creek** or **Bash Bish Falls**. **Queechy Lake** and **Kinderhook Lake** allow fishing from car-top boats only. A New York State fishing license is required at all locations.

Several **state forests** allow hunting in season: **New Forge** (New Forge Rd., off Route 82, Taghkanic), **Beebe Hill** (County Rd. 5,

Austerlitz), and **Harvey Mountain** (East Hill Rd., off Route 22). Call the local state ranger (518/828-0236) for information. **Taconic State Park** permits bow and rifle hunting for deer only. **Lido's Game Farm** (68 Berkshire Rd., off County Rd. 11, 518/329-1551) is a private club in the town of Hillsdale.

Golf

A dozen golf courses are scattered among Columbia County's rolling hills. **Undermountain Golf Course** (274 Undermountain Rd., Copake, 518/329-4444, www.undermountaingolf.com, 7am-7pm Mon.-Fri., 7am-6:30pm Sat.-Sun., Mon.-Fri. $22.75, Sat.-Sun. and holidays $27.50, seniors and juniors $21) operates a public 18-hole course with views of the Taconic Range, the Berkshire Mountains, and the Catskills.

Copake Country Club (44 Golf Course Rd., off County Rd. 11, Copake Lake, 518/325-4338, www.copakecountryclub.com, 7am-7pm daily Mar.-Nov., Mon.-Fri. 18 holes $30, Sat.-Sun. 9 holes $40, 18 holes $59) is an 18-hole par-72 course overlooking Copake Lake with distant views of the Catskills across the Hudson. The club offers cart rentals, a pro shop, lessons, and a restaurant.

Cycling

Cyclists have many options for touring country roads and trails in this part of the Hudson River Valley. The **Grand Tour of Columbia County** (www.roberts-1.com), an aggressive 83-mile road ride with a 60-mile option, traverses nearly every major town in the county on back roads that meander by old homes, farms, rolling hills, and waterfalls. For an easier ride, the paved **Harlem Valley Rail Trail** (51 S. Center St., Millerton, 518/789-9591, www.hvrt.org) follows a set of old railroad tracks along the base of the Taconic Range. Two completed sections now total 15 miles of car-free paths. Access the path at Undermountain Road, off Route 22 in Ancram or at the Taconic State Park entrance in Copake Falls. The same rail trail continues into Dutchess County, connecting the towns of Millerton, Amenia, and Wassaic. The section from Millerton to Undermountain Road remains under development.

Mountain bikers will find 20 miles of trails with 3,000 feet of possible climbing in **Beebe Hill and Harvey Mountain State Forests** (http://dec.ny.gov)—short loops for beginners, longer routes for riders with some skills, and advanced terrain for the experts. Start at the East Hill Road, Barrett Pond, or Fog Hill Road parking areas, all located off Route 22 in Austerlitz. Visit the Columbia County Mountain Bike Alliance (http://mtballiance.cc) for the latest updates on new trail development. The group hosts Thursday-evening rides as well.

Steiner's Sports (301 Warren St., Hudson, 518/828-5063, www.steinersskibike.com, 10am-6pm Mon.-Fri., 10am-5pm Sat., 11am-4pm Sun.) carries high-end ski, bike, and kayak equipment in three locations: Hudson, Valatie, and Glenmont. Stop in for maps, supplies, and route advice. You can also rent bikes for a cruise around town.

Yoga and Spas

Bodhi Spa (543 Warren St., Hudson, 518/828-2233, www.bodhiholisticspa.com) offers massage and facial treatments plus a full schedule of yoga classes. A Yin Yoga class is especially relaxing before or after your spa treatment.

ENTERTAINMENT AND EVENTS
Performing Arts

After three decades of neglect, Hudson's 19th-century city hall building reopened in 1998 as a local performing arts center, **Hudson Hall** (327 Warren St., Hudson, 518/822-1438, http://hudsonhall.org, 9am-5pm Tues.-Fri, noon-5pm Sat.-Sun., tickets free-$20). Artist exhibitions and concerts are hosted throughout the year. **Basilica Hudson** (110 Front St., Hudson, 518/822-1050, http://basilicahudson.org) hosts a wide range of artists, musicians, and filmmakers in a converted 1880s factory building down by the train station.

Set in an 1847 schoolhouse, the **Spencertown Academy Arts Center** (790 Rte. 203, Spencertown, 518/392-3693, www.spencertownacademy.org, 1pm-5pm Thurs.-Sun. Feb.-Dec.) has a 140-seat auditorium and four exhibit spaces. Events range from jazz and classical concerts to yoga classes. The quaint **Mac-Haydn Theatre** (1925 Rte. 203, Chatham, 518/392-9292, www.machaydntheatre.org, tickets $42), on a hilltop overlooking the town of Chatham, has a 50-year history of producing musicals, with a summer children's theater. The theater runs seven or eight shows per season.

Bars and Nightlife

Hudson residents congregate at the **Red Dot** (321 Warren St., Hudson, 518/828-3657, www.reddotrestaurant.com, 5pm-9:30pm Thurs.-Fri. and Mon., 11am-3pm and 5pm-9:30pm Sat.-Sun.) after work to drink Morland Old Speckled Hen by the pint.

For live music in a hip dinner-theater setting, **Club Helsinki** (405 Columbia St., Hudson, 518/828-4800, www.helsinkihudson.com) is a win. It's open for concerts and special events. The reservation process is a bit confusing at first. You can buy general admission tickets online, but in order to reserve a seat for the show, you must call ahead to reserve a table in the club. Tables are arranged in front of the small stage and on a mezzanine level above. You can also skip the table and watch from a seat at the bar. This is a popular venue for the local residents, and shows frequently sell out, even on rainy weekday nights. An adjoining restaurant (in the same building, out of earshot of the club) serves dinner (from 5pm daily). Performances have included Black Francis of the Pixies and Shawn Colvin. When the music of the evening plays the sounds of the south, Louisiana native chef Hugh Horner plans a special menu of Creole dishes such as deep-fried okra and Savannah-style low-country boil.

For maritime entertainment, **Hudson Cruises** (518/822-1014, www.hudsoncruises.com) offers afternoon or evening cruises with dinner, dancing, and scenic river views. Boats depart from Henry Hudson Riverfront Park on Front Street in Hudson at various days and times.

Chatham Brewing (59 Main St., Chatham, 518/392-1026, www.chathambrewing.com, 4pm-8pm Mon., noon-9pm Wed.-Thurs., noon-10pm Fri.-Sat., noon-8pm Sun.) serves craft beers made on-site. The setting is small and somewhat quiet for a bar, so you'll be able to have a conversation with a friend. Stop in for a taste or a pint.

For a little nightlife during the day, plan a visit to **Hillrock Estate Distillery** (408 Pooles Hill Rd., Ancram, 518/329-1023, www. hillrockdistillery.com). On a 200-acre barley farm, the former head distiller of Maker's Mark is experimenting with the Solera system of aging whiskey—sort of blending a little old with a little new—to get the complex flavors that connoisseurs desire. The bourbon is then finished in 20-year-old oloroso sherry casks to add the final touch. Call or book online to arrange a tour.

Hudson Valley Distillers (1727 Rte. 9, Claremont, 518/537-6820, www. hudsondistillers.com, noon-6pm daily) makes vodka from local apples and gin distilled from local wines. Shop its beverage market or order a drink at the Cocktail Grove.

Festivals

Folk dancers and bluegrass music lovers attend the popular **Falcon Ridge Folk Festival** (Dodds Farm, 44 County Rd. 7D, Hillsdale, 860/364-0366, www. falconridgefolk.com) each July to watch up to 40 bands perform on three stages, with plenty of flat areas for camping. The **Columbia County Fair** (Columbia County Fairgrounds, Rte. 66 and Rte. 203, Chatham Village, 518/392-2121 or 518/758-1811, www. columbiafair.com) is an old-fashioned fair with live music, a rodeo, tractor pulls, and amusement rides. It takes place on Labor Day weekend. And the Clermont hosts various festivals and educational events throughout the year, including a sheep festival in April.

The **Tour of the Catskills** (www. tourofthecatskills.com) is a challenging multiday cycling event held in early August. Hundreds of amateur and professional cyclists compete in a Friday time trial and two stages Saturday and Sunday. The route follows some of the most scenic country roads through Greene and Ulster Counties. The town of Windham is a good place to watch the action.

SHOPPING
Antiques and Boutiques

The town of Hudson is chock-full of boutiques and galleries, where you can find everything from contemporary art and jewelry to vintage records, first-edition books, and loose-leaf tea. Start your tour of Hudson's antiques shops at **Hudson Market** (310-312 Warren St., Hudson, 518/822-0028, www. hudsonmarket.com, 11am-5pm Sun.-Thurs., 11am-6pm Fri.-Sat.), a collective of six dealers that occupies a former grocery store. **Five and Diamond Vintage Clothing** (502 Columbia St., Hudson, 518/828-4140, www. fiveanddiamond.blogspot.com, noon-5pm Thurs.-Sun. and by appointment) houses a well-curated selection of vintage men's and women's clothing. Owner Lisa does all the buying and offers customers her personal expertise and knowledge of fashion history.

The **Bees Knees** (725 Warren St., Hudson, 518/697-0888, www.thebeeskneeshudson. com, 11am-5pm Mon. and Wed.-Thurs., 10am-5pm Fri.-Sat., noon-4pm Sun.) is a cute children's store and community center for parents—the perfect place to find an eco-friendly baby gift or a new toy for the rest of your travels.

Designer **Nikki Chasin** (553 Warren St., Hudson, no phone, 11am-6pm Thurs.-Mon.) has opened a Hudson shop to complement her online women's fashion boutique. Simple but polished apparel is her specialty, including unfussy sweaters and unique dresses and jumpsuits.

Away from the Warren Street bustle, **Copake Auction** (266 Rte. 7A, Copake, 518/329-1142, www.copakeauction.com,

What Grows When

Each season brings a new crop of fruits and vegetables to market. Harvest times change year to year depending on the weather, but here are some general guidelines for what to expect throughout the growing season.

SPRING

The first veggies to appear in local farmers markets are leafy greens that can handle the cold, such as spinach, chard, lettuce, and kale. Asparagus spears reach for the sky in April and May. Fiddleheads, wild mushrooms, garlic scapes, and edible pea pods come next, followed by strawberries in early June.

SUMMER

The longer days of summer ripen cherries, blueberries, raspberries, currants, and peaches. Sweet corn, summer squash, broccoli, beets, potatoes, peppers, beans, garlic, and tomatoes are abundant in August.

FALL

The first frost sweetens the flavor of brussels sprouts and cauliflower. Butternut squash and pumpkins grow large on the vine, while apples and pears reach their peak.

8am-4pm Mon.-Fri.) has specialized in the sale of Americana items for the past 50 years. Its annual antique bicycle auction draws cycling enthusiasts from across the nation and overseas.

If you are looking for homey gifts, step into **Classic Country** (2948 County Rd. 9, East Chatham, 518/392-2211, http://classiccountry. com, 10am-5pm Wed.-Sat., 11am-4pm Sun.), where you will find a wide selection of hand-picked furniture, linens, baby gifts, blankets, soaps, and other trinkets.

Books

Bookworms will want to spend an hour or two browsing the shelves at **Librarium** (126 Black Bridge Rd. II, East Chatham, 518/392-5209, www.thelibrarium.com) or **Rodgers Book Barn** (467 Rodman Rd., Hillsdale, 518/325-3610, www.rodgersbookbarn.com, 11am-4pm Fri.-Sun., 1pm-4pm Mon., other times by chance or appointment). Better yet, save time for both. Each shop houses tens of thousands of titles in a converted barn that sets the mood for reading. For current fiction and nonfiction, along with a pint of ale on tap, wander into **The Spotty Dog Books & Ale** (440 Warren St., 518/671-6006, www.thespottydog. com, 11am-9pm Mon.-Sat., noon-8pm Sun.). There is a special section of books and toys for kids, plus frequent author events.

Farm Stands and Local Products

There is at least one farm stand, farmers market, or pick-your-own orchard in every town in Columbia County. The **Hudson Farmers' Market** (518/851-7515, www. hudsonfarmersmarketny.com, 9am-1pm Sat. May-Nov.), at 6th Street and Columbia Street, has meat, eggs, plants, flowers, cheese, wool, and fruits and veggies in season. To the east, near Claverack, you can pick apples and pears at **Philip Orchards** (518/851-6351, https:// philiporchardsny.com).

Pop into the **Olde Hudson** (449 Warren St., Hudson, 518/828-6923, http://oldehudson. com) pantry to pick up gourmet ingredients for a picnic or homemade dinner.

Green Acres Farm (269 Schneider Rd., Hudson, 518/851-7460, www. greenacreshudson.com, 9am-6pm Fri.-Mon.) opens with the summer's first harvest of tomatoes, peaches, and corn. Stop in for a weekend's worth of fresh produce and irresistible pastries baked right on the premises. The stand closes precisely at noon on Thanksgiving Day, after the holiday's homemade pies are delivered to its loyal customers. **Fix Brothers Fruit Farm** (215 White Birch Rd., Hudson, 518/828-7560, www.fixbrosfruitfarm.com) runs a popular you-pick apple farm just off Route 9G, between Bard College and Hudson. Pick any mix of Honeycrisp, Fuji, Macoun, Golden Delicious, Mutsu, and Cortland apples for $1 per pound.

Deer, buffalo, elk, antelope, and llamas are just some of the animals that share the pastures at **Highland Farm** (283 County Rd. 6, Germantown, 518/537-6397, www.eatbetter-meat.com). The farm sells venison and smoked venison products, breeds animals for zoos, and shelters endangered species, all under one roof.

Otto's Market (215 Main St., Germantown, 518/537-7200, www.ottosmarket.com, 8am-7pm Thurs.-Tues.) stocks some standard food brands but also maintains a wide selection of unique and local products. Owner Otto Leuschel makes an effort to cover the basics in a more personal setting. The beer selection is impressive. The market also has a deli serving baked goods made fresh daily, a breakfast selection including a variety of breakfast burritos, and specialty hot and cold sandwiches.

FOOD
Along the Hudson: Route 9G
★ **Gaskins** (2 Church Ave., Germantown, 518/537-2107, www.gaskinsny.com, 5pm-10pm Thurs.-Mon., $18-28) has earned the respect of foodies near and far with its community-first approach to incredible food. Chef Nick sources ingredients from nearby farms, including Montgomery Place Orchards, while host Sarah makes you feel right at home. Pork belly, grass-fed burgers, and homemade ice cream tend to stay on the menu, but the produce changes with the seasons. Heirloom tomatoes star in late summer, while apples and kabocha squash make appearances in the fall.

The list of trendsetting eateries in Hudson is changing all the time, and many deliver dining experiences on par with what you'd find in New York City. ★ **Grazin' Farm-to-Table Direct** (717 Warren St., Hudson, 518/822-9323, www.grazinburger.com, noon-8pm daily, $12-20) resembles a classic diner on the outside, but makes its chili, burgers, hot dogs, and sausages all from grass-fed beef and pastured pork. Most of the meat comes from Grazin' Angus Acres farm in Ghent. Prices are high, but you will taste the difference.

A young couple transplanted to Hudson in 2013 and lovingly restored the building that eventually became ★ **Wm Farmer & Sons** (20 S. Front St., Hudson, 518/828-1635, www.wmfarmerandsons.com, 5pm-9pm Thurs. and Sun., 5pm-10pm Fri.-Sat., $29-37). The nightly selection of oysters makes a great starter. Small plates might feature crispy octopus cazuela, fried chicken livers, or roasted Florentino cauliflower; larger plates could include a Hudson Valley steelhead, duck confit, or heritage pork loin roast. If you're staying the weekend, consider booking a room in one of their boarding houses next door.

Swoon Kitchenbar (340 Warren St., Hudson, 518/822-8938, www.swoonkitchenbar.com, 4pm-9pm Thurs., 4pm-10pm Fri., noon-10pm Sat., noon-9pm Sun., $25-30) quickly cornered the market for New American cuisine. **Wasabi** (807 Warren St., Hudson, 518/822-1888, 11:30am-2:30pm and 4:30pm-9:30pm Mon. and Wed.-Thurs., 11:30am-2:30pm and 4:30pm-10:30pm Fri.-Sat., 3pm-9:30pm Sun., $15-25) filled the void for Japanese with creative sushi rolls and some hot dishes as well.

Locals fill the **Red Dot Restaurant & Bar** (321 Warren St., Hudson, 518/828-3657, www.reddotrestaurant.com, 5pm-9:30pm Thurs.-Mon., 11am-3pm Sat.-Sun., $16-26) on weekend evenings, even in the dead of winter. Entrées range from fish and chips

---

1: one of many sustainable farms selling at the Hudson Farmers' Market **2:** Hudson Cruises **3:** a corn maze at the Fix Brothers Fruit Farm **4:** lunch specials at The Farmer's Wife

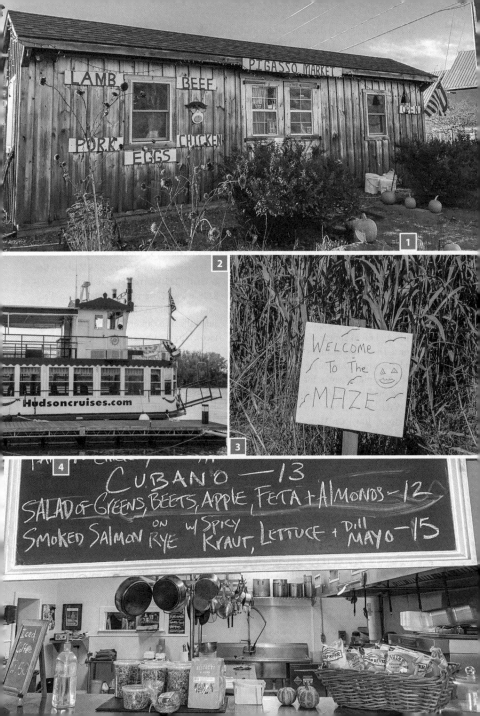

1. LAMB BEEF PIGASSO MARKET OPEN PORK EGGS CHICKEN
2. Hudsoncruises.com
3. WELCOME To The MAZE
4. CUBANO —13
SALAD of GREENS, BEETS, APPLE, FETA + ALMONDS — 12
Smoked Salmon ON RYE w/ SPICY KRAUT, LETTUCE + DILL MAYO — 15
Iced Coffee

to Thai curried vegetables. **Mexican Radio** (537 Warren St., Hudson, 518/828-7770, www.mexrad.com, 4pm-9pm Wed.-Thurs., 4pm-10pm Fri., noon-10pm Sat., noon-7pm Sun., $17-20) serves traditional and vegetarian Mexican cuisine, with plenty of gluten-free options too. House favorites include Mexican spring rolls, the Cajun burrito, and Baja-style fish tacos. **Wunderbar & Bistro** (744 Warren St., Hudson, 518/828-0555, www. wunderbarbistro.com, 11am-9pm daily, lunch $7-27, dinners $10-29) up the street serves dependable Austrian and Hungarian dishes at reasonable prices. Sports fans can watch the game on four large-screen TVs in a recently extended dining area. **Baba Louie's Pizza** (517 Warren St., Hudson, 518/751-2155, www. babalouiespizza.com, 4:30pm-8pm Mon. and Thurs., noon-3pm and 5pm-9pm Fri.-Sat., noon-3pm and 5pm-8pm Sun., $13-20) makes its pies from a sourdough crust. Toppings are fresh and often appear in creative combinations. The menu includes soups and salads, and the casual atmosphere is perfect for families. The menu works for vegetarians, and house-made soups are vegan.

With locations in Hudson and Cortona, Italy, **Ca'Mea Ristorante** (333 Warren St., Hudson, 518/822-0005, www. camearestaurant.com, noon-3pm and 5pm-8:30pm Tues.-Thurs., noon-3pm and 5pm-9pm Fri.-Sat., $20-32) is wildly popular with pasta lovers. House-made ravioli are stuffed with spinach and ricotta. Gnocchi come with a zucchini basil pesto and cherry tomatoes. Go for a half-portion so you have room for an entrée afterward.

Feast & Floret (13 S. 3rd St., Hudson, 518/822-1500, www.feastandfloret.com, 5pm-9pm Wed.-Fri., noon-3pm and 5pm-9pm Sat.-Sun., $17-27) serves a rotating menu of Italian-inspired dishes made from seasonal ingredients. Unusual entrées include a squid ink *soprese* pasta and roasted half octopus. The owners make their own dried botanicals, tinctured honeys, and finishing salts, which you can taste and purchase.

★ **Verdigris Tea & Chocolate Bar** (135 Warren St., Hudson, 518/828-3139, www. verdigristea.com, 10am-6pm Mon., Wed., and Fri.-Sun., 10am-8pm Thurs.) is paradise for those serious about tea. Choose a black, white, green, chai, or herbal tea and have a fresh pot brewed at the bar, or buy an ounce to go. Along with the tea itself, all manner of accessories are sold here, including pots, infusers, mugs, and timers. The chocolate bar features chocolates from around the world and serves up homemade pastries and chocolate drinks that are pure indulgence. Try the classic hot chocolate, which is a rich ganache of melted dark chocolate blended with milk and topped with whipped cream and chocolate shavings; you won't be sorry.

On warm summer days, **225 Warren Bar & Grill** (225 Warren St., Hudson, 518/697-8225, www.225warren.com, noon-9pm Wed.-Sat., $8-14) has inviting tables set up on the sidewalk. You can order fried calamari, fish tacos, burgers, Caesar salad, club sandwiches, and the like.

Along the Taconic State Parkway

Jackson's Old Chatham House (Village Square, Old Chatham, 518/794-7373, www. jacksonsoldchathamhouse.com, 11am-9pm daily, mains $17-36) serves reliable tavern-style food, including burgers, steaks, pork chops, and still the best prime rib around. The wood-burning fireplace is a plus in winter months. Nearby, the **Old Chatham Country Store & Cafe** (639 Albany Turnpike, Old Chatham, 518/794-6227, www.oldchathamcountrystore. com, 8am-3pm Thurs.-Mon., 5:30pm-8:30pm Fri.-Sat., reservations required, mains $10-20) has homemade soups and sandwiches in a casual setting. You can order a weekend dinner to go for Sunday if you call ahead by the previous Monday.

Blue Plate (1 Kinderhook St., Chatham, 518/392-7711, www.chathamblueplate.net, 5:30pm-9pm Tues.-Sat., 5pm-9:30pm Sun., $15-22) is an American bistro with some twists, where you can begin the meal with a butternut squash bisque and move on to a grass-fed burger, Blue Plate meatloaf, or vegetable pad thai. Comfort food is the theme at the newer and very popular **Chatham Grill** (34 Hudson Ave., Chatham, 518/392-1471, http://chathamgrill.com, 11am-8pm Mon.-Fri., 3pm-8pm Sat.-Sun., $10-24).

The People's Pub (36 Main St., Chatham, 518/392-2337, www.thepeoplespub.com, 4pm-late Tues.-Sun., $15-22) changed from a Welsh pub to a sustainable food eatery that celebrates local growers and farmers. On the menu are a burger, shrimp tacos, falafel plate, and Hudson Valley steelhead.

Along Route 22

The popular chain **Four Brothers Pizza Inn** (2828 Rte. 23, Hillsdale, 518/325-7300, www.fourbrotherspizzainn.com, 11:30am-9pm daily, $10-19) is open late, serving Italian, Greek, and American dishes. The restaurant is one of nine pizzerias in the Hudson River Valley, which, as the name implies, were established by four Greek brothers who immigrated to the United States.

Eight miles from the town of Hudson and 10 miles from Catamount, ★ **Local 111** (111 Main St., Philmont, 518/672-7801, www.local111.com, 5:30pm-9pm Wed.-Sat., 11am-2pm Sun., $22-32) continues to lead Columbia County's farm-to-table movement from a converted service station in a rather run-down mill town off Route 82. At least 18 local farmers contribute foods; some of them deliver their goods in the morning and return for dinner that night.

After a round of golf at the Copake Country Club, enjoy lunch or dinner at The **Greens** (Copake Country Club, 44 Golf Course Rd., Copake Lake, 518/325-0019, www.thegreensatcopake.com, 3pm-8pm Mon.-Thurs., 11am-9pm Fri.-Sat., 11am-8pm Sun., closed Tues.-Wed. off-season, $24-42), which serves a club menu of appetizers, salads, pizzas, and sandwiches, and a dinner menu featuring seafood, beef, pork, and duck dishes. Many of the ingredients are harvested locally.

An unassuming farmhouse along County Route 8 holds a delightful eatery, ★ **The Farmer's Wife** (3 County Rte. 8, Ancramdale, 518/329-5431, www.thefarmerswife.biz, 8:30am-3pm Wed.-Sun., $8-14). You might order a bowl of smoked chicken chili, a salad made of local greens, or a cheesesteak sandwich for lunch. Ingredients come from Herondale and other neighboring Columbia County farms. If you're in a hurry to see the sights, the grab-and-go menu is a great option.

ACCOMMODATIONS

Aside from a couple of modern hotels that cater to business travelers, places to stay in Columbia County tend toward the upscale. An increasing number of bed-and-breakfast inns and interesting vacation rentals are opening throughout the county; many of them are clustered in and around the town of Hudson.

$100-150

The **Hudson City B&B** (326 Allen St., Hudson, 518/822-8044, www.hudsoncitybnb.com, $125-175) occupies the former residence of Joshua T. Waterman, four-term mayor of Hudson beginning in 1853. The house is painted green with cream trim and sits within walking distance of the Warren Street antiques shops. Its comfortable rooms are decorated in 19th-century furnishings.

Inn at Ca'Mea (333 Warren St., Hudson, 518/303-6650, www.innatcamea.com, $130-280) consists of three updated buildings right in the heart of Hudson—one a Victorian mansion, another a Craftsman cottage, and the third an 18th-century historic home.

$150-200

Under new ownership, the **Inn at the Shaker Mill Falls** (40 Cherry Lane, Canaan, 518/794-9345, www.shakermillfalls.com) puts you a short drive from Berkshires attractions, including summer performances at Tanglewood, 10 miles away. Guest rooms occupy a converted 1834 mill.

Close to the river and train station, **The Wick** (41 Cross St., Hudson, 518/249-6825, www.thewickhotel.com, $176-189) is a new Marriott property set in an 1860s candle factory with 55 modern rooms and suites.

At the edge of the Berkshires, pine floors, antique trunks, and down comforters lend a cozy feel to guest rooms at ★ **The Inn at Silver Maple Farm** (1871 Rte. 295, Canaan, 518/781-3600, www.silvermaplefarm.com, $180-335). Breakfast includes homemade breads and muffins.

★ **The Hudson Whaler Hotel** (542 Warren St., Hudson, 518/217-4334, https://hudsonwhaler.com, $179-280), formerly the Barlow Hotel, underwent a complete restoration in early 2021. This small hotel now has a contemporary nautical theme, with 16 suites spread across three floors; some rooms are accessible and pet-friendly. Best of all, the location is ideal for walking to all that Hudson has to offer.

Over $200

Batterby House (formerly The Country Squire, 251 Allen St., Hudson, 518/822-9229, www.batterbyhousehudson.com, $200-365) also changed hands in recent years, but remains a cozy and stylish home with five inviting guest rooms and beds of all sizes. The new owners love vinyl; accordingly, each room has its own record player and a collection of 20-30 albums to play—swap with your fellow guests for more variety. This place is within walking distance of all the action on Warren Street.

The Inn at 34 (34 S. 2nd St., Hudson, 888/279-0365, www.innat34.com, $230-290) has been furnished with English antiques in keeping with the home's 1840s history. The innkeepers serve homemade granola, baby pancakes, and steel-cut oats for breakfast.

For a group trip, you might consider renting out the entire **Mount Merino Manor** (4317 Rte. 23, Hudson, 518/828-5583, www. mountmerinomanor.com, $1,795/night), which used to be a B&B and now is offered only as a private vacation rental. It has seven guest rooms and suites, all with private baths, king or queen beds, air-conditioning, and high-quality bed linens. Some have fireplaces, soaking tubs, and spa showers.

Campgrounds

Woodland Hills Campground (386 Fog Hill Rd., Austerlitz, 518/392-3557, www.whcg. net, May 15-Columbus Day, $45 tents, $60-80 full hookups, near the intersection of the Taconic State Parkway and the Massachusetts Turnpike (I-90), has 200 sites for tents and RVs. Amenities include hot showers, laundry, and family activities.

Taconic State Park (Rte. 344, off Rte. 22, Copake Falls, 518/329-3993, year-round) offers two recreational areas—Copake Falls and Rudd Pond—with campsites, trailer sites, and cabins (mid-May-Nov., sites $15-27, cabins $140-175). Deer hunting is allowed in season, and camping is extended for hunters. Reserve online (www.reserveamerica.com). The Rudd Pond Area is located off Route 22 on Route 62, two miles north of Millerton.

Camp Waubeeka Family Campground (133 Farm Rd., Copake, 518/329-4681, www. campwaubeeka.com) has four rustic cabins ($70-239) as well as campsites (tents $29-49) and trailer hookups ($57-87).

INFORMATION AND SERVICES

The **Columbia County Office of Tourism** (401 State St., Hudson, 518/828-3375 or 800/724-1846, www.columbiacountyny.org, 8:30am-4pm Mon.-Fri.) has maps and brochures covering the county as well as the greater Hudson River Valley. The **Columbia County Chamber of Commerce** (1 N. Front St., Hudson, 518/828-4417, www. columbiachamber-ny.com) can also provide visitor information.

GETTING THERE AND AROUND

Bus

Trailways of New York (800/858-8555, www.trailways.com) stops across the river in the village of Catskill, eight miles from downtown Hudson. Ride-shares and taxis are available, and some hotels offer free shuttle service.

Train

Hudson is a two-hour train ride from New York City's Penn Station. The **Amtrak Rail Station** (69 S. Front St., Hudson, 800/872-7245, www.amtrak.com) is located at the water's edge. A one-way ticket from Penn Station to Hudson costs $54-73. You can hop a cab from the train station or rent a car from **Enterprise Rent-a-Car** (78-80 Green St., Hudson, 518/828-5492, www.enterprise.com).

Car

From New England, turn off I-90 at exit B2 to reach the northern end of the Taconic State Parkway, the speediest north-south route through Columbia County. Route 23 crosses northern Columbia County, connecting Hillsdale to Hudson. Route 9 and its many spinoffs form a major commercial corridor along the river, while the more rural Route 22 runs along the base of the Taconic Range at the eastern edge of the county.

The Capital-Saratoga Region

The Capital-Saratoga Region of Albany,

Rensselaer County, and Saratoga Springs marks the end of the tidal Hudson River and serves as a bookend to a journey through the Hudson River Valley. After Albany and Troy, the river becomes part of the Champlain Canal before veering west to its origin, high in the Adirondack Mountains.

Henry Hudson reached Albany in September 1609 and had to turn the 122-ton *Half Moon* around when the river became too shallow. Word spread after that maiden voyage, and Fort Orange became one of the earliest and largest Dutch settlements along the river. Today's state capital is a destination in its own right, but with an international

Highlights

Look for ★ to find recommended sights, activities, dining, and lodging.

★ **Empire State Plaza:** The centerpiece of downtown Albany is a 98-acre plaza with an impressive collection of art displayed indoors and out (page 270).

★ **The Capitol Building:** Elaborate stone carvings line the imposing outdoor stairway that leads from the Empire State Plaza to the entrance of the headquarters for the New York State Assembly (page 271).

★ **Lark Street and Washington Park:** Downtown Albany has a bohemian enclave at the east end of Washington Park, with several blocks of eclectic boutiques and trendy restaurants (page 272).

★ **Grafton Lakes State Park:** A pleasant sandy beach and rare peace pagoda draw visitors from near and far to this corner of Rensselaer County (page 286).

★ **Saratoga Spa State Park:** Natural hot springs, towering pine trees, and an outdoor concert venue are highlights of this 2,300-acre park (page 290).

★ **Saratoga Race Course:** Thanks to the oldest continuously operating thoroughbred track in the United States, the city's population triples during the summer racing season (page 291).

★ **The Frances Young Tang Teaching Museum and Art Gallery:** Skidmore College has a state-of-the-art museum dedicated to presenting and teaching contemporary works (page 292).

The Capital-Saratoga Region

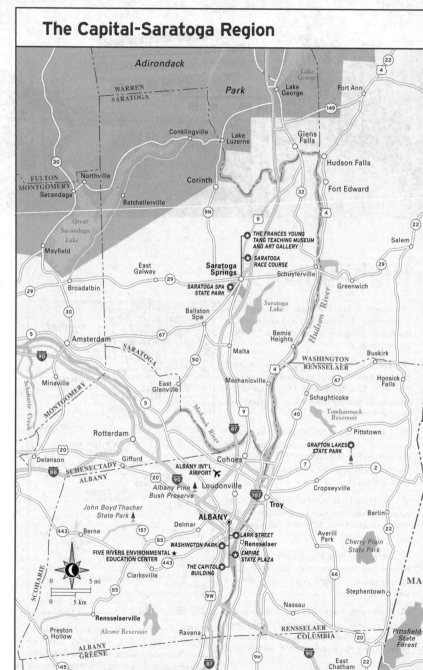

© MOON.COM

airport and a modern train station, the city also serves as a gateway to surrounding towns and wilderness areas.

Across the Hudson River from Albany lies sleepy Rensselaer County, home of the nation's first engineering school, Rensselaer Polytechnic Institute (RPI); two attractive state parks; and a large concentration of Tiffany glass.

Although it's best known for its summer horse-racing scene, Saratoga Springs offers a much wider appeal. A Victorian-era village is packed with boutique shops selling treasures old and new. Wellness spas, historic homes, a world-class outdoor performing arts theater, and several chefs of Food Network television fame make for a rich and varied travel experience. Apple orchards and art shows also have their place. Ideally situated at the edge of the Adirondack Park, the largest publicly protected area in the contiguous United States, this small city of 27,000 residents offers hikers and backpackers convenient access to supplies and outfitters. Lake George is just 30 minutes farther up the Northway (I-87) for summer swimming and boating.

PLANNING YOUR TIME

One day allows plenty of time to explore most of downtown Albany, but you'll need extra time to schedule a tour of the capitol building or the Executive Mansion. Popular Albany itineraries include dinner downtown followed by an evening event at the **Times Union Center** (www.timesunioncenter-albany.com), a weekend of historic colonial sights, or a day of holiday shopping at the malls.

Rensselaer County is easily explored in a day or two of scenic back roads driving. The trip from Albany to Saratoga Springs should take about half an hour with light traffic; however, a large number of government workers commute into Albany each day, so be sure to time your drive to avoid the rush. Ideal as a weekend getaway, Saratoga Springs also can work well as a side trip from Lake George, or as a day of civilization before or after a multiday hike through the Adirondack backcountry.

Albany

From names like Ten Broeck to its annual tulip festival, New York's capital city retains much of its early Dutch roots. As the New York State capital since 1797, the city has also preserved much of its 19th- and 20th-century architecture. Walk a few of the city's historical blocks and you'll find many examples of the Italianate, Federal, and Greek Revival styles, in conditions ranging from perfectly restored to borderline run-down.

Albany today contains an appealing mix of architectural masterpieces, art collections, and historic sights. Meanwhile, students from several area colleges support a vibrant sports and nightlife scene. With a population of 100,000, the city is large enough to offer a rich urban experience—yet compact enough that you can tour the downtown in a day. Unfortunately, however, many parts of Albany have yet to recover from the economic turmoil of the mid-20th century. As a result, showy state government buildings intermingle with signs of urban misfortune.

DOWNTOWN ALBANY

The modern Empire State Plaza and giant Times Union Center have done much to revitalize downtown Albany since most of its factories shut down in the 1950s; however, the

Previous: Lark Street historic houses in Albany; New York State's capitol building; New York State Museum.

Albany

© MOON.COM

new and restored buildings contrast sharply with the low-income neighborhoods that surround them. City leaders have wooed high-tech companies—making everything from nanotechnology to fuel cells—as a key source of economic growth.

The majority of visitors find themselves in Albany for one of three reasons: a business convention, a school field trip, or a concert or sporting event. Whatever the draw, it's well worth the time to absorb a slice of New York state history while you're in town.

★ Empire State Plaza

The centerpiece of downtown Albany is the 98-acre Empire State Plaza on State Street, where most of the government's employees show up for work each day. Ten dazzling skyscrapers surround an open plaza and fountain, including the Corning Tower, which at 42 stories is the state's tallest building outside New York City.

In the 1960s, then-governor Nelson A. Rockefeller envisioned an architectural wonder and cultural center that would bring jobs and visitors to downtown Albany again. He commissioned Wallace Harrison, the same architect who built Rockefeller Center, and construction began in 1965. Thirteen years later, the city had a gorgeous new public space. The best view in town is found atop the Corning Tower Observation Deck (Corning Tower, 42nd Fl., off the Empire Plaza exit in Albany, 518/474-2418, 10am-4pm Mon.-Fri.).

One of the most unusual sights on the plaza is a sculpture-like building called The Egg (Empire State Plaza, 518/473-1061, www.theegg.org), a custom-built performing arts center with two theaters and state-of-the-art acoustics.

Key to Rockefeller's vision was the incorporation of art into public spaces. (His mother, Abby Aldrich Rockefeller, had been instrumental in the founding of the Museum of Modern Art in New York City.) Accordingly, scattered throughout the plaza, inside and out, are pieces of the impressive New York State Art Collection (2978 Corning Tower, 1 Empire State Plaza, 518/474-2418, 7am-6pm Mon.-Fri.), featuring the work of New York State artists from the 1960s and 1970s. It is considered one of the most important collections of modern art in the country.

Currently, there are 92 paintings, sculptures, and tapestries displayed on the concourse, in building lobbies, and in outdoor spaces. The collection is especially strong in abstract art. Alexander Caldwell and Mark Rothko are among the best-known artists in the collection. Visitors may view the works anytime government offices are open.

The Plaza Visitor Center (518/474-2418, http://ogs.ny.gov), located off the main concourse, near The Egg, has maps and information on tours. Additional information booths are located at the north and south ends of the concourse. Take the Empire Plaza exit from I-787. There are several visitor parking lots around the plaza on Madison and Grand Streets, but it can be maddeningly difficult to find the entrances amid ongoing construction. Rates vary based on time of day, but $10 per day is about the going rate midweek, $5 per day on weekends and holidays.

New York State Museum

At the south end of the plaza, the New York State Museum (Madison Ave., 518/474-5877, www.nysm.nysed.gov, 9:30am-5pm Tues.-Sun., free) began in 1836 as a center for geological and natural history exhibits. Over the years, it has maintained a core focus on geology, biology, anthropology, and history as they relate to the state. Exhibits are organized by regions of the state covering everything from the Adirondack Wilderness to the marshland of the Long Island Sound and the A Train to Brooklyn. Particularly moving is the 9/11 exhibit, which includes artifacts recovered from the wreckage of the Twin Towers. The fourth-floor carousel is popular with children. They can ride any of 36 horses, two donkeys, and two deer—all carved around 1895 by Charles Dare of Brooklyn and acquired by the museum in 1975.

The Executive Mansion

The state's governor lives in the New York Executive Mansion (138 Eagle St., 518/473-7521, www.governor.ny.gov), one block south of the Empire State Plaza. The home was built in the 1850s and has housed governors and their families since 1875, including Theodore Roosevelt and Franklin Delano Roosevelt. Public rooms contain exquisite artwork and furnishings from the 18th, 19th, and 20th centuries. Guided tours (10am, 11am, noon, 1pm, and 2pm Thurs. Sept.-June) are for groups of 10-30, reservations required.

★ The Capitol Building

The Capitol Building (Washington Ave., 518/474-2418) that towers over State Street hill, adjacent to the north end of the Empire State Plaza, looks more like a European castle than a U.S. state capitol. A stunning set of stairs climbs up to three grand archways, featuring elaborate stone carvings. Construction began by hand in 1867 and took 30 years to complete, by which time Theodore Roosevelt had become governor. The final price tag was an astronomical $25 million.

The New York State Assembly conducts its business inside. You can take a free **guided tour** of the building (10am, noon, 2pm, and 3pm Mon.-Fri., excluding holidays). A number of lively inns and restaurants are clustered along State Street, within a short walk for business travelers and midweek lunch-goers.

From the Empire State Plaza, it is a short walk down State Street to Broadway and one of Albany's newest outdoor spaces: The **Hudson River Way** is a pedestrian bridge that crosses over I-787 to **Albany Riverfront Park,** in the Corning Preserve (518/434-2032), where residents come to walk their dogs or read a book on warm afternoons. Along the path, murals depict Albany's long and colorful history.

Follow Broadway a few blocks farther north to reach the **Albany Heritage Area Visitors Center** (25 Quackenbush Square, 800/258-3582, www.albany.org, 9am-4pm Mon.-Fri., 10am-3pm Sat., 11am-3pm Sun.), a good place to get an overview of the history and culture of the Capital Region and then enjoy a cold beer at the adjoining microbrewery.

From there, it's a short drive to the handsome **Ten Broeck Mansion** (9 Ten Broeck Place, 518/436-9826, www.tenbroeckmansion. org, 10am-4pm Thurs.-Fri., 1pm-4pm Sat.-Sun. mid May-mid Oct., adults $5, students and seniors $4, under age 13 $3), where the Albany County Historical Association has set up shop. The Federal-style home was originally built by Abraham Ten Broeck, a distinguished general and statesman who fought at the Battle of Saratoga and later served as mayor of Albany. More than two decades after the wealthy Olcott family had donated the renovated building to the city, museum staff discovered a fully stocked wine cellar in the basement. Many of the surrounding buildings in the once-exclusive Arbor Hill district have been converted into urban apartments. Mansion tours must be booked in advance. On Wednesdays, there is an outdoor Architecture & Garden Talk offered at 1pm.

★ Lark Street and Washington Park

Many of Albany's events, including the popular spring tulip festival, take place in **Washington Park** (www. washingtonparkconservancy.org), a 90-acre green space in the center of the city that has been public property since the 17th century. Jogging trails circle a small lake and a handful of statues and monuments across the park. A bronze statue of Scottish poet Robert Burns was created by a local sculptor in 1888. The King Fountain was made of rocks from Storm King Mountain in Orange County. Though the park is well loved, it's rarely crowded, and students can always find a quiet place to read. Playgrounds are a draw for kids.

At the east end of the park, bohemian Lark Street is Albany's answer to Manhattan's East Village. This is the neighborhood of choice for Friday drinks or Sunday brunch. Several blocks of funky shops and trendy eateries between State and Madison Streets attract the city's hippest residents. You'll find everything from vintage video games to boutique clothing and jewelry designers and espresso art.

The historic Center Square neighborhood, bound by Lark, State, Swan, and Jay Streets, connects the Lark Street district to the Empire State Plaza. Stroll through its quiet streets to see rows of brick, brownstone, and clapboard houses more than 100 years old.

Albany Institute of History and Art

For a lasting impression of Hudson River Valley history and culture, save a few hours to visit one of the oldest museums in the United States. Outdating the Smithsonian, the Metropolitan Museum of Art, and even the Louvre, the **Albany Institute of History and Art** (125 Washington Ave., 518/463-4478, www.albanyinstitute.org, 10am-5pm Wed.-Sat., noon-5pm Sun., adults $10, seniors and students $8, ages 6-12 $6, under age 6

1: Albany Tulip Festival at Washington Park
2: Empire State Plaza

free, free to all 5pm-8pm Thurs.) was established in 1791. The museum has increasingly broadened its focus over the years to include Hudson River School paintings, artifacts from colonial times, and 19th-century American sculpture. You can easily spend a couple of hours here and still want to return for more.

Schuyler Mansion State Historic Site

Major General Philip Schuyler's home (32 Catherine St., 518/434-0834, http://parks. ny.gov, 11am-5pm Wed.-Sun. mid-May-Oct., adults $5, seniors and students $4, under age 13 free) was an important base of operations during the Revolutionary War and is now a New York state historic site. Tours begin on the hour, and the last tour begins at 4pm. The house was closed for renovations in 2021.

USS *Slater*

The only restored World War II destroyer escort, once part of a fleet of more than 500 ships, now rests on the Hudson River at the Port of Albany, as a monument, memorial, and museum dedicated to all the destroyer escorts and their crews. The Allied forces used destroyer escorts to protect convoys of supply ships that were essential to the war effort. The USS *Slater* DE766 is a cannon-class destroyer that was built in less than one month and commissioned in May 1944. It served in both the Atlantic and Pacific theaters.

After the war, the ship was transferred to Greece as part of the Military Defense Assistance Program. The ship was active in Greece until 1991, and in 1993, the Destroyer Escort Sailors Association raised enough funding to bring the USS *Slater* back to the United States. Restoration has been ongoing for nearly two decades, entirely funded by volunteers. A group of veterans visits each fall and stays on board for a week to chip, repaint, and polish various parts of the vessel. Their work is highly detailed—cabins, bunks, and even the refrigeration room look just as they did in the 1940s, thanks to many donated artifacts.

In spring, summer, and fall, the ship is open for **guided tours** (141 Broadway, Albany, 518/431-1943, www.ussslater.org, 10am-4pm Wed.-Sun. Apr.-Nov., adults $9, seniors $8, ages 6-14 $7, under age 6 free). In winter, it moves one mile south to Rensselaer. The one-hour tour covers several levels of the ship, including the galley, captain's cabin, officers' cabins, and the communications center. Visitors are led up and down ladders and through the narrow hallways of the lower decks. Kids may be invited to try on a helmet and sit in the cannon seats. One of the most interesting aspects of the tour is the retelling of stories shared by previous visitors who served in the military during World War II. The USS *Slater* does not receive taxpayer funding; donations are greatly appreciated.

ALBANY COUNTY

Historic Cherry Hill

South of downtown Albany, **Historic Cherry Hill** (523½ S. Pearl St., 518/434-4791, www. historiccherryhill.org, guided tours 1pm, 2pm, and 3pm Fri., 10am-4pm Sat., adults $6, seniors and students $5, ages 12-18 $3) was once the center of a working farm that belonged to the Van Rensselaer family. A hodgepodge of collections inside the 1787 Colonial-style home document the lives of four generations of the family, ending with Catherine Bogart Putnam Rankin, the great-granddaughter of Philip and Maria Van Rensselaer. On display are ceramics, silver, textiles, books, and photographs.

The home is also known as the site of a famous murder in 1827. Author Louis C. Jones chronicled the story in a book called *Murder at Cherry Hill* and also referred to the murder in a better-known book of ghost stories, *Things That Go Bump in the Night*. From I-787, take exit 2.

Watervliet Shaker Historic District

In the shadow of the Albany Airport stands an intriguing slice of history, the **Watervliet Shaker Historic District** (875 Watervliet

Shaker Rd., 518/456-7890, http://home.shakerheritage.org, 10am-4pm Tues.-Sat. Mar.-Oct., 11am-5pm Tues.-Sun. mid-Oct.-mid-Dec.) and the site of the first American Shaker settlement. The first group of Shakers arrived here in 1776 with the founder of the movement, Ann Lee, and built a log cabin as the first communal dwelling. Over the years, the community grew to 350 people, and the last members left the site in 1938.

Visitors can explore several buildings, beginning with a museum in the 1848 Shaker Meeting House. Outside are an herb garden, barnyard, and network of trails around a nature preserve. Lee and other early members are buried in the Shaker Cemetery on the property. Guided tours (11:30am and 1:30pm Sat. June-Oct.) are offered. This is a convenient place to let young kids run around before or after a long flight to or from Albany.

Albany Pine Bush Preserve

A dry and sandy 3,200-acre preserve just outside of Albany is a geological wonder because it looks like it belongs on the coast, with pitch pines and scrub oak dotting the landscape. This is prime habitat for the endangered Karner blue butterfly, which feeds on blue lupine growing in the dry clearings of the rare pine barrens ecosystem. Visit the **Albany Pine Bush Discovery Center** (195 New Karner Rd., Albany, 518/456-0655, www.albanypinebush.org, 9am-4pm Thurs.-Fri., 10am-4pm Sat.-Sun., free) to get acquainted with the wildlife and trails in the preserve. The preserve is open 24 hours daily year-round for hiking and recreation. Keep an eye out for creatures large and small: Fishers, white-tailed deer, cottontail rabbits, and red and gray foxes all call this area home. Plan your visit in late May, when the lupine is in full bloom, to increase your chances of seeing the Karner blue butterfly.

John Boyd Thacher State Park

West of Albany, **John Boyd Thacher State Park** (1 Hailes Cave Rd., Voorheesville,

518/872-1237, http://parks.ny.gov, 8am-dusk daily, vehicles $6) celebrated its 100th anniversary in 2014. It encompasses the **Helderberg Escarpment,** a six-mile-long limestone cliff that contains billion-year-old fossils and rock formations. Even amateur geologists will be able to spot the distinct change in rock formations as they climb and descend the staircases of the **Indian Ladder,** an 80-foot cliff on top of the escarpment. The ladder itself is only 0.4 mile each way; an easy loop hike (2.5 miles) leads one back to the time when the area surrounding Albany was covered by a warm tropical sea. (Note the trail is closed November-April.) For an informative geology lesson, call to sign up for a **guided tour** (518/872-0800) with the park interpreter.

Besides the geological features, the park offers panoramic views of the Adirondack and Berkshire Mountains and of Vermont's Green Mountains. Residents fought hard to keep this park open when budget cuts swept the state. Twelve miles of trails accommodate hiking, mountain biking, cross-country skiing, snowshoeing, and snowmobiling. Also on the premises are an Olympic-size swimming pool, basketball and volleyball courts, playgrounds, ball fields, and picnic areas.

Rensselaerville

In the southwest corner of Albany County lies the 200-year-old hamlet of Rensselaerville (not to be confused with the Rensselaer County city of Rensselaer), named for the Dutch patroon who ran the local manor. Due to its remote location, the site was settled relatively late by colonial standards—in the 1780s—by Revolutionary War veterans from Long Island and New England. A number of handsome 19th-century buildings have been preserved along Main Street, including the original gristmill. **The Grist Mill Museum** (Main St., Rensselaerville, 10am-3pm Wed. and noon-2pm Sat. Memorial Day-Labor Day) is part of the local historical society. Today, they house a dozen antiques shops and restaurants. There is also a 2,000-acre preserve with 10 miles of trails for hiking and exploring the

Walt Whitman's Long Path

The 326-mile Long Path got its name from a line in a famous Walt Whitman poem, "Song of the Open Road":

Afoot and light-hearted I take to the open road, Healthy, free, the world before me, The long brown path before me leading wherever I choose.

The trail begins at the George Washington Bridge between Upper Manhattan and Fort Lee, New Jersey, and meanders up and across the Hudson River Valley, eventually making its way to the northern terminus at John Boyd Thacher State Park.

Catskill Creek. To get to Rensselaerville, take I-90 to Route 85 west, and follow Route 85 for 12 miles.

Five Rivers Environmental Education Center

Ten miles of trails meander across fields and streams at this New York State Department of Environmental Conservation park. The **visitors center** (56 Game Farm Rd., Delmar, 518/475-0291, www.dec.ny.gov) has nature-themed exhibits, maps, and guides. A variety of outdoor education programs are held throughout the year. Wildlife includes the eastern bluebird, pileated woodpecker, wood duck, snapping turtle, and great horned owl.

RECREATION
Winter Sports

Hockey and figure skating are popular winter activities in the Albany area. Empire State Plaza and the Albany County Hockey Training Facility have rinks with public skate sessions. Nordic skiers will find trails at John Boyd Thacher State Park and at the 400-acre **Five Rivers Environmental Education Center** (56 Game Farm Rd., Delmar, 518/475-0291, www.dec.ny.gov). For downhill skiers, Windham and Hunter Mountains are a half-hour away in the Upper Hudson River Valley, while the higher and steeper slopes of Gore Mountain await in the Adirondacks.

The **Empire State Plaza Ice Rink** (279 Madison Ave., 877/659-4377, www.winter. empirestateplaza.org, noon-8pm Tues.-Sun.

Dec.-Mar., $4 adults, $3 children) offers views of the state capitol during winter skating excursions. The rink provides rentals and also has a skate lounge with lockers and music, as well as an on-site café. Note that some form of collateral, such as a driver's license, is required for rentals. The rink often hosts special events, such as meet-and-greets with Olympic skaters and special skate clinics.

Hiking

Several short hiking trails meander through **John Boyd Thacher State Park** (1 Hailes Cave Rd., Voorheesville, 518/872-1237, http:// parks.ny.gov). The longest is the final stretch of the **Long Path** (3.2 miles one-way, moderate), with several valley views and two waterfalls to see. The **Nature Center Trail** (1.1 miles) makes for an easy wooded loop from Thompson's Lake, with waterfall views.

The **Albany Pine Bush Preserve** (http:// albanypinebush.org) has about 20 miles of multiple-use trails. Most of the loops are about a mile long. For example, from the Blueberry Hill West parking area, you can follow the red trail 1.1 miles to the top of a dune that presents views to the south and west.

At the **Five Rivers Environmental Education Center,** the **North Loop** (2 miles) takes you through forests along the property boundary for a moderately challenging route.

Backpackers should continue north to the Adirondack Park for overnight hikes in the backcountry.

Cycling and Mountain Biking

The 41-mile-long **Mohawk-Hudson Bikeway** connects Albany, Schenectady, and Troy along the Hudson and Mohawk Rivers. Call 518/372-5656 for a free map. The **Mohawk-Hudson Cycling Club** (www. mohawkhudsoncyclingclub.org) organizes road and mountain biking trips within an 80-mile radius of the Albany-Schenectady-Troy area, including a September Century Weekend that begins in Saratoga Spa State Park and Mountain Bike Festival at **Grafton Lakes State Park** (100 Grafton Lakes State Park Way, Grafton, 518/279-1155, http://parks. ny.gov) outside Troy.

In addition, several hundred cyclists participate each summer in the **Cycling the Erie Canal Tour** (518/434-1583, www.ptny. org/canaltour, $1,200), an eight-day ride from Buffalo to Albany covering roughly 50 miles a day. The fee includes camping, meals, entertainment, and riding support.

Albany also can be the starting point for a multiday self-guided bike tour of the Hudson River Valley. Order a guide with step-by-step directions and detailed maps from **Parks & Trails New York** (www.ptny.org).

Stop by the **Downtube Bicycle Works** (466 Madison Ave., 518/434-1711, www. downtubebicycleworks.com, noon-6pm Tues.-Fri., 11am-4pm Sat.) in a convenient downtown location, for gear and information.

Mountain bikers can find lengthy trail systems at John Boyd Thacher State Park, Grafton Lakes State Park, and Albany Pine Bush Preserve.

Golf

Capital Hills at Albany (65 O'Neil Rd., 518/438-2208, www.caphills.com, $32-41), designed in 1929, maintains a challenging public course (18 holes) with tough closing holes and considerable elevation change. Rent a cart unless you're looking for a cardio workout. Ten miles north of Albany, **Mill Road Acres Golf Course** (30 Mill Rd., Latham, 518/785-4653, www.millroadacres.com, $27.50-31.50) has a well-maintained nine-hole course.

River Cruises

Dutch Apple Cruises (Madison Ave. and Broadway, Albany, 518/463-0220, www. dutchapplecruises.com) operates several sightseeing tours per week from Snow Dock in the Port of Albany, right next to the USS *Slater* museum.

ENTERTAINMENT AND EVENTS
Performing Arts

The twin theaters inside **The Egg** (Empire State Plaza, 518/473-1061, box office 518/473-1845, www.theegg.org) showcase theater, dance, music, and comedy. Performances at The Egg have included George Thorogood & The Destroyers, Keb' Mo', Béla Fleck & The Flecktones, Ray Manzarek and Robby Krieger of The Doors, Golden Dragon Chinese Acrobats, Hot Tuna, and Steven Wright.

Spectrum 8 Theatres (290 Delaware Ave., 518/449-8995, www.spectrum8.com, adults $10, seniors $8, under age 14 $7.50) is the place to catch an indie film along with some of the best movie snacks around.

Founded in 1931, the **Albany Symphony Orchestra** (19 Clinton Ave., 518/465-4755, www.albanysymphony.com) plays at the Palace Theatre near Quackenbush Square. Its programs often emphasize contemporary or overlooked American works.

Steamer No. 10 Theatre (500 Western Ave., 518/438-5503, www.steamer10theatre. org) is a nonprofit group that produces and presents shows for children and families, as well as tours schools and theaters throughout the Northeast. In addition to its professional cast, there is a children's theater that holds family-friendly productions, special acting classes, and children's workshops, as well as Shakespeare in the Park each July-August in Lincoln Park.

The Rolling Stones once played at the **Palace Theatre** (19 Clinton Ave., 518/465-3334, www.palacealbany.com), a restored 1933 theater that has hosted the likes of Chris Tucker, Stone Temple Pilots, and the Moscow Ballet.

Bars and Nightlife

Albany boasts a colorful nightlife scene, with many bars and clubs along Pearl and Lark Streets. **Speakeasy 518** (42 Howard St., 518/449-2332, www.speakeasy518.com, 7pm-close Thurs.-Sat.) is an upscale bar in true 1920s style, complete with oil lamps on each table, brick walls, a roaring fire, and a menu of Prohibition era-inspired drinks. Cell phones are not welcome, and reservations are required.

Nine Pin Cider Works (929 Broadway, 518/449-9999, www.ninepincider.com) makes hard ciders from apples grown in the Capital District and throughout the Hudson River Valley. The tasting room (11am-9pm Mon.-Wed., 11am-10pm Thurs., 11am-11pm Fri.-Sat., 11am-7pm Sun.) is an opportunity to try a glass of cider or purchase merchandise. Tours are also available by appointment.

ADCo Bar & Bottle Shop (75 Livingston Ave., 518/621-7191, www.albanydistilling.com, 4pm-10pm Tues.-Thurs., 4pm-midnight Fri., 2pm-midnight Sat.) is the first licensed distillery in Albany since Prohibition. On the tasting menu are its small-production whiskies, rums, and vodkas. Tours of the distillery (78 Montgomery St., 3pm most Sat.) are offered; reserve on the website.

In the historic telephone company building, **City Beer Hall** (42 Howard St., 518/449-2337, http://thecitybeerhall.com, 4pm-midnight Wed.-Thurs., 4pm-2am Fri., 11am-2am Sat., 11am-3pm Sun.) has 18 rotating beers and ciders on tap, plus a long list of special brews and a full bar. On weekend nights, the upper level becomes a dance floor, with DJs spinning tunes until 2am.

The Hollow Bar + Kitchen (79 N. Pearl St., 518/426-8550, www.thehollowalbany.com, 4pm-10pm Mon.-Tues., 11:30am-10pm Wed.-Thurs., 11:30am-midnight Fri., 4pm-midnight Sat.) occupies another historic building within walking distance to the Times Union Center.

This is a great place to enjoy craft beer with live music, or in warmer months, a cocktail on the sidewalk patio. The eclectic menu includes pub fare, salads, burgers, and heartier entrées, with lots of gluten-free and vegetarian options.

Festivals

For almost 60 years, Albany residents have celebrated their Dutch heritage with the annual **Albany Tulip Festival** (Washington Park, 518/434-2032, www.albanyevents.org), which coincides each year with Mother's Day in May. Sample an array of foods and live music while you admire the massive display of flowers. Lark Street has a festival for just about every season. One Saturday each September, the street closes to traffic to host **LarkFEST,** with music, food, and entertainment. **Art on Lark** takes place in June, with hundreds of artists exhibiting or performing their works. And **Winter WonderLARK** is a December event, complete with ice sculptures, holiday shopping, and runners sprinting the length of the street in their Speedos. Details for all of these events are at www.larkstreet.org.

Spectator Sports

Before visiting Albany, check the **Times Union Center** (formerly the Pepsi Arena, 51 S. Pearl St., 518/487-2000, www.timesunioncenter-albany.com) website for upcoming events. You might be able to catch a monster truck show, the latest mega-concert, or an NBA game. The arena is the home to the AHL (American Hockey League) Albany Devils, Albany Firebirds (arena football), and the Siena Saints college basketball team.

SHOPPING

Albany-area shopping malls draw consumers from hours away for a healthy dose of retail therapy. With key stores including Dick's Sporting Goods, Athleta, Apple, Macy's, and H&M, the **Crossgates Mall** (1 Crossgates Mall Rd., 518/869-9565, www.shopcrossgates.com, 10am-9pm daily), in Guilderland, a

1: The Egg, a performing arts venue **2:** a trail in John Boyd Thacher State Park **3:** sightseeing with Dutch Apple Cruises suburb of Albany, may be the largest remaining mall in New York State.

For a funkier selection of clothing and locally made crafts, head to the shops on Lark Street in downtown Albany. Among the many boutiques and antiques shops is **Elissa Halloran Designs** (229 Lark St., 518/432-7090, noon-6pm Tues.-Sun.), which carries women's apparel and handmade jewelry. Lark Street also has a fun retro video game store, **Pastime Legends Video Games** (292 Lark St., 518/512-5353, www.pastimelegends.com, noon-5pm Mon., 11am-6pm Tues. and Sun., 10am-7pm Fri.-Sat.).

Bookstores

The Book House of Stuyvesant Plaza (1475 Western Ave. and Fuller Rd., 518/489-4761, www.bhny.com, 10am-6pm Mon.-Sat., noon-5pm Sun.) is a delightful independent bookstore featuring local authors in Albany's Stuyvesant Plaza outlet mall.

Farm Stands

After checking out the Helderberg Escarpment, pay a visit in spring, summer, or early fall to **Indian Ladder Farms** (342 Altamont Voorheesville Rd., Altamont, 518/765-2956, www.indianladderfarms. com, store 10am-4pm Wed.-Fri., 10am-5pm Sat.-Sun.) to pick your own apples, raspberries, and blueberries. You can also pick your own strawberries in season at **Altamont Orchards** (6654 Dunnsville Rd., Altamont, 518/861-6515, www.altamontorchards.com, store 10am-5pm Mon.-Fri., 9:30am-4:30pm Sat.-Sun.).

The **Empire State Plaza Farmers Market** (10am-2pm Wed. and Fri. May-Oct.) happens twice a week in summer and then moves indoors to the concourse (10am-2pm Wed. only Oct.-Apr.). The **Downtown Albany Farmers Market** gets going at SUNY Plaza (Broadway and State St., 11am-2pm Thurs.). And the **Delmar Farmers Market** can be found at Bethlehem Middle School (332 Kenwood Ave., Delmar, 9am-1pm Sat. May-Oct.). Among other local goods, you can buy all kinds of maple products from Maple Hill Farms, which is based in Cobleskill.

Near Grafton Lakes State Park, **Soul Fire Farm** (1972 NY-2, Petersburg, 518/880-9372, www.soulfirefarm.org, by appointment) is a unique, mission-driven organization that follows ancestral farming practices and Afro-Indigenous agroforestry principles to restore food sovereignty. The farm offers monthly tours during the growing season, as well as events and workshops related to its charter.

FOOD

There are hundreds of restaurants to choose from in the Albany metropolitan area. A steady stream of politicians and financial executives support a diverse and upscale restaurant scene downtown.

Surf and Turf

One of the oldest and most traditional establishments is ★ **Jack's Oyster House** (42 State St., 518/465-8854, www.jacksoysterhouse.com, 5pm-9pm Mon.-Sat., 3pm-8pm Sun., $22-54), a turn-of-the-20th-century tavern with a dark wood interior that creates a formal but not stuffy atmosphere. During the busy lunch hour, waiters dressed in snappy uniforms whisk about the dining room carrying trays of fresh oysters from the raw bar. Steaks pair well with the restaurant's private-label red wine from Silverado Vineyards in California.

Inside the Hampton Inn & Suites, **Yono's Restaurant** (25 Chapel St., 518/436-7747, www.yonos.com, 5pm-10pm Mon.-Wed. and Fri.-Sat., $21-36) feels a bit old-fashioned with its ornate dining room, round tables, live piano music, and formal service. But the food is first-rate, representing a who's who of Hudson River Valley farms. Flavors hint of Indonesian and continental cuisine: hand-rolled vegetable *lumpia, satay* four ways, pan-seared Hudson River Valley foie gras, and lobster curry tamarind soup.

Chef Yono also oversees the more casual **dp: An American Brasserie** (25 Chapel St., 518/436-3737, www.dpbrasserie.com,

5pm-10pm Mon.-Wed. and Fri.-Sat., $16-39), with a menu of small plates, steak frites, salad entrées, and burgers. A Pimm's cocktail at the casual bar hits the spot on a summer evening. ★ **Angelo's 677 Prime** (677 Broadway, at Clinton Ave., 518/427-7463, www.677prime. com, 5pm-10pm Mon.-Sat., $25-179) is an excellent steak house and wine bar centrally located in Albany's theater district. Chopped or wedge salads, caviar, and a full raw bar complement a menu of Kobe beef, steak au poivre, and a 40-ounce porterhouse for two. You can also start with French onion soup or lobster bisque or crispy cauliflower cakes.

Taverns and Pubs

Savoy Taproom (301 Lark St., 518/599-5140, www.savoyonlark.com, 5pm-midnight Sun.-Thurs., 5pm-1am Fri.-Sat., $16-32) dates all the way back to 1936. It continues to stay open late, with a rotating old-fashioned cocktail and an entire menu of Moscow Mule selections. The dinner menu covers a lot of ground, from stir fry to steak frites.

Next door to the visitors center, ★ **C. H. Evans Brewing Company at the Albany Pump Station** (19 Quackenbush Square, 518/447-9000, www.evansale.com, noon-8pm Wed.-Thurs., noon-10pm Fri.-Sat., noon-8pm Sun., $15-25) occupies the 1874 pump station, which once drew water from the Hudson River to the tune of seven billion gallons a year. The owner comes from a family with a long history of brewing in the area. The original Evans family brewery was located in Hudson. The modern-day microbrewery and restaurant serves award-winning brews that include the Quackenbush Blonde, Evans Whit, and the Kick-Ass Brown. Beer influences the menu as well, appearing in the pale-ale battered red onion rings and beer-battered fish-and-chips. Other notable dishes include the grass-fed beef smoked chili and harvest medley salad.

The **City Beer Hall** (42 Howard St., 518/449-2337, http://thecitybeerhall.com, 4pm-midnight Wed.-Thurs., 4pm-2am Fri., 11am-2am Sat., 11am-3pm Sun., $10-17) is

a nice spot for Sunday brunch, with entrées such as a creole breakfast bowl, steak and eggs, or the beer hall burger. Other times of day, you get a free slice of pizza with your drink, or you can order small and large plates of southern fried chicken, pulled pork, falafel, and ramen. Late night snacks include pickles, potato chips, and maple bacon peanuts.

Close to the airport, **Innovo Kitchen** (1214 Troy-Schenectady Rd., Latham, 518/608-1466, https://innovokitchen.com, 11:30am-9pm Mon.-Sat., $15-46) has a fantastic Bloody Mary bar with all the fixin's. Food on the wide-ranging menu tastes pretty good, too. Stop by for the popular Taco Tuesday menu, served 3pm-9pm.

Authentic Cajun culture defines the experience at **Parish Public House** (388 Broadway, 518/465-0444, www.parishpublichouse.com, 11am-10pm Mon.-Fri., noon-10pm Sat., noon-8pm Sun., $12-25), a lively venue for food, drinks, and live music. You'll eat plates of jambalaya, crawfish, or shrimp and grits while local bands and ensembles perform for the crowd.

Choose from 26 beers on tap at **McGeary's Irish Pub** (4 Clinton Square, 518/463-1455, www.mcgearyspub.com, 11am-10pm daily, $9-18). Outdoor dining is offered in a small front patio in Clinton Square, near the intersection of North Pearl and Clinton Streets.

International

Athos Restaurant (1814 Western Ave., 518/608-6400, www.athosrestaurant.com, 4:30pm-close Mon.-Thurs., 4pm-close Fri.-Sun., $22-36) brings the flavors of Greece to the Capital District. Chef Lou graduated from the Culinary Institute and worked previously at Jack's Oyster House.

El Mariachi Tapas (289 Hamilton St., 518/432-7580, 11:30am-9pm Mon.-Thurs., 11:30am-10pm Fri., 3pm-10pm Sat.; 271 Lark St., 518/465-2568, 4pm-10pm Thurs.-Sat., www.elmariachisrestaurant.com, $10-26) serves both Spanish- and Mexican-themed small plates. The full tequila bar and homemade sangria are a plus. Local students prefer the cheap eats and Ms. Pac-Man game at **Bombers Burrito Bar** (258 Lark St., 518/463-9636, www.bombersburritobar. com, 11am-2am Mon.-Wed., 11am-3am Thurs.-Sat., 11am-1am Sun., $9-15). Look for a second location downtown in the Empire State Plaza food court. For a modern take on Mexican street food, head downtown to ★ **Ama Cocina** (4 Sheridan Ave., 518/776-4550, www.amacocina.com, 5pm-8pm Tues.-Wed., noon-9pm Thurs., noon-10pm Fri.-Sat., $10-15). Everything is made in-house, from plates of *chicharrones* to the Big Bad-Ass Burrito Box and the signature chili-seasoned street corn.

More than 100 Italian restaurants are scattered across the Albany area, but a few of them manage to rise above the rest. For northern Italian convenient to downtown, grab a table at **Café Capriccio** (49 Grand St., 518/465-0439, www.cafecapriccio.com, 5pm-9pm daily, $20-55). For a little romance and Italian fare with a sophisticated twist, head to **Nicole's Restaurant** (556 Delaware Ave., 518/436-4952, www.nicolescatering.com, 5pm-9pm Wed.-Thurs., 5pm-10pm Fri.-Sat., 4pm-8pm Sun., $18-39), with a quiet courtyard surrounded by flowers. Supersize plates of pasta and giant bottles of chianti define the southern Italian experience at **Buca di Beppo** (44 Wolff Rd., Colonie, 518/459-2822, www.bucadibeppo.com, 11am-9:30pm daily, $15-25), outside Albany.

Bistros

The focal point of the **New World Bistro Bar** (300 Delaware Ave., 518/694-0520, 5pm-9pm Tues.-Sat., $22-38), an 80-seat gastro pub in Albany's Delaware Avenue neighborhood, is an art deco mahogany bar from the 1939 World's Fair. Menus here rotate seasonally to allow for organic, locally sourced ingredients. Classics such as a grass-fed double cheeseburger and pork schnitzel join innovative dishes that include smoked trout cakes and a vegetarian cassoulet. Vegan and gluten-free menus are also available. Reservations are strongly recommended.

Cafés and Quick Bites

Paesan's (289 Ontario St., 518/435-0312, www.paesanspizza.com, 11am-midnight Sun.-Thurs., 11am-1am Fri.-Sat., $10-25) has mastered the art of the thin-crust pizza. Most weekdays, a host of vendors congregate on the lawn behind the capitol building serving lunch to go. A slice of pizza or a couple of tacos are among the best deals around.

In business since 1976, **The Daily Grind** (204 Lark St., 888/876-3222, www.dailygrind. com, 7am-3pm daily) is a European-style coffee bar and café that roasts its own beans. Breakfast and lunch dishes range $7-10.

The **Iron Gate Café** (182A Washington Ave., 518/445-3555, www.irongatecafe.com, 9am-3pm Wed.-Mon., $7-16) appeals to weekday lunch-goers. Sandwiches include a mushroom melt, turkey BLAT, and ever-popular buffalo chicken.

Cheesemongers

The Cheese Traveler (540 Delaware Ave., 518/443-0440, www.thecheesetraveler.com, 11am-6pm Tues.-Wed., 11am-7pm Thurs.-Fri., 10am-5pm Sat., noon-5pm Sun., $6-10) is owned by cheesemonger Eric Paul. He personally takes customers through the process of selecting just the right cheeses, while also providing background info and insight. The sandwich menu is small but impressive, featuring choices like the Sweet and Savory, which consists of Pawlett cheese, smoked duck breast, and blueberry jam on rustic Italian bread.

Culinary Events

In mid-April, the Downtown Albany Business Improvement District (http://downtownalbany.org, $25) organizes **Restaurant Week,** inviting thousands of diners to enjoy a three-course meal at participating eateries across the city. More than a dozen establishments participate, including Jack's Oyster House, The Albany Pump Station, and Café Capriccio.

If you're visiting in August, check the calendar for the **New York State Food Festival** (www.albany.com), a one-day event including a farmers market, more than 50 food vendors, and live music.

ACCOMMODATIONS

Albany's many business hotels are clustered downtown and near the airport. Unique properties are more difficult but not impossible to come by. Look near Washington Park and the Empire State Plaza.

$100-150

In the shadow of the state capitol buildings, the ★ **State Street Mansion Bed & Breakfast** (281 State St., 518/462-6780 or 800/673-5750, www.statestreetmansion. com, $130-165) is a three-story brownstone B&B with 12 amply furnished rooms and off-street parking. Smaller doubles with private bath run $130, while larger rooms with two queens go for $165. Flat-screen TVs with cable, wireless internet, and continental breakfast included.

The **Washington Park Inn** (634 Madison St., 518/930-4700, www.washingtonparkinn. com, $145) offers seven guest rooms plus a small business center in a great location on the park.

At the **Hilton Garden Inn-Albany Airport** (800 Albany Shaker Rd., 518/464-6666, $125), adjacent to the Albany Airport, the night staff has a tradition of buying breakfast for the last visitor to arrive for the night. A small pantry in the lobby has a variety of healthy snack foods for sale, since restaurants are hard to find at off hours. Rooms come with microwave ovens for simple meal preparation. This property completed a multimillion-dollar renovation in 2011, giving rooms and commons areas a modern look and feel. Rooms with one king or two full beds are basic but pleasant enough for a one-night stay, and you can't get any closer to the airport. The hotel has an inviting lobby, a swimming pool, free Wi-Fi, and high-definition TVs. Accessible rooms have modified baths to accommodate wheelchairs.

At the intersection of Wolf Road and the airport access road, **Hotel Indigo** (254 Old Wolf Rd., Latham, 518/869-9100, www. hotelindigo.com, $125-150) is a dressed-up motel, with contemporary decor and a small café on-site. The suites have small kitchenettes that work well for families. Guest rooms have parquet floors and brightly colored linens. Hotel amenities include a sauna, a fitness room, and internet access.

$150-200

Two heated pools and a day spa are among the amenities at **The Desmond** (660 Albany Shaker Rd., 518/869-8100, www. desmondhotelsalbany.com, from $151), primarily a business hotel and conference center with basic rooms in a complex of brick buildings near the airport. The on-site restaurant, Mr. D's, has an outdoor patio and American menu. Weekend packages include rooms and meals at discounted rates. Take exit 4 from I-87.

Among the most upscale accommodations in Albany is the four-room ★ **Morgan State House** (393 State St., 518/427-6063, www. statehouse.com, $150-254), where feather beds, robes, and down comforters make for a cozy night's stay. A 12-foot ceiling with skylights makes room 4B one of the best in the house.

One block from the state capitol and the Times Union Center, the **Hilton Albany** (40 Lodge St., 518/462-6611, www.hiltonalbany. com, $164-370) includes 384 modern rooms on 15 floors, plus a health club and a business center. Many rooms have views of either the Hudson River or capitol building.

INFORMATION AND SERVICES

The **Albany Visitors Center** (25 Quackenbush Square, 518/434-1217 or 800/258-3582, www.albany.org, 9am-4pm Mon.-Fri., 10am-3pm Sat., 11am-3pm Sun.) has a wealth of information on local attractions.

GETTING THERE AND AROUND

As a major transportation hub for the Catskill and Capital regions, Albany is easily reached by air, train, car, or bus. Many residents as far south as Dutchess County prefer to fly in and out of Albany International Airport than fight traffic around the New York City airports.

Bus

Dozens of local bus lines serve the Albany metro area. Check the website of the **Capital District Transportation Authority** (www. cdta.org, base fare $1.50 for three rides, unlimited day pass $3.90) for current routes and schedules.

Train

One of the most pleasant ways to get from New York City to the Capital Region is to board an **Amtrak** (800/872-7245, www. amtrak.com) train at Penn Station and follow the Hudson River for two hours north. Be sure to get a seat on the left side to catch the views the whole way up the river. Ride-shares and cabs are readily available from the Rensselaer station (525 East St., Rensselaer).

Car

Albany is a major metropolitan area with heavy traffic during commuting hours. I-87 and I-787 are the main north-south highways. The Albany Airport is at exit 13N on I-87. You can rent a car from any of the major chains at the Albany Airport.

Rensselaer County

The Taconic, Berkshire, and Green Mountains provide the backdrop for the pastoral setting of east Rensselaer County, while the cities of Troy and Rensselaer hug the Hudson River on the county's western side.

Members of the Van Rensselaer family were the original patroons of the area around Albany, and their name graces not only the county but also the town and the original engineering school in this country—Rensselaer Polytechnic Institute.

The meatpacking industry produced Troy's arguably best-known resident, Samuel Wilson (Uncle Sam), whose statue pays tribute to him near **Riverfront Park** downtown. Industry brought great wealth to the area, as witnessed by the elegant homes and the plethora of Tiffany glass found in this community.

The city quickly gives way to quieter small-town settings that dot the rest of the county. Opportunity for outdoor recreation abounds in two state parks, Grafton Lakes and Cherry Plain. Sinuous roads lead to oft-surprising small treasures of communities tucked away in the country. Farmers markets sell honey, maple sugar, and produce and range from small roadside stands to larger, well-developed markets.

TROY AND RENSSELAER

Troy

Known as the Collar City, Troy was at the heart of the Industrial Revolution. Stroll along its streets to see some of the finest examples of urban architecture in a concentrated area. The streetscapes appeared in the 1993 movie *The Age of Innocence.*

Known for its superb acoustic properties, the **Troy Savings Bank Music Hall** (30 2nd St., 518/273-0038, www.troymusichall.org) reflects beaux arts and French Renaissance influences. George B. Post, who also designed Chickering Hall in New York City, was the architect. The building was completed in 1875.

Just a few steps away, the **Rensselaer County Historical Society** (57 2nd St., 518/272-7232, www.rchsonline.org, noon-5pm Thurs.-Sat. Feb.-Dec. 23, closed major holidays) is located in the Joseph B. Carr Building. You can tour the neighboring

Troy

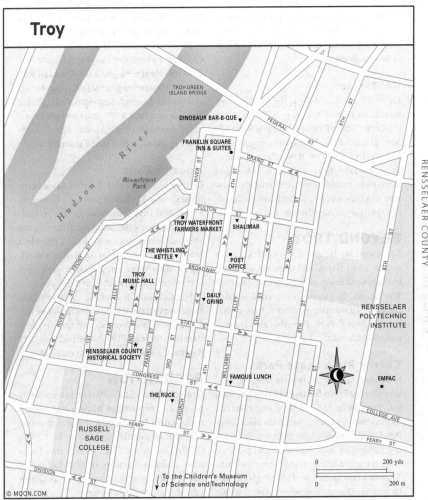

Federal-style **Hart-Cluett House** on the second Saturday of each month. Guided walking tours of Troy are also offered at 2pm on Saturdays.

Antiques shops, restaurants, and other stores line the streets of the downtown area. The **Troy Waterfront Farmers Market** (www.troymarket.org) is held outdoors in the summer at Monument Square (290 River St., 9am-2pm Sat. May-Oct.) and moves indoors for the winter at the Troy Atrium (49 4th St., 9am-2pm Sat. Nov.-Apr.).

South of downtown is the **Burden Iron Works Museum** (1 E. Industrial Pkwy., 518/274-5267, https://hudsonmohawkgateway. org, hours vary, call ahead), which used to cast bells, including the Centennial Bell that hangs in Independence Hall in Philadelphia, but now offers tours of Troy with themes including Tiffany glass and the Iron Works.

The **Children's Museum of Science and Technology** (250 Jordan Rd., 518/235-2120, www.cmost.org, 10am-5pm Mon.-Sat. July-Aug., $8) brings STEAM education to life with hands-on exhibits and daily planetarium shows. Young ones can tinker, craft, learn about nature, and explore the wonders of nanotechnology.

Rensselaer

Eight miles south of Troy, the smaller community of Rensselaer (pop. 9,392) features the Crailo State Historic Site (9½ Riverside Ave., 518/463-8738, http://parks.ny.gov, tours $5). Part of the Van Rensselaer patroonship, this farm bears the name of the Van Rensselaer estate in the Netherlands. Now used as a museum, its exhibits focus on the colonial history of New Netherland in the area.

BEYOND TROY

The urban landscape of Troy quickly gives way to small towns and open vistas as you travel toward the eastern parts of the county. The Taconic, Berkshire, and Green Mountains come into view as you pass through towns that include Averill Park, Petersburgh, Grafton, and Hoosick Falls.

Cherry Plain State Park

Near the Massachusetts state line, the 175-acre Cherry Plain State Park (10 State Park Rd., Petersburg, 518/733-5400, https://parks.ny.gov) features a sandy beach on Black River Pond. You can enjoy hike-in or trailer camping; fishing for bass, bullhead, and pickerel; and hiking and biking along the nature trails. There is a boat launch, and hunting is allowed in season. During the winter months, this park is a popular place for ice fishing, snowmobiling, and cross country skiing.

★ Grafton Lakes State Park

Local residents vote Long Pond Beach at pretty Grafton Lakes State Park (254 Grafton Lakes State Park Way, off Rte. 2, Grafton, 518/279-1155, http://parks.ny.gov, vehicles $6-8) the best in the Capital Region, beating out even Lake George in the Adirondacks. The park actually has six ponds, which appeal to anglers in search of rainbow and brown trout, as well as pickerel, perch, and bass. There are

25 miles of trails to explore and boat ramps with rentals at each of the ponds.

Watch for the tiny sign on Route 2, near Grafton Lakes, for the entrance to the Grafton Peace Pagoda (87 Crandall Rd., 518/658-9301, www.graftonpeacepagoda.org, call for information 8am-5pm daily). Peace pagodas date back 2,000 years and are a symbol of nonviolence. This is one of only a few peace pagodas located in the United States.

Hoosick Falls

Celebrated American folk artist Anna Mary Moses, who became known as Grandma Moses, was first discovered in this present-day town of a few thousand residents near the Vermont border. The town boasts a Grandma Moses-inspired mural on the wall of a building on Main Street, and the artist was buried here when she died in 1961 at the age of 101.

Hoosick Falls is also the gateway to the Bennington Battlefield (north side of Rte. 67 between Walloomsac and the Vermont state line, 518/686-7190, http://parks.ny.gov), the site of a Revolutionary War encounter.

RECREATION

Grafton Lakes State Park is known for its network of mountain biking and hiking trails. Long Pond Loop (2.5 miles) is one of the most popular to take by foot. Both Grafton Lakes and Cherry Plain State Parks offer swimming holes in the shadows of the mountains to the east, as well as cross-country ski trails in winter.

ENTERTAINMENT AND EVENTS

Nationally known artists perform at the Troy Savings Bank Music Hall (30 2nd St., Troy, 518/273-0038, www.troymusichall.org) throughout the year. Music at Noon is a free concert series usually held the second Tuesday of the month October-May. Check the website for a current schedule of events.

The Experimental Media and Performing Arts Center (8th St. and Congress St., Troy, 518/276-3921, www.

empac.rpi.edu) is housed at Rensselaer Polytechnic University. EMPAC is an effort to bridge the arts, sciences, and technology. Four different spaces host artists and researchers who are creating new ways to experience the senses. A full-service café (noon-3pm daily) is also open during performances, screenings, and events.

FOOD

Ask the innkeepers in the eastern part of the county what they recommend for dining, and they will suggest eating in Troy. Restaurants are few and far between in the east, but you will find a few local establishments in some of the larger villages.

Known for hot dogs that it ships worldwide, **Famous Lunch** (111 Congress St., Troy, 518/272-9481, www.famouslunch.net, 7am-10pm Mon.-Sat., under $10) is a Troy institution serving breakfast, lunch, and dinner.

For an ethnic food fix, **Shalimar** (407 Fulton St., Troy, 518/273-8744, www.shalimartroyny.com, noon-10pm daily, $11-16) offers a lunch buffet of Indian and Pakistani dishes.

Carnivores can rejoice in the selection at **Dinosaur Bar-B-Que** (377 River St., Troy, 518/308-0400, www.dinosaurbarbque.com, 11:30am-9pm Sun.-Mon., 11:30am-10pm Wed.-Thurs., 11:30am-11pm Fri.-Sat., $11-30), which serves a variety of chicken, pork, beef, and seafood in sauces like hoisin sesame, Memphis style, and Cajun. Sides are traditional barbecue fare, and 25 varieties of beer are on tap. Vegetarian options are sparse, but there are gluten-free options.

The outdoor patio and live music is the reason for a meal at **Paolo Lombardi's Ristorante** (104 W. Sand Lake Rd., Wyantskill, 518/283-0202, www.paolo lombardis.com, 4pm-9pm Tues.-Sat., 4pm-8pm Sun., mains $17-37). Traditional Italian dishes fill out the menu, with a few flourishes, including calamari that can be prepared in three different styles (classic, *aioli al limone*, or balsamic), a selection of seasonal risottos,

and the catch of the day prepared with lemon butter and herbs.

Since 1998, **The Ruck** (104 3rd St., Troy, 518/273-1872, www.getrucked.com, 4pm-midnight Mon.-Thurs., noon-2am Fri., 11am-2am Sat., 11am-midnight Sun.) has transformed from a dive bar into an establishment known for hearty pub fare and an impressive selection of foreign and domestic craft beers. The "Hangover Brunch" happens every Saturday and Sunday. If you order nothing else to eat, try the wings.

At the Gregory House inn, **La Perla** (3016 Rte. 43, Averill Park, 518/674-3774, www.gregoryhouse.com, 4pm-9pm Mon. and Wed.-Thurs., 4pm-10pm Fri.-Sat., 3pm-9pm Sun., $14-43) serves pizza, pasta, veal, beef, chicken, and seafood.

The ★ **Whistling Kettle Tea Stop & Cafe** (254 Broadway, Troy, 518/874-1938, www.thewhistlingkettle.com, 11am-6:30pm daily, $9-11) has a wide selection of teas (plus smoothies and hot chocolate) that you can sip with a scone or crepe—or buy a tin to go. Afternoon Tea service ($16) is a special treat. The shop has a second location in Ballston Spa and a third location in nearby Schenectady.

ACCOMMODATIONS

The options in Rensselaer County are limited, and you will need to book in advance if your trip coincides with a graduation or other important weekend. There are a few bed-and-breakfast inns scattered throughout the region and some interesting motels from which to choose. Downtown Albany accommodations are only a short drive away.

$100-150

Twelve uniquely themed rooms, including a Nautical Room, Adirondack Room, and Rose Garden, welcome guests to the ★ **Gregory House** (3016 Rte. 43, Averill Park, 518/674-3774, www.gregoryhouse.com, $125-160). All 12 rooms have private baths, and there is a pool for guests. The on-site restaurant offers authentic Italian cuisine.

Franklin Square Inn & Suites (1 4th St., Troy, 518/274-8800, www.franklinsquareinn. com, $110-300) is a Best Western property with 63 rooms and suites. Centrally located in downtown Troy, the inn is within walking distance of the Hudson River and downtown attractions. Rooms include continental breakfast; complimentary coffee, tea, and juice are available around the clock.

$150-200

Hidden off the road, the hilltop setting of the contemporary-style **Berkshire Mountain House** (150 Berkshire Way, Stephentown, 518/733-6923, $200) allows panoramic views of the nearby mountains. The main house consists of nine individually decorated rooms and one apartment. A separate house can accommodate up to 12 people or be rented as two separate two-bedroom apartments. Guests may walk the trail or take a dip in the pond. The inn is pet-friendly.

INFORMATION AND SERVICES

Troy no longer has a visitor center, but the **RiverSpark Hudson-Mohawk Heritage Area** website has current information at www.riverspark.org.

GETTING THERE AND AROUND

Bus

The **Capital District Transportation Authority** (110 Watervliet Ave., Albany, 518/482-8822, www.cdta.org) provides public bus service within Troy and to surrounding cities. The base fare is $1.50; an unlimited day pass is $3.90. The nearest Greyhound station is in downtown Albany.

Train

The closest rail connection is the Albany-Rensselaer **Amtrak station** (525 E. St., Rensselaer), approximately eight miles south of Troy and across the river from Albany. Taxis are available at the station.

Car

Rental cars are available at the Albany Airport; it takes approximately 20 minutes to reach Troy from the airport, depending on traffic.

Saratoga County

For the 40-mile stretch from Troy to Fort Edward, the Hudson River becomes an industrial conduit for the Champlain Canal, a shipping channel built in the early 19th century that extends all the way to the Canadian border. A series of locks and dams enables ships to navigate the changing elevation. The most impressive feat of aquatic engineering takes place at Waterford, where the Hudson merges with its largest tributary, the Mohawk River. Managing an elevation difference of 165 feet, the **Waterford Flight of Locks** are the highest in the world.

Route 4 follows the Hudson shoreline northward, passing by a handful of historic sites: On October 17, 1777, British General John Burgoyne surrendered to American General Horatio Gates in a decisive victory that convinced the French to join the American cause and marked the turning point of the Revolutionary War. **Saratoga National Historical Park** (648 Rte. 32, Stillwater, 518/664-9821, www.nps.gov/sara, free, pets OK) commemorates the battles of Saratoga and is now an admission-free park. A nine-mile tour road (Apr.-mid-Nov.) open to motorists, cyclists, walkers, joggers, and cross-country skiers winds through the 3,000-acre park and reenacts the battles that took place on surrounding farmlands and woods. The scenery alone is worth a side trip from Saratoga Springs. Watch for white-tailed deer,

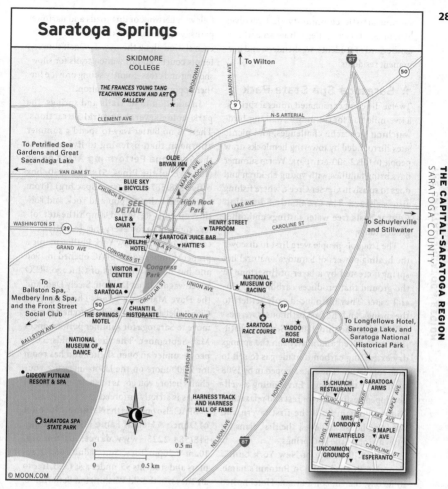

Saratoga Springs

red fox, and wild turkeys in the woods and fields, while red-tailed hawks and turkey vultures soar overhead. Park facilities include a visitors center, a museum, and a bookstore. The Battlefield Visitors Center is open 9am-5pm daily.

George Washington, Alexander Hamilton, and the Marquis de Lafayette all stayed at the summer residence of General Philip Schuyler, a few miles north in Schuylerville. Visitors can tour the **General Schuyler House** (Rte. 4, Schuylerville, 518/664-9821, free). It has guided tours (9:30am-4:30pm Fri.-Mon.

Memorial Day-Columbus Day); however, the house was closed in 2021 for renovations. Just off Route 4 is the 155-foot-tall **Saratoga Monument** (Rte. 4 and Rte. 32, Victory, 518/664-9821), built in 1877 to honor the historic Revolutionary War victory. It also was undergoing repair work in late 2021.

SARATOGA SPRINGS

The main reason to visit Saratoga County is to explore the Victorian town of Saratoga Springs. Natural hot springs, world-class horse racing, autumn apple picking, and a vibrant artistic community that revolves around Skidmore College draw an enthusiastic crowd of students, weekenders, and permanent residents.

★ Saratoga Spa State Park

Twelve different carbonated mineral springs, a five-mile trail for running or walking, birdwatching, geocache challenges, and picnic sites surrounded by towering hemlocks draw people to this 2,300-acre park. Warm summer days bring families with young children and dogs to splash in Geyser Creek, where fishing also is allowed. The Creekside Education Center hosts free water tastings and other guided tours.

The Iroquois people were first to discover the healing powers of Saratoga's natural hot springs, created by a layer of limestone in the ground that produces carbonated mineral water. They introduced early settlers to the springs, and the first bathhouses were established in the mid-1800s. Sensing profit, industry arrived and nearly ran the springs dry extracting carbon dioxide gas to sell to soda companies. The state stepped in by 1908 to preserve the springs. Envisioning a well-developed destination for rest and relaxation, Gideon Putnam built the first tavern and boarding house and drew the first plans for a town around the hot springs.

In 1930, the state of New York built a Georgian Revival hotel in Putnam's name. In its day, the Gideon Putnam Hotel hosted the likes of entertainers Bob Hope and Fred Astaire, as well as Chief Justice of the U.S. Supreme Court Charles Evans Hughes.

Today, visitors to Saratoga Spa State Park (19 Roosevelt Dr., 518/584-2535, http://parks.ny.gov, $10 per vehicle) can access the mineral baths through the Gideon Putnam Resort & Spa or the Lincoln Mineral Baths. The family-oriented Peerless Pool (adults $2, children $1) has a zero-depth entry and a waterslide. A second swimming area, the Victoria Pool (adults $8, children $4), is surrounded by brick buildings and arched walkways. The Five Mile Trail is an easy loop that

follows a network of dirt roads and narrower paths; you can sample the mineral water at each station along the way. Two golf courses, tennis courts, and in winter, trails for snowshoeing and cross-country skiing provide further opportunities for recreation.

In addition to its trails and springs, the park holds several cultural attractions: There is no better way to spend a summer afternoon than listening to live music at the Saratoga Performing Arts Center (108 Ave. of the Pines, 518/584-9330, box office 518/587-3330, www.spac.org). From opera and ballet to pop and rock and roll, this custom-designed amphitheater offers something for everyone. Initially conceived to give the New York Philharmonic a proper summer home, SPAC opened in 1966 and has hosted the likes of Chicago, REO Speedwagon, Janet Jackson, Steely Dan, and the Dave Matthews Band. The New York City Ballet and Philadelphia Orchestra both move to Saratoga for summer performances May-September. The theater holds 5,000 people under an open shelter and has room for 7,000 more on the lawn—measure your chairs before you go, as the height limit of 24 inches is strictly enforced.

SPAC also operates the National Museum of Dance & Hall of Fame (99 S. Broadway, 518/584-2225, www.dancemuseum.org, 10am-4:30pm Tues.-Sun., adults $6.50, seniors and students $5, under age 13 $3, free to all Tues.), in the old Washington Bath House, built in 1918. The Greek Revival building contains five galleries full of photographs, videos, books, and costumes that document all forms of dance, from ballet to tap. The museum hosts dance workshops, yoga classes, and special events.

The original Roosevelt Bathhouse, constructed in 1930, is part of the Gideon Putnam Resort & Spa (24 Gideon Putnam Rd., 866/890-1171, www.gideonputnam.com, $400). It holds a 13,000-square-foot spa with 42 private spa rooms. Guest rooms were renovated in 2018 after a major flood.

The Saratoga Automobile Museum

(110 Ave. of the Pines, 518/587-1935, www.saratogaautomuseum.org, 10am-5pm Wed.-Sun. Jan.-Mar., 10am-5pm daily Apr.-Sept., 10am-5pm Tues.-Sun. Oct.-Dec., adults $12, children $10) is located in a restored bottling plant inside the park. Ongoing exhibits celebrate the auto industry and racing in New York State, while visiting exhibits have included Cars & Culture of the 1950s as well as auto-themed photography and paintings.

★ Saratoga Race Course

At the next exit on I-87 is Saratoga's other main attraction, the **Saratoga Race Course** (267 Union Ave., 718/641-4700, www.nyra.com/saratoga, free parking). Featured in the contemporary book and movie *Seabiscuit*, the racetrack dates to 1863, making it the oldest continuously operating thoroughbred track in the country. Horse racing became wildly popular in the 1940s and 1950s, and the Saratoga Race Course has been a local institution ever since.

Saratoga's population of 27,000 triples during the monthlong summer racing season, from the end of July through Labor Day weekend. Tickets are affordable, and the scene is at once traditional and exciting. Women still don their Sunday best to watch from the grandstand. At the other end of the spectrum, diehard fans barbecue at their cars and watch from the parking lot without buying tickets at all. The hoopla concludes each year with the famous **Travers Stakes,** named for racetrack cofounder William Travers.

Day-of tickets go on sale at 8am each morning for the day's races. Purchase them at the Union Avenue Gate (limit four per person, $10, cash only unless you go to the box office and will-call). Advance-purchase tickets are available through Ticketmaster starting in early May or at the box office starting mid-July. You can rent binoculars at the track for up-close viewing. Take exit 14 (Union Ave.) from I-87.

For information before or after the racing season, call 718/641-4700 or 516/488-6000. For information during the season (late July-Labor Day), call 518/584-6200.

National Museum of Racing

Across from the racetrack, an informative museum demonstrates what traits make the best thoroughbreds and recreates famous scenes on the track. Recent additions to the **National Museum of Racing** (191 Union Ave., www.racingmuseum.org, 518/584-0400, 10am-4pm Wed.-Sun. Oct.-May, adults $20,

Saratoga Race Course

seniors $15, students $10, under age 5 free) include newspaper articles from the mid-19th century. On your visit, you can watch the museum's signature film, *What It Takes: Journey to the Hall of Fame.*

Beyond the racetrack and museum on Union Avenue is the 400-acre Yaddo estate, an artists' community established in 1900 and housed in an imposing Tudor mansion. Its terraced **Yaddo Rose Garden** (312 Union Ave., 518/584-0746, www.yaddo.org, 8am-dusk daily), modeled after classical Italian designs, has been gradually restored since the founding of the Yaddo Garden Association in 1991. Docent-led garden tours are offered (Sat.-Sun. late June-early Sept., $5 pp). During the Saratoga thoroughbred racecourse season (late July-Labor Day), the guided garden tours are also offered Tuesday.

Downtown Saratoga Springs

Broadway and Union Avenue both lead to the open lawns of **Congress Park** and the heart of Saratoga Springs. Kids will want to head straight to the park's working carousel or to feed the ducks in the pond. The **Canfield Casino** (Congress Park, 518/584-6920, www.saratogahistory.org, 10am-4pm daily Memorial Day-Labor Day, 10am-4pm Wed.-Sun. Labor Day-Memorial Day, adults $10, seniors and students $5, under age 12 free), a major attraction during the spa town's heyday, is now a local history museum.

Along Broadway, between Congress and Van Dam Streets, is a host of tempting options for shopping, entertainment, and dining out. To get oriented, stop by the information booth at the corner of Broadway and Congress Street. Then continue up Broadway to one of Saratoga Springs' most famous landmarks, the **Adelphi Hotel** (365 Broadway, 518/678-6000, www.theadelphihotel.com, $329), a four-story Victorian that has stayed in business since the turn of the 20th century. The hotel got a fresh look in 2017 with an inviting bar on the main floor. Let the bartender surprise you with the evening's special cocktail.

★ The Frances Young Tang Teaching Museum and Art Gallery

North Broadway leads to the Skidmore College campus and an innovative museum that hosts programs with titles like "Why Is Contemporary Art So Weird?" **The Frances Young Tang Teaching Museum and Art Gallery** (815 N. Broadway, 518/580-8080, http://tang.skidmore.edu, noon-9pm Thurs., noon-5pm Fri.-Sun. mid-Jan. to mid-May and mid-July to mid-Dec., suggested donation adults $5, children $3) combines an outstanding permanent collection with provocative lecture topics to engage an audience of students, as well as adults and children in the local community. Exhibits are designed to involve other college departments, from dance to history. Rooftop concerts are a favorite local pastime in summer.

RECREATION
Winter Sports

When a good nor'easter buries the North Country in snow, **Saratoga Spa State Park** becomes a winter play land, and the cross-country skiing is sublime. You can rent equipment at a ski shop at the golf course and ski (or snowshoe) 20 kilometers of trails. **Lapland Lake** (139 Lapland Lake Rd., Northville, 518/863-4974, www.laplandlake.com, 10am-4:30pm Mon.-Fri., 9am-4:30pm Sat.-Sun. and holidays, adults $20, juniors $10) has another 38 kilometers of groomed trails for classic and skating-style cross-country. Rentals and lessons are available. For off-site skiing and snowshoeing, try one of the local apple orchards.

Downhill skiers continue farther north to resorts in the **Adirondack Park,** including **Gore Mountain** (Peaceful Valley Rd., North Creek, 518/251-2411, www.goremountain.com). Adult lift tickets cost $79 on weekends. Teens are $60, juniors $45, and $10 under age 6.

1: mineral water spout at a spring in Saratoga Spa State Park **2:** outdoor play in Congress Park **3:** the Five Mile Trail in Saratoga Spa State Park **4:** entrance to the Yaddo Rose Garden

Adirondack Park Facts

- The original forest preserve was established in 1885.

- The park encompasses approximately six million acres.

- It is larger than Yellowstone, the Everglades, Glacier, and Grand Canyon National Parks combined.

- About half of the park is constitutionally protected to remain a "forever wild" forest preserve.

- The remaining half of the park is designated private land, which includes settlements, farms, timberlands, businesses, homes, and camps.

- There are more than 3,000 lakes and 30,000 miles of streams and rivers inside the park.

- Between seven million and ten million people visit the park annually.

- It is the largest area without a city in New York State.

the author heading out on a kayak in Adirondack Park

Hiking

As the gateway to the Adirondack Mountains, the Capital Region affords convenient access to some of the best—and most challenging—hiking and backpacking in the Northeast. The highest peaks in New York State, including 5,344-foot Mount Marcy, are within a 100-mile drive. The **Mount Marcy Trail** (14.8 miles round-trip) starts at Adirondack Loj on Heart Lake. Bugs and black bears can be minor or major annoyances, depending on your tolerance. The steep and rocky terrain will challenge even the strongest of hikers: Routes are often longer than they look at first glance, and it's not unusual to encounter thunderstorms, mosquitoes, bears, and flat-out fatigue all in one overnight hike.

Cycling and Mountain Biking

The **Saratoga Mountain Biking Association** (518/587-0455, www.saratogamtb.org) maintains trails on 538 acres north of Skidmore College. Trails suit riders of all abilities, with single track, steep climbs, and fast descents. If you want to plan a biking tour of the Saratoga area, or need to pick up gear and supplies, head over to **Blue Sky Bicycles** (71 Church St., 518/583-0600, www.blueskybicycles.com, 10am-6pm Mon.-Sat,, noon-5pm Sun.), where the friendly team will be happy to assist. A 44-mile road route takes you from the shop around Saratoga Lake and out to the Saratoga Battlefield and back. Blue Sky does not have rentals, but you can find everything else from spare tubes and carbon dioxide cartridges to bike shorts and tri gear.

Golf

There are at least a dozen golf courses in the immediate Saratoga area. One of the best is **Saratoga Spa Golf Course** (60 Roosevelt Dr., 518/584-2006, www.saratogaspagolf.com, late May-Oct., $31-53), a 27-hole complex with a 7,098-yard championship course. Before your round, you can hit a bucket of balls from the grass tees at the driving range. Private pilots should reserve a tee time at the **Airway Meadows Golf Course** (262 Brownville Rd., Gansevoort, 518/792-4144, www.airwaymeadowsgolf.com, Sat.-Sun. $34, Mon.-Fri. $29), adjacent to an airstrip and sky-diving school.

Adirondack Park

CANADA

UNITED STATES

Malone

Plattsburgh

Lake Champlain

Canton

Keeseville

Burlington

Tupper Lake

Whiteface Mtn

Lake Placid

Saranac Lakes

Porter Mtn

Street Mtn

Seward Mtn

Mt Marcy

Seymour Mtn

Allen Mtn

Star Lake

Cranberry Lake

Tupper Lake

Middlebury

Long Lake

Newcomb

Ticonderoga

Raquette Lake

Adirondack Park

Indian Lake

GORE MOUNTAIN SKI RESORT

Whitehall

Fair Haven

Warrensburg

Lake George

Lake George

Hudson Falls

VT

Great Sacandaga Lake

Utica

Saratoga Springs

Hudson River

Amsterdam

Richfield Springs

Fort Plaine

Schenectady

MA

0   25 mi

0   25 km

Cobleskill

Troy

ALBANY

© MOON.COM

Slide into a GPS-equipped cart at the **Saratoga National Golf Club** (458 Union Ave., 518/583-4653, www.golfsaratoga.com, $130-220), and you'll forget about the money you paid to get away from the crowds. Tee times get booked up to a month in advance, and rates are highest during the racetrack season.

Elevation changes are a challenge at the **Saratoga Lake Golf Club** (35 Grace Moore Rd., 518/581-6616, www.saratogalakegolf. com), where you can enjoy unlimited holes with a golf cart included for just $30.

Swimming and Boating

The busiest lake in the Capital Region is **Lake George,** 30 minutes from downtown Saratoga Springs along I-87. Known for its clear water and summer resort scene, the lake measures 32 miles long and three miles across. Several towns have public beaches. Scuba divers can explore underwater shipwrecks with remarkably good freshwater visibility. **Million Dollar Beach** has public parking. An **Antique Classic Boat Show** takes place in August.

In addition to Lake George, several smaller lakes offer ample space for aquatic adventures. You can rent a kayak, canoe, or rowboat from **The Kayak Shak** (Saratoga Outdoor Center, 251 Staffords Bridge Rd., 518/587-9788, www. kayakshak.com, 9am-7pm daily, weather permitting, single kayak $25 half-day, $45 full-day) to paddle around **Saratoga Lake.** Give stand-up paddleboard yoga classes a try in summer.

The larger **Great Sacandaga Lake,** west of Saratoga Springs near Gloversville, is an artificial lake that allows powerboats, personal watercraft, and fishing. Swimming and windsurfing are also popular summer activities. **Moreau Lake State Park** (605 Old Saratoga Rd., Gansevoort, 518/793-0511, http://parks. ny.gov) has a sandy beach and wooded campsites, though it tends to be crowded in summertime. Boating and fishing are allowed.

1: views along Mount Marcy Trail **2:** Lake George

Fishing

Anglers cast for largemouth bass, northern pike, and panfish in **Saratoga Lake.** You can rent a boat and stock up on tackle at **Lake Lonely Boat Livery** (378 Crescent Ave., 518/587-1721, call ahead for hours). For more serious sportfishing and charter operations, head to **Lake George,** where the catch includes lake trout and landlocked salmon as well as bass.

Yoga and Spas

The Roosevelt Baths & Spa (39 Roosevelt Dr., 800/452-7275, ext. 4, www. rooseveltbathsandspa.com, 9am-5pm daily) at the Gideon Putnam Resort & Spa has been a bathhouse since the 1930s. Today, spagoers continue to soak in the healing mineral waters ($50 for 40 minutes) as part of their wellness routine. A full menu of treatments includes massages, facials, body scrubs, and aromatherapy.

Saratoga Botanicals Organic Spa & Wellness Store (80 Henry St., 518/306-4108, www.saratogabotanicals.com, 9am-4pm daily) sells organic skin-care products and offers holistic health services, from facials and massage to nutritional counseling and acupuncture. Check the website for special workshops and talks on topics like DIY face masks and natural remedies for kids.

At **Yoga Mandali** (454 Broadway, 518/584-0807, http://yogamandali.com), your first class is free, and drop-ins are welcome. Classes range from Vinyasa Flow to restorative and meditative styles.

ENTERTAINMENT AND EVENTS
Performing Arts

The story goes that the **Saratoga Performing Arts Center** (108 Ave. of the Pines, 518/584-9330, box office 518/587-3330, www.spac.org) was originally built to keep the New York Philharmonic from moving to Vermont for its summer home. While the philharmonic never came to Saratoga Springs, the new venue did become one of the largest producers of first-rate music, dance, and opera performances in the state. Performers have included everyone from Stevie Nicks and Toby Keith to Blink 182. A night of ballet or opera here is simply unforgettable. For opera aficionados, **Opera Saratoga** (480 Broadway, Suite LL16, 518/584-6018, www.operasaratoga.org), formerly Lake George Opera, stages performances at the Spa Little Theater in Saratoga Spa State Park.

The local visitors center produces a series of free concerts in Congress Park during the summer months.

Bars and Nightlife

Between its racetrack spectators and student population, Saratoga Springs has earned a reputation as a party town: Jazz bars, dance clubs, and Irish pubs, as well as coffeehouses and wine bars, offer venues for spirited entertainment. Several of the late-night establishments are on Caroline Street.

Located in a 19th-century brick building on Broadway, **The Wine Bar** (417 Broadway, 518/584-8777, www.thewinebarofsaratoga. com, 4pm-midnight Mon.-Sat., food $7-40, wine flights $12-20) has earned recognition from *Wine Spectator* for its ever-changing list of 45 wines by the glass. Patrons like the small plates that pair nicely with the pours. Happy hour takes place 4pm-6pm Wednesday-Friday and 2pm-6pm Saturday-Sunday.

Druthers Brewing Company (381 Broadway, 518/306-5275, www.druthers brewing.com, noon-9pm Sun.-Thurs., noon-10pm Fri.-Sat.) brews its own craft beers, including an unusual apple beer that uses apple cider from nearby Indian Ladder Farms. Also on tap are the Druthers Golden Ale, Against the Grain Weizen wheat beer, Triple Wit, and more. Lunch and dinner fare ($15-20) includes salads, burgers, mac and cheese, and sandwiches.

One block off Broadway, jazz aficionados settle in at the beautiful wooden bar of **9 Maple Avenue** (9 Maple Ave., 518/583-2582, www.9mapleave.com, from 4pm daily) for a night of live music, well-made cocktails, and a large selection of single malts. **The Parting Glass** (40-42 Lake Ave., 518/583-1916, www. partingglasspub.com) plays live Irish music. **Saratoga Gaming & Harness Raceway** (Crescent Ave., 518/584-2110 or 800/727-2990, www.saratogacasino.com) has 1,300 video gaming machines.

Festivals

Each September since 2001, SPAC has hosted the popular **Saratoga Wine & Food Festival** (Saratoga Performing Arts Center, 108 Ave. of the Pines, 518/584-9330, ext. 3021, www.spac.org), drawing food and wine enthusiasts from across New England and the mid-Atlantic states.

SHOPPING

Storefronts crowd both sides of Broadway in Saratoga Springs, offering a mix of boutique jewelry and apparel, high-end retail chains, and straight-up kitsch. Some seasonal boutiques set up shops only for the summer months. **Silverado Jewelry Gallery** (446 Broadway, 518/584-1044, www. silveradonewyork.com, 10am-5pm Mon.-Wed., 10am-6pm Thurs.-Sat., 11am-5pm Sun.) sells unique silver and semiprecious jewelry from a number of New York City artists. At the corner of Broadway and Phila Street, you can browse the selection of sundresses, hats, and handbags at **Lifestyles** (436 Broadway, 518/584-4665, www.lifestylesofsaratoga.com, 10am-6pm Sun.-Wed., 10am-7pm Thurs.-Sat.). **Symmetry Gallery** (348 Broadway, 518/584-5090, www.symmetrygallery.com, 11am-6pm Mon.-Sat., by appointment Sun.), also on Broadway, features art-glass works by local artists. As the name implies, the **Pink Paddock** (358 Broadway, Suite 1, 518/587-4344, www.lillypulitzer.com, 10am-6pm Mon.-Wed. and Fri.-Sat., 10am-8pm Thurs., 11am-5pm Sun.) sells a unique collection of pink apparel, as well as other shades. You'll find everything from seersucker pants and argyle sweaters to ribbon headbands, flip-flops, and flirty summer dresses.

The friendly staff at **Saratoga Trunk** (493

Broadway, 518/584-3543, www.saratogatrunk. com, 10am-6pm Mon.-Sat.) will help you find a beautiful dress for a special occasion or a designer hat for opening day at the racetrack. **Hatsational** (510 Broadway, 518/587-1022, www.hatsational.com, 10am-6pm Sun.-Tues., 10am-7pm Wed.-Sat.) is another place to look for his and hers hats for race day.

Farm Stands and Local Products
The **Saratoga Farmers Market** (High Rock Ave., 800/806-3276, www. saratogafarmersmarket.org, 9am-1pm Sat., 3pm-6pm Wed. May-Oct., 9:30am-1:30pm Sat. Nov.-Apr.) is a summer tradition, with 50 local vendors set up under a permanent pavilion. If you're planning a whole meal, pick up some fresh-baked bread, organic beef, and smoked salmon while you're here.

Putnam Market (435 Broadway, 518/587-3663, www.putnammarket.com, 10am-6pm Mon.-Sat., 10am-5pm Sun.) supplies the gourmands in town with an impressive display of cheeses and pâtés. Order sandwiches, desserts, and chocolates or pick up fresh fish to cook yourself. The adjoining wine store (Putnam Wines) offers free tastings every day and stays open on Sunday.

Visit **Bowman Orchards** (141 Sugar Hill Rd., Rexford, 518/371-2042, www. bowmanorchards.com) or **Charlton Orchards** (140 Charlton Rd., Ballston Lake, 518/381-3601) for an afternoon of apple-picking and cider-sipping.

Bookstores
Lyrical Ballad Bookstore (7 Phila St., 518/584-8779, www.lyricalballadbooks.com, 11am-5pm Sun.-Mon., 11am-6pm Wed.-Sat.) displays some of its fine old books and prints in a former bank vault. **Northshire Bookstore** (424 Broadway, 518/682-4200, www.northshire.com, 10am-9pm Sun.-Wed., 10am-10pm Thurs.-Sat.) is an offshoot of an independent bookseller based in Manchester, Vermont. Browse the collection of new titles, or check the calendar for upcoming author events.

FOOD
The food scene in Saratoga Springs evolves a bit with every season. Today, you can find everything from classic French and traditional Italian to international cuisine—and everywhere are chefs who make the most of the farm-fresh ingredients at their fingertips.

Fresh seafood is flown in daily to ★ **15 Church Restaurant** (15 Church St., 518/587-1515, www.15churchrestaurant.com, from 5pm daily, $18-56). Sea bass, sea trout, and scallops make regular appearances on the menu. Meat entrées range from rabbit and duck to filet mignon with gorgonzola butter. Produce is sourced locally when in season. Creative cocktails and tempting desserts round out the dining experience.

Wheatfields (440 Broadway, 518/587-0534, www.wheatfields.com, 11:30am-9pm Wed.-Thurs., 11:30am-10pm Fri.-Sat., 10am-8pm Sun., $13-28) offers family meals to go that feed 4-6 people and include an entrée, pasta, sauce, and garlic bread. Favorites here include homemade pasta dishes, steak salad, and the bistro chicken, which can be prepared marsala or parmesan style. Choose a sidewalk table on a warm summer evening.

★ **Henry Street Taproom** (86 Henry St., 518/886-8938, www.henrystreettaproom. com, 4pm-10pm Tues.-Fri., 2pm-10pm Sat., 2pm-9pm Sun., $12-18) serves a menu of fish-and-chips, double-patty burgers, farm toast, and market salads to complement the lineup of craft beer and special mixed drinks.

The **Olde Bryan Inn** (123 Maple Ave., 518/587-2990, www.oldebryaninn.com, 11:30am-8:30pm Wed.-Sun., $16-35) is a historic affair serving a lighter menu of fish and chips, sandwiches, and mac and cheese. Heartier options include prime rib, chicken and prosciutto saltimbocca, and baked haddock and rock shrimp scampi, along with a gluten-free menu.

Hattie's (45 Phila St., 518/584-4790, www. hattiesrestaurant.com, 5pm-9pm Wed.-Fri., 10am-2pm and 5pm-9pm Sat., 10am-2pm Sun., $15-25) serves Nashville-style hot chicken in a pleasant courtyard in town. The original "shack" (3057 Rte. 50, Wilton Plaza, 518/226-0000, www.hattieschickenshacks. com) serves gluten-free fried chicken daily. **Chianti II Ristorante** (18 Division St., 518/580-0025, www.chiantiristorante.com, 5pm-9pm Wed.-Thurs. and Sun., 5pm-10pm Fri.-Sat., $16-33) serves a full menu of Italian specialties, from pasta to risotto to beef tenderloin and the fresh catch of the day. Some of the restaurant's produce is grown on a newly purchased property called DZ Farm; the rest comes from local growers whenever possible. Order a bottle of red and enjoy the outdoor patio.

Inside the Adelphi Hotel, **Salt & Char** (353 Broadway, 518/450-7500, https:// saltandcharsaratoga.com, 5pm-9pm Tues.-Thurs., 5pm-9:30pm Fri.-Sat., $24-75) is a steakhouse that serves buffalo tenderloin, tomahawk steaks, New York strip, and the like. You can start with a plate of raw oysters and finish with profiteroles.

Cafés and Quick Bites

Don't leave Saratoga without sampling a pastry at ★ **Mrs. London's** (464 Broadway, 518/581-1652, www.mrslondonsbakery.com, 7am-6pm daily, $7-15). Savory options include a grilled panini on ciabatta and a rotating menu of soups and sandwiches. Delicate meringues are a perfect sweet fix after the meal.

Vegetarians and visitors with a case of late-night munchies won't go hungry at **Esperanto** (6½ Caroline St., 518/587-4236, http://esperantosaratoga.com, noon-7pm Sun. and Tues.-Wed., noon-2:30am Thurs., noon-4am Fri.-Sat., $7-13). It has a tempting selection of quick eats, including burritos, pizza, and the Oboy: sautéed chicken blended with cheese, scallions, and spices, baked in their own pizza dough.

Greenhouse (33 Railroad Place, 518/450-1036, www.greenhousesalad.com, 10am-8pm Mon.-Sat., $10-15) serves up a healthy menu of chopped salads. Customers begin by choosing a green and may add four toppings that range from meats and cheeses to nuts and other vegetables. Salads are tossed with one of several homemade dressings. Soups, wraps, and a variety of cookies, chips, and pretzels are also available.

★ **Uncommon Grounds** (402 Broadway, 518/581-0656, www.uncommongrounds. com, 6am-9pm daily) serves espresso drinks, smoothies, sandwiches, pastries, and other coffeehouse fare. Comfy chairs and board games are a good way to pass the time on a rainy day; enjoy the sidewalk tables in nicer weather.

The **Saratoga Juice Bar** (382 Broadway, 518/583-1108, http://legacyjuiceworks.com, 7:30am-6pm daily) blends health remedies, preventive treatments, and ordinary refreshing cold drinks. A number of cold-pressed juice blends are prepared ahead of time; others can be custom-made on the spot. Key ingredients include spinach, kale, beets, carrots, and ginger.

ACCOMMODATIONS

Overnight visitors to Saratoga Springs have more than 100 establishments to choose from, including business hotels, smaller inns, motels, and bed-and-breakfasts. Expect sky-high rates and crazy crowds during the monthlong horse-racing season. Centrally located chains, not covered here, include Hilton Garden Inn, Hampton Inn, Comfort Inn, Residence Inn, and Holiday Inn.

$100-150

The Springs Motel (189 Broadway, 518/584-6336, www.springsmotel.com, $99-225) has clean and comfortable rooms at great rates. Amenities include free Wi-Fi and flat-screen TVs. You can walk to the racecourse and Saratoga Spa State Park from the motel.

Located on Union Avenue, near Saratoga Lake and across the highway from the racetrack, **Longfellows Hotel** (500 Union Ave., 518/587-0108, www.longfellows.com, from $139) is a large conference center that hosts

1: freshly baked loaves at Mrs. London's
2: Henry Street Taproom

weddings and other special events. Rooms and suites are modern and businesslike.

A convenient location and filling breakfast make **The Inn at Saratoga** (231 Broadway, 518/583-1890, www.theinnatsaratoga. com, from $129) a top pick for many repeat Saratoga visitors. This is the oldest operating hotel in town, and fittingly, the rooms are furnished in an antique motif. Wi-Fi is free, as is use of the bikes. Guests get free access to the YMCA and Victoria Pool in Saratoga Spa State Park.

$150-200

Six miles south of Saratoga Springs in the town of Ballston Spa, the **Medbery Inn and Day Spa** (48 Front St., Ballston Spa, 518/885-7727, www.medberyinnandspa.com, $185-225) has 11 rooms decorated in pastel colors and floral linens. Data ports and whirlpool tubs lend a modern touch to the 200-year-old property. There is a day spa on-site, and you can dine in a speakeasy setting at the **Front Street Social Club** (52 Front St., Balston Spa, 518/309-3245, www.frontstreetsocialclub.com, 4pm-9pm Sun. and Wed.-Thurs., 4pm-10pm Fri.-Sat., $15-38) next door. Note that children under 12 are not encouraged to stay at the inn.

Over $200

Spacious guest rooms and suites cost up to $550 at the restored **Gideon Putnam Resort & Spa** (24 Gideon Putnam Rd., 866/890-1171, www.gideonputnam.com, $400). You'll be within walking distance of SPAC, but beware that rates go way up during the monthlong horse-racing season. The Roosevelt Baths & Spa (9am-5pm daily) on-site offers a full menu of relaxing body treatments, including a signature mineral water bath.

Centrally located, the ★ **Saratoga Arms** (497 Broadway, 518/584-1775, www. saratogaarms.com, $209-269) has 31 quiet guest rooms with comfortable queen or king beds, luxury linens, fireplaces, and whirlpool tubs as well as a fitness center and spa. Friendly service makes for a most enjoyable stay.

The ★ **Adelphi Hotel** (365 Broadway, 518/678-6000, www.theadelphihotel.com, $329) closed for renovations for a few years, then reopened to much fanfare in 2017. Its updated rooms and suites have hardwood floors, radiant heat in the baths, and a modern-antique look. Nespresso machines are an added plus. You'll also want to dine at the hotel's new farm-to-table steakhouse, Salt & Char.

the Adelphi Hotel

Campgrounds

You can pitch a tent or park an RV under the pine trees at the **Whispering Pines Campsites & RV Park** (550 Sand Hill Rd., Greenfield Center, 518/893-0416, www. saratogacamping.com, tent sites $35-40). Services include hot showers, a swimming pool, a trout brook, and two ponds.

INFORMATION AND SERVICES

In Saratoga Springs, the **Saratoga County Chamber of Commerce** (28 Clinton St., 518/584-3255, www.saratoga.org, 9am-5pm Mon.-Thurs., 9am-4pm Fri., late June-Labor Day) operates an information center near Congress Park. Daily guided walking tours are offered July-August.

GETTING THERE AND AROUND

Bus

The **Saratoga Springs Summer Trolley** stops at Congress Park, National Museum of Dance, Roosevelt Baths & Spa, Saratoga Race Course, SPAC, and other points of interest. Trolleys leave SPAC every 40 minutes, with the North Loop operating 11am-7:40pm daily and the South Loop 10am-7:20pm daily. The **Capital District Transportation Authority** (110 Watervliet Ave., Albany, 518/482-8822, www.cdta.org) provides public bus service within Saratoga Springs and to surrounding cities. The base fare is $1.50; an unlimited day pass is $3.90.

Train

Saratoga Springs has a modern **rail station** (26 Station Lane, at West Ave., 518/587-8354) with Enterprise and Thrifty car rentals on-site.

Car

The Capital Region is a major metropolitan area with heavy traffic during commuting hours. I-87 and I-787 are the main north-south highways. The Albany Airport is at exit 13N on I-87; Saratoga Springs is at exit 14. You can rent a car from the Albany Airport or from several independent companies in the Saratoga area.

Background

The Landscape

Abundant natural resources in the Hudson River Valley played a critical role in the development of trade and commerce in colonial America. The lush display of trees, bushes, and wildflowers astounded Henry Hudson when he first sailed up the river. Native American and European settlers found ample water, arable land, and lumber, fish, and game to support their growing communities.

Nearly half the land in the Hudson River Valley has been developed for urban, residential, and agricultural use, and the rest remains second- and third-growth forest. Elevation in the region ranges from 150 feet

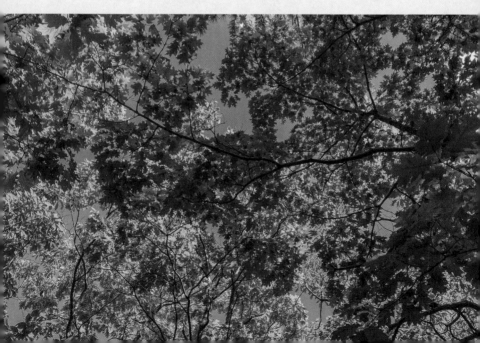

in the lowlands to 4,000 feet in the mountains. Lowlands consist of fertile farmland, rolling hills, marshes, and swamps. Mountainous areas feature sheer cliffs, escarpments, and rocky lookout points. In addition, the Catskill region is known for its red clay soil.

GEOLOGY

Dramatic rock formations in the Hudson River Valley tell a story of mountain-building, erosion, and glacial movement that began a billion years ago. The oldest exposed bedrock in the region is found in the Hudson Highlands of Orange and Putnam Counties. Limestone and shale marine sediments remind us that the valley was once the edge of a shallow tropical sea, much like the Red Sea, complete with pink sand and delicate coral formations.

The Taconic Mountains were formed next in an event known as an orogeny, followed by the Acadian Mountains, which stretched as high as the Himalayas. Runoffs from the mountain range deposited sandstone and shale to create the Devonian Catskill Delta, which forms the Catskill and Shawangunk Mountains of today. Farther south, molten rock carved the sheer cliffs of the Palisades.

In recent geologic history, 40,000 years ago, glaciers carved the fjord we now call the Hudson River. When the ice melted, it formed glacial Lake Albany and a submarine canyon that extends 500 miles offshore from Manhattan.

GEOGRAPHY

The Hudson River Valley is bounded by New York City and New Jersey to the south, New England to the east, the Adirondack Mountains to the north, and the Appalachian Plateau and Mohawk Valley to the west. At the center of the valley is the river itself, 315 miles long, 3.5 miles across at its widest point, and 216 feet at its deepest. The river originates from Lake Tear of the Clouds in the Adirondack Mountains and becomes navigable at Troy, above Albany. Dozens of tributaries feed the Hudson, draining the Catskill Mountains to the west and the Taconic Range to the east. The largest rivers and creeks include the Croton, Wallkill, Rondout, Esopus, and Catskill.

A second major river, the Delaware, traverses the western part of the region and empties into the Atlantic to the south.

CLIMATE

The Hudson River Valley enjoys a temperate, continental climate. Four distinct seasons range from the muggy days of summer to the crisp, clear-blue days of fall and below-freezing temperatures in winter. The first frost comes in late September, ending a growing season that lasts 160-180 days. According to U.S. Department of Agriculture Forest Service data, average rainfall is about 40 inches, while snowfall measures 165 inches at the mountaintops and 40-60 inches on the valley floor. Extreme weather events include ice storms and blizzards in winter and thunderstorms and the occasional hurricane in summer and fall. The fall foliage season lasts mid-September through late October, with the peak typically around Columbus Day weekend.

ENVIRONMENTAL ISSUES

The Hudson River absorbed a barrage of industrial waste, raw sewage, and agricultural runoff during the late 19th and early 20th centuries. The river was thought to be on the verge of recovery by the 1970s, when scientists tested striped bass for polychlorinated biphenyls (PCBs) and found alarming levels of contamination. The discovery shut down all commercial fisheries along the river, and in 1977, General Electric (GE) was ordered to stop dumping PCBs into the river. But the Hudson was unable to heal itself. The U.S.

Average Temperature by Month

Month	High (°F)	Low (°F)
January	34	15
February	38	16
March	47	26
April	59	36
May	70	46
June	78	55
July	84	60
August	82	59
September	74	50
October	62	38
November	51	30
December	39	21

Environmental Protection Agency finally agreed in 2002 to conduct a massive dredging effort to clean up the river, but GE continued to fight the decision for years. By August 2007, GE had begun construction of processing and transportation facilities that will store sediment dredged from the river. The first phase of dredging began in 2009, and in 2011, the second and much larger phase of dredging began near Fort Edward, 50 miles north of Albany.

The dredging was completed in 2015, and five years later, the EPA issued a completion statement, indicating the cleanup project had succeeded. PCB rates at two testing locations remained at acceptable low levels through 2020, and the river is considered to be safe once again for swimming, wading, boating, and even as a source of treated drinking water. In all, the dredging project removed 2.76 million cubic yards of sediment and 310,000 pounds of PCBs. Besides removal of contaminated sediment, the project also involved adding 1.4 million new plants and treating more than 2 billion gallons of water. For more interesting stats and FAQs, visit www.hudsondredging.com.

During this monumental 30-year effort, a number of influential environmental organizations stepped in to accelerate the recovery efforts. The New York State Department of Environmental Conservation's **Hudson River Estuary Program** (www.dec.ny.gov) works to protect the local watershed for Hudson River Valley residents. The **Beacon Institute for Rivers and Estuaries** (199 Main St., Beacon, 845/838-1600, www.bire. org) studies and protects rivers, estuaries, and watersheds in the area.

Modeled after the Dutch vessels that sailed the Hudson in the late 18th century, a sloop called *Clearwater* was conceived in the 1960s as a call to action to clean up the river before it was too late. In a unique classroom setting, *Clearwater* volunteers educate local residents about the importance of environmental awareness and conservation. Beginning in 1966, the watchdog organization has battled GE on the dumping of PCBs into the river, prosecuted Clean Water Act offenders, and pioneered the model of encouraging environmental advocacy through a hands-on sailing experience (www.clearwater.org).

Plants and Animals

The constant mixing of saltwater and freshwater as far north as Albany creates a rich supply of nutrients that in turn support a remarkably diverse set of interdependent plants and animals.

TREES

Sixty percent of the entire Hudson River Valley is covered in second- or third-growth forest. Towering red and white oaks and a variety of northern hardwoods—white and yellow birch, sugar maple, hickory, basswood, and ash—make up the majority of the deciduous forest. Acorns and beechnuts provide a key source of food for wildlife populations. Common conifers include blue spruce, hemlock, white pine, and yellow pine. The sand plains around Albany support the growth of pitch pine-scrub oak forests.

FLOWERS

Across the Hudson River Valley, bright yellow forsythias mark the arrival of spring, adding the first splash of color to the barren winter landscape each May. Cultivated daffodils and tulips are close behind, and more than 100 different kinds of wildflowers bloom by midsummer, including goldenrod, buttercups, and daisies, as well as jack-in-the-pulpit, sarsaparilla, and winterberry.

MAMMALS

A variety of critters big and small make their home in wooded valleys, fields, and mountainous areas. Among them are the black bear, gray squirrel, coyote, raccoon, river otter, and bobcat. In addition, many of the Hudson River Valley's suburbs are overrun with white-tailed deer that munch on everything in sight, from geraniums to apple blossoms.

SEALIFE

The Hudson River once held a large number of saltwater creatures, including oysters, mussels, crabs, and turtles. Most of the shellfish are gone today—blue crabs are an exception—but the river still supports more than 150 types of fish, such as bass, shad, and sturgeon, many of which are prized catches for determined anglers. At the water's edge, muskrats, snapping turtles, and ospreys feed on cattails and other marsh plants.

BIRDS

Ornithologists flock to the Hudson River Valley's wilderness areas to view more than 100 types of nesting birds, migrating raptors, and waterfowl. Among the more unusual species are the red-eyed vireo, found in woodland areas; American redstart, which arrives to nest in late spring to early summer; gray and yellow Canada warbler, found at lower levels of the forest; and Western wood-pewee, which prefers the dense upper canopy. Wild turkeys, grouse, and pheasant are abundant in wooded areas as well. The noisy pileated woodpecker likes a moist habitat where it can feed on carpenter ants. Observing one in action is a treat. Mallard ducks paddle through calm, sheltered waters across the valley, while Canada geese enjoy spending the winter near local golf courses. And the American bald eagle has made a comeback along the Delaware River, with sightings as far east as Greenwood Lake.

REPTILES AND AMPHIBIANS

The Hudson River Valley has its share of snakes, frogs, salamanders, and turtles. The friendly garter snake, water snake, and white striped milk snake are common. The only two poisonous snakes are the copperhead, found south of Kingston, and the timber rattlesnake, which lives in parts of the Catskills and along the river valley.

Come March, spring peepers fill the evening air with a familiar song. One of the most common amphibians in the region, peepers

Making Maple Syrup

A handful of Hudson River Valley farmers continue to produce real maple syrup the old-fashioned way. They drill holes in hard maple trees, collect the sap that drips out, and boil excess water away in a wood-fired evaporator. The end result is Grade A maple syrup that turns a quick breakfast into a gourmet feast.

Once an off-season income supplement for dairy farms, maple sugarhouses today draw late-season skiers and other visitors for a lesson in culinary science. The process begins in late February or early March, when temperatures climb into the 40s during the day and return to the low 20s at night. For four to six weeks, the fluctuating temperatures move tree sap from roots to leaves and back again, allowing the farmer to catch some of the flow without harming the tree. The most authentic sugarhouses hang aluminum buckets on each trunk to collect the sap, although larger operations have upgraded to plastic pipes in order to speed up the process.

sap buckets hanging on a maple tree in the Catskills

Straight out of the tree, sap runs clear, with just a hint of sweetness. Back in the sugarhouse, the farmer boils the frothy liquid in the long flutes of a steel evaporator, staying up all night when necessary to finish the day's harvest. An instrument called a hydrometer measures the specific gravity of the liquid and tells the boiler when the sap has officially reached the distinctive amber color and thickness we associate with the real stuff. It's a precise and labor-intensive operation—for every 40 gallons of raw sap, a sugarhouse will produce approximately 1 gallon of syrup.

SUGARHOUSES IN THE HUDSON RIVER VALLEY

Delaware County

- **Catskill Mountain Maple,** 65 Charlie Wood Rd., DeLancey, 607/746-6215, www.catskillmountainmaple.com

- **Shaver-Hill Maple Farm,** Shaver Rd., Harpersfield, 607/652-6792, www.shaverhillfarm.com

Greene County

- **Maple Glen Farm,** 1288 Scribner Hollow Rd., East Jewett, 518/589-5319

- **Maple Hill Farms,** 107 C Crapser Rd., Cobleskill, 518/234-4858 or 866/291-8100, https://maplehillsyrup.com (sold seasonally at the Delmar Farmers Market and year-round online)

Sullivan County

- **Andersen's Maple Farm,** 534 Andersen Rd., Long Eddy, 845/887-4817

- **Muthig Farm,** near the Neversink Reservoir, 1036 Muthig Rd., Parksville, 845/292-7838

Ulster County

- **Lyonsville Sugarhouse,** 591 County Rd. 2 (Krumville Rd.), Kripplebush/Accord, 845/687-2518 live anywhere that standing water is found. Other types of frogs and toads live at the water's edge, including wood frogs, bullfrogs, green frogs, and two dark-spotted frogs, the northern leopard and the pickerel.

Motorists often encounter feisty snapping turtles crossing back roads to lay their eggs. Painted turtles are another common species. Less common are the box turtle, wood turtle, the yellow-spotted Blanding's turtle in the lower Hudson River Valley, and the map turtle in the Hudson River. A dozen kinds of salamander also inhabit area rivers and ponds. The mudpuppy is found in the Hudson, while the hellbender lives in the southern part of the region.

INSECTS

Mosquitoes and mayflies are a nuisance in wet and wooded areas May through July, while fireflies light up the forest on hot summer nights. Deer ticks, found in fields and woods, can spread Lyme disease.

History

EARLY INHABITANTS

Anthropologists believe that the Hudson River Valley's earliest inhabitants settled the region as many as 10,000 years ago. By the 17th century, three main Native American nations lived along the river: the Mohican (Algonquin) people claimed the east bank of the river, from Long Island Sound to Albany, as well as the west bank from Albany to Catskill; the Mohawk (Iroquois) people lived in the Catskill area; and the Lenni Lenape (Delaware) people occupied the west, from the Catskills south to the Potomac. Modern town names like Wappingers, Tappan, Hackensack, and Minisink all refer to Native American tribes.

EUROPEAN EXPLORATION AND SETTLEMENT

Technically speaking, Giovanni Verrazzano was the first European explorer to enter the Hudson River at New York Harbor in 1524. But it was Henry Hudson, commissioned by the Dutch, who made it famous. Hudson sailed the *Half Moon* as far north as Troy in 1609, in search of a northwest passage to the Indies. Hudson did not succeed and turned around when the river became too shallow near Troy, but Dutch settlers returned soon after to settle Fort Orange at present-day Albany.

Despite ongoing conflicts, the Native American and European populations began to trade fur, tobacco, wheat, oysters, beans, corn, pumpkins, and other goods. Dutch settlements grew at Albany, Manhattan, and Kingston.

The Dutch introduced the patroon system of land management, in which an individual was granted proprietary rights to a tract of land in return for bringing 50 new settlers to the colony. When the English took over in the mid-17th century, they introduced a similar approach, the manor system. Robert Livingston, Frederick Philipse, and other historic figures were all benefactors of these preferential land-management practices.

REVOLUTIONARY WAR

Nearly two centuries after the first Europeans arrived, the Hudson River Valley's communities found themselves in the crossfire of the war for independence. Major battles took place at Stony Point, Kingston, White Plains, and Saratoga. Soldiers wheeled cannons along Route 23 between the Hudson and the Berkshires. George Washington established headquarters in Newburgh and other towns along the river, and West Point was fortified to keep the British out.

EARLY INDUSTRY

After the revolution, abundant natural resources created the foundation for industry in the newly independent country: tanneries, bluestone quarries, sawmills, and gristmills opened to support a growing population. Dairy farms and orchards flourished, and the first icehouses appeared along the Hudson.

STEAMBOAT TRAVEL

Inventor Robert Fulton shattered previous Hudson River records on August 14, 1807, when he made the first successful steamboat journey from New York to Albany in 32 hours. Backing the venture was Chancellor Robert R. Livingston, who had met Fulton in France a decade earlier.

Engines powered by steam would eventually revolutionize the transport of goods and passengers on the Hudson, spurring a new wave of economic development. Change might have proceeded at a faster clip had New York State not granted Livingston a 20-year monopoly on steamboat travel between New York City and Albany. Livingston and Fulton were free to seize and impose fines on any competitors. But the sovereign state of New Jersey understandably objected to the arrangement, and the Supreme Court intervened to settle the dispute. In the landmark 1824 decision *Ogden v. Gibbons,* the court ruled to end the monopoly, setting a precedent for federal control over interstate commerce. In the wake of the decision, between 1819 and 1840, the number of steamboats on the river rose from 8 to more than 100.

RAIL TRAVEL AND RIVERSIDE ESTATES

The advent of the railroad brought a new wave of prosperity to the Hudson River Valley and Catskill Mountain towns. Summer resorts flourished in Greene, Sullivan, and Delaware Counties. Westchester County became a commuter base as early as the 1800s, when rail travel made it possible to

Revolutionary War Timeline

1774	New York "Tea Party"
1775	Americans capture Fort Ticonderoga and Crown Point
1776	British invade New York City
1777	Saratoga Campaign— the turning point
1778	Fortress West Point begun
1779	Battle of Stony Point
1780	Benedict Arnold and John André treason
1781	Siege of New York City and Battle of Yorktown
1783	British evacuate New York City

reach New York City in just a few hours. In this era of prosperity, families including the Rockefellers, Vanderbilts, Philipses, and Van Cortlandts built or expanded their sprawling country estates along the banks of the Hudson.

INDUSTRIAL REVOLUTION

Factories grew like weeds along the banks of the Hudson during the early 20th century, manufacturing everything from cars to paper to poultry. General Electric began to make appliances in Troy, and IBM settled near Poughkeepsie. As the industrial economy transformed into the information economy and jobs moved overseas, most of these factories shut down. Today's many abandoned plants in Beacon, Newburgh, Poughkeepsie, and other river cities testify to the volume of industry that once thrived across the valley. By the 1960s, the Hudson had earned designation as an industrial river—a body of water polluted beyond repair.

Tour the Hudson River Valley's grand estates, and experience an architectural history that spans 400 years, from the earliest Dutch and English influences to the revivalist movements of the 19th and 20th centuries. Here are a few examples of the styles that have been preserved in modern times.

DUTCH COLONIAL

· Late 19th century to the 1930s

· Symmetrical two-sided roof with two slanted sides (gambrel) and curved roof edges

· Example: Eleanor Roosevelt's Val-Kill Cottage

FEDERAL

· 1780-1830

· Low-pitched roof, semicircle over the front door, and large windows with usually six panes per window

· Example: Clermont

GREEK REVIVAL

· Late 18th and early 19th centuries

· Greek detailing applied to American homes

· Example: 1911 Roxbury Arts Center

NEOCLASSICAL-CLASSICAL REVIVAL

· Late 1800s to the early 1900s

· Symmetry and differences in hierarchy; grand entrances and staircases

· Example: Mills mansion at Staatsburg State Historic Site

RECESSION AND REVIVAL

Modern auto, rail, and jet travel changed the region forever, sending would-be visitors to ever more exotic destinations in the same amount of time it once took to reach the Catskills from New York City. Farmers, manufacturers, and vacation resorts alike struggled to compete on the international stage, and most towns along the Hudson River fell into a deep and prolonged recession.

The economic boom of the late 1990s triggered a long overdue recovery for many area towns. Weekenders bought second homes, supporting riverfront restaurants and festivals from Newburgh to Kingston. After the attacks on 9/11, many of those urban weekenders became permanent residents, changing small-town dynamics once again.

Government and Economy

ORGANIZATION AND POLITICAL PARTIES

New York State comprises 64 counties, 11 of which are covered in this handbook. Four of the 11 counties were established when the first New York General Assembly convened in 1683, with the rest to follow by the early 19th century. Several Hudson River Valley cities, including Fishkill, Poughkeepsie, and Kingston, hosted the early state government, before it eventually settled in Albany.

Hudson River Valley communities have representation in 10 of the state senate's 63 districts, and following the latest elections, the region overall has a slight leaning toward the Democratic Party. The New York State Assembly is the lower house of the state legislature. It is made up of 150 districts, with one representative from each.

AGRICULTURE

Some 4,000 farms cover nearly 20 percent of all land in the Hudson River Valley, producing everything from beef, poultry, milk, and cheese to apples, sweet corn, organic produce, wine, hay, and flowers. Most of the area's longtime farmers are struggling to make ends meet in the globalized economy. They face a host of challenges, from achieving profitability and resisting development pressure to updating infrastructure and raising public awareness and support for an endangered way of life.

The locavore movement, which continues to gain momentum across the nation, stands to benefit responsible growers in the Hudson River Valley. Community-supported agriculture and "agritourism" activities such as farm tours, tasting rooms, and educational programs promise a more sustainable future for farmer and community alike.

INDUSTRY

The larger cities and towns along the Hudson River reached their peak at the height of the Industrial Revolution, when area factories

New York's Notable Governors

- **George Clinton** (first, 1777-1798) is remembered as the Father of New York.

- **DeWitt Clinton** (sixth) served two nonconsecutive terms in 1817-1822 and 1825-1828, during which he led the construction of the Erie Canal.

- **Martin Van Buren** (ninth, January-March 1829) was known as Old Kinderhook. His tenure as governor is the second shortest on record for the state.

- **Theodore Roosevelt** (33rd, 1899-1901) was elected in 1899 after returning from the Spanish-American War. He served for two years before becoming vice president to William McKinley.

- **Franklin Delano Roosevelt** (44th, 1928-1932) mobilized New York State's government to aid the economy during the Great Depression.

- **W. Averell Harriman** (48th, 1955-1959) was famous for his diplomacy skills. Prior to becoming New York's 48th governor, he served as ambassador to the Soviet Union and Great Britain.

- **Nelson A. Rockefeller** (49th, 1959-1973) was elected governor of New York four times. He grew the State University of New York into the largest provider of public higher education in the country and also improved and expanded the New York State Parks system.

Hudson Valley Population and Income

	Population	Median Household Income
Albany County	308,506	$64,535
Columbia County	59,461	$63,032
Dutchess County	294,218	$78,028
Greene County	47.188	$53,617
Orange County	384,940	$76,716
Putnam County	93,320	$102,183
Rensselaer County	158,714	$65,851
Rockland County	325,789	$91,108
Ulster County	177,573	$63,348
Westchester County	967,506	$92,758

Source: https://hvmag.com/life-style/history/hudson-valley-statistics/

made everything from automotive parts to ball bearings to men's shirt collars. In the 1980s and 1990s, globalization sent most of those jobs overseas, shutting the old factories down.

Today, employment in the manufacturing sector continues to decline as the services sector grows. Most new jobs of late are appearing in real estate; educational services; arts, entertainment, and recreation; and health care and social assistance industries. The largest employers (excluding agriculture) in the area are in the government, health care, retail, and food and accommodations sectors.

Despite periodic cutbacks since the early 1990s, IBM remains one of the largest employers in the region, with offices and plants from Somers to Hawthorne and Poughkeepsie to East Fishkill. Health care and pharmaceuticals account for the next largest group of jobs. Retailers Home Depot and Walmart have a significant presence in the job market as well.

DISTRIBUTION OF WEALTH

Household income varies widely across the valley. In Westchester, Rockland, Putnam, Orange, and Dutchess Counties, it is well above the state and national averages, while the rest of the counties fall at or below the mean. Property values fell significantly throughout the region during the Great Recession, but then recovered to levels not seen since the previous peak in 2005. The COVID-19 pandemic has triggered a new housing bubble with affluent families leaving the city to displace longtime local residents in many of the rural towns.

More than 80 percent of residents in the Hudson Valley drive or carpool to work. As the area becomes its own economic center, distinct from New York City, it is encountering the associated challenges of providing affordable housing and managing traffic congestion.

TOURISM

Tourism is a growing part of the overall Hudson River Valley economy, as historical sights, museums, farms, and cultural attractions draw visitors from New York City, the greater Tri-State area, and beyond. West Point alone draws more than three million visitors a year and is one of the top three tourist destinations in New York State.

The People

DEMOGRAPHICS

Historically, Hudson River Valley immigrants were German, Dutch, or Irish. Today, more than two million area residents represent a mix of many nations from Central America to Asia. They are commuters to New York City, farmers, small-business owners, artists, students, second-home owners, and blue-collar workers. The majority of counties in the region exceed the national average in the percentage of high school and college graduates within the population. The migration of creative types from New York City continues, with Hudson and Kingston among the most popular destinations of late.

ETHNIC GROUPS

All major socioeconomic groups are represented in the Hudson River Valley, and the ethnic makeup has become increasingly diverse as new immigrants arrive in New York City and gradually make their way north in search of jobs and homes. Black, Hispanic, and Asian minorities live throughout the region, representing the highest percentages of total population in Westchester and Rockland Counties.

Although they played a pivotal historical role in the development of the Hudson River Valley, Native Americans unfortunately have little presence in modern-day communities. In Ulster and Sullivan Counties, several tribes have been in negotiations with government officials to open casinos that some argue could revive struggling local economies, as well as benefit the tribes; however, a strong contingent opposes this kind of development on the grounds that it would encourage the spread of gambling without generating the kind of economic momentum that's promised.

As immigrant communities take hold and expand in more remote areas, they are introducing international foods and traditions that were once limited to urban areas like New York City. The result for residents and visitors alike is an increasingly diverse mix of options for culture, dining, and entertainment throughout the region.

Essentials

Transportation

AIR

The Hudson River Valley is easily accessible from several international airports, including **John F. Kennedy** (JFK, Van Wyck Expressway, 718/244-4444), **LaGuardia** (LGA, Grand Central Pkwy., 718/533-3400), and **Newark** (EWR, I-95 and I-78, 973/961-6000) in the New York City area, as well as upstate airports **Albany** (ALB, 737 Albany-Shaker Rd., Albany, 518/242-2200, www.albanyairport.com), **Stewart** (SWF, 1180 First St., New Windsor, 845/564-7200), and **Westchester** (HPN, 240 Airport Rd., White Plains, 914/995-4860, http://airport.

westchestergov.com). Numerous county and private airstrips provide local shuttle service.

Stewart and Albany offer convenient access to many Hudson River Valley attractions; however, the busier New York City airports often have better rates and flight-time choices for travelers coming from afar.

Stewart Airport has just one terminal with several rental car agencies on-site. Ride shares and taxis are readily available. The only food option inside the terminal is a Euro Café diner between gates 3 and 4. Hudson News has limited grab-and-go convenience food options. There is an ATM near baggage claim.

Newark is closest to destinations in Orange and Rockland Counties, while JFK and LaGuardia serve Westchester and Putnam Counties best. Newark also has the best public transportation to and from New York City. Its AirTrain service connects to NJ Transit and Amtrak, which offer frequent express trains from Penn Station. Rail service to JFK is a trickier proposition that requires a long subway ride to Queens and then an AirTrain connection to the terminals. Information about all three New York City airports and Stewart, as well as AirTrain services at Newark and JFK, is available at the Port Authority of New York and New Jersey website (www.panynj. gov/airports).

Car services are often the best option for getting to and from Stewart and Albany airports, and listings are available on the airport websites; cabs, rental cars, and shuttle services are also readily available to most destinations.

TRAIN

Metro-North (800/638-7646, www.mta. info/mnr) and **NJ Transit** (973/275-5555, www.njtransit.com) run commuter lines from New York City's Grand Central and Penn Stations, reaching Poughkeepsie and Wassaic in the north, Port Jervis in the west, and Connecticut in the east. Metro-North offers discount rail fare and admission to

popular destinations (www.mta.info/mnr) including Boscobel, Clearwater, Dia:Beacon, and Kykuit/The Rockefeller Estate.

Amtrak (800/872-7245, www.amtrak.com) offers service beyond the commuter zone, following the eastern bank of the Hudson all the way to Albany and Saratoga Springs. Taxis and ride shares are readily available at most major stations.

BUS

Greyhound (800/229-9424, www. greyhound.com) buses stop in major cities and towns throughout the valley, including Albany, New Paltz, Newburgh, Poughkeepsie, Saratoga Springs, and White Plains. **Shortline Bus** (800/631-8405, www. coachusa.com) and **Trailways of New York** (800/776-7548, www.trailwaysny.com) offer regional connections and package trips.

Public transportation gets less reliable the farther you travel into the countryside, but most counties run some sort of local bus system to connect major town centers and some rural areas.

BOAT

Several companies run daytime and evening cruises along the river. Major ports include Newburgh, Kingston, and Hudson. The Hudson River Sloop *Clearwater,* based in Poughkeepsie, produces environmental education programs and riverfront festivals. **NY Waterway** (800/533-3779, www.nywaterway. com) runs commuter ferries as well as sightseeing tours to and from Manhattan. Some packages include admission to popular destinations.

CAR

Traveling by car affords the opportunity to meander along scenic back roads, across one-lane bridges, and down bumpy dirt roads; however, drivers should be aware that along with the rural scenery comes some inevitable

---

Previous: the Delaware & Ulster Railroad in Arkville.

run-ins with traffic congestion. And once you leave the highway, few roads are straight and flat; hills and curves are part of any Hudson River Valley road trip.

Two major interstates traverse the Hudson River Valley: I-84 connects Pennsylvania to Connecticut through southern Dutchess County. And I-87, the New York State Thruway, runs from New York City to Albany and then on to Buffalo.

Toll Roads

The New York State Thruway (I-87) holds the record as the longest toll highway in the United States. It costs $6.50 to drive the length of the Hudson River Valley northbound, from the New York City line to the downtown Albany exit (141 miles). The return trip costs $11.50, due to one-way bridge fees. Exits are often 15 miles or more apart, so watch carefully for signs to avoid missing your turn. Occasional rest areas have gas, restrooms, and fast food, including Starbucks. Many rental cars are equipped with an E-ZPass transponder that will bill the tolls to your account—a big time saver during busy travel times.

The following four Hudson River crossings have a toll:

- Bear Mountain Bridge (Westchester and Orange): $1.50
- Newburgh-Beacon Bridge (I-84): $1
- Kingston-Rhinecliff Bridge (northern Dutchess and Ulster): $1
- Rip Van Winkle Bridge (Columbia and Greene): $1

There is a $5.75 toll to cross the Tappan Zee Bridge (renamed the Governor Mario M. Cuomo Bridge in 2018) between Westchester and Rockland Counties, and a $16 toll for the George Washington Bridge. All bridges and toll roads in New York State are equipped with the E-ZPass (www.ezpassny.com) automatic transponder system, which is compatible with most systems in the Northeast. Some crossings now only have E-ZPass or pay online/by mail options. Some agencies, including Avis, rent cars with E-ZPass installed. If available, cash-only lanes are clearly marked at the toll plaza.

Highway Information

Aside from your smart phone, the next-best sources of real-time traffic updates for the Lower Hudson Valley and New York metropolitan area are WCBS AM 880 radio "on the eights" (1:08, 1:18, 1:28, etc.) and AM 1010 WINS "on the ones" (1:01, 1:11, 1:21, etc.). **Radio Catskill** is a hydropowered community radio station serving the Catskills, the Upper Delaware, and Mid-Hudson regions (FM 90.5 and FM 94.5, www.wjffradio.org). In Albany, tune to **WAMC Northeast Public Radio** (FM 90.3 in Albany and FM 90.9 in Kingston, www.wamc.org).

Consult www.nycroads.com/crossings/hudson-river for bridge conditions. Also online is the New York State Travel Information Gateway (www.511ny.org), with information by region.

The Taconic State Parkway

The scenic Taconic State Parkway runs north-south from the Sprain Brook Parkway, which comes out of New York City, to I-90 near the Massachusetts state line and offers convenient access to many of the Hudson River Valley's inland towns. Unlike the six-lane interstates that run parallel to it, the Taconic has just two lanes in each direction with a wide, green median in between. It crosses some of the prettiest woodlands, marshes, and fields of Westchester, Dutchess, and Columbia Counties, making it a popular route for motorists.

Several risks make the route one of the more dangerous in the state. When driving the Taconic for the first time, take these factors into consideration:

- **Narrow lanes:** The Taconic's narrow lanes are unforgiving, particularly on icy or wet roads. There are drains every few hundred feet on both sides and no emergency breakdown lanes. If you must stop for any reason, pull all the way onto the grass, as far as possible away from traffic.

- **Cross traffic:** Except for a few of the busiest intersections, the Taconic does not have on- and off-ramps. After one too many accidents, the state closed most of the hazardous crossroads in Dutchess County, but many in Columbia County remain open. Watch for cars braking suddenly in the left lane to turn, or for cars accelerating slowly in the right lane.

- **Deer:** The Hudson River Valley supports a healthy population of white-tailed deer, and many of them feed on the shrubs and bushes that line both sides of the Taconic. They cross roads most frequently during the fall rutting period in October-November. Watch for eyes at night, and remember that a deer caught in the glare of oncoming headlights will often freeze in its tracks. When you see one, others likely are feeding nearby.

- **Speed traps:** The speed limit on the Taconic is 55 miles per hour, and New York State troopers are serious about enforcing it. Although traffic moves much faster during rush hour, troopers frequently lurk in the median to catch drivers who exceed the limit by as little as five miles per hour. Bulls Head Road near Rhinebeck and the town of Fishkill are known hot spots.

U.S. Route 9 and Route 9W on the east and west sides of the Hudson River are slower north-south routes along the valley.

Driving Guidelines

The maximum speed limit on New York State highways is 65 miles per hour, and limits are often lower through congested areas or on older highways. Seatbelts are required at all times, and it is illegal to talk on a cell phone while driving, unless you have a hands-free connection. Speed limits in construction zones are strictly enforced. Speed traps are common along major roads and highways. Right turns on red are permissible outside New York City, unless otherwise marked.

Rental Cars

Rental agencies are easy to come by in the Lower Hudson Valley, but more difficult as you venture north, until you reach Albany. Major brands cluster around the airports, and most sizable towns have at least one independent rental service.

Car rentals generally are much less expensive in the Hudson River Valley than they are at the New York City airports. If you are traveling from these airports to the Mid-Hudson region or farther and plan to stay more than a couple of days, try this cost-saving strategy: Arrange a one-way rental at the higher airport rate, then return the car the next day and reserve a new vehicle at the lower upstate rate for the remainder of your trip.

BICYCLE

Mountain bikes and hybrids are easier to find as rentals than road bikes, but a few shops in the area cater to the cycling community. Cycling enthusiasts Ken Roberts and Sharon Marsh Roberts have posted a wealth of useful information, including maps, online (www.roberts-1.com/bikehudson). You can travel with bikes on Shortline Bus and Metro-North.

Recreation

Excellent outdoor recreation is one of the top reasons people come to the Hudson River Valley. You can escape the crowds in summer or winter on the expansive network of trails in the Catskills or in one of the region's many state parks. Approximately 100,000 acres of wilderness are preserved in more than a dozen state parks, including Bear Mountain, Harriman, Minnewaska, and Saratoga Spa. Catskill Park encompasses another 900 square miles of "forever wild" state land. And the expansive Taconic State Park encompasses 5,000 acres at the base of the Taconic Range, near the Massachusetts and Connecticut state lines. Hiking, boating, and fishing rank among the most popular activities.

State Parks

All told, the Hudson River Valley, Catskills, and Capital-Saratoga regions encompass more than 40 state parks and 20 designated state historic sites. The state plays an active role in preserving the Catskill Park: It runs the Belleayre Mountain ski resort, maintains a network of 33 trails, stocks rivers and creeks with fish, and operates a number of campgrounds. See individual chapters for specific park profiles. Or contact the New York State Office of Parks, Recreation and Historic Preservation (518/474-0456, nysparks.state.ny.us) at Empire State Plaza in downtown Albany. The New York State Historic Preservation Office is located at the Peebles Island Resource Center in Waterford (518/237-8643). For camping reservations, call Reserve America (800/456-2267, www.reserveamerica.com).

Hiking

Most state parks maintain their own trail systems and camping facilities, and some 200 miles of trails traverse the Catskill Forest Preserve. High above the Hudson River Valley are Kaaterskill Falls and the Escarpment Trail, a magical wilderness setting where the Hudson River School of painters found inspiration and the Catskill Mountain House entertained prominent guests. Slide Mountain in Ulster County is the highest peak in the Catskills and offers a challenging day hike.

In Minnewaska State Park, part of the Shawangunk Ridge, hikers may see two rare species: the dwarf pitch pine and the peregrine falcon. Taconic State Park has Bash Bish Falls, as well as miles of trails that invite exploration.

Camping in all of these areas is unrestricted below 3,500 feet, although backpackers are encouraged to camp in designated areas to diminish the impact on the forest.

Cycling

Cyclists enjoy endless miles of rolling hills on quiet country roads, and several counties have converted long stretches of abandoned train tracks into paths for walking, jogging, or biking. Piermont and New Paltz are popular cycling towns, and many local clubs plan group rides on summer weekends. You might tour one county at a time, or attempt the 180-mile multi-day ride from New York City to Albany. Include as many bridge crossings as possible, and allow time to take in some of the sights along the way. Several companies offer guided bike tours of the area; an amateur bike race is another way to discover many of the back roads.

Saratoga Springs-based Escapades Bike Tours (877/880-2453, www.escapadesbiketours.com) organizes a six-day fall-foliage tour in October for cyclists of all levels. Average daily mileage is 25-45, depending on individual preferences and abilities.

The Tour of the Catskills (www.tourofthecatskills.com) is a challenging multiday cycling event held in early August. Hundreds of amateur and professional cyclists compete in a Friday time trial and two stages

Saturday and Sunday. The route follows some of the most scenic country roads through Greene and Ulster Counties. The town of Windham is a good place to watch the action.

Swimming and Boating

The Hudson and its tributaries support all manner of water sports. Boats are available for rent at marinas on both shores—the **Village of Catskill** is a good place to launch. Tubing on the **Esopus** in Ulster County is especially popular in summer. Sailing school is an option out of Kingston. **Greenwood Lake** in Orange County, **Lake Taghkanic** in Columbia County, and several lakes near Saratoga Springs have beaches for swimming and facilities for boats.

Kayakers can paddle lakes, ponds, creeks, and of course the Hudson River in Dutchess County. **The River Connection** (9 W. Market St., Hyde Park, 845/229-0595, www. the-river-connection.com) offers water sports instruction, as well as equipment sales and rentals. Certified instructors lead trips from various launch points along the river, including Norrie Point (Staatsburg), Tivoli, Croton Point, and Poughkeepsie. Experienced paddlers may join the guided day trips from Athens to Saugerties, Saugerties to Norrie Point, and Cold Spring to Annsville Creek, which make up the annual Great Hudson River Paddle.

Fishing

Anglers can fish the tidal Hudson River, freshwater creeks and streams, or reservoirs.

Guided tours are available in many locations, including the Willowemoc Creek and Beaver Kill river near **Roscoe (Trout Town USA)** and the **Pepacton Reservoir.** Popular catches include American shad, striped bass, perch, herring, and sturgeon in the Hudson, and wild trout and bass in lakes, streams, creeks, and ponds throughout the region. The **Catskill Fly Fishing Center and Museum** in Sullivan County pays tribute to the founders of the sport in a series of informative exhibits. Bass tournaments draw large crowds to the river near the town of Catskill in summer.

Winter Sports

New Yorkers flock to **Windham Mountain, Hunter Ski Bowl, Plattekill, Catamount,** and **Belleayre Mountain** for downhill skiing and snowboarding. Runs are relatively short at all three resorts; **Belleayre** (Belleayre Ski Center, Rte. 28, Highmount, 845/254-5600, www.belleayre.com) caters to beginners, while **Windham** (Rte. 23, Windham, 800/754-9463, www.windhammountain.com) and **Hunter** (Rte. 23A, Hunter, 800/367-7669, www.huntermtn.com) have more terrain for experienced skiers and boarders. Resorts with snowmaking equipment open in late November-early December, as soon as temperatures dip below freezing. Spring conditions typically last through the end of March.

For more of a wilderness experience, many state parks—especially **Harriman, Minnewaska,** and **Saratoga Spa**—maintain trails for cross country skiing, snowshoeing, tubing, and tobogganing.

Food and Accommodations

FOOD

Whether you intend to plan a trip around the valley's good eats or you simply want to know where to get sustenance while you're on the go, it will be extremely difficult to go hungry in this part of New York State. Gourmet restaurants are scattered all over the area, while numerous taverns, pubs, delis, and diners reflect their individual locations and communities. Many of the best places to eat are not centrally located in the valley's towns and villages, but either a few miles away on a scenic country back road or hidden in a commercial plaza. Either way, it's often worth the drive to seek out a memorable culinary experience.

In summer, you can get your fill roaming from one roadside farm stand to the next, with an occasional pause to pick your own fruit and vegetables. During summer, ice cream stands pop up in every town, and the hardest decision will be whether to choose homemade or soft-serve. If all of this fails to please, fast-food chains are everywhere, too.

ACCOMMODATIONS

Hudson River Valley accommodations range from budget motels to modest inns to luxury resorts and vacation rentals. In most counties, there is an appealing option for just about every type of trip and budget.

Resorts

Scattered throughout the region—mostly in the Catskill Mountains—are a handful of full-service resorts that offer golf, spa treatments, and other activities on-site. Prices are often given per person per week and include meals. The **Mohonk Mountain House** (1000 Mountain Rest Rd., New Paltz, 855/883-3798, www.mohonk.com) near New Paltz and the **Emerson Resort and Spa** (5340 Rte. 28, Mt. Tremper, 877/688-2828 or 845/688-2828, www.emersonresort.com) near Woodstock are a couple of examples.

Most of the area's ski resorts have a variety of slope-side and nearby rooms and condos for rent.

Hotels and Motels

You can find everything from major chains to boutique hotels along the Hudson River. Some of the most charming properties are housed in historical homes that have been restored and converted for guest use. Many of the top establishments also run award-winning restaurants, staffed by graduates of the prestigious Culinary Institute of America in Hyde Park.

Bed-and-Breakfast Inns

By far the most popular places to stay in the Hudson River Valley are bed-and-breakfast inns, which range from a few rooms in a private home to rooms with private entries in a converted barn or carriage house. With these types of accommodations, you may have the opportunity (or obligation, depending on how you see it) to socialize with the owners over breakfast. Another bonus: Innkeepers often hire CIA graduates to prepare gourmet country-style breakfasts. Some B&Bs are centrally located in the valley's most popular towns; others are more remote. Quality varies widely too, so it pays to do your homework before you book.

Efficiency Cabins

Many motels and campgrounds also provide rustic one-room cabins with kitchenettes. These are often heated by wood-burning stoves or fireplaces. Expect a cozy atmosphere but very basic amenities in this type of lodging.

Camping

From dozens of state parks to the Catskills and Shawangunks, outdoors enthusiasts can choose from hundreds of appealing places to pitch a tent. For car camping, Yogi Bear's

Jellystone Camp-Resort has several locations in the Mid-Hudson region. Some parks, such as Taconic State Park, also rent cabins for year-round activities. Backpackers can camp anywhere below 3,500 feet elevation in the Catskills, but rangers ask that you choose designated camping areas out of consideration for the forest.

Other Options

Simple guesthouses—a room or two in someone's home—are another possibility, as are vacation rental properties listed on sites like Airbnb and VRBO. Some of the newer restaurants in the region offer these types of accommodations for guests, ranging from a single bedroom above the kitchen to standalone cottages and cabins nearby. The **Brushland Eating House** (1927 County Rd. 6, Bovina, 607/832-4861, www.brushlandeatinghouse.com) is a good example.

Yoga institutes and alternative lifestyle centers like the **Omega Institute** (150 Lake Dr., Rhinebeck, 845/266-4444, www.eomega. org) offer yet more choices in accommodations. Another interesting option is the rustic two-room **Saugerties Lighthouse** (168 Lighthouse Dr., off Mynderse St., Saugerties, 845/247-0656, www.saugertieslighthouse.com).

Travel Tips

STUDENTS

Students will find a range of programs at the Hudson River Valley's many colleges and universities. The **State University of New York** (www.suny.edu) has campuses in Albany, New Paltz, and Purchase. Private institutions include **Vassar College** (www.vassar. edu), **Marist College** (www.marist.edu), **Bard College** (www.bard.edu), **Skidmore College** (www.skidmore.edu), and the **Culinary Institute of America** (www. ciachef.edu). Job seekers should consult online resources, local newspapers, and county websites for current listings.

FEMALE TRAVELERS

Women traveling alone should feel safe throughout the Hudson River Valley, but be aware of surroundings when exploring urban areas like Albany, Newburgh, and Poughkeepsie. Get detailed directions for places you want to visit in these areas so you don't wander too far off course, and leave valuables behind. In general, take the same precautions you would in any midsize U.S. city.

LGBTQ+ TRAVELERS

Back in 2004, the town of New Paltz brought same-sex marriage to the national spotlight. A year later, the New Paltz Pride March and Festival brought together a group of volunteers who soon after formed the **Hudson Valley LGBTQ Community Center** (300 Wall St., Kingston, 845/331-5300, www. lgbtqcenter.org). Among other awareness- and community-building initiatives, the center sponsors an annual Spring Pride event.

While many of the Hudson River Valley's towns are progressive in their way of thinking, LGBTQ+ travelers may encounter a quietly conservative attitude in some rural areas. For accommodations, New Paltz, Woodstock, Rhinebeck, and Hyde Park all have a number of inns that are especially welcoming to gay couples—specifically, **Cromwell Manor Historic Inn** (174 Angola Rd., Cornwall, 845/534-7136, www.cromwellmanorinn.com) and **Morgan State House** (393 State St., Albany, 518/427-6063, www.statehouse.com). **The Day to Be Gay in the Catskills Festival** draws a crowd of residents and visitors typically over Labor Day weekend with music and entertainment. The website for **Out in the Catskills** (www.outinthecatskills.com) provides a list of gay-friendly establishments in Sullivan County. New York City-based *Go Magazine* (www.gomag.com) occasionally features lesbian-friendly destinations in the Hudson River Valley. **Big Gay Hudson Valley** (https://biggayhudsonvalley.com) is a great online resource with its own newsletter, blog, and events directory. Each year, Hudson Valley magazine publishes a list of events that take place during Pride month each June.

TRAVELERS OF COLOR

People of color live throughout the Hudson Valley region, representing the highest percentages of total population in Westchester and Rockland Counties, and the cities of Albany, Poughkeepsie, Newburgh, and Monticello. Unfortunately, recent studies find that racial tensions have risen in many local neighborhoods of upstate New York since 2010, but people and organizations are working harder than ever before to address the complex issues of diversity, equity, and inclusion in all aspects of local life.

Since June 2020, the local publication **Chronogram** (www.chronogram.com) has been maintaining an updated list of resources for racial justice. For example, Hudson-based **Kite's Nest** (www.kitesnest.org) is an innovative education center that develops young leaders to bring about personal transformation, social connection, healing, and systemic change. There are many Black and minority-owned businesses to seek out and support across the Hudson Valley, from farms and restaurants to consultancies and creative agencies. **Edible Hudson Valley** (https://ediblehudsonvalley.ediblecommunities.com) published a compilation of businesses and resources, called "Take Action Now: How to Support BIPOC in the Hudson Valley."

Every year **The Conference on Black History in the Hudson Valley** (www.hrmm.org/black-history-conference.html) is hosted by the Hudson River Maritime Museum, The Library at the A.J. Williams-Myers African Roots Center, TMI Project's Black Stories Matter, the Underground Railroad Education Center, and Harambee/the Pine Street African Burial Ground. This important event for researchers has taken place at the SUNY Ulster campus in Stone Ridge since 2018.

TRAVELERS WITH DISABILITIES

With a few exceptions, travelers with disabilities will find most major attractions in the region easily accessible. The exceptions are some of the outdoor garden tours, which may not be wheelchair-friendly. Travel plazas along the New York State Thruway are fully accessible, and people with disabilities can purchase full-service fuel at self-serve rates.

FAMILIES TRAVELING WITH CHILDREN

Families will find many kid-friendly establishments across the Hudson River Valley, including historic museums, interpretive nature trails, and water parks. Restaurants often have special menus for children, and many historic sights and attractions offer reduced admission fees for families. Students also often receive preferential rates. A few of the region's luxury inns do not allow young children. Check before making reservations.

SENIORS

Senior citizens enjoy reduced admission fees at most attractions throughout the region; however, some walking tours of historic homes and gardens, such as the Rockefeller Estate, may be dangerous for travelers with limited balance or mobility. If you're concerned, call ahead for details.

PETS

Pets are welcome at many, but not all, outdoor spaces throughout the Hudson River Valley. Inquire at inns and hotels before bringing your dog along. Restaurants do not allow pets

At the time of writing in March 2022, the Hudson River Valley and Catskills were significantly impacted by the effects of the coronavirus and statewide public health mandates, but the situation is constantly evolving. Many places remained closed without expected reopening dates; many that had reopened were understaffed and operating with limited hours. Small businesses across the region were struggling to stay afloat. Most museums, historic sites, and other attractions implemented reservation systems and other requirements to limit crowds.

Now more than ever, Moon encourages readers to be courteous and ethical in their travel. Be respectful to residents and mindful of the evolving situation in your chosen destination when planning your trip. Get vaccinated if your health allows, and if possible, test regularly before, during, and after your trip to ensure you continue to test negative for COVID-19.

LOCAL CONDITIONS AND RESTRICTIONS

Check local websites for local restrictions and the overall health status of your destination and your point of origin. If you're traveling to or from a COVID-19 hotspot, or anticipate potential cancellations or quarantine requirements, you may want to reconsider your trip.

Some destinations may require proof of vaccination or a recent, negative COVID test result before arrival; other tests and potentially a self-quarantine period, once you've arrived; or proof of a negative test to re-enter your original point of departure. You may also be required to wear a mask and/or provide proof of vaccination or a negative COVID test to enter indoor businesses such as restaurants, bars, and museums. For proof of a negative COVID test, a PCR test is often required. It's a good idea to research places that offer tests in your destination, and possibly make some testing appointments, before your trip.

TRAVEL REQUIREMENTS

If you plan to fly, check with your airline and the destination's health authority for updated travel requirements. Some airlines may be taking more steps than others to help you travel safely. Check their websites for more information before buying your ticket, and consider an early or late flight to limit exposure. Flights may be more infrequent, with increased cancellations.

Masks may still be required to ride local trains and buses. As of March 2022, proof of vaccination is no longer required to enter restaurants and other businesses statewide; however, individual business owners may choose to request this from their customers at their discretion.

PLANNING YOUR TRIP

Check the website of any venues you wish to patronize to confirm opening hours and to learn about any specific visitation requirements, such as testing, mask, and vaccination

---

inside, but many don't mind if your pooch curls up at your feet outside.

FISHING AND HUNTING

Trout fishing on lakes and streams is permitted April 1-October 15. You can fish for crappie, whitefish, shad, and perch year-round. Certain rivers and counties have additional restrictions. Trout fishing on New York City reservoirs is open year-round with size limitations. A free New York City Public Access permit is required to fish on the reservoirs. The application can be downloaded and printed from the Department of Environmental Protection at https://www1.nyc.gov/site/dep/recreation/fishing.page.

A wide variety of game is available for hunting in designated seasons within the Hudson River Valley. Deer, turkey, bear, ducks, and upland game are popular species. You'll know you're in a hunting town when you see signs advertising Hunter Breakfasts. New York State is divided into four hunting

policies; mandatory reservations; or **limited occupancy.** Check Google, the venue's website, and even their social media to get the most up-to-date information on hours and whether they're open.

More than ever, it's a good idea to plan your meals and accommodations and make reservations well in advance. You may want to consider restaurants with outdoor dining options or accommodations where you can cook meals on your own.

Expect general disruptions. Events may be postponed or cancelled. Some tours and venues may require reservations, enforce limits on the number of guests, operate during different hours than the ones listed, or be closed entirely. Be diligent and continue to research all the way up to your time of departure, as things are likely to change.

WHAT TO PACK

Pack **hand sanitizer,** a **thermometer,** and plenty of **face masks.** Though cloth masks may be sufficient for local requirements, a well-fitting N95, KN95, or KF94 mask is generally considered more effective at reducing the risk of transmission of COVID-19. If possible, stock up on **at-home rapid tests** to take throughout your travels.

Be prepared for possible closures and reduced services over the course of your travels. Consider packing snacks, bottled water, a cooler, or anything else you might need to limit the number of stops along your route.

RESOURCES

- New York Times Coronavirus Map: https://www.nytimes.com/interactive/2020/world/coronavirus-maps.html

- New York State Coronavirus Mandates: https://coronavirus.health.ny.gov/home

- MTA Service: https://new.mta.info/coronavirus

- World Health Organization: https://www.who.int/emergencies/diseases/novel-coronavirus-2019/travel-advice

- CDC: https://www.cdc.gov/coronavirus/2019-ncov/travelers

- International Air Transport Organization: https://www.iatatravelcentre.com/world.php

- U.S. State Department: https://travel.state.gov/content/travel/en/traveladvisories/ea/covid-19-information.html

zones: Northern, Southern, Westchester, and Suffolk. Seasons are divided into regular (for rifles), archery, and special firearms. Hunting season dates and regulations vary from year to year.

Before hunting or fishing, make sure you have the correct license, tag, and federal stamps. Licenses are available in many sporting goods stores. Contact the **New York State Department of Environmental Conservation** (518/402-8845, www.dec.ny.gov) for the latest information.

HEALTH AND SAFETY

The Hudson River Valley has a severe and worsening problem with ticks and Lyme disease. Wear long sleeves and pants when hiking in grassy or wooded areas, use effective insect spray, and always check for ticks when you return. See a doctor immediately if you discover you've been bitten. Poison ivy is another nuisance that can cause minor skin irritation and itching.

Hypothermia is a concern for hikers, paddlers, and cyclists who may be subject to rapid temperature changes. Bring layers and plenty of fluids for any outdoor adventure.

Campers need to take precautions against black bears, who often visit campsites in search of food. Don't cook near your tent, and remember to bring rope or a bear canister to store your food out of reach.

Deer are a perennial hazard when driving roads at night; take it slow and watch for the glow of eyes in the bushes.

Dial 911 for emergencies, or 0 for the operator. Area hospitals are open around the clock to treat injuries and illnesses. Bring proof of medical coverage.

Crime in New York State remains below the national average, and many Hudson River Valley communities are known to be among the safest in the state. Crime rates in the largest towns and cities measure average or better across the valley. Albany and Newburgh are the exceptions, with the highest crime rates in the region. Take the same precautions you would at home.

Information and Services

Businesses in New York are generally open 9am-5pm Monday-Friday. Banks close earlier, around 3pm, although some are open on Saturday morning as well, and ATMs are accessible 24 hours daily. Shops in tourist destinations stay open on Saturday and part or all of Sunday, and some supermarket chains stay open 24 hours.

Most stores, hotels, and restaurants accept credit cards for payment, but there are exceptions, so be sure to ask before you attempt to pay with plastic. The state sales tax is 4 percent, but when you add local county taxes, the markup usually exceeds 8 percent.

MAPS AND TOURIST INFORMATION

Printed road maps are a thing of the past, but Jimapco used to publish one of the best atlases to the region. The spiral-bound *Hudson Valley Street Atlas* is out of print but may be found. Individual county maps still can be found in convenience stores throughout the region.

COMMUNICATIONS AND MEDIA

Post offices, found in even the most rural towns, are generally open 8:30am-5pm Monday-Friday and 8:30am-noon Saturday.

Public libraries across the region offer internet access free or for a nominal charge. In addition, free Wi-Fi is ubiquitous at McDonald's, Barnes & Noble, Starbucks, and most coffee shops.

Telephone Area Codes

There are four main area codes in the Hudson River Valley.

- 518: Albany, Saratoga, Greene, Columbia
- 607: Parts of Delaware
- 845: Rockland, Putnam, Orange, Sullivan, Dutchess, Ulster, and parts of Delaware
- 914: Westchester

Local Media

The *New York Times* (www.nytimes.com) features regular coverage of upstate towns and issues. The *Poughkeepsie Journal* (www.poughkeepsiejournal.com) is owned by a national publisher. Many other towns have low-circulation newspapers, and several regional magazines contain useful information for travelers: *Hudson Valley Magazine* (Suburban Publishing, www.hvmag.com), *Westchester Magazine* (Today Media, www.westchestermagazine.com), and *Kaatskill Life* (The Delaware County Times, www.kaatslife.com). *Chronogram* (www.chronogram.com) is a free large-format print magazine focused on art and culture in the valley. Look for copies in tourism offices, hotel lobbies, and visitors centers. *The Hudson River Valley Review,* published by the Hudson River Valley Institute at Marist College (3399 North Rd., Poughkeepsie, 845/575-3052, www.hudsonrivervalley.org/review), prints scholarly research and literature connected with the region.

Most local television networks are based in New York City or Albany. Albany radio station WAMC (FM 90.3) is an NPR-member station, as is WNYC (FM 93.9) from New York City.

Resources

Suggested Reading

CULINARY

Baehrel, Damon. *Native Harvest*. New York: Lightbulb Press, 2016. Gorgeous reflection on Hudson Valley ingredients that have defined this chef's journey over a 30-year career.

Greenberg, Jan. *Hudson Valley Harvest: A Food Lover's Guide to Farms, Restaurants and Open-Air Markets*. Woodstock, VT: Countryman Press, 2003. This overview of the region's microterroirs covers everything from heirloom beans to shiitake mushrooms. Chapters are organized by type of food.

Manikowski, John. *Wild Fish & Game Cookbook*. New York: Artisan, 1997. Not only is Manikowski an accomplished outdoorsman and writer, he also illustrated his own book.

The Valley Table. The Valley Table Inc. This quarterly print publication maintains an informative website (www.valleytable.com) of local culinary news and events.

FICTION

Adams, Arthur G., ed. *The Hudson River in Literature: An Anthology*. New York: Fordham University Press, 1980. This anthology, which includes the writings of James Fenimore Cooper and William Cullen Bryant, provides a good overview of writers who wrote about and were influenced by the Hudson River Valley.

Cooper, James Fenimore. *The Last of the Mohicans*. New York: Bantam Classics, 1982. The second Leatherstocking Tale and the most popular of Cooper's novels, this adventure of the French and Indian War in the Lake George region takes place in 1757.

Cooper, James Fenimore. *The Leatherstocking Tales*. New York: Library of America, 1985. The five books that make up Cooper's tales are set in the Hudson River Valley.

Donahoe, Kathleen. *Ghosts of the Missing*. Mariner Books, 2020. Set in a fictional Hudson Valley town, much of the action revolves around a writer's colony that's based in one of the area's historic grand estates.

George, Jean Craighead. *My Side of the Mountain*. New York: Puffin Books, 1988. Many young readers have fallen in love with this story about a boy who runs away from home to the Catskills.

Goodman, Allegra. *Kaaterskill Falls*. New York: Delta, 1999. This book, about three Jewish families who spend summers in the Catskills, was contemporary novelist Allegra Goodman's first.

Goodman, Carol. *The Widow's House*. New York: HarperCollins, 2017. A story of two writers who leave New York City for a haunted house in the country.

Irving, Washington. "The Legend of Sleepy Hollow." Rockville, MD: Wildside Press, 2004. Washington Irving lived in Sleepy Hollow and found inspiration for his writing in local residents and villages.

Irving, Washington. "Rip Van Winkle." Hensonville, NY: Black Dome Press Corp, 2003. Irving's classic tale of a very sleepy man takes place in the Catskills.

Keane, Mary Beth. *Ask Again, Yes*. Scribner, 2019. This intense story of two families in the 1970s is set in a fictional version of Pearl River.

Kennedy, William J. *Ironweed*. Penguin, 1984. This Pulitzer Prize winner is set in Depression-era Albany.

Salter, James. *Light Years*. Vintage, 1995. Winner of the PEN/Faulkner award, this book is a classic portrait of marriage set in the Hudson Valley.

Straub, Emma. *All Adults Here*. Riverhead Books, 2020. This page-turner of a family drama is set in an unnamed, modern-day Hudson Valley town.

HISTORY

Benjamin, Vernon. *The History of the Hudson River Valley: from Wilderness to the Civil War*. New York: The Overlook Press, 2014.

Chernow, Ron. *Titan: The Life of John D. Rockefeller, Sr.* New York: Vintage Books, 2004. This biography has sections on Kykuit and the Pocantico Hills and gives a good overview of the economy and culture that defined the Hudson River Valley in the 19th century.

Diamant, Lincoln. *Chaining the Hudson: The Fight for the River in the American Revolution*. New York: Fordham University Press,

2004. This book provides a historical account of defending the river at West Point.

Evers, Alf. *The Catskills: From Wilderness to Woodstock*. Woodstock, NY: Overlook Press, 1982. This book serves as the definitive history of the Catskills.

Hall, Bruce Edward. *Diamond Street: The Story of the Little Town with the Big Red Light District*. Hensonville, NY: Black Dome Press, 1994. Hudson's red-light district is researched and explained.

Lewis, Tom. *The Hudson: A History*. New Haven, CT: Yale University Press, 2007. A professor at Skidmore College tells the story of the Hudson River, from early explorers to modern times.

Richardson, Judith. *Possessions: The History and Uses of Haunting in the Hudson Valley*. Harvard University Press, 2005. Take a tour of the folklore, origins, and lasting effects of the region's most famous ghost stories.

Rinaldi, Thomas E., and Robert J. Yasinac. *Hudson Valley Ruins: Forgotten Landmarks of an American Landscape*. Hanover, NH: University Press of New England, 2006. The authors portray lesser-known historic sites and abandoned buildings across the Hudson Valley in photos and text.

Ruttenber, E. M. *Indian Tribes of Hudson's River to 1700* and *Indian Tribes of Hudson's River 1700-1850*. Saugerties, NY: Hope Farm Press, 1992. These two titles present a thorough history of the Native Americans who first inhabited the valley.

Van Zandt, Roland. *The Catskill Mountain House: America's Grandest Hotel*. Hensonville, NY: Black Dome Press, 1991. Roland Van Zandt offers an in-depth look at one of the most famous hotels in the nation's history.

MEMOIR

Bounds, Gwendolyn. *Little Chapel on the River*. William Morrow Paperbacks, 2006. A post-9/11 story of leaving Manhattan for the river town of Garrison.

DuLong, Jessica. *My River Chronicles: Rediscovering the Work that Built America*. Atria Books, 2009. Past and present meet in this memoir of the author's work in the engine room of an antique fireboat.

Jorrín, Sylvia. *Sylvia's Farm: The Journal of an Improbable Shepherd*. New York: Bloomsbury, 2004. A Delaware County farmer reflects on her experience of learning to raise sheep in the Catskills.

Mullen, Jim. *It Takes a Village Idiot*. New York: Simon & Schuster, 2001. A humorous account of an urbanite's adjustment to country life.

Philip, Leila. *A Family Place: A Hudson Valley Farm, Three Centuries, Five Wars, One Family*. Excelsior Editions, 2009. Personal account of life on a multigeneration family orchard.

NATURE

Boyle, Robert H. *The Hudson River: A Natural and Unnatural History*. New York: W. W. Norton, 1979. This is required reading for anyone who takes an environmental interest in the Hudson River.

Burroughs, John. *In the Catskills*. Charleston, SC: BiblioBazaar, 2007. One of America's first conservationists and a contemporary of Walt Whitman and John Muir, Burroughs writes about Slide Mountain and his hometown of Roxbury in a collection of eight essays.

Cole, Thomas. *Thomas Cole's Poetry: The Collected Poems of America's Foremost Painter of the Hudson River School*. York, PA:

George Shumway Publisher, 1972. Cole was a poet as well as a painter. More than 100 of his poems and a chronology of his life are included in this edition.

Klinkenborg, Verlyn. *The Rural Life*. New York: Back Bay Books, 2002. This memoir of life on a farm takes place largely in Columbia County.

Titus, Robert and Joanna. *The Catskills: A Geological Guide*. Fleischmanns, NY: Purple Mountain Press, 2016. This must-read for armchair geologists contains basic explanations and recommended field trips.

Titus, Robert and Joanna. *The Hudson Valley in the Ice Age: A Geological History & Tour*. Fleischmanns, NY: Purple Mountain Press, 2012. A work from the valley's foremost geological experts. Follow their articles at https://thecatskillgeologist.com.

TRAIL GUIDES

Henry, Edward G. *Catskill Trails: A Ranger's Guide to the High Peaks*. Hensonville, NY: Black Dome Press, 2000. This pair of trail guides is an essential resource for hikers. Book 1 covers the Northern Catskills, and Book 2 covers the Southern Catskills.

Kick, Peter. *Catskill Mountain Guide (Hiking Guide Series)*. Boston: Appalachian Mountain Club Books, 2002. A guide to more than 90 trails and a pullout map by a local outdoorsman.

Kick, Peter. *25 Mountain Bike Tours in the Hudson Valley: A Backcountry Guide (25 Bicycle Tours)*. Woodstock, VT: Countryman Press, 2006. An updated edition on rail trails, bikeways, and shops.

New York-New Jersey Trail Conference. *Explorer's Guide 50 Hikes in the Lower Hudson Valley: Hikes and Walks from Westchester County to Albany County*. Woodstock, VT:

Countryman Press, 2014. Hikes on both sides of the Lower Hudson are detailed in this latest edition.

Parks and Trails New York. *Cycling the Hudson Valley*. Albany: Parks and Trails New York, 2022. This edition has expanded coverage for biking and sightseeing around the Hudson and Champlain Valleys.

TRAVEL ESSAYS

Carmer, Carl. *The Hudson*. New York: Farrar and Rinehart, 1939. In the early 20th century, Carl Carmer wrote a guide to the region, filled with personal anecdotes and observations.

James, Henry. *The American Scene*. Reprinted in *Henry James: Collected Travel Writings*. New York: Library of America, 1993. This book, first published at the turn of the 20th century, captures Henry James's reflections on his return to upstate New York.

Lossing, Benson J. *The Hudson: From the Wilderness to the Sea*. Hensonville, NY: Nabu Press, 2010. Lossing presents a 19th-century perspective of the region in a travel narrative format.

Lourie, Peter. *River of Mountains: A Canoe Journey down the Hudson*. Syracuse, NY: Syracuse University Press, 1998. This contemporary travel narrative follows a paddler from the Adirondacks to New York Harbor.

Van Zandt, Roland. *Chronicles of the Hudson: Three Centuries of Travel and Adventure*. Hensonville, NY: Black Dome Press, 1992. This book captures an interesting cross-section of travel writing related to the Hudson River.

Internet Resources

Most New York State counties maintain a tourism website with information on attractions, activities, lodging, and dining out. In addition, most establishments maintain at least a basic website with general information. Here are some of the unique sites that cover broader issues and trends in the region.

Black Dome Press
www.blackdomepress.com
This publisher has a large online catalog of regional fiction and nonfiction titles.

Chronogram
www.chronogram.com
Online version of the free monthly print publication dedicated to supporting the arts in the Hudson Valley.

Clearwater
www.clearwater.org
This organization gathers information about the ongoing cleanup of the Hudson River.

Hike the Hudson Valley
www.hikethehudsonvalley.com
This should be your go-to resource for entertaining vignettes and practical details on just about any Hudson Valley hike.

Historic Hudson Valley
www.hudsonvalley.org
This organization publishes information about visiting several national historic landmarks in the area, including Kykuit/The Rockefeller Estate, Philipsburg Manor, and Montgomery Place.

The Hudson River Valley Institute
www.hudsonrivervalley.net
This Marist College organization is dedicated to scholarly research and writing about the Hudson River Valley National Heritage Area.

Hudson Valley Magazine
www.hvmag.com
This regional print publication has timely information for residents and visitors and articles about local food, business, and culture.

Hudson Valley Tourism
www.travelhudsonvalley.org
A promotional agency, connected with the I Love New York state tourism office, representing the counties in the region with a detailed calendar of events.

I Love NY
www.iloveny.com
The central New York State tourism site contains trip ideas, event information, and more.

Index

List of Maps

Photo Credits

Dedication

This edition of *Moon Hudson Valley & the Catskills* came together while I was biking the Wallkill Valley Rail Trail, fishing with the kids at Green Lake, hiking to Inspiration Point, stocking up on coffee at Irving Farm, and having many other adventures. But the most memorable of them all was the trip to Rhinebeck in November 2021 to celebrate my grandma's 100th birthday.

© GARY GOTH

Ruth Ellen Williams Goth lived most of her long life in the Hudson Valley, first in New Rochelle and then in Poughkeepsie, with frequent trips "up country." We spent countless hours together in my childhood years and stayed close for decades, despite living far apart.

On visits back home, we shared pastries at the CIA's Apple Pie Bakery Café, marveled at the river views from the deck at Shadows, and dined on the waterfront at Frank Guido's Port of Call. She loved to walk through parks, get dressed up for weddings, tell stories and laugh on the porch, and keep tabs on her 20 great-grandchildren. In the final days of my work on this edition, she passed away at the age of 100 years and four months. This book is dedicated to her memory.

Spending only a few days in a park? Try Moon's Best of Parks guides.

Asia & Pacific

Latin America

MOON
BALI & LOMBOK
CHANTAE REDEN

MOON
FIJI

MOON
Japan

MOON
NEW ZEALAND
JAMIE CHRISTIAN DESPLACES

MOON
BAJA
JENNIFER KRAMER

MOON
BELIZE

MOON
CARTAGENA
& COLOMBIA'S
CARIBBEAN COAST

MOON
CHILE

COSTA RICA
NIKKI SOLANO

TRIP OF A LIFETIME
GALÁPAGOS ISLANDS

MOON
ECUADOR
& THE GALÁPAGOS ISLANDS

MOON
TRIP OF A LIFETIME
MACHU PICCHU
RYAN DUBE

MOON
OAXACA

MOON
TRIP OF A LIFETIME
PATAGONIA
WAYNE BERNHARDSON

MOON
TIJUANA, ENSENADA &
VALLE DE GUADALUPE,
WINE COUNTRY

MOON
YUCATÁN
PENINSULA

BAHAMAS

DOMINICAN REPUBLIC

JAMAICA

PUERTO RICO

AMALFI COAST

AMSTERDAM
BRUSSELS & BRUGES

EGYPT

Greek Islands
& ATHENS

ICELAND

IRELAND

MOROCCO

NORMANDY
& BRITTANY

PRAGUE, VIENNA
& BUDAPEST

ROME,
FLORENCE
& VENICE

Scotland

SOUTHERN
ITALY

Get inspired for your next adventure

Follow @**moonguides** on Instagram or subscribe to our newsletter at **moon.com**

#TravelWithMoon

MAP SYMBOLS

▦▦▦ Expressway	○ City/Town	✈ Airport	⚓ Golf Course
▬▬ Primary Road	◉ State Capital	✕ Airfield	🅿 Parking Area
▬ Secondary Road	⊛ National Capital	▲ Mountain	⛺ Archaeological Site
┄┄┄ Unpaved Road	✪ Highlight	✛ Unique Natural Feature	⛪ Church
╌╌╌ Trail	★ Point of Interest		⛽ Gas Station
⋯⋯ Ferry	• Accommodation	🦅 Waterfall	🌀 Glacier
┈┈ Railroad	▼ Restaurant/Bar	⚐ Park	Mangrove
▦ Pedestrian Walkway	■ Other Location	⊤ Trailhead	Reef
▥ Stairs	△ Campground	🎿 Skiing Area	Swamp

CONVERSION TABLES

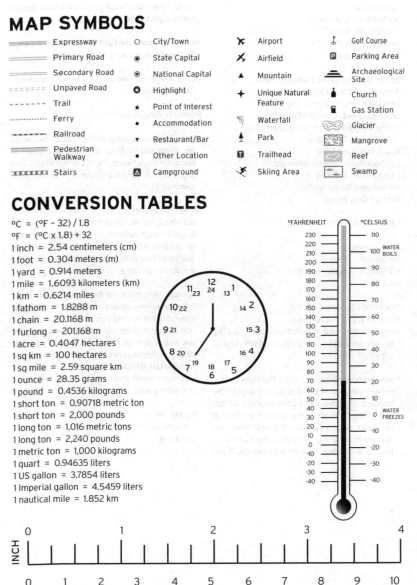

°C = (°F - 32) / 1.8
°F = (°C x 1.8) + 32
1 inch = 2.54 centimeters (cm)
1 foot = 0.304 meters (m)
1 yard = 0.914 meters
1 mile = 1.6093 kilometers (km)
1 km = 0.6214 miles
1 fathom = 1.8288 m
1 chain = 20.1168 m
1 furlong = 201.168 m
1 acre = 0.4047 hectares
1 sq km = 100 hectares
1 sq mile = 2.59 square km
1 ounce = 28.35 grams
1 pound = 0.4536 kilograms
1 short ton = 0.90718 metric ton
1 short ton = 2,000 pounds
1 long ton = 1.016 metric tons
1 long ton = 2,240 pounds
1 metric ton = 1,000 kilograms
1 quart = 0.94635 liters
1 US gallon = 3.7854 liters
1 Imperial gallon = 4.5459 liters
1 nautical mile = 1.852 km

**MOON HUDSON VALLEY
& THE CATSKILLS**
Avalon Travel
Hachette Book Group
1700 Fourth Street
Berkeley, CA 94710, USA
www.moon.com

Editors: Rachael Sablik, Kathryn Ettinger
Acquiring Editor: Nikki Ioakimedes
Series Manager: Kathryn Ettinger
Graphics Coordinator: Rue Flaherty
Production Coordinator: Rue Flaherty
Cover Design: Toni Tajima
Map Editor: Karin Dahl
Cartographers: Lohnes and Wright,
  Larissa Gatt, and Karin Dahl
Proofreader: Deana Shields
Indexer: Greg Jewett

ISBN-13: 978-1-64049-609-5

Printing History
1st Edition — 2005
6th Edition — November 2022
5 4 3 2 1

Front cover photo: the Catskills in autumn © Diana Robinson Photography / Getty Images

Back cover photo: Cold Spring © James Andrews | Dreamstime.com

Printed in Malaysia for Imago